The New Urban Paradigm

The New Urban Paradigm
Critical Perspectives on the City

Joe R. Feagin

ROWMAN & LITTLEFIELD PUBLISHERS, INC.
Lanham • Boulder • New York • Oxford

ROWMAN & LITTLEFIELD PUBLISHERS, INC.

Published in the United States of America
by Rowman & Littlefield Publishers, Inc.
4720 Boston Way, Lanham, Maryland 20706

12 Hid's Copse Road
Cummor Hill, Oxford OX2 9JJ, England

British Library Cataloguing in Publication Information Available

Library of Congress Cataloging-in-Publication Data

Feagin, Joe R.
    The new urban paradigm : critical perspectives on the city / Joe
R. Feagin.
        p.   cm.
    Includes bibliographical references and index.
    ISBN 0-8476-8498-9 (cloth). — ISBN 0-8476-8499-7 (paper)
    1. Cities and towns—United States. I. Title.
HT123.F38   1998
307.76' 0973—dc21   97-26345
                                                              CIP

ISBN 0-8476-8498-9 (cloth : alk. paper)
ISBN 0-8476-8499-7 (pbk. : alk. paper)

Printed in the United States of America

♾ ™ The paper used in this publication meets the minimum requirements of
    American National Standard for Information Services—Permanence of Pa-
per for Printed Library Materials, ANSI Z39.48-1984.

TO
Tom Pettigrew and Charles Tilly

Contents

Preface

Cities are the heart of contemporary societies, as they have been in many societies for millennia. They are economic, political, educational, and cultural centers. In spite of the Cassandras who periodically lament their demise or imminent death, cities in countries like the United States have a way of coming back from their low points.

The central reality of cities is that they are, at base, places where ordinary people strive hard to build viable lives, strong families, and vital communities. As a rule each new generation of urbanites, including immigrants from elsewhere, brings the hope, energy, and effort that keeps cities alive and full of change and dynamism. Generally, U.S. cities remain lively concentrations of Americans seeking a better life for themselves and their families.

This does not mean that cities are fundamentally controlled by ordinary urbanites. Much of what they do and create is done under the limitations and restrictions of the macrostructures and social processes within which they find themselves. By birth or migration they come into cities that have preexisting histories, collective memories, and hierarchical structures. In the U.S. the realities of contemporary urban life are disproportionately and heavily shaped by the underlying systems of capitalism, racism, and patriarchy, oppressive systems that are heavily reinforced and implemented in the actions of powerful elites. This book is largely about the role of the underlying systems of class and racial inequality in the historical development and current realities of U.S. cities. It is also about the major agents who shape urban change and development, the often invisible but very powerful elites. And it is about the microlevel conditions and problems that ordinary urbanites encounter as a result of the underlying systems and elite decisions.

Given these critical issues, it is surprising that cities in general seem to be of little interest today to most social scientists, policy makers, and public commentators. Indeed, a recent search of hundreds of thousands of print media articles in the Lexis/Nexis database by the author turned up no broad and probing discussions of the character or general problems of U.S. cities and little reference to recent research by urban social scientists.

Because of this lack of visibility, some observers suggest that urban social science may be dying. Certainly, some social science departments no longer offer urban courses or offer them less often. Yet this fear is exaggerated. Knowledgeable observers in the American Sociological Association suggest that the number of urban sociology courses has stayed steady in recent years, and in many large cities, particularly those that are booming, college teachers report great student interest in urban issues, particularly social problems such as crime, poverty, and racial conflict. One reason that it is sometimes hard to find out what is going on in urban social science is that urban research is scattered across many departments in colleges and universities. Urban studies can now be found in such programs as sociology, urban planning, ethnic studies, history, political science, geography, criminal justice, and social work. While there may be some decline in interest in urban issues in some disciplines or departments, there is actually a boom in interest in others. For example, historians are doing much exciting work on cities these days. One urban history network on the Internet now has twelve hundred subscribers and has seen important discussions about cities across the globe.

Still, we need new ideas and a new thrust in our study of cities. We need to focus more heavily on their political-economic histories and the rise and fall of their social institutions; on the character and impact of their underlying systems of capitalism, racism, and patriarchy; and on how all of this plays out in the everyday lives of contemporary urbanites.

In spite of the well-crafted articulations of this new urban paradigm in the social science literature, most social science textbooks and handbooks still provide little serious discussion of critical class, racial, and gender issues. Most offer little more than a rehash of older urban materials and concepts, such as a discussion of concentric zones, or some urban demographic data. The new *Blackwell Dictionary of Sociology*, for example, has no entry for urban sociology and only brief conventional treatments of the topics of "urban ecology" and "urbanization and urbanism." A look at social science journals reveals that most urban research reported there makes little or no use of the new urban paradigm. A large portion of that research, in my judgment, is not as creative or insightful as it should be. Today, too many urban research projects are atheoretical or are linked to dated or unimaginative ecological, demographic, or urban problems perspectives.

One advantage of the new urban paradigm central to the research presented in this book is that, for all its diversity, it offers important insights into how various urban realities are interconnected. Topics as diverse as job flight from central cities, unemployment, poverty, crime, racial segregation, and suburbanization have underlying connections that a critical perspective accenting class/racial/gender inequality draws out and elucidates.

Acknowledgments

I have spent most of my life in large cities, mainly in Houston; Boston; Riverside, Calif.; Austin; and Gainesville, Florida. Living in Houston early on stimulated me to think about significant class and racial issues. Over the decades I have been indebted to numerous people who have helped sharpen my insights into the character of cities. While I was doing graduate work at Harvard, Tom Pettigrew and Gordon Allport consistently encouraged my interest in studying racial relations and conflict in cities, and Chuck Tilly pressed me to become conversant with community research and urban theory. In the mid-1970s, when I was preparing a second edition of the reader, *The Urban Scene*, I first discovered the pioneering contributions to the new paradigm of geographer David Harvey and sociologist Manuel Castells. Encounters with Harvey's and Castells' probing writings, and conversations with Castells, significantly shaped my political-economy perspective on cities. During the late 1970s and 1980s, when I became involved in field studies of real estate development and particular global cities, I had stimulating and informative conversations with a number of fine urban scholars, particularly Gideon Sjoberg, Tony Orum, Mark Gottdiener, Bryan Roberts, and Michael Peter Smith, to whom I owe a substantial intellectual debt. Other urbanists who contributed significantly to my understanding of cities were Bob Parker, Stella Capek, John Gilderbloom, Nestor Rodriguez, and Bob Bullard. During the late 1980s and 1990s my new project on discrimination in cities began with personal tutoring from Melvin Sikes and Diane Smith about the painful reality of being a person of color in U.S. cities.

For comments on portions of this volume, I am indebted to Bob Parker, Yanick St. Jean, Nancy Di Tomaso, Tony Orum, and Hernan Vera. I am grateful to Mark Gottdiener and John Gilderbloom for taking the time to provide their insightful review-and-reprise articles for the end of this volume. I would also like to thank the many fellow urbanists who gave me, at various points, their comments and insights on the articles and chapters contained in this collection. I would like to thank the various publishers for permission to reprint the articles and Dean Birkenkamp, editor extraordinaire, for his strong support for this book project.

Introduction

Urban social science is now beginning its second century of research and theory. U.S. social scientists began to study cities in depth in the late nineteenth century. During this early period they often worked with a nonprofit organization concerned with urban problems and city reform. One of the most important of these urban social scientists was William E. B. Du Bois, who in 1899 pioneered the first systematic field study of everyday life in an urban community, a study published as *The Philadelphia Negro*.

Spending many hours in the field, Du Bois (1973 [1899]) interviewed 2,500 families and created a complex portrait of Philadelphia's Seventh Ward. He prepared the first monograph giving major recognition to a community of poor urbanites as a "striving, palpitating group, and not an inert, sick body" (Du Bois 1968, 198–99). He also assessed the role racist barriers played in creating the terrible conditions faced by African Americans in Philadelphia: "Such discrimination is morally wrong, politically dangerous, industrially wasteful, and socially silly. It is the duty of whites to stop it, and to do so primarily for their own sakes" (Du Bois 1899, 394). At a time when leading white sociologists espoused negative prejudices against immigrants and African Americans, Du Bois was the only social scientist to conduct a major and objective study of African Americans in the burgeoning cities.

Although he was a path-breaking researcher, Du Bois has not generally been given credit for being one of the founders, if not *the* founder, of urban social science in the United States. This is likely because, until recently, white academics have given little attention to the work of critical black scholars who accent matters of racial oppression in assessing problems of city development. The emergence of sociology as a major social science discipline in the 1920s at a few elite white universities, particularly at the University of Chicago, was coupled with a focus on urban research, yet with no significant use of the pioneering racial analysis of Du Bois or the antipoverty analysis of activist-sociologists like Jane Addams (see Park and Burgess 1921). Note that Du Bois left academia in the 1910s in part because of its conservatism on racial matters. From its beginning, the new social science of cities failed to set the critical factors of racial and class domination at the center of its analysis of city growth, development, and decline.

The Chicago School

The famous Chicago school of urban sociology, which came into prominence in the 1920s, centered around the major sociologists Robert Park and Ernest Burgess. These influential social scientists were interested in the processes of urban development and the life patterns of residents of distinctive areas within cities. They approached urban development from a viewpoint that came to be called "human ecology," a perspective that was quasi-biological and accented demographic and economic competition of groups within urban areas. The human ecology tradition emphasizes the "struggle" of human groups for "survival" within physical environments and probes demographic trends such as mobility and migration of population groups as well as population concentrations within cities. For Park, Burgess, and their colleagues, cities spread outward from the center as population grows, with the more affluent groups moving outward and new and poorer migrants settling in the center. The image of concentric zones of different urban uses spreading out from the center of a city has been a staple of urban social science for several decades (see Park, Burgess, and McKenzie 1925).

The researchers associated with the Chicago school not only studied the population geography of cities but also prepared important urban ethnographies published by the University of Chicago press. The approach in most of these books drew on Park's view that cities were composed of "moral regions" where values were often different from the "dominant moral order" (Schwendinger and Schwendinger 1974, 476). Focusing on the culture of poverty (a concept they seem to have given modern sociology) and urban "disorganization," none of the studies seriously probed the realities of racial and class oppression as they shaped cities. Instead, these social scientists saw urban phenomena such as prostitution, slums, racial ghettos, and the homeless primarily as topics for objective research or as technical problems that professional experts could fix without confronting problems of oppression (see Schwendinger and Schwendinger, 1974:

480–86). This myopia about racial and class matters has had serious consequences for urban analysis ever since.

Indeed, many of these urban researchers accepted some of the racist ideas of the day. In his writings Park (1918, 40; see also Park 1950, 387) suggested that racial characteristics, seen as "innate biological interests," determine characteristic features of groups, including their "racial temperaments." However, Park was opposed to racial discrimination and argued, naively, that there is a long-term trend toward (one-way) assimilation of subordinated racial groups like black Americans.

In regard to class issues, Park, Burgess, and most of their associates took a corporate-liberal approach that views capitalism as basically a good system but one requiring modest government regulation. Viewing urban problems from a modified "free-market" point of view, they saw cities as held together by social consensus. They and their more recent followers have studied urban markets and interethnic or interracial competition in cities without a clear recognition of the underlying racial and class domination. As the Schwendingers (1974, 397) note, the corollary of the consensus notion "was that the stability of communities composed of black sharecroppers and white planters as well as that of societies composed of workers and capitalists did *not*, ultimately, rest on the ideological control and management of public opinion, or on the operation of the police, the judges, and the armies of the state."

The Chicago school spawned two traditions that came to dominate subsequent urban research, one accenting human ecology and population analysis and another accenting ethnographic portraits of local communities. The ecological approach is common in contemporary urban research and emphasizes population trends in and around cities. Perhaps because of the theoretical sterility of much of this analysis, urban social science went into decline from the 1940s to the 1970s. By the late 1960s, however, urban conflicts and other dramatic changes in cities insured that there would new interest in cities among social scientists.

Creating social theory about cities involves the process of abstracting from what Karl Marx called the "real concrete" to the "abstract concrete." However, many urban social scientists are abstractors who have not thought critically about the notions of cities that academia has traditionally offered. The habitual abstractions about cities made by many mainstream urbanists represent the concerns of business and political elites with population growth, technology, or the "underclass." The mainstream ecological tradition seems primarily interested in describing the growth and geographical layout of cities and relies heavily on government data, such as that from the U.S. censuses. Much urban ecology theory accents phenomena like technological and population change as driving factors behind city development.

The other mainstream tradition accents community studies and ethnographies, which provide detailed descriptions of urban communities but usually with little theory or critical analysis. What theory there is in this community ethnography tradition is devoted to showing that traditional images of urban communities are incorrect. On occasion, urban ethnographers have probed important questions not favored by elites, such as the fine work of Herbert Gans (1962) on the negative impact of highly touted government urban renewal on a working-class community in Boston.

Many urban social scientists working on demographic and community studies have given little attention to the impact of class and racial (or gender) domination in U.S. cities. Some (see Vaughn, Sjoberg, and Reynolds 1993) suggest that one reason for this neglect is the dependence of many U.S. researchers on grants from corporate foundations or government agencies. In addition, much of the data used by urban social scientists comes from governmental sources such as census data. A heavy dependence on the state or business-generated foundations for research funding or data generally does not encourage a critical perspective on city development and problems. Another weakness in much mainstream social science is the technocratic impulse seen early on among researchers associated with the Chicago school. In this tradition many urban social scientists are more concerned with being professional experts for the dominant elites in business or government than with bringing significant and positive changes for the less affluent communities they often study.

The New Urban Paradigm

In the late 1960s urban social science in the United States was ripe for change. Too many urban social scientists accepted uncritically the dominant assumptions about cities and passed these along to subsequent generations of researchers. In *The Structure of Scientific Revolutions* Thomas Kuhn (1962: 165–66) criticized scientific education for being too "narrow and rigid" and for not producing students "who will easily discover a fresh approach." Gideon Sjoberg and his associates (see Vaughn, Sjoberg, and Reynolds 1993) have called for a countersystem approach in social science, one in which social scientists try to step outside the thought patterns of the dominant paradigm to look much more critically at their society.

Since the late 1960s a new approach to the study of cities has developed. Usually called the "critical political-economy" or "sociospatial" perspective, this approach probes not only the what of cities but also the how and the why. The new urban paradigm developed by these researchers emphasizes several major dimensions of cities: (1) the importance of class and racial (and, to a lesser extent, gender) domination in shaping urban development; (2) the central role of powerful economic actors, particularly those in the real estate industry, in building cities; (3) the role of growth-assisting government actors in city development; (4) the importance of symbols, meanings, and culture to the shaping of cities; and (5) the global contexts of urban development.

One of the first to break new ground in dealing with the centrality of class in the making of cities was Henri Lefebvre, who in the 1960s began to write about how the geographical spaces called "cities" are treated, under the system of capitalism, just like other commodities. These spaces of human habitation have both exchange value and use value, two evaluations that often come into conflict. Lefebvre made the influential distinction between primary and secondary circuits of capital. The primary circuit involved capital flowing into and out of production (e.g., manufacturing), while the secondary circuit referred to capital investment in land and buildings. In capitalist systems both circuits of capital play an important role in the development of cities (Lefebvre 1991; Lefebvre 1996; see also Gottdiener 1994, 127).

One of the most visible of the early representatives of the new urban paradigm was the Spanish sociologist Manuel Castells. In an early essay Castells (1976 [1968]) raised the critical question, "Is there an urban sociology?" His answer was that there was nothing especially "urban" about issues researched under the traditional label of "urban sociology." For that reason, in his work over the next two decades Castells proposed that a reinvigorated urban social science should focus on the collective consumption characteristic of urbanized countries with welfare states. He emphasized the study of class struggles around collective consumption and welfare state issues and also explored the way in which urban social movements are generated (Castells 1983).

In 1976 Castells' essay on the urban question (and two others), originally published in French, was made available in English in a path-breaking collection edited by Chris Pickvance (1976). By the late 1970s many British scholars and a few American scholars (including this author) were influenced by the new French work of Lefebvre, Castells, and others. Influenced by Lefebvre, British geographer David Harvey (1973) developed an influential argument that the central issue to be understood in making sense of cities was not collective consumption but the more basic Marxist concern of capital accumulation.

Gradually, U.S. social scientists also began to look at capital accumulation and at the economic actors who directed this capital accumulation. In the mid-1970s Harvey Molotch (1976) analyzed the urban "growth machine," the coalition of powerful urban real estate and political actors concerned with city growth. In the early 1980s I contributed to this analysis with a typology and discussion of the powerful economic and political agents that shape urban space so fundamentally (see chapter 4). Important theoretical work was undertaken by Mark Gottdiener (1985) in his brilliant book *The Social Production of Urban Space*. Gottdiener prefers the term "sociospatial perspective" for the new urban paradigm, a term that accents that cities are complex, multifaceted expressions of interactions between people and geographical spaces. Settlement spaces take on significant symbolic meaning for those who settle them.

Gottdiener has examined how "themed" environments such as Disneyland illustrate how the "current consumption-dominated, themed economy is tied to the production of desires through information flow and image circulation, on the one hand, and the flow of money from consumers to businesses on the other" (1997, 159). Accenting the symbolic character of group struggles over urban space is an important contribution of the new urban paradigm.

Gottdiener's analysis offers useful cautions against some recent postmodern analysis that views cities as a buzzing confusion of often unconnected cultural symbols and communities (for critical discussion, see Smith 1992; Zukin 1995, 293). His research suggests how much urban symbolism, for a range of otherwise divergent social groups, is constructed and manipulated by corporate centers of cultural management, including entertainment, media, advertising, and public relations firms. These insights carry over to many other types of urban symbolism beyond the themed environments.

We should note here that what has been called "postmodern urban analysis" has been useful in pointing up the varieties of cultures and symbolism in cities, as well as the impact of city residents ("recentering" them) who have often been ignored in urban analysis. However, a postmodern analysis that privileges cultural complexity and diffuseness in cities runs the danger of ignoring or playing down the still central structure-process factors of class, race, and gender (see, for example, Ellin 1996; Best and Kellner, 1991). There is no need yet to move beyond the new urban paradigm in this regard. Too much emphasis on the anarchy of urban subcultures can help legitimate the severely inegalitarian class, racial, and gender hierarchies that still profoundly shape cities.

Powerful Economic and Political Actors

Central to the new paradigm is a concern with the role of capitalism and capitalists in shaping cities. A critical question neglected by mainstream ecologists and community ethnographers is one that is central to the critical political-economy perspective: *Who* creates cities? One important answer is that cities are built environments that have been shaped by powerful development actors, both those in the private sector and those in government, working within the capital accumulation structure of modern capitalism.

The traditional urban approach accents demographic factors or decisions of many anonymous residents as the major determinants of city development. No individual or small group of individuals has a major determinate influence on urban land and building development. Urban housing and land markets are "free," that is, they are determined by competitive bidding by thousands of consumers and firms. Yet this unquestioned "free market" is an illusion, for certain select and powerful human agents have a disproportionate and determining impact on the economic values, social and business networks, and institutions basic to city development. Working within a capitalist framework of class domination, a small group of powerful decision makers, including major investors, speculators, builders, and developers, do far more to shape land and building markets than simply outbid their competitors. Economic systems and governments do not develop out of an inevitable structural necessity but rather in a contingent manner. They result from conscious actions taken by individual decision makers in certain class and racial groups acting in particular historical circumstances.

The broader social and historical contexts of urban development vary, and they must be factored into an adequate understanding of a particular city's development. While interest in cities seems to have waned in recent years among many social scientists, it seems to have increased among historians, who have done some excellent work documenting the history of powerful economic and political agents in making and destroying cities, as well as in reflecting and remaking the character of U.S. capitalism.

Take the case of suburban developments, where about half of all Americans now live. In mainstream urban analysis these outlying residential areas are seen as the result of technological developments, such as the centrality of the automobile, and of the desires of millions for a house with space. Yet, from the beginning of significant suburban subdividing in the 1890s to the rise of huge developers such as Levitt and Sons in the 1940s, the larger homebuilders became dominant in the building of suburbs by using government to displace smaller builders. In his research Marc Weiss (1987) has shown that larger developers worked with the American City Planning Institute to issue a statement that became the basis for the federal government's document, *A Standard City Planning and Enabling Act,* which in turn became the basis for much local planning legislation. By the 1930s larger developers associated with major real estate organizations felt that existing land-use laws did not provide the desired stability for profitable development. Major finance and real estate associations worked *for* the passage of the government's 1934 National Housing Act, which created federal housing regulation. With a staff recruited from the private development sector, the new Federal Housing Administration (FHA) wrote regulations that buttressed the U.S. lending industry by insuring individual mortgages and standardized subdivision development nationwide, thereby giving the large developers great power in shaping and creating suburbanization.

In her historical research Ann Keating (1989) has shown that metropolitan patterns of racial, ethnic, and class segregation have their roots in the first suburbs created around large U.S. cities such as Chicago. The growth of local suburban areas with their own governments reflected developer decisions. Before the emergence of suburban governments, there were segregated settlement patterns fostered by nineteenth-century real estate developers and their affluent (white) middle-class customers. Suburban areas reflected the intentional development goals of racial and ethnic homogeneity.

Historical studies such as these put large land speculators and land and housing developers at the heart of city expansion. Thousands of local residents and smaller builders made their decisions largely *within* a framework created by powerful real estate (and allied government) actors with narrow class and racial interests. Drawing on historical studies like these and on contemporary research, the new urban political economists can focus major attention on class and racial domination in the shaping of U.S. cities.

Racialized Cities: Creating and Maintaining Apartheid

In the work of the Chicago school and most of its contemporary followers in urban ecology and demography, the main interest in racial-ethnic issues has been in demographic patterns such as urban migration or the displacement of older ethnic groups by newer ones in an ongoing "invasion-succession" process. For example, in the sixth edition of their major influential textbook, *Urban Society,* Noel Gist and Sylvia Fava (1974) did not deal with racial stratification issues beyond some descriptive demographic data. There is no discussion of the role of racial or class domination in urban growth or development. Similarly, in the second edition of his major textbook, *Urban Society: An Ecological Approach,* prominent human ecology theorist Amos Hawley (1981, 270) offers no discussion of the role of class or racial stratification in city development beyond a brief comment that "the ghetto is a slum enclosed by a wall of discrimination." Other brief references to black Americans in cities are limited to a little data on migration and segregation (Hawley 1981, 270–75). Even after hundreds of violent uprisings in the cities during the 1960s and early 1970s, mainstream urban social science textbooks did not give racial or class oppression serious attention in analyzing city life or change.

Moving Racial Domination to the Center

As I see it, the processes and structures of racial stratification and domination must be placed at the center of serious urban analysis. The aforementioned powerful real estate actors represent and articulate, historically and in the present, the racial interests of white Americans. Since at least the middle of the nineteenth century, white agents of city development have been concerned with creating urban spaces where whites are in command and are protected from migrants of color coming to cities from rural areas, the South, and overseas. To understand fully and deeply the sociospatial character of cities, one must understand not only class domination but also the often-related phenomenon of racial domination.

As late as 1900, nine in ten African Americans still lived in the South, mostly in rural areas. Declining agriculture and the brutality of segregation stimulated millions to migrate to the economic "promised land" of northern cities. Once there, however, they were forced to settle in segregated areas already forced upon earlier generations of black families. Racial divisions in the cities were enforced by white violence, discriminatory law, and informal discrimination (Feagin and Feagin 1996, 249–50). When large suburbs were created after World War II, they too were rooted in discrimination. One leading housing analyst of the 1940s—who later became the first black member of a presidential cabinet—described white reaction to the black immigrants: "Whites began to flee before the never-ending stream of Negro migrants. Enterprising realtors, anticipating inflated prices, commissions, and rentals often manipulated the evacuation of whites by crying 'Wolf' " (Weaver 1948, 29).

Gunnar Myrdal and his associates (1964 [1944] 2,618) argued that housing segregation is basic to segregation generally: "Because Negro people do not live near white people, they cannot . . . associate with each other in the many activities founded on common neighborhood. Residential segregation also often becomes reflected in uniracial schools, hospital and other institutions." Since the basic unit of human reality is not the individual human being but rather a dense cluster of social relations around an individual that extends in many directions in space, this walling off of urban areas is central to creating close linkages between space and social life. The new political economy perspective accents this sociospatial reality of cities. The experiential reality of enforced separate spaces is at the heart of racial relations, and sociospatial freedom is limited most seriously for urbanites of color. Over time the system comes to seem natural, at least for those in power. "The lived experience of people in a segregated society links the perceived natural quality of the world we inhabit with its racialized characteristics—giving the social construction of a race a quality that seems both natural and inevitable" (Mahoney 1995, 1659–60).

Everyday segregation in cities reflects and reinforces socially created concepts of race. Historically, whites, particularly those in the middle class and in elite positions, have made use of different strategies to inscribe patterns of apartheid on the face of cities. Initially, cities like San Francisco, Louisville, and Baltimore used municipal ordinances to create and reinforce rigidly segregated residential areas (Ringer 1983, 254–55). When this strategy was knocked down in a 1917 Supreme Court decision, whites developed the highly effective strategy of restrictive housing covenants. For large cities the majority of residential areas were covered by racist covenants designed to keep black urbanites out of white residential areas. When the large developers began to accelerate suburbanization, many built racial restrictions into their operations. For example, the sales contract for houses sold in Levittown, Pennsylvania, had this clause: "No dwelling shall be used or occupied by members of other than the Caucasian race" (quoted in Cross 1984, 117). Not until 1948 did the United States Supreme Court rule that governments could not enforce these housing agreements, but they could still be enforced privately in the practices of homeowners and real estate agents. Moreover, until the 1960s federal government agencies and developers, small and large, promoted housing discrimination against African Americans and other Americans of color (Ringer 1983, 259–61). In addition, housing discrimination has long been reinforced by overt and covert discrimination by school officials and private employers.

Although in 1968 a new civil rights act officially banned most housing discrimination, this and subsequent housing laws have been weakly enforced, and discriminatory practices persist widely across the nation. Late 1990s' housing audit studies in major U.S. cities have found very high discrimination rates (60–80 percent) for black applicants (testers paired with white testers) seeking rental housing. In addition to this widespread housing discrimination, another major reason for persisting or increasing racial segregation and inequality is the movement of capital and jobs out of central cities to the suburbs or outside the country. Over the last several decades most new jobs in metropolitan areas have been created outside central cities where most Americans of color reside. In their work on residential segregation Douglas Massey and Nancy Denton (1993, 8) have reiterated the point that "residential segregation is the institutional apparatus that supports other racially discriminatory processes and binds them together into a coherent and uniquely effective system of racial subordination."

For more than a century multiple and reinforcing practices of discrimination against Americans of color have guaranteed that cities will be territorially and institutionally segregated. From the beginning, most suburban rings around the cities were designed using a variety of means—racially and socially restrictive ordinances and covenants, informal real estate practices, zoning—to be homogeneous. A major force creating the modern city has been whites segregating people of color, and at the heart of this process have been the large land and real estate developers. Urban apartheid is not a chance occurrence, or the reflection simply of the noncoordinated choices of millions of individuals, but has long been an intentional creation. Today, as in the past, the spatial and social realities of U.S. cities are clear reflections of "slavery unwilling to die" (see chapter 10).

The Growing Scale of Urban Apartheid

Racial apartheid is still very much the sociospatial face of U.S. cities, and it is growing in scale as we move into the twenty-first century. Between 1980 and 1992 the population in U.S. metropolitan areas grew nearly 15 percent, from 178 million to 203 million. Since the 1960s the United States has seen a dramatic increase in the percentage of the population living in suburban areas, to about half of the population today, with the percentages in central cities and rural areas declining. The central cities have had a decrease in white population, while most of the growing suburbs have exclusively or heavily white populations. Today about three quarters of whites live in suburbs or nonmetropolitan areas, while the majority of people of color live in cities, not in suburbs or rural areas (Wilson 1995, 3). Most cities over one million now have residential populations that are at least half people of color. As of the 1990 census, the proportions of the eight largest cities that are black, Latino, American Indian, and Asian/Pacific Americans are as follows: New York (60.5 percent), Los Angeles (65.2 percent), Chicago (62.7 percent), Houston (60.1 percent), Philadelphia (48.4 percent), San Diego (42.5 percent), Detroit (79.7 percent), Dallas (53.1 percent). By the year 2000 it is likely that all these cities will have majority populations that are Americans of color. It is also significant that non-European immigrant families, including children and grandchildren, are now concentrated in large East and West coast cities. Not coincidentally, these cities are all international centers with complex ties to cities across the globe. Most of the suburban areas of the large cities, in contrast, are heavily and disproportionately white and nonimmigrant in composition. Ever larger numbers of Americans are living out the reality of spatial apartheid within, and sometimes between, the metropolitan areas.

This continuing residential and social apartheid is now accompanied by another demographic trend. Over the next several decades it seems likely that Americans of European descent will become a statistical minority of the populations in a majority of cities of all sizes, and they will eventually become a minority of the nation's population. The U.S. Census Bureau recently estimated that around the year 2050 the U.S. population will be 400 million, about half of whom will be Americans of color (McLeod 1996, A3).

These demographic trends, when coupled with the segregation of most white Americans and Americans of color from each other, will likely force major shifts and changes in U.S. society both inside and outside the cities. Since the nineteenth century many white Americans have articulated the fear that cities are becoming centers for too many residents who are neither white nor European. Sociologist Sharon Zukin (1995, 41) has suggested that "as urban public spaces have included more strangers, those who look and talk so differently they are considered 'Others,' the Americans who used them before have abandoned them, leaving them to a generalized ethnic Other, a victim of the politics of fear." Some demographic analysts (see Frey 1979) have discussed "white flight" to suburbia and concluded that the prejudices of whites did not generate the general desire for suburbanization, but did channel choices to suburban areas reserved for whites. Yet such analysis underestimates the strength of white prejudices and racial fears.

Today, white fears about the new sociospatial reality of cities are increasing. Ironically, whites now fear what they have created, over more than a century of exclusionary racial practices. The image of the large city in most white minds is frequently linked to stereotypes of people of color. As William J. Wilson (1995, 3) put it, "Thus in the eyes of many in the dominant white population, the minorities symbolize the ugly urban scene left behind. Today, the divide between the suburbs and the city is, in many respects, a racial divide." Fearfulness about non-European immigrants is seen in speeches of Republican presidential candidate Patrick Buchanan, such as this comment to the 1992 Republican convention: "And as those boys [National Guard at 1992 riot] took back the streets of Los Angeles, block by block, my friends, we must take back our cities, and take back our culture, and take back our country" (quoted in Zukin 1995, 47). Buchanan wishes to take back the cities from growing numbers of non-European residents. *Forbes* editor Peter Brimelow (1995, 5–10, 59) has written that the United States is facing "the greatest wave of immigration it has ever faced," suggesting that the white population of the cities and nation is in decline. He further suggests that "the American nation has always had a specific ethnic core. And that core has been white." Not too long ago 90 percent of Americans, he argues, "looked like me. That is, they were of European stock. And in those days, they had another name for this thing dismissed so contemptuously as 'the racial hegemony of white Americans.' They called it 'America.'" Today, many white Americans fear demographic changes in the cities and seem to desire a return to whiter cities.

Yet it is unlikely that white fears or fear-motivated actions will return the nation to an imagined much-whiter America. Major social changes are well underway. How fast more large-scale social, economic, and political changes will come is hard to predict, and few urban social scientists seem to be seriously researching these issues. But certain changes seem likely. Relatively soon these population changes will likely end traditional white dominance of political and judicial systems in the majority of the larger cities, and perhaps in some major states. These demographic changes mean that democratic institutions, including universal suffrage and the peer-jury system, will no longer be reliable ways for whites to maintain their political and social dominance. This demographic transition will be difficult to stop, and it is likely the United States will face increasing pressures to desegregate its social, economic, and political institutions as well as to redistribute its socioeconomic resources.

How great white resistance to these changes will be is unclear, but there will undoubtedly be substantial resistance. Some desegregation and redistribution must come unless whites decide to create a fascist system like the old South Africa with its highly repressive, but ultimately unstable, white minority rule. It is possible that some may devise new types of racial exclusion such as new literacy tests or poll taxes in a campaign for "responsible citizenship." It is also possible that some whites may seek out certain non-European groups with which to ally politically so as to forestall non-European political coalitions against traditional white hegemony.

As of the late twentieth century, the signals from white leaders and masses are not favorable for substantial desegregation and the creation of a new sociospatial reality in our cities and nation. Whites *in extremis* may react in increasingly repressive and embattled ways. Indeed, there are numerous reports around the nation of whites developing more of their own suburban enclaves, creating gated communities and developing private school systems and security forces. Today, there are more than eighty-two thousand local governments, with many created for suburban residential areas. In recent years a conservative U.S. Congress has reduced the federal government's role in cities and made local governments play a much greater role in dealing with city problems. This renewed focus on local and state governments perpetuates and extends major class and racial biases in the shaping of cities. As Richard Briffault (1990, 346) says, "The proliferation of municipalities in metropolitan areas translates race and wealth differences into territorial segregation and fiscal separation. The interplay of local incorporation law and state decentralization of fiscal and regulatory responsibilities turns poor places into poor municipalities." Without access to resources outside their communities, poor Americans face greater difficulties in mobilizing against the powerful players in the urban sociopolitical system. "By enabling affluent localities and their residents to separate themselves from their poorer neighbors and by providing them with an ideology that justifies their resistance to the claims of the larger society outside their borders, localism further empowers the already powerful" (Briffault 1990, 346). Such political action by affluent whites is not new; it perpetuates the sociospatial apartheid of the cities.

The New Urban Paradigm and Racial Domination

These profound racial realities, which in one sense *are* "the cities," have not received the attention from social scientists or policy analysts that they deserve. Traditional assessments have either ignored racial-ethnic matters or constructed them within rather atheoretical ecological-demographic or ethnographic frameworks. Those researchers constructing the new critical political-economy paradigm have given more attention to matters of racial stratification and domination than mainstream urbanists. In one major review, John Logan and Harvey Molotch provide a general overview of political-economic development in cities, with central emphasis on class domination and some attention to racism. They show how difficult it has been for black urbanites to build up the necessary savings and wealth because of exclusionary barriers that deny them good jobs and stable businesses. They conclude that the ghettoized situation of African Americans is not the result of "recent trends like suburbanization or high-tech displacement. These patterns represent a historically consistent, sequentially reinforcing practice of repression" (Logan and Molotch 1987, 131). While providing insight into the repressive origins of urban apartheid, their analysis is brief and focused on "the dilemma of the ghetto."

In a book on New York City, researchers John Mollenkopf and Manuel Castells (1991, 413–16), two leading contributors to the new urban paradigm, note the increasing segregation of white middle-class residential areas from racially and ethnically diverse residential areas. However, while there is some discussion of racial-ethnic demography and segregated job distributions, not one of the authors in this edited volume gives central attention to racial-ethnic domination in New York City's development as a segregated city. For all their acumen in regard to role of class in cities, many of the new-paradigm researchers have not given enough attention to racial stratification and domination in the shaping and development of U.S. cities. This neglect needs to be rectified by the next generation of urban scholars.

The Global Context of Urban Racial and Class Struggles

One reason why racial-ethnic issues will probably become ever more important for U.S. cities, and for the nation as a whole, is that most of the world's residents are neither white nor European. These peoples and nations (including Japan, India, China, and Korea) are becoming more influential in the world's economic and political systems.

Yet, surprisingly, much U.S. social science is still framed wholly within the framework of the U.S. nation-state. This is true generally for mainstream urban social science. Excessive dependence on this nation-state framework, particularly on its hidden assumptions about U.S. superiority or uniqueness, means that global trends, contexts, and structures are not attended to as closely as they should be. For example, many of the world's economic engines, such as most of the major banks, are no longer housed in U.S. cities. And a growing number of organizations such as the World Bank and of corporations such as Exxon are substantially autonomous of particular governments, including that of the United States. Many U.S.-owned corporations are moving jobs in large numbers from U.S. cities to cities and rural areas overseas. This has had a major negative impact on many U.S. cities. Moreover, international agreements, such as the U.N.'s Universal Declaration of Human Rights, are setting new international standards for societies, such as standards of human relations (for example, the right to a decent-paying job) that go well beyond those of the U.S. civil rights tradition. Mainstream social science in the United States has given too little attention to these changes on the international scene and their implications for the development or decline of U.S. cities. It is scholars in the critical political-economy tradition who have most diligently pursued these global issues (see Chase-Dunn 1985; Smith and Feagin 1987; Smith 1996; Vaughn, Sjoberg, and Reynolds 1993).

Interestingly, as we move into the twenty-first century, many large cities' growth coalitions are seizing on the sobriquet of "global city." A recent reading of the national and international press by the author revealed that the term "global city" has been used for cities as diverse as Singapore, London, Miami, Atlanta, Orlando, Los Angeles, and Chicago. Clearly, some U.S. business and political leaders are already more attuned to the international ties and dimensions of cities than many urban social scientists. Recently, a business leader spoke to Chicago's elite Commercial Club and asked: "Twenty years from now, will Chicago be a global city or a once-great city? And if the club, representing the region's major corporations, doesn't respond, who else will?" (quoted in Krieg, 1997, 11). One hundred CEOs there are now working toward a new development plan for Chicago focused on land use, economic development, transportation, government, and education. As in the past, these business leaders have in mind large-scale government infrastructure projects to bring the city to the level they require to do this global business profitably (see Krieg 1997, 11; see also Sassen 1994).

An increasing number of white business and political leaders now recognize the links between the changing racial-ethnic demography of cities and the future of the nation's systems of class and racial domination. Analysts like Pat Buchanan and Peter Brimelow are pressing to "take back" the cities from their growing non-European populations. In contrast, a few liberal white leaders are beginning to recognize that nativism is not the answer for cities of the future. Defining contemporary Los Angeles as "paradise lost," California State Senator and mayoral aspirant Tom Hayden has recently commented on the city's future: "There's got to be balance between racial and ethnic groups, between our economy and nature and between our striving and our seeking peace of mind. The city is always vibrating with negative tension, envy, hostility, and underlying violence because it's out of balance. A mayor can establish a vision that protects our diversity and all of our citizens . . . This could be the great global city, but only if there's local healing" (quoted in Olney 1997, 9). Racial-ethnic conflict, a lack of healing, is seen as barring the development of Los Angeles as a great global city.

Living in all-white or nearly all-white enclaves does not prepare white Americans for dealing with a world that is composed mostly of people of color. This lack of ability to deal with diversity—and the lack of willingness to redress racial-ethnic oppressions and their negative effects—is a chronic reaction of most white Americans, including powerful whites who shape the development of cities and the society generally. A leading scholar of desegregation, Gary Orfield, has argued that future white leaders who grow up in suburban enclaves will have "no skills in relating to or communicating with minorities" (quoted in Church 1987, 17). This isolation will become even more of a serious handicap for whites as the United States moves into the twenty-first century, over the course of which whites will eventually become a minority of both the metropolitan and national populations.

Bringing Gender to the Center

Until very recently, the processes and structures of gender domination, of patriarchy, have received little attention in urban social science. Indeed, in 1989
Chicago urban sociologist Gerald Suttles (1989) published a book called *The
Man Made City*. As of the mid-1990s, we are beginning to get substantial sociological analysis of the role of gender in the shaping of U.S. cities. Some pioneers of the new urban paradigm gave brief but important attention to gender
issues. In his work on urban social movements Castells (1983, 29–271) examined the role of women in the Paris Commune, the Glasgow rent strike, inner-
city revolts in the U.S., and Madrid neighborhood associations. Within cities
women have regularly mobilized on behalf of the economic and other needs of
families, thereby accenting use-value and everyday experience over the exchange-value logic of capitalism. From this class-oriented mobilization many
women moved, Castells (1983, 309) argues, in the direction of a greater feminist consciousness challenging the patriachal foundations of all social life.

Writing about the same time, urban planner Dolores Hayden (1981, 27–29)
showed how much some urban physical patterns are linked to patriarchy, in
particular how much suburban housing is built around the model of men working outside and women working at home. More recently, analysts like Gottdiener (1994: 158–164) have suggested that middle-class women moving outside
the home into the workplace have had an impact in generating commercial and
spatial changes (e.g., fast food restaurants) in suburban areas. Even here, however, there are some important historical cautions. Many American women,
particularly women of color, have always had to work outside the home. They
have long made the trek between employment areas and residential areas (see
Garber and Turner 1995, xii–xix). Suburbia was developed primarily for white
families. This is an area where much additional research and theory is needed.

Recent work by the few sociologists now working on patriarchy and city development has highlighted a number of other urban issues that need more research. In pioneering work Spain (1992; 1995) has explored how urban spaces
are gendered. She (1995, 256–268) provides as one example public housing,
where the original model of housing for poor married couples has given way
to warehousing unmarried poor women—which Spain suggests is a threat to
the patriarchal order. Probing variations across cities, Appleton (1995, 4–49)
distinguishes between private patriarchy (the gender regime of man-at-work/
woman-at-home typical of suburbs) and public patriarchy (the gender regime
of central cities, with more women-headed households, more economic independence for women, and more dependence on government for income). Het-
erogeneous central cities provide more opportunities for women to resist
patriarchy and develop independently from men, while homogeneous suburbs
enshrine a more incapacitating and entrenched form of patriarchy.

A few urban analysts (see Sassen 1994) have researched or touched on the global dimensions of women's lives. For example, U.S. capitalists have sought out women workers around the globe, who must often work for low wages in rigid patriarchal systems. This job and capital flight reshapes not only rural areas and cities overseas but also areas in the United States, as jobs move out of central cities.

People Fighting Back

An accurate history of cities must encompass the attempts of ordinary people to make city neighborhoods supportive places to live lives and raise families. Ethnographers from those of the Chicago school to recent case study researchers like Herbert Gans (1962), Elijah Anderson (1990), and Anthony Orum (1995) have taught us that cities only "work" because of the people working in them. All urban life is lived in a particular place in space and time, not at the abstract level of the city or urbanization. For that reason, neighborhoods in cities become places of hope or despair, of life or death, of successful or unsuccessful families. They become places of memories and meaning. They are not just about profit and exchange value; they become "home."

When class or racial domination become too burdensome, residents of cities tend to organize and rebel. Some of the best urban analysis, often from those accenting the new urban paradigm, stresses the ways in which people struggle to make cities their own. Urbanites struggle against powerful elites that strive to maintain cities as arenas of class and racial domination. Yet, these movements are local and usually do not target, and cannot readily change, the national or global political-economic systems. This remains a critical problem in urban organizing. Issues of urban political movements have been emphasized by a number of the researchers who have helped to create the new urban paradigm (see Castells 1983; Feagin 1983).

Since at least the 1960s U.S. cities have seen citizen movements involved in power struggles against class and racial domination. These groups provide one source of pressure for the large-scale societal changes mentioned previously. Poor and working-class urbanites, particularly oppressed groups of color, have periodically asserted desires for control over their urban spaces and for much better lives. For example, in San Antonio, Mexican American communities have long suffered neglect from the Anglo establishment in regard to such things as neighborhood flooding and poor governmental services, even while the Anglo elite has found city funds for its preferred development projects. In the mid-1970s community protest against this neglect was harnessed in an activist group called Communities Organized for Public Service (COPS). Organized through family networks and local Catholic parishes, COPS targeted community residents' demands to do something about community services, housing, drugs, and education (Boyte 1984, 139–46). Mexican Americans were elected to political office, and COPS was able to get major concessions from Anglo business and political leaders for neighborhood and other improvements. City government was forced to support many millions of dollars worth of new housing, roads, and other public improvements in Mexican American areas of the city (Feagin and Capek 1989). Still politically effective in the late 1990s, COPS has become a model for racially and ethnically based movements among the formerly disempowered in U.S. cities. Moreover, ACORN organizers, who represent the largest grass-roots organization across the United States, have recently accelerated efforts in organizing Americans of color and other poor urbanites against reactionary programs targeting welfare mothers, in developing campaigns to increase minimum-wage levels, and in attempts to place poor families in abandoned housing in the cities.

Not all protest against class and racial domination has been, or will be, nonviolent. Violence against domination is a common feature of the history of U.S. cities. For example, the 1960s and early 1970s saw several hundred urban uprisings by black Americans living in historically segregated city areas. These urban uprisings were racially and class based although white elites denied their political significance and claimed that they had more to do with the "pathology" of the "underclass" (Feagin and Hahn 1973). The same interpretation has been offered by white political and business leaders for recent riots, such as the April 1992 Los Angeles riot, which started after the acquittal of police officers in the beating of a black man named Rodney King. By the time that uprising was over, ten thousand rioters had been arrested and more than fifty people had been killed. For the first time in the twentieth-century history of major urban uprisings, the majority of those arrested were Latino (Feagin and Vera 1995). Here too we see the impact of the aforementioned demographic changes. In the future the nation's cities will likely see more such revolts if racial desegregation and economic redistribution do not take place.

If urban social scientists are to help in generating nonviolent change in the direction of group empowerment and redistribution of resources, and if they are to develop a more accurate understanding of present and future cities, they must devote much more attention to how, when, and where community groups fight against serious intrusions of class and racial domination into their communities.

Conclusion

In his brilliant book, *The World and Africa*, Du Bois showed that the extreme degradation and poverty in European colonies overseas was "a main cause of wealth and luxury in Europe. The results of this poverty were disease, ignorance, and crime. Yet these had to be represented as natural characteristics of backward peoples" (1965 [1946], 37). Similarly, the new urban paradigm forces us—as social scientists and as citizens—to consider how the wealth and luxury of rich or affluent urbanites and suburbanites is connected to such "urban problems" as the poverty, disease, and crime of the much less affluent. In public discussions and chamber of commerce brochures U.S. cities are often portrayed in terms of large economic development projects, new homes in nicely landscaped suburbs, gleaming office towers, and new multilaned highways. In addition, the local mass media in cities accent everyday discussions of city problems such as poverty, crime, and violence.

Yet, seldom are these two discussions brought together. The latter problems exist substantially because of the former developments, which are generally in the interests of the rich and affluent. Large-scale development projects, such as highways and economic development projects, usually come at the expense of better housing, jobs, and services for the working-class residents of cities, including those in communities of color. Low wages for the many who hold construction and service jobs, which increase profits for the capitalists, help create or maintain low-income communities, which in turn have the fabled "urban problems." Not only residential segregation and spatial isolation but unemployment and underemployment become recurring realities for those in many urban communities, while the rich and affluent classes move to the suburbs and profit from cheap services or good business profits. The realities of city prosperity, "greatness," and "urbanity," are often based, at least in part, on the realities of labor exploitation, racial domination, and business-centered disinvestment or economic development.

The new political-economic approach decenters the more conventional discussions of urban ecology, the impersonal forces such as urbanization and industrialization, and the "culture of poverty" by forcing consideration of the class and racial domination at the heart of urban growth, development, affluence, and decline. This approach suggests that insights about the character of cities stemming from the oppressed are often much better than those of the affluent, because the former experience daily the grim realities of city life. One's perspective on urban development is quite different when issues of class and racial oppression are moved from the margin to the center of analysis. Understanding class oppression and racism is central to an accurate comprehension of how cities have developed and how they continue to be shaped and reshaped (for parallel arguments on sexism, see Bologh 1990, 37; Benokraitis and Feagin 1995).

Moving class and racial oppression to the center does a number of important things for urban analysis. It makes clear that we must go beyond the discussion of suburban or office tower developments for the affluent, or the cruelties of life for the less affluent, to examine how these cruelties are connected to what at first appear to be the positive developments for and by the affluent. It helps us move beyond much mainstream discussion that blames the values, behaviors, and cultures of the poor or of people of color for urban problems. Some can live in prosperous urban enclaves. *because* others must labor in poverty and racial degradation.

In the chapters which follow I have tried to assess many urban questions from this new critical political-economy perspective. I place class and racial domination at the heart of the analysis of city life, change, and development. Framing urban questions this way not only puts the actions of the powerful at the forefront of analysis but also raises questions about their ill-gotten privileges. It features the historical conditions and institutions that protect class and racial privileges. This examination, in turn, makes clearer why people in cities rebel and why, in my judgment, we as social scientists must take a lesson from these urban rebellions and center future research and policy analyses on large-scale city and societal transformation in the direction of class and racial justice and equality.

References

Anderson, Elijah. 1990. *Street Wise: Race, Class, and Change in an Urban Community*. Chicago: University of Chicago Press.

Appleton, Lynn M. 1995. "The gender regimes of American cities." In *Gender in Urban Research*, edited by Judith A. Garber and Robyne S. Turner, 44–59. *Gender in Urban Research*. Thousand Oaks: Sage.

Benokraitis, Nijole and Joe R. Feagin. 1995. *Modern Sexism: Blatant, Subtle and Covert Discrimination*. Englewood Cliffs, N.J.: Prentice-Hall.

Best, Steven and Douglas Kellner. 1991. *Postmodern Theory: Critical Interrogations*. New York: Guilford.

Bologh, Roslyn W. 1990. *Love or Greatness: Max Weber and Masculine Thinking—A Feminist Inquiry*. London: Unwin Hyman.

Boyte, Harry C. 1984. *Community Is Possible*. New York: Harper and Row.

Briffault, Richard. 1990. "Our localism: Part II—Localism and legal theory." *Columbia Law Review* (March) 90:346–452.

Brimelow, Peter. 1995. *Alien Nation: Common Sense about America's Immigration Disaster*. New York: Random House.

Capek, Stella, and Joe R. Feagin. "Grassroots movements in a class perspective." In *Research in Political Sociology*, edited by P. C. Washburn, 27–53. Greenwich, Conn.: JAI Press, 1991).

Castells, Manuel. 1976 [1968]. "Is there an urban sociology?" In *Urban Sociology: Critical Essays*, edited by Chris G. Pickvance, 33–59. London: Tavistock.

Castells, Manuel. 1983. *The City and the Grassroots: A Cross-Cultural Theory of Urban Social Movements*. Berkeley: University of California Press.

Chase-Dunn, Christopher. 1985. "The system of world cities, A.D. 800–1975." In *Urbanization in the World Economy*, edited by Michael Timberlake, 269–92. New York: Academic Press.

Church, George J. 1987. "The boom towns," *Time*. 15 June, 17.

Cross, Theodore. 1984. *The Black Power Imperative: Racial Inequality and the Politics of Nonviolence*. New York: Faulkner.

Du Bois, William E. B. 1965 [1946]. *The World and Africa.* New York: International Publishers.

Du Bois, William E. B. 1968. *The Autobiography of W. E. B. Du Bois.* New York: International Publishers.

Du Bois, William E. B. 1973 [1899]. *The Philadelphia Negro.* Millwood, N.Y.: Kraus-Thomson.

Ellin, Nan. 1996. *Postmodern Urbanism.* Oxford: Blackwell.

Feagin, Joe R. 1983. *The Urban Real Estate Game.* Englewood Cliffs, N.J.: Prentice-Hall.

Feagin, Joe R., and Clairece B. Feagin. 1996. *Racial and Ethnic Relations.* 5th edition. Englewood Cliffs, N.J.: Prentice-Hall.

Feagin, Joe R., and Harlan Hahn. 1973. *Ghetto Revolts: The Politics of Violence in American Cities.* New York: Macmillan.

Feagin, Joe R., and Hernan Vera. 1995. *White Racism: The Basics.* New York: Routledge.

Frey, William H. 1979. "Population movement and city-suburban redistribution: An analytic framework." *Demography* 13:571–88.

Gans, Herbert J. 1962. *The Urban Villagers.* Glencoe, Ill.: Free Press.

Garber, Judith A. and Robyne S. Turner. 1995. "Introduction." In *Gender in Urban Research,* edited by Judith A. Garber and Robyne S. Turner, x–xxvi. *Gender in Urban Research.* Thousand Oaks: Sage.

Gist, Noel P., and Sylvia Fleis Fava. 1974. *Urban Society.* 6th ed. New York: Crowell.

Gottdiener, Mark, 1985. *The Social Production of Urban Space.* Austin: University of Texas Press.

Gottdiener, Mark. 1994. *The New Urban Sociology.* New York: McGraw-Hill.

Gottdiener, Mark. 1997. *The Theming of America: Dreams, Visions, and Commercial Spaces.* Boulder, Colo.: Westview.

Harvey, David. 1973. *Social Justice and the City.* Baltimore: Johns Hopkins University Press.

Hawley, Amos H. 1981. *Urban Society: An Ecological Approach.* 2d ed., New York: Wiley.

Hayden, Dolores. 1981. *The Grand Domestic Revolution.* Cambridge: MIT Press.

Keating, Ann Durkin. 1989. *Building Chicago: Suburban Developers and the Creation of a Divided Metropolis.* Columbus: Ohio University Press.

Krieg, Richard M. 1997. "Talking politics: A second Burnham plan: Will it succeed?" *Crain's Chicago Business.* 21 April, 11.

Kuhn, Thomas. 1962. *The Structure of Scientific Revolutions.* Chicago: University of Chicago Press.

Lefebvre, Henri. 1991. *The Production of Space.* Oxford: Blackwell.

Lefebvre, Henri. 1996. *Writings on Cities.* Oxford: Blackwell.

Logan, John R., and Harvey L. Molotch. 1987. *Urban Fortunes: The Political Economy of Place.* Berkeley: University of California Press.

Massey, Douglas S., and Nancy A. Denton. 1993. *American Apartheid: Segregation and the Making of the Underclass.* Cambridge: Harvard University Press.

McLeod, Ramon G. 1996. "U.S. population expected to be half minorities by 2050." *San Francisco Chronicle*. 14 March, A3.

Mahoney, Martha R. 1995. "Shaping American communities: Segregation, housing and the urban poor: Segregation, whiteness, and transformation." *University of Pennsylvania Law Review* (May) 143:1659–84.

Mollenkopf, John, and Manuel Castells. 1991. "Conclusion: Is New York a dual city?" In *Dual City: Restructuring New York*, edited by John Mollenkopf and Manuel Castells, New York: Russell Sage.

Molotch, Harvey. 1976. "The city as a growth machine." *American Journal of Sociology* 82 (September): 309–32.

Myrdal, Gunnar. 1964 [1944]. *An American Dilemma*. Vol. 2. New York: McGraw-Hill.

Olney, Warren, 1997. "Commentary; perspectives on the mayor's race; two views of what Los Angeles is and what it needs." *Los Angeles Times*. 2 April. B9.

Orum, Anthony M. 1995. *City-Building in America*. Boulder, Colo.: Westview.

Park, Robert E. 1918. "Education in its relation to the conflict and fusion of cultures: With special reference to the problems of the immigrant, the Negro, and missions." *Publications of the American Sociological Society*. Vol. 13.

Park, Robert E. 1950. *Race and Culture*. New York: Free Press.

Park, Robert E., Ernest W. Burgess, and Roderick D. McKenzie. 1925. *The City*. Chicago: University of Chicago Press.

Park, Robert E., and Ernest W. Burgess. 1921. *Introduction to the Science of Sociology*. Chicago: University of Chicago Press.

Ringer, Benjamin B. 1983. *"We the People" and Others*. New York: Tavistock.

Sassen, Saskia. 1994. *Cities in a World Economy*. Thousand Oaks, Calif.: Pine Forge Press.

Schwendinger, Herman, and Julia Schwendinger. 1974. *The Sociologists of the Chair: A Radical Analysis of the Formative Years of North American Sociology (1883–1922)*. New York: Basic Books.

Smith, David A. 1996. *Third World Cities in Global Perspective: The Political Economy of Uneven Urbanization*. Boulder, Colo.: Westview.

Smith, Michael Peter, ed. 1992. *After Modernism: Global Restructuring and the Changing Boundaries of City Life*. New Brunswick: Transaction Publishers.

Smith, Michael Peter, and Joe R. Feagin, eds. 1987. *The Capitalist City: Global Restructuring and Community Politics*. London: Blackwell.

Spain, Daphne. 1992. *Gendered Spaces*. Chapel Hill: University of North Carolina Press.

Spain, Daphne. 1995. "Public Housing and the Beguinage." In *Gender in Urban Research*, edited by Judith A. Garber and Robyne S. Turner, 256–70. *Gender in Urban Research*. Thousand Oaks: Sage.

Suttles, Gerald. 1989. *The Man Made City*. Chicago: University of Chicago Press.

Vaughn, Ted R., Gideon Sjoberg, and Larry Reynolds. 1993. *A Critique of Contemporary American Sociology*. New York: General Hall.

Weaver, Robert C. 1948. *The Negro Ghetto*. New York: Russell and Russell.

Weiss, Marc A. 1987. *The Rise of the Community Builders: The American Real Estate Industry and Urban Land Planning*. New York: Columbia University Press.

Wilson, William Julius. 1995. "The political economy and urban racial tensions." *American Economist* (March) 39:3–6.

Zukin, Sharon. 1995. *The Cultures of Cities*. London: Blackwell.

I

CITIES IN GLOBAL PERSPECTIVE

Section I includes three articles that probe the global contexts of city formation and growth. In chapter 1, "Cities and the New International Division of Labor: An Overview," Michael Peter Smith and I provided an introduction for the first major book to deal centrally and empirically with how the development of large cities is linked to the world capitalist economy, its large multinational corporations, and its processes of economic restructuring across the globe. In this introduction to an edited book, we press the new urban political-economy paradigm in a global direction and suggest where and how major international cities specialize in certain areas of the capitalist world economy, how this specialization and other economic restructuring is supported by state action, and how the internationalization of metropolitan development has an impact on, and is shaped by, household and community action and restructuring.

In chapter 2, "The Global Context of Metropolitan Growth: Houston and the Oil Industry," I examine a major international city, one with ties to economic regions and cities across the globe. Called both the "oil capital of the world" and the "capital of the Sunbelt," Houston has been at the center of the economic boom in the Sunbelt. For many decades, Houston's oil-driven economy has spurred economic and demographic expansion, though with periodic boom and bust cycles linked to the fortunes of the world's oil-gas industry. This case study shows that the new critical political-economy paradigm offers more utility than older paradigms for making theoretical sense out of the development of global cities. Houston's sociospatial development is linked both to shifts in the capitalist mode of production and to the assisting role of state officials working with capitalistic interests to create strong, and "free enterprise," urban development. Since World War II many billions of dollars' worth of oil-gas contracts have been made between Houston companies and oil fields and firms in many areas of the world's oil-gas economy, from Malaysia to the North Sea. Thus, this metropolis's development reveals that the world context of cities must be examined carefully in order to understand the causes, character, and significance of contemporary trends in urbanization.

In chapter 3, I provide a comparative analysis of Houston with Europe's reputed "oil capital," Aberdeen, Scotland. As with Houston, I use not only government and historical data but also numerous field interviews with those at the center of local development to draw an in-depth portrait of the character and consequences of extractive (oil-gas) development. One issue here is how the placement and impact of extractive industries like oil and gas in core capitalist countries differs from that in the rest of the world. One difference is that prior economic development in core countries has enabled them to create infrastructures facilitating later advanced economic development. Here I also explore differences in Houston's and Aberdeen's development within their own regions and the significance of the timing of capitalist investment in the emergence of urban regions. Both have been greatly influenced by the investment decisions of the multinational oil-gas corporations, but Aberdeen's later expansion brought large-firm dominance earlier than in the case of Houston, whose earlier entry and stronger state-assisted development meant that it actually helped to create or foster large multinational firms in the oil and gas industry. This meant that the people in the Aberdeen region did not get the development of new firms as they expected, and they did not develop the national political clout of the Houston region.

Taken together, these articles show that corporate expansion in the world capitalist system does not exist in a vacuum, but has a major impact on urban regions around the globe. Corporate investment and disinvestment are linked constantly to state action and have major economic, social, and political effects on urban households and communities. The capitalist world economy is integrated economically but situated geographically in those human spaces we call cities. The activities of capitalists and their state allies create urban contradictions and thus have a fundamental impact on the activities of households, on how they live their lives, on whether they can find jobs, on whether they stay or immigrate, and on whether they mobilize to oppose the oppressiveness of class domination in the world's cities.

1

Cities and the New International Division of Labor: An Overview[1]

Joe R. Feagin and Michael Peter Smith

Introduction

The world of modern capitalism is both a worldwide net of corporations and a global network of cities. There are world command cities such as New York, London, and Tokyo, which have extraordinary concentrations of top corporate decision makers representing financial, industrial, commercial,

---

This chapter is reprinted with minor revisions from Feagin, Joe R., and Michael P. Smith. 1987. Cities and the new international division of labor: An overview. Chap. 1. pp.3-34 in *The Capitalist City*, edited by M. P. Smith and J. R. Feagin. London: Basil Blackwell.

[1] In this introduction we note the following articles in our edited volume: Michael Timberlake, "World-system theory and the study of comparative urbanization"; Norman J. Glickman, "Cities and the international division of labor"; Michael Peter Smith and Richard Tardanico, "Urban theory reconsidered: Production, reproduction and collective action"; David C. Perry, "The politics of dependency in deindustrializing America: The case of Buffalo, New York"; Saskia Sassen-Koob, "Growth and informalization at the core: A preliminary report on New York City"; Richard Child Hill and Joe R. Feagin, "Detroit and Houston: Two cities in global perspective"; Edward W. Soja, "Economic restructuring and the internationalization of the Los Angeles region"; Patricia Ann Wilson, "Lima and the new international division of labor"; Desmond S. King, "The state, capital and urban change in Britain"; Sophie Body-Gendrot, "Plant closures in socialist France"; Helen I. Safa, "Urbanization, the informal economy and state policy in Latin America"; June Nash, "Community and corporations in the restructuring of industry"; Enzo Mingione, "Urban survival strategies, family structure and informal practices"; Susan S. Fainstein, "Local mobilization and economic discontent"; Margit Mayer, "Restructuring and popular opposition in West German cities"; and John Walton, "Urban protest and the global political economy: The IMF riots."

law, and media corporations. Even a cursory examination of such "first-tier" cities shows the intimate relationship between the weblike organization of modern capitalism and the network of cities across the globe. The major organizational units in the capitalist web are the large international banks and transnational corporations; the latter today account for 70–80 percent of world trade outside the centrally planned socialist countries (Clairmonte and Cavanagh 1981, 5). The top 500–1,000 multinational corporations not only sit at the summit of a pyramid of interrelated capitalistic firms of all sizes, but they also create a truly transnational economy, one whose primary geographical nodes are the world's cities.

But most cities are not at the world command level; indeed, different cities occupy a variety of niches in the capitalist world economy. There are the specialized command cities which concentrate the headquarters operations of particular industries, such as the auto companies in Detroit, Michigan, and the rubber companies in Akron, Ohio. There are divisional command cities like Houston, Texas, with its absence of top oil firm headquarters and its high concentration of major divisions of top oil firms. There are cities specializing in a particular type of manufacturing production such as steel-making in Birmingham, Alabama, and car manufacturing in Birmingham, England. There are state command cities like Washington, D.C., and Brazilia. And there are numerous cities which are difficult to classify because of the diversity of their economic and state functions, such as the huge cities of Singapore, Mexico City, and São Paulo in the "Third World." Nonetheless, all these cities are linked together by the organizational web of transnational corporations, their facilities, subsidiaries, suppliers, and subcontractors. Major cities, as the places where the transnational corporate web is grounded physically, are the cotter pins holding the capitalist world economy together.

These interconnected networks of firms and cities have been described in terms of such concepts as a capitalist world economy or "the new international division of labor." The latter phrase has become particularly common since the publication of the seminal book of the same name by Fröbel, Heinrichs, and Kreye. Published in 1980, this book defined the new international division of labor as the shifting world market for labor coupled with the shifting world market for production sites (cf. also Cohen 1981). Plant closures in core industrial countries are part of these changing markets, as are new plant startups in Third World countries. Disinvestment and unemployment in one city in one nation can be linked to investment and employment in another nation. The shifting investments of transnational corporations can determine the future of labor, production sites, cities, and nations.

Before we examine this changing global economy in detail, we should note that a shifting international division of labour is not, in fact, new. For at least two centuries capitalists have expanded operations across state boundaries to exploit raw materials, labor, production sites, and overseas markets. Writing in the mid-nineteenth century, Marx (1967, 451) described the 'new and international division of labor' that this global expansion entailed:

> By constantly making a part of the hands [workers] "supernumerary" modern history, in all countries where it has taken root, gives a spur to emigration and to the colonisation of foreign lands, which are thereby converted into settlements for growing the raw materials of the mother country; just as Australia, for example, was converted into a colony for growing wool. A new and international division of labor, a division suited to the requirements of the chief centres of industry, springs up, and converts one part of the globe into a chief agricultural field of production, for supplying the other part which remains a chiefly industrial field.

This was a major step in the global division of labor under capitalism—peripheral agricultural dependency on core industrial centers—but over time nations outside the core became much more than suppliers of agricultural and raw materials for the "chief centers of industry." Gradually, their agricultural and raw materials production for export was paralleled by industrial production for export. The newly industrialized nations and their cities thus became increasingly important in the world economic order. In recent decades a new international division of labor has emerged, one that no longer involves medium-sized firms with distinctive national identities exchanging goods across national boundaries, but rather one that increasingly involves transnational firms investing heavily in many countries and trading goods and services with one another, or transnational firms' subsidiaries trading within the globally extended framework of one large corporation.

The scholarly contributions to this volume highlight several important propositions about urban development in this transforming global economy of modern-capitalism.

1. The causes, character, and significance of urban development can best be understood by analyzing cities in terms of their transnational linkages, especially their connections within the world capitalistic economy, its dominant multinational firms, and its processes of economic restructuring.
2. Moving through stages of economic growth and change, many major cities in the world economy tend to specialize in particular raw materials, production, distribution, marketing, and financial and other 'service' activities, while other cities house complex combinations of such activities.
3. The restructuring of global, national, and local economies is intimately intertwined with state action and mediation; the role of the state can be generative or reactive.

4. Economic restructuring and state restructuring are intrinsically associated with household and community restructuring, and thus with geographical (spatial) transformation.

5. Household and community restructuring are not mere by-products of economic and state restructuring; the everyday activities of people living in households and communities—informalization, immigration, formation of networks, and political action—are constitutive elements in the process of urban transformation; they shape as well as reflect the global flows of labor and capital and the character of state policies.

The Global Economy of Capitalism: Structuring and Restructuring

Foreign Investment

A distinguishing feature of global restructuring has been the expansion of U.S. investment abroad and the sharp increase in foreign investment in the United States, both trends which Glickman's chapter in this book (see chapter 3) examines in some detail. Glickman notes that U.S. assets abroad in 1983 were $226 billion, a tripling of assets since 1970, while direct foreign investment in the U.S. went up tenfold, from $13 billion to $134 billion, in the same period. Large multinational firms have been moving capital in both directions. These capital flows signal the scale of the global economic restructuring which has been taking place since at least the late 1960s. The capitalist world system periodically undergoes global restructuring, typically in response to shifts in international competition. There are a number of forces and processes here: the concentration of investment capital in a decreasing number of firms, peripheral industrialization and the 'global assembly line', intensified transnational competition, changes in the mode of production, large-scale labor migration flows, and capital restructuring by core country multinationals to reestablish favorable conditions for profitability in an increasingly competitive global environment.

Corporate Cities

Noting the global context of urban economies is becoming commonplace in the social science literature, but clarity about what this global context means is much less common. The central economic actors in the international division of labor are the top 500–1,000 multinational corporations. These major organizations have created an integrated, worldwide network of production, exchange, finance and corporate services arranged in a complex hierarchical system of cities. The headquarters executives of these corporations are particularly effective at global scanning for the optimal labor costs and control factors, resource costs, markets, and state subsidies. Clearly, these large companies have been able to integrate their operations on a global scale (Cohen 1981, 302–4). As can be seen in Table 1.1, the headquarters facilities of the largest five hundred multinational firms (excluding banks) are disproportionately located in the major cities of core countries.

The New York metropolitan area is the headquarters capital of the core cities, capturing 59 of the top 500 transnational firms, including 18 of the top 100. London and Tokyo are at roughly the same level in the 1980s; both now house the headquarters of more than 30 of the top transnationals. Somewhat less important are Paris, Chicago, Essen, Osaka, and Los Angeles with 14–26 each of the top 500 companies, followed by an industrial grouping including Houston, Pittsburgh, and Hamburg. All cities with five or more of the top 500 companies are in the United States, Great Britain, France, Germany, Italy, Canada, Sweden, and Japan. More countries are included when we examine cities with only 2–4 of the top 500 firms. These include Australia, Belgium, the Netherlands, and the first "Third World" country, South Korea. (South Africa is an ambiguous case.) When cities with only one large transnational firm are examined, we find many more countries represented, including a scattering of firms in underdeveloped countries from Brazil to India.

Another instructive way of examining the relationship between transnational firms and cities is to list the 17 largest cities in the world using 1984 data (see table 1.2). This population ranking may have changed somewhat since the 1984 survey, but five of the world's largest cities here have *no* transnational headquarters. Two of these, not surprisingly, are in the People's Republic of China, but the other three are in Brazil, India, and Egypt. And four other cities, in Argentina, Brazil, Mexico, and India, have only one transnational firm. While most of the world's largest corporations are in large cities, it is clear that city size is not necessarily correlated with economic power. In short, a handful of cities house *all* the top firms. If we extend this list to the world's cities over one million (a total of 162) we find that 75 percent have *no* multinational firms' headquarters.

Multinational corporations have expanded dramatically since the Second World War, both in their outreach into noncapitalist areas of the globe and in their own corporate structure. This industrial expansion typically involves investment in labor and fixed capital, ranging from factories, headquarters offices and warehouses, to ports and toxic waste disposal facilities. The decisions as to where to locate these fixed capital activities are shaped by a complex array of political and economic issues and relationships, not just those pertaining to a particular firm or set of firms, but also to the trends in the world economy. Moreover, this worldwide network of fixed capital and labor investments by transnationals has been matched by the creation of a web of international banking corporations and markets, a development that John Walton's paper (chapter 17) highlights. Coupled with the growth of the financial

Table 1.1 Headquarters location of the world's largest transnational firms, 1984

	City	Metropolitan area population (000s)	Number of firms
1	New York	17,082	59
2	London	11,100	37
3	Tokyo	26,200	34
4	Paris	9,650	26
5	Chicago	7,865	18
6	Essen	5,050	18
7	Osaka	15,900	15
8	Los Angeles	10,519	14
9	Houston	3,109	11
10	Pittsburgh	2,171	10
11	Hamburg	2,250	10
12	Dallas	3,232	9
13	St. Louis	2,228	8
14	Detroit	4,315	7
15	Toronto	2,998	7
16	Frankfurt	1,880	7
17	Minneapolis	2,041	7
18	San Francisco	4,920	6
19	Rome	3,115	6
20	Stockholm	1,402	6
21	Turin	1,191	5
22	Hartford, CT	1,020	5
23	Fairfield, CT	100	5
24	Seoul	6,889	4
25	Atlanta	2,196	4
26	Montreal	2,828	3
27	Stuttgart	1,835	3
28	Cologne	1,810	3
29	Cleveland	2,174	3
30	Milan	3,775	3
31	Basel	580	3
32	Eindhoven, Netherlands	374	3
33	Midland, MI	100	3
34	Genoa	830	2
35	Zurich	780	2
36	Akron, OH	606	2
37	Winston–Salem, NC	291	2
38	Peoria, IL	320	2
39	Ashland, KY	100	2
40	Wilmington, DE	100	2
41	Bethlehem, PA	100	2
42	Southfield, MI	100	2
43	Moline, IL	100	2

Table 1.1 (Continued)
Headquarters location of the world's largest transnational firms, 1984

	City	Metropolitan area population (000s)	Number of firms
44	Philadelphia	5,254	2
45	Johannesburg	3,650	2
46	Madrid	4,515	2
47	Melbourne	2,722	2
48	Munich	1,955	2
49	San Diego	1,788	2
50	Cincinnati	1,481	2
51	Rotterdam	1,090	2

Sources: Rand McNally Commercial Atlas & Marketing Guide, Rand McNally & Co.: Chicago, 1986; *Statistical Abstract of the U.S.,* U.S. Department of Commerce Bureau of the Census, 1985; *Ward's Business Directory,* vol. 3, Information Access Co.: Belmont, CA, 1985.

Banks are excluded from the data sources. Size is in terms of sales. The population figures listed above are Ranally Metropolitan Areas (RMAs), which include outlying urbanized areas (e.g. suburban towns) around the city giving the area its name.

web has been the expansion of other transnational-related services, such as law, accounting and advertising corporations (cf. Cohen 1981, 288). And, perhaps most important of all, the large transnational firms are the foundation on which not only service-related firms, but also a huge array of small to middle-sized commercial and industrial corporations, are grounded. A little-researched dimension of the modern global economy is the major multiplier effect that the top multinationals have on the diffuse urban economies in which they operate. A great many, perhaps most smaller corporations, as well as the office and shopping center developments in which they are located, would not exist were it not for the multinationals operating in or headquartered there.

Capital Centralization and Export Industrialization

A major driving force behind the expansion of this capitalist world economy is the centralization of capital, the process whereby smaller firms merge into or are taken over by a larger firm, or large firms come together. Mergers and takeovers proliferate in times of economic crisis, as healthier firms take over those in economic difficulty. This increase in capital under a unified command can facilitate a more rapid shift in large-scale productive activities from one region to another than would be possible under a smaller firm. It also allows larger-scale investments. With the development of large concentrations of capital under a unified command, it is easier for the larger firms to take advantage of worldwide labor conditions (N. Smith 1984, 146). Together with competition and periodic crises in profitability, concentration generated the search for

Table 1.2 Firms in the world's 17 largest cities

City	Metropolitan area population (000s)	Firms
1 Tokyo	26,200	34
2 New York	17,082	59
3 Mexico City	14,600	1
4 Osaka	15,900	15
5 São Paulo	12,700	0
6 Seoul	11,200	4
7 London	11,100	37
8 Calcutta	11,100	0
9 Buenos Aires	10,700	1
10 Los Angeles	10,519	14
11 Bombay	9,950	1
12 Paris	9,650	26
13 Peking	9,340	0
14 Rio de Janeiro	9,200	1
15 Cairo	8,500	0
16 Shanghai	8,300	0
17 Chicago	7,865	18

Source: See table 1.1.

cheaper and more 'disciplined' labor pools. In addition, a sharp drop in the cost of sea and air transport and satellite communications has facilitated corporation decision makers to utilize the huge disparities in wages across cities, regions and nations. Thus Third World nations and their cities have been able to compete with core countries in labor-intensive production, as well as with state subsidies for production. In response to this competition, three reactions have taken place in core countries: (1) the general exporting of older labor-intensive jobs; (2) the automating of core jobs to increase the productivity of the higher-wage workers there; and (3) as Sassen-Koob points out in this book (chapter 6), the creation of new low-wage jobs concentrated in a few large core cities as a result of increased subcontracting, customized production for affluent markets, and labor-intensive, mass production for low-income markets in those cities.

Direct foreign investment in labor-intensive production by transnational firms is not new. However, from the 1910s to the late 1960s much of that capital investment was for plants to produce for *local* markets overseas. Since the 1970s manufacturing in foreign countries for reexport to the United States and other core countries has grown dramatically, catapulting cities in the periphery into much greater importance as industrial cities. This is a central dimension of the new international division of labor. In the last two decades the world capitalist system has switched substantially, and for the first time in its history, to overseas volume production of manufactured products in Third World cities for reexport to the home markets in core cities. One analysis of Asian countries found that the proportion of reexport sales increased from less than 10 percent to more than 25 percent between 1966 and 1977 for U.S.-affiliated firms: the proportion was a remarkable 70 percent for electrical machinery (Grunwald and Flamm 1985, 3). By 1981 about 22 percent of manufacturing imports into the United States from developing countries were assembled abroad by U.S. firms for reexport. The process of globalization of manufacturing, vertically integrated across national boundaries, began with textiles and garment manufacturing, then spread to radios, TVs, and automobiles. Most recently, high-tech electronics products (e.g., semiconductors) have become part of this global factory (Grunwald and Flamm 1985, 6–7).

"Export" industrialization has brought major changes to cities in both developed and developing nations, since their links to the world economy are increased and their dependence upon multinational firms and outside investors is increased. In the Third World, the net effect of this type of industrialization is usually negative in terms of inequality, dependency and the costs of urban growth (Grunwald and Flamm 1985, 8). Capitalist expansion has emphasized the goal of accumulation, which creates a situation of affluent development in certain areas of the core cities at one "pole" of the world economy and dependent development or underdevelopment in peripheral cities at the other. Yet the pockets of affluence created in core cities, in turn, generate demands for customized production and personal services performed by low-wage workers, thereby contributing to uneven development within growing cities at the core. As Perry makes clear (chapter 5), the new pattern of capitalist expansion has also made peripheral previously prosperous core industrial cities like Buffalo, New York.

Yet the underdeveloped capitalist countries are not identical. One should make a clear distinction between the leading eight or nine 'underdeveloped' capitalist economies and the rest; indeed these leading countries account for an estimated three-quarters of manufactured exports, such as textiles, clothing and electronics, from all underdeveloped capitalist economies. The expansionist industrial bourgeoisies in countries such as South Korea, Hong Kong, Singapore, Taiwan, Malaysia, India, Indonesia, Brazil, and Mexico not only facilitate core country transnational penetration of their own economies with free trade zones, tax write-offs, and weak regulation but also develop their own transnational corporations (e.g., South Korea's huge Hyundai conglomerate) which exploit the more undeveloped capitalistic economies.

In addition, private-public partnerships to promote economic development are common in the leading underdeveloped countries. As Clairmonte and Cavanagh (1981, 5) note, export manufacturing is dominated by subsidiaries of multinational firms, "but the pattern is changing toward one of dependent partnership by domestic state and private capital." Big firms in these countries are sometimes jointly owned private—state oligopolies. The critical urban aspect of this second-tier of peripheral capitalist economies can be seen in the fact that the principal cities in such leading underdeveloped countries play a much more important role in the world economy (and politics) than those cities in the dozens of lesser peripheral nations such as Peru, a country discussed in Wilson's article (chapter 9) in this volume.

Some Contradictions

As is suggested by the increasing tendency towards uneven development within leading urban growth poles at the core, the globalization of production has inherent contradictions for the developed 'pole' nations. One contradiction can be seen in the abandonment of existing fixed capital in plants, warehouses, offices, and the like in declining cities of core industrial countries. The abandoned fixed capital investments of U.S. industrial corporations in Detroit, Buffalo, and Pittsburgh illustrate this—a point highlighted in Hill and Feagin's and Perry's chapters in this book (7 and 5). From the 1920s to the 1980s the movement of surplus capital into Third World countries, as well as into Europe after World War II, at first created prosperity for U.S. export-oriented corporations. Yet this export capital has periodically created new corporate competitors, which come back later to threaten and reduce the profitability of U.S. corporations, and thus generate a search for enhanced profitability. Meanwhile, U.S. workers face plant closures that are linked to the flight of capital overseas. For example, the move of capital overseas in the seven-year period 1975–82 displaced 170,000 workers in the textile/garment industry alone, and another 75,000 jobs in the electrical industry (Grunwald and Flamm 1985, 223).

Global expansion of core country multinationals is also linked to the global expansion of the United States and its NATO allies' military establishments. While corporate capitalists like to speak of themselves as 'peacemongers' desiring to integrate even the Communist bloc into their world economy, it is also the case that the United States and other NATO navies guarantee multinational access to harbors on all the oceans. In times of energy crisis, for example, the U.S. Sixth Fleet protects the interests of U.S. firms in Middle East oil. U.S. military power is still seen as crucial to the political stability necessary to ensure corporate profitability in many developing countries. The constant threat of class- or religious-based revolutions (e.g., Iran), as well as of political terrorism directed against the core nations of the capitalist world economy, has led to the systematic expansion of the military of these core nations since 1945. Thus in 1985 the United States alone had 241,000 sailors at sea and 480,000 soldiers stationed overseas, the latter not only in West Germany, but in 39 other countries and territories including Bermuda (1380), Panama (10,270), Italy (10,170), Greece (2900), Spain (12,000), Turkey (3800), Japan (71,760),

South Korea (44,160), Egypt (1500), and the Philippines (17,410). There are in fact thousands of U.S. military bases and installations in these forty countries and territories. In addition, half the world's nations today have military dictatorships, most with extensive trade with U.S. transnationals tied to the U.S. military—industrial complex (Sivard 1985, 13; Arkin and Fieldhouse 1985, 147). These countries also have cities which are havens for corporations seeking a docile labor force, a friendly government and supportive state policies.

After World War II, the Pentagon divided the globe into regions for military planning, with a high-ranking military officer in command, an arrangement no other country has established (Anon. 1986, 2). This global military planning does not distinguish clearly between the needs of the nation–state and those of its transnationals. As an Air Force General expressed it in a National War College study, an 'indirect' national security strategy argues for the protection of Americans through the proliferation of American values around the globe, using as one dissemination mechanism "multinational enterprise," whose "growing arsenal of foreign-based business operations is working for us around the clock. Its osmotic action transmits and transfuses not only American methods of business operation, banking, and marketing techniques; but our legal systems and concepts, our political philosophies" (Barnet and Muller 1974, 101). The multinational corporation is part of the broad American national security plan, which includes the most massive global military organization in world history.

Yet this global military expansion has its own built-in contradictions. The hundreds of billions of dollars spent to buttress this expansion have produced a very heavy drain on the tax resources available to the United States and its NATO allies. This drain is now so great that it threatens the international banks which are an essential part of the debt structure created to finance the military expansion. In addition, the massive military expenditures are a major reason for the sharp curtailment of welfare state programs in core countries, an austerity which, in turn, has created conditions conducive to popular mobilization, particularly in Europe.

In the United States, where the modern mass consumption paradise has been enshrined, the key American values of individualized consumption and personal security in homogeneous local communities have nonetheless been threatened by the labor market restructuring and spatial reorganization of U.S. cities that is occasioned by global economic restructuring. Thus, a final contradiction is that even in the most advanced capitalist country, the fundamental bases of mass consent—anticipated improved standards of middle-income mass consumption and the availability of 'good communities' and urban facilities for social reproduction—are being undermined by the $300 billion commitments to military hegemony. Some of the political implications of this contradiction are discussed below in the chapters by Nash, Perry, Fainstein, and Smith and Tardanico (chapters 13, 5, 15, and 4).

The Restructuring of Cities

Fundamental economic restructuring at the global level means restructuring in those other critical contexts within which the world's households live, including the city and the community. We shall now focus upon the city. We visualize five basic types of urban restructuring that are part of the global revolution that analysts since Marx have called the "new international division of labor":

a. economic restructuring in cities;
b. state restructuring in cities;
c. household restructuring (including migration) in cities;
d. community (and community politics) restructuring in cities; and
e. spatial restructuring in cities.

Economic Restructuring

Economic Change in U.S. Cities

In order to make sense of the economic restructuring which underlies the many changes in households, communities, cities, and states, we shall start with a breakdown of the changes which characterize major U.S. cities such as Detroit, Houston, Los Angeles, and New York. We shall then examine European and Third World cities. In looking at U.S. cities one can distinguish at least five different aspects of the economic restructuring there. These are (1) plant closure, (2) plant start-ups, (3) corporate center development, (4) the expansion of service and other types of jobs related to the office developments, and (5) corporate expansion in outlying areas.

Plant closures have become commonplace in the U.S. and European cities, as manufacturing decentralizes around the globe. In chapter 8 of this volume, Soja notes the loss of thousands of manufacturing jobs in Los Angeles in older unionized industries such as autos, rubber and steel. Similarly, New York City lost half a million jobs between the 1960s and 1980s. The chapter by Hill and Feagin (chapter 7) documents the fact that plant closures and disinvestment can occur in any city, whether it be an old industrial city like Detroit or a more recent industrial "boom town" like Houston. The reasons for economic restructuring in these cities have been variously ascribed, and they include renewed competition from Europe and Japan, profit cycles in mature industries, and the desire of industrial capital in core countries to renegotiate the terms of past concessions to organized labor. Indeed, many of the lost manufacturing jobs were well-paid, and were so because of decades of political struggle by core country trade unions.

Although plant closures receive considerable media attention, they are not the only sign of economic change. Another feature of economic restructuring can be seen in plant start-ups, even in those U.S. cities which have suffered many plant closures. In the 1970s and 1980s an estimated six thousand manufacturing 'sweatshops' were opened in New York, Los Angeles, and Chicago, employing a total of 85,000 workers, particularly immigrant women workers from Asia, Mexico, and Central America (Anon. 1984, 7). One reason for the rise of these sweatshops in garment and electronics manufacturing is the requirement of engineers and designers to have some manufacturing facilities nearby for prototype and related production requirements. Moreover, it is important to note that the movement of capital, interregionally or internationally, is linked to the migration of labor. The availability of a vast reservoir of illegal immigrant labor lacking the basic right of citizenship and willing to work for low wages is a major factor contributing to the rise of these new sweatshops and their spatial concentration in large U.S. core cities (M. P. Smith 1987). As documented by Sassen-Koob (chapter 6), other factors contributing to the growth of new labor-intensive, low-wage manufacturing facilities in core cities include: (a) subcontracting by formal sector firms to informal sector subcontractors to avoid state regulation of the labor process; (b) the growth of a low-income mass market of immigrants and displaced workers who can only consume cheaply produced goods; and (c) the increased demand for customized products by retailers catering to gentrified high-income service workers in restructured metropolitan cores.

The expansion of office-related corporate activities in core cities has increased white-collar employment, from top corporate executives to typists and filing clerks. This is a critical feature of the economic restructuring in many, but by no means all American cities. The construction of millions of square feet of office space in central cities has been linked to the centralization of corporate decision making and communications functions in corporate headquarters and in major subsidiary facilities, as well as in the very large number of firms (e.g., law firms) servicing corporate headquarters (Feagin 1983, 64–65). From London to New York or Tokyo major transnational firms have created not only a huge nested complex of personal and business service firms, but also an array of small and medium-sized commercial and industrial corporations crucially dependent on the transnational enterprises. This organizational centralization of transnationals is associated with a number of organizational trends among large corporations, including the tens of thousands of mergers since 1960, reorganization in the face of increased foreign competition, and "economies of scale" that come from a centralized communications center. The concentration and centralization of capital in fewer firms is often associated with a concentration of office headquarters and major subdivisions in selected cities. Most jobs in the corporate centers are distributed across three basic categories: better-paying managerial and professional jobs, lower-paying clerical and sales jobs, and low-paid service jobs. Rapid growth in headquarters cities, or in the central core of such cities, can also bring a range of social costs, such as inadequate water and sewerage supplies (Feagin 1985).

The number of low-paid service jobs has increased so dramatically in many cities that it is sometimes viewed as a distinct type of economic restructuring. In part, this is because personal, commercial and clerical service work has grown in such places as a kind of multiplier effect of the conversion of these core cities to corporate headquarters operations and to tourist, professional service, restaurant, and entertainment meccas (Sassen-Koob, 1983; and chapter 6). While some producer service jobs pay a good wage, the majority of jobs are low-waged. For example, "more than 60 percent of the service jobs in New York City pay salaries below the Bureau of Labor Statistics' living standard for a low-income family of four, while 25 percent of full-time service workers earn less than the poverty level" (McGahey 1983, 23). The numerous office complexes in central cities require large numbers of low-paid workers to clean them, as well as a large cohort of restaurant workers, laundry workers, dog walkers, residential construction workers, and the like to serve the better-paid white-collar workers who work in the complexes or who reside in central city areas. Indeed, many low-paid "service" and construction workers serve the higher-paid "service" workers; a fact which suggests the basic flaw in the idea of a unified 'service society' found in much of the social science literature. Here again we see capital flows into the central city linked to labor migration from the underdeveloped countries.

A fifth major type of economic restructuring, especially in larger U.S. cities, has involved corporate expansion in suburban areas (M. P. Smith 1979, 238–40). In numerous U.S. cities the downtown corporate center development has been paralleled by a decentralized pattern of development in outlying areas. Office and industrial parks sprawl outwards across the landscape to the hinterlands of cities from San Francisco, Los Angeles and Houston; to Atlanta and Boston. New industrial complexes, some with thousands of firms like northern California's Silicon Valley, have been constructed on the outskirts of large cities (Rogers and Larsen, 1984). In the case of Los Angeles (described in Soja, chapter 8) plant closures on a large scale have coexisted not only with corporate center development but also with extensive new plant openings in the electronics and aerospace industries, high-technology firms which are clustered in outer cities, mostly on the western edge of the Los Angeles basin. This coexistence of different types of economic restructuring is common in U.S. and other core country cities. Yet it does not mean that the U.S. economy and other core economies are becoming 'post-industrial' in composition. Deindustrialization is often followed by reindustrialization. As Soja emphasizes in regard to Los Angeles, the manufacturing sector there has indeed changed, from old industrial to high-tech production and garment sweatshops, but the fundamental rationalization and labor processes of capitalism have not been significantly altered.

Economic Restructuring: The Level of Region

So far we have emphasized economic restructuring *within* cities, from the corporate center to the 'second round' of corporation-related suburbanization. Moving up a level to that of regional economics, we should note briefly the often-cited regional economic restructuring which has affected particular groups of cities and their hinterlands. A leading example in the United States is the economic surge of cities in the Sunbelt (southern tier) states from the 1960s to the 1980s and the decline of many cities in the industrial heartland of the Midwest. In the last decade we have also seen uneven city development in New England. Boston, for example, once an area in decline, in the late 1970s and early 1980s was booming in the fields of electronics and computers. In this economic restructuring it is usually sets of cities within the regions that are the primary sites of the economic trends. For example, in many ways the restructuring in Detroit (noted by Hill and Feagin, chapter 7) is similar to that in Youngstown, Cleveland, and Pittsburgh, cities in the same region. The economic restructuring in Los Angeles discussed by Soja, moreover, is in a number of ways similar to the economic shifts in San Francisco and other West Coast cities. And economic restructuring in New York has some parallels in Boston and Philadelphia, although in the latter cases there are perhaps more differences than similarities.

A major caveat to a simplistic approach to regional restructuring is that all regions contain cities which diverge from what may be commonly called the dominant trend. Thus in the economically troubled industrial heartland there are cities which remain economically healthy, like Minneapolis, which has a diversified economy with a dozen major corporations' headquarters there (and in the twin city of St. Paul)—companies ranging from food giants like General Mills to the high-tech firms 3M and Control Data. With a major university and leading medical center, this city has a well-educated labor force and a high quality of life. Minneapolis and, to a substantial extent, Milwaukee demonstrate that some cities in the midwestern region prosper in a sea of industrial decline. The reverse phenomenon can be seen in the Sunbelt region during the 1960s to 1980s. While Dallas, Houston, and Phoenix were booming, cities like New Orleans and Birmingham were stagnating or in decline. In a 1977 University of New Orleans survey the city of New Orleans was rated the poorest of the fifty largest U.S. cities and was also notorious for its overcrowded housing and police-community conflict (Macdonald 1984, 88–89). Despite extensive efforts by its local state officials throughout the 1970s and 1980s, New Orleans has been unable to diversify its tourist and oil-dependent economy (Smith and Keller, 1983). By the late 1970s Birmingham was a dying steel town, the only major metropolitan area in the Sunbelt with two-figure unemployment rates. A lack of economic diversity, a focus on steel-related industry, made Birmingham vulnerable to the same sort of disinvestment as that found in Youngstown and Pittsburgh in the industrial heartland (Macdonald 1984, 84–85). *Within* U.S. regions there is as much differentiation in urban economic health as there is *between* regions.

State Restructuring in Cities

Uneven development across cities, regions, and nations is not a mechanical process of economic relations in isolation from other important factors. Cities change not only as a result of the requirements of global or local capital but also as a result of state policy at the local and national level. There are, in effect, two worldwide "logics," an economic (capitalistic) logic and a state logic; these have for a century or more been inextricably interrelated. Changing urban development patterns are best understood as the long-term outcomes of actions taken by economic and political *actors* operating within a complex and changing matrix of global and national economic and political *forces*. It is historically specific political-economic processes through which contemporary corporations must work rather than expressing general economic laws of capitalist development.

Indeed, even a cursory glance at the contemporary world scene reveals many examples of these processes, including free trade zones, varying tax concessions, public-private organizations like MITI in Japan, and legislation requiring that manufactured products have some local content. A distinctive political-economic history accounts for the uneven pattern of urban development in the United States. This is why the particular forms of uneven urban development in the United States—declining inner cities, sprawling suburban development, extreme race and class segmentation of residential communities, and pronounced population dispersal of affluent communities to the hinterlands—are not found in the same form in other advanced capitalist states. For example government action over many decades has established a tax system in the United States which allows rapid depreciation of fixed capital investments, such as plants and office building, for tax purposes. Rapid depreciation has facilitated unprecedented levels of plant closures and also of office block construction—two dimensions of economic restructuring just examined. These tax laws represent economic growth-oriented state action as well as reflecting the substantial lobbying of a coalition of powerful real estate corporations since the 1930s (Feagin 1983).

Paralleling each type of urban economic restructuring previously discussed for cities are distinctive types of government action, mediation or involvement. In the case of plant closures it is usually the undiversified cities which depend on one economic sector that face the most difficulty. Locational specialization, which may be functional for producers operating on a global scale, leaves specialized localities highly vulnerable to economic crisis and marginalization, to the problem of large numbers of displaced workers, and to heightened pressure on national and local government officials to intervene to save the steel mill or car plant. Local and national governments have responded in a variety of ways to plant closures. In the United States the market-centered ideologies of local growth coalitions have led them to lobby local governments to set up economic development commissions to attract new industries to replace those in decline. In chapter 13 June Nash examines the impact of the restructuring of General Electric plants on the city of Pittsfield, Massachusetts. Major plant closures there were met by a proliferation of development commissions and private consulting firms working with local government officials to promote Pittsfield as a place for new industry; the relatively high wage levels of unionized workers there were seen by the local growth coalition as antibusiness elements in need of change.

Moreover, as Glickman explains (chapter 3), a variety of capital–labor coalitions have developed to lobby local and federal governments to deal with the impact of global restructuring on U.S. cities. Thus the city government of Detroit, the Chrysler Corporation and the United Auto Workers union worked together for a federal loan guarantee for an auto firm in serious trouble because of foreign competition. In some cases the local or regional state has become involved in negotiations with firms threatening an imminent departure—negotiations involving state intervention in regard to tax concessions. For example, in 1985–86 many Michigan cities faced great pressure from General Motors to reduce local taxes on GM plants; otherwise they would be closed down.

Sometimes new state structures are created in the most unlikely places, such as generally *laissez-faire* South Carolina, which regularly advertises itself as the state which would never 'kill the goose that laid the golden egg'. The South Carolina government created an Agency for Displaced Workers to cope with the state of plant closures in textiles, machine products and light manufacturing which have blighted the area in the last decade. Underlining the global roots of these developments, a skilled, displaced textile worker was recently recruited to go to Guatemala to train workers there to operate the textile machine he once operated in South Carolina, but which a local machinery salesman had sold to a factory owner in Guatemala. When confronted with the fact that his temporary job would only intensify displacement of other U.S. textile workers, since the Guatemalan firm produced for export to the U.S. market, the worker simply replied: "I've got to look out for me and my wife" (Anon. 1985, 19). In this instance, the textile mill worker's household survival strategy was an impediment to the development of either community or class consciousness as a collective basis for resisting more plant closures at home.

As a result of the, admittedly scattered, grassroots worker resistance to plant closures in the United States, the U.S. Congress has introduced plant closure legislation, and some city and regional governments have actually passed limited plant closure laws. However, in the U.S. government response to plant closures has for the most part been more market-driven and concessionary than in some European countries, a point documented in Nash and Body-Gendrot (chapters 13 and 11).

More generally, the federal state has come under increased pressure to protect U.S. firms and and workers against the adverse effects of renewed international competition. Aggressive foreign policy has attempted to reassert economic hegemony with the tools of the state. Glickman (chapter 3) discusses the protectionist pressures which have forced the federal state to legislate on behalf of U.S.-based firms and unionized workers, such as the "voluntary" quotas on imported Japanese cars.

The other dimensions of urban economic restructuring we discussed in the previous section have also involved other forms of state action. Direct state involvement in the opening of sweatshops in certain U.S. cities has been limited. Some government agencies turn a blind eye to violations of labor, health and safety laws. Federal involvement is indirect, but it does include the encouragement of some Third World (e.g., Vietnamese) immigration that provides low-wage garment and electronics workers. Broadly considered, the foreign policy of the U.S. government has accelerated some types of immigration from Mexico, Central America, and parts of Asia.

Urban Redevelopment and the State

Corporate expansion in U.S. central cities has involved the most extensive state intervention and mediation. Beginning in the 1950s, federally funded, large-scale urban redevelopment and urban renewal programs facilitated the development of office buildings, shopping centers, convention centers, hotels, and tourist attractions. Billions of dollars were spent by local and federal governments to demolish older housing and other buildings in inner-city areas. Private investment flowed into the construction of new buildings on the government-susidized, cleared land. Local governments also provided other substantial subsidies in the form of tax concessions, relaxation of regulations, and public capital investments in infrastructure (Fainstein et al. 1983; Feagin 1983).

By the 1970s conventional urban renewal and the massive clearance programs had been scrapped to be replaced by new forms of public–private partnership. In the face of the accelerated movement of capital investment on the global scale in the past decade, a multitude of alliances have been forged at the state and local levels between public officials and various business interests to promote new business investment, particulary in inner cities. These political alliances have played a key role in exacerbating uneven urban development patterns. The primary tool used to extract resources to support the goals of this network of economic and political elites has been the tax concession. These partnerships are managed by quasi-public development organizations variously called Downtown Development Authorities (DDAs), Economic Development Corporations (EDCs), and Local Development Companies (LDCs). They usually implement their decisions without referenda or legislative approval of specific projects. They have a great deal of discretion over the use of public funds and the granting of tax concessions. When viewed in isolation, the achievements of these organizational networks have been impressive in revitalizing declining areas.

For example, in the case of Atlanta, a new kind of metropolitan-wide growth coalition has been formed in response to the economic crisis there. Using a network of international business contacts made as a result of his United Nations ambassadorship, Mayor Andrew Young initiated an aggressive campaign to attract international business. Atlanta and its six surrounding counties have launched a $3 million campaign to promote the metropolitan area as an attractive location for services, sales, distribution, and high-technology industries. Atlanta's effort to forge metropolitan-wide political unity in the face of intensified competition for international capital investment illustrates a major political consequence for local government officials of the most common current definition of urban crisis — an awareness that both too rapid growth and too little growth in the economic base of local community life can expand the role of the state as a facilitator and regulator of economic growth processes and as a mediator of economic decline.

In the case of Houston's unprecedented economic decline in the mid-1980s, the local Chamber of Commerce created an Economic Development Council, composed of developers, bankers, and newspaper editors (the "growth coalition"), with an annual budget of $3 million to advertise and promote the city as a good place to do business. Pressure was put on city and county governments to provide half the funding for what has become a *private*–public partnership. Too little growth in this case was the trigger for the local growth coalition to create in 1984 a new organization, rare in the Sunbelt region of the United States, designed to seek a greater diversity of capital investments for a city long tied to the exigencies of the petroleum and petrochemical industries (Feagin 1987).

The expansion of low-wage service (and construction) jobs in large cities has involved the same indirect state involvement as in the case of sweatshops, particularly U.S. foreign policy action which has encouraged or accelerated Third World migration to the United States. These immigrants not only undertake low-wage factory jobs but also do a substantial part of the low-wage service work in cities. This immigration has had other political impacts as well. The rapid infusion of migrants tied to new localities through either informal kinship, friendship, neighborhood, or village networks or through more formalized associational support networks (e.g., the social movement in California to grant "sanctuary" to refugees from Central America) may create service and political management problems for local government officials. In Miami, Cuban and Haitian migration, and massive government support for the Cubans, contributed to the anger seen in black rioting there in the early 1980s (Macdonald 1984, 59–72; Smith 1987). And in many cities of the Southwest there have been loud complaints about illegal immigrants taking jobs local citizens could do. The pressure on the local state to restrict social services for these immigrants has been great, as has similar pressure on the federal government to impose legislated barriers to their immigration.

State involvement in corporate expansion in the localities outside central cities has also included tax concessions and other tax subsidies, as well as direct capital investments in waterways, roads, and other types of infrastructure facilities. Public–private partnerships similar to those in downtown areas have developed in many outlying localities of major U.S. cities.

State Reaction in European Nations

State involvement is not unique to U.S. cities. Three authors in this volume consider the reaction of European states to global economic restructuring and to the impact that restructuring has had on cities and on people's movements. For example, international competition has had a severe impact on the French auto and steel industries. In her chapter in this book (chapter 11), Sophie Body-Gendrot (cf. also Body-Gendrot 1982, 272–88) discusses the large-scale state intervention which this competition has caused. The extreme centralization of state power in a country like France means that local officials do not have to experience great popular pressure to take actions in the face of plant closures and high unemployment in their cities. Whatever the central state's political composition (Socialist or Gaullist), it has taken the blame for localized deindustrialization and plant closures. One of the ironies of recent French history is that urban workers have had to endure a high rate of unemployment and massive industrial restructuring under a Socialist government. State action in France oscillated between a leftist Keynesianism of state intervention on behalf of ailing industries and a more conservative policy, since 1983, focusing on industrial competitiveness and austerity. The failure of left-wing governments in France to deal with unemployment and deindustrialization has in turn precipitated strikes and new right-wing movements calling for the expulsion of immigrant workers.

Desmond King (chapter 10) details similar deindustrialization problems and market-oriented state responses in Great Britain. Thus London lost 40 percent of its manufacturing jobs between 1959 and 1975, a loss which is a key cause of uneven development in London and urban decline in many other industrial cities. King attributes much of the decline in London and other older, densely concentrated cities to changes in the global economy favoring investment in cities in developing countries. In his view older European cities cannot adapt readily to the rapidly changing needs of new corporate investments. The Thatcher government in Britain has not ignored distressed areas, but rather has aligned itself with market-oriented public policies. In Great Britain, central state action has often taken the form of encouraging and facilitating private investment in decaying areas of cities, using such market-oriented solutions as urban enterprise zones. As an example, King notes the sale in 1981 of publicly owned land in the depressed Docklands area of London to private developers, a development strategy opposed by local residents.

In her article on West German cities in this volume Mayer (chapter 16) documents processes of economic restructuring—urban disinvestment, redevelopment, gentrification—similar to those in U.S. cities. In West Germany the federal state's industrial policy has worked in recent years to restructure industrial production towards industries which are the most competitive on the world market. Moreover, state intervention in central city redevelopment has come to West Germany later than in the United States, although the reason has been the same—to enhance the profitability of corporations operating in inner city areas. Thus in 1971 West Germany's Urban Development Act increased state power to redevelop inner city areas. This intervention at the local level, as in the United States, gave community-based protest groups a centralized target. There have been squatter movements pressing for housing reform, as well as an array of community movements protesting against redevelopment, airport expansion, and a general lack of access to state decision making. Mayer notes that, because political access at the local level is much less available to community groups in West Germany, these groups have moved to participation in the new alternative political parties (e.g., the Greens) at the national level. Yet many of these citizen groups have been coopted into existing administrative structures but have not significantly expanded local democracy in West German cities. Mayer even suggests that a hidden function of these urban movements has been to facilitate urban redevelopment programs under state control.

Restructuring of Urban Households in Cities

Each type of economic restructuring in core country cities can also be linked to a restructuring of urban households. Enzo Mingione (chapter 14) deals with the survival strategies of worker households in industrialized nations of the United States and Western Europe in crisis periods, as well as in normal times. The expansion of informal economies, of such things as maintenance work, has become very important in areas with large-scale disinvestment; it is clear that women are central to these informal economies. This expansion of informal economies is, in part, a response to cutbacks in welfare programs by governments around the globe.

Plant closures are often very disruptive to workers and their households, as well as to other households (e.g., small businesses) serving the local economy. In U.S. cities, as elsewhere, plant closures can force household restructuring, from moonlighting, to family breakdown and divorce, to serial migration (that is, migration of successive family members) to other cities. At the very least, plant closures place a great burden on the basic building blocks of communities and cities—the household units.

Economic restructuring in the form of sweatshop expansion in U.S. cities affects yet other urban households. Often crossing national borders, households in Third World countries "loan" themselves, or selected members, for work in U.S. sweatshops. The provision of low-wage work in New York, Los Angeles, or Chicago can mean the relocation of Mexican, Asian, or Caribbean households to American cities. Households may be temporarily or permanently restructured across national boundaries in line with shifting capital investments.

Corporate center restructuring has had an impact not only on the households directly tied to the office workplace, but also to households displaced by corporate center construction. In this case household restructuring involves the migration of better-paid managerial and professional workers to inner-city areas, often to luxury apartments or gentrified homes, whose construction involves the displacement of middle- and low-income households. Other corporate center employees become involved in the major segregation of households in the suburbs and workplaces in the inner city.

As in the case of sweatshop expansion, the increase in service (and construction) jobs associated with corporate center expansion has had an impact on household restructuring, particularly for immigrant and ethnic minority households in inner-city areas. As in the sweatshop case, the Third World immigrant households supply workers for the lower-paid service positions, thus breaking up and reconstituting families across national borders. Moreover, local minority (citizen) families working in this service sector may secure employment as a result of corporate center expansion, yet still be a victim of higher rents or displacement resulting from corporate growth and urban displacement.

Economic restructuring in the form of corporate expansion to outlying areas has an effect on worker households which varies by wage level. The affluent upper tier can locate in nuclear family units in outlying small communities or luxury suburban apartments, with the segregation and isolation for household members that these residential patterns entail. The lower tiers of workers may face a reverse commuter scenario, commuting from inner-city areas to corporate offices and plants in outlying suburbs, a daily journey which can produce a serious financial and psychological drain on moderate-income households.

Restructuring of Communities and Community Politics

Even though the processes producing community change are encapsulated in wider political and economic structures and are affected by international processes of investment, production and trade, the point of impact for people is not only the household but also the particular *place*, the community space, which is the locus of interhousehold organization, the cares of everyday life, and community politics. These microsocial structures—neighborhoods and communities—are the bases of acculturation and thus of the creation of human and family identity. Hence local practices, springing from the actions of people in households, neighborhoods, community organizations, and local political jurisdictions, are the central elements in collective action that the chapters by Smith and Tardanico (chapter 4), Fainstein (chapter 15) and Mayer (chapter 16) chronicle.

The unfolding of capital restructuring creates profoundingly destabilizing conditions of everyday life in the cities most immediately affected. Recent research has sought to connect the unfolding world economy to the arena of grassroots politics in both core and peripheral cities. Smith and Tardanico (chapter 4) explore the web of interconnections linking the microstructures of household and neighborhood life in core and peripheral cities to the wider arenas of the global economy, the state and community politics. Starting from the premise that the processes of production and reproduction are inseparably connected to the dynamics of local community life, Smith and Tardanico draw upon the previously only loosely connected literatures on global restructuring, household survival strategies and collective action theory to draw out the actual means by which the consciousness, intentionality and everyday practices of common people force changes in the planning, implementation and consequences of state and business policies, thereby shaping and reshaping urban culture, economy, and politics. Their chapter extends the discussion of households in the informal economy to encompass activities taking place within, between, and outside households that contribute to the formation of the social networks that become the building blocks of collective responses to the economic crisis ranging from group migration to community protest action.

One of the key collective responses to urban restructuring has been the urban social movement. Such popular movements, as Fainstein's chapter illustrates, are often based in residential projects and neighborhoods and reflect demands for improved public services and expanded input into the political sphere. While urban social movements are often successful on specific local issues, they are not easily integrated into citywide or regional movements. Fainstein's analysis, as well as recent work by Castells (1983), attempts to deal with the possibilities for a coalition of the hundreds of community groups resisting public service deterioration in the face of corporate disinvestment.

In her chapter on Pittsfield, Massachusetts, Nash (chapter 13) concludes
with the important point that corporate dominance over workers has historically involved an implied commitment to a community and to people who
work in production: a type of social contract. But the rapid movement of jobs
overseas and the creation of automated plants in the United States, Nash argues, is destroying the legitimation for that corporate hegemony, as workers
gradually perceive the destruction of the social contract between capital and labor. Thus, in the current crisis, the workplace as well as the community remain
a potential local focus of collective action against the destruction of human
structures. The forms of resistance or accommodation to local crises of disinvestment, unregulated growth or uneven development have varied from nation
to nation and place to place (Smith and Judd 1984). Where popular resistance
has occurred, its form, development and effectiveness have depended upon the
issue being targeted; the resources available; the political channels available
for expressing discontent; the character of existing or emergent forms of community organization connecting affected individuals, households, and social
networks to the political process; and the prevailing structure and culture of local politics (M. P. Smith 1987).

Economic restructuring such as plant closure has a major impact on communities, not only because households are situated in spatially defined communities, but also because communities are usually linked to major corporations
in a symbiotic way. Communities grow up, historically speaking, with local investments in plant and other means of production and distribution. As the
building blocks of towns and cities, communities are situated localities with
homes, churches, schools, small businesses, and the like woven together into
a social fabric that is both a daily network of everyday life and a household
safety net. Thus plant closures not only break up families but also disrupt, often quickly, the social mesh of community life. In the United States, for instance, in industrially declining communities such as Detroit, Michigan; and
Youngstown, Ohio, school taxes are not paid, and school governing bodies
must close down schools or reorganize, even though there are still children of
unemployed workers to be taught. Local services may deteriorate. Small businesses, even churches, may go bankrupt.

Sweatshop expansion in cities can create new urban communities, such as
in the new Central American and Asian enclaves in Los Angeles, New York,
Chicago, and Houston, as well as in the immigrant enclaves of London. These
are the new ghettos of U.S. inner cities and are often differentiated themselves,
as can be seen in the distinctive Salvadorean, Gautamalan, Honduran, and
Mexican areas of cities like Los Angeles and Houston. These communities are
relatively new, and they range from relatively stable family-centered communities to areas with high turnover and transiency. Many such immigrant communities are further impoverished in effect, when their residents send large
amounts of money back to their poverty-stricken families in their countries of

origin. Demands on the local state for public assistance may eventually emanate from these new community areas, as the new residents come to identify themselves with their new territory. However, substantial barriers to the development of such community consciousness, such as lack of citizenship and persisting identification with places of origin, must first be overcome for such local demands to develop, not to mention the resistance of the indigenous residents.

Past corporate center redevelopment has destroyed some older communities in central areas, particularly minority (e.g., black, Puerto Rican) areas and those with large concentrations of retired and elderly, as in the South of Market area in San Francisco (Hartman 1984). Urban renewal not only remade the physical profile of central cities from Boston to San Francisco, but also displaced and destroyed whole communities of 'disposable' human beings, often numbering in the thousands. Homes, friendship networks, and living space for low- and middle-income city dwellers have been destroyed, sometimes precipitating significant community conflict ranging from lawsuits slowing urban renewal in the South of Market area in San Francisco to the large-scale ghetto disturbances in Newark, Detroit, and Los Angeles.

The expansion of services in inner cities has had similar effects on communities as sweatshop expansion. Indeed, some cities in core countries have seen new immigrant communities, linked to service jobs, develop distinct from older immigrant communities. For example, research by Rodriguez (1986) on Houston's Latin American immigrants indicates that the development of different undocumented ("illegal") immigrant communities is related to different phases of economic development. Houston's older undocumented Hispanic communities provided labor for the area's earlier industrialization phases in the 1925–65 period, while undocumented communities that are developing today provide labor for services. Today's new undocumented communities still provide workers for labor-intensive industrial enterprises, but these communities additionally provide workers for jobs associated with the developing business service sector. Examples of jobs directly connected to business are messengers and office cleaners, while the jobs indirectly connected range from restaurant workers to housemaids. Moreover, even without collective protest, new communities of Third World immigrants may indirectly put new political pressures on the local state for better services and housing. For example, the indigenous minorities who perform the service jobs have had some difficulty in finding decent housing in central city areas which have undergone urban renewal. The presence of new immigrant groups intensifies demand for the limited supply of cheap rented housing, thus driving up rents. Subletting in other minority communities has sometimes been the result, yet another underlying condition behind ghetto riots.

Corporate expansion in outlying city areas has fed the development or redevelopment of suburban communities, sometimes bringing the classic range of urban problems to suburbia. This can be seen in the Silicon Valley development south of San Francisco. This high-tech industry expansion has created serious environmental (e.g., toxic waste) and housing problems for local communities, as well as a crisis in local infrastructure and taxation. It has sometimes created new suburban and ex-urban enclaves of better-paid computer and electronics workers, as well as enclaves of low-paid Asian and Mexican workers (Rogers and Larsen 1984, 184–229). Rising housing costs have sometimes forced lower-paid workers to abandon original communities of settlement in areas like Silicon Valley. In addition, in cities like Los Angeles and Houston suburban corporate development has brought a scattering of office tower blocks to the suburbs and major residential and shopping center developments twenty miles from the city center. Thus, economic restructuring in U.S. cities can also entail a great deal of metropolitan sprawl.

Restructuring Urban Space in Cities

As the foregoing discussion has suggested, the physical and geographical profile of urban development has been shaped in many ways by the interplay of global capitalism, the state, and the activities of urban residents. Perhaps because of its scale and scope the impact of global capitalism has been easiest to identify. Major economic investment and location decisions shape the built environment of cities, from the expansion of outlying residential areas to the number and location of ancillary industries, office towers, and shopping precincts. Surplus capital from existing manufacturing industries may be channeled into real estate projects; and new manufacturing industries attract real estate capital into Sunbelt cities. As manufacturing industries change in response to the global reorganization of capitalism, the built environment of cities also experiences physical change. Private property and industrial investment are central dimensions of modern capitalism, and they set the broad parameters within which land and housing patterns emerge. Each type of economic restructuring involves investment or disinvestment in the physical facilities of production—plants, offices, warehouses, shops—and in the housing for workers in those means of production. Production and consumption (housing) construction require a complex of other constructions, from roads, water and sewerage systems to government offices.

Disinvestment in the form of plant closures has a negative multiplier effect on urban development. It means not only abandoned factories but also abandoned offices, warehouses, shops, and housing. And it means a deterioration in state infrastructure facilities (e.g., water systems) which are paid for by the taxes on production. Most urban decay is the physical outcome of corporate decisions to move fixed capital expenditures to other areas of a city or to other cities around the nation or around the globe. A plant closing can mean urban decay in only one part of a city as in the uneven development pattern which can be seen in Cleveland, Buffalo, or Detroit; or it can devastate an entire city, as in Youngstown, Ohio.

New plants in inner cities, particularly the sweatshops of Los Angeles, Chicago, and New York, have made only a modest impact on the built environment. Most have been located in existing, even abandoned, buildings. But they do signal the cyclical process of disinvestment and investment which proceeds in a series of stages over a particular city's lifetime. Many a city area has been abandoned, thus reducing the price of land and building so providing the framework for later economic development. Some urban areas may be in permanent physical decline, while others experience periodic resuscitation.

Corporate centralization restructuring has brought office development to major central cities, literally elevating the skylines. Clusters of office towers are characteristic of San Francisco, Los Angeles, Chicago, Minneapolis, Detroit, New York, and Houston, as well as a dozen other major cities. Billions in investment capital have flowed into this distinctive type of fixed capital. Harvey (1985), building on the insights of Lefebvre (1970), has argued that the secondary circuit of real estate investment is an important outlet for surplus capital which cannot find opportunities for above-average profit in production (e.g., manufacturing) investments. (See Gottdiener, 1985, for a detailed critique of Harvey's position.) Coupled with office construction has been the building of related facilities, often government-subsidized through urban renewal, such as hotels, convention centers, and quality department stores. Even though some older cities have successfully converted to corporate–professional cities, it should not be assumed that this developmental pattern is likely to become the typical pattern of urban transformation. Research has documented the robust growth of service employment in the past decade, along with continuing industrial decline. The data support the conclusion that, despite notable exceptions like New York and Los Angeles, overall the central city share of the new dynamic has not been adequate to provide real economic regeneration in most older cities.

This expansion of office space is a major reason for the large numbers of inner-city service employees, who must maintain, in the most direct sense, the massive physical plant. Many of these employees are housed in inner-city slum areas, the large areas of deteriorating housing into which little private or public investment flows. They make their own investments in the older, central-city housing, generally slowing its deterioration and abandonment.

The spatial impact of corporate investment in outlying areas of large cities in the United States has in a number of cases been dramatic. Silicon Valley, for example, has plants and offices for two thousand companies where there was once mostly open space. Residential communities have proliferated. In Houston decentralized development in the seventeen business activity centers outside the downtown area has proliferated an assortment of office complexes and shopping facilities at the periphery. There is a biomodal distribution of development, in the center and in the outlying ring.

State policies, sometimes in support of capital accumulation, sometimes more autonomously, sometimes intentionally and sometimes by their unintended effects, have also played a key role in restructuring urban space. National and local taxation policies promote particular patterns of investment and household consumption; regulatory policies affect the flow of credit, mediate the labor process in the formal sector, and manage (or fail to manage) the flow of immigrants across national borders. State policies allocating responsibility for the social costs of capitalist production, such as pollution control and assisting displaced workers, vary across regions and nations, entering into the calculus of factors affecting investment decisions and capital flows between core and periphery.

Depending on the balance of social forces embodied in state policies, the economic development policies of the local and regional state vary from purely capital-serving tax concessions to more balanced 'linkage' development policies where local state officials are able to impose pro-neighborhood and other political conditions on the development process. Concessions of the latter sort have been extracted from developers by progressive governments in cities such as San Francisco, Boston, Los Angeles, and Santa Monica, California, where neighborhood pressure has been an important factor in local politics (see Clarke 1987).

The crucial variable producing popular responsive policies affecting urban development is the extent to which the networks of ordinary people in households, communities, and workplaces can combine to produce forms of organization leading to the effective expression of demands for better neighborhood and working conditions, improved urban public services, and the self-management of their communities. From the Third World squatter settlements, discussed in the next section, to core country women's organizations demanding child-care facilities, to the progressive neighborhood movements in the United States, to urban social movements in Europe, it is clear that popular praxis matters. It is an essential element in community politics; and when it is present, the balance of power within the state, and hence the state role in urban restructuring, becomes more than a matter of capital accumulation.

Cities in the Third World: The Global Assembly Line

As we noted previously, global restructuring has had major consequences for cities in the core countries, including plant closures and job losses linked to such phenomena as reexport manufacturing in countries in the periphery. Much of the global assembly line is now located in the city economies of the Third World, from Mexico City, to São Paulo, Singapore, Seoul, and Manila.

In Third World nations a dominant city often develops, one that is six to fifteen times the size of the next largest city. Reviewing the literature on these 'primate' cities, Timberlake (chapter 2) notes that this urbanization phenomenon occurs for several reasons, including the fact that Third World export-oriented economies usually need only one shipping outlet, as well as the fact that the development of railroads has usually focused on transit to that one city. In addition, the destruction of local industry and trade by the increase of multinational investment tends to reduce the number of large cities. And the primate city, unlike cities in the United States, is usually the only city with a significant finance capital market centered on facilitating exports and foreign investment.

In many Third World cities the new international division of labor has had two major effects: (1) an increase in export-processing industries, and (2) a significant increase in the use of the informal economic sector to support these formal sector industries. We have already discussed these export-processing industries. Their increase has led to a significant expansion of the manufacturing proletariat in Third World cities, a segregated work force with men tending to work in basic industries (e.g., steel) and women working on consumer products (e.g., television sets). Today the occupational structure of industrializing cities in the Third World also includes a large tertiary or informal sector which some analysts have termed as "marginal." Reviewing the literature, Timberlake notes that this work (e.g., scavenging, domestic work, piecework at home) is not marginal but is inexorably linked to a system of modern capitalistic production. Moreover, the home workers also help reproduce industrial workers.

This combination of formal sector jobs and informal sector support activities has been a spur to economic development in many Third World cities, even though it is development dependent on the needs of multinational corporations. Even so, some cities in underdeveloped countries have been bypassed by this distorted type of transnational development. Cities like Lima are losers in the new international division of labor, for Lima has captured little of the new reexport industrial production characteristic of the global assembly line. As described by Patricia Ann Wilson (chapter 9), Lima has faced a distinctive type of economic restructuring. Once a center of assembly-line production for local markets, Lima has become a peripheral, backwater city, as production for export markets, even for Peru, has shifted to cities like Mexico City and São Paulo.

In her chapter (chapter 12) Helen Safa examines dependent urbanization in Latin America, the most urban of all developing regions. Latin American cities, initially colonial markets exporting raw materials, have recently been dominated by export-led growth linked to manufacturing. The increasing internationalization of manufacturing production has created a competitive search for cost cutting. This competitive search has led to much subcontracting to the informal sector, not only in garments, but also toys and electronics.

Safa discusses in detail the importance of these informal economies in Latin American cities. The informal sector produces many goods and services for the formal sector. Enterprises in the formal sector often subcontract production to the informal sector, just as is the case in the sweatshops of Los Angeles, Chicago, and New York. Noteworthy here is the role of the state. Latin American governments have facilitated the use of home, and other informal sector, production to reduce the labor costs of transnational corporations. A key role of the state in Latin American cities has been to facilitate production and, wherever possible, to repress worker organization and dissent. The state also mediates the contradictions of this pattern of development by attempting to respond to the demands of urban social movements by cooptative management of neighborhood services and state-sponsored citizen participation schemes.

We see here an impact as well on households and communities. Women workers are important not only in manufacturing but also in the informal economy. One type of work segregation in Latin American cities involves the use of younger, single women in export-oriented manufacturing plants, with older, married women with children working in their households and thus in the informal sector, a point Safa's chapter emphasizes. In Third World cities much of the labor in the informal sector, as well as in agriculture, is done by women and children. This is true of subsistence farming in the rural areas from which men have migrated to work in urban industries. In his article Timberlake cites studies documenting the fact that the penetration of foreign capital into Third World cities exacerbates the existing patriarchal family relationships there, often thus leading to a type of superexploitation of women workers as a group.

In Third World cities, as elsewhere, communities are the seedbeds of protest. Citizen protest has become characteristic of many of these cities in the last decade. One reason is the austerity forced on governments in underdeveloped capitalist countries by the principal organs of finance capital in the core capitalist countries. As John Walton notes (chapter 17), the current international debt crisis which affects most Third World countries is rooted in the attempt by the United States to regain a favorable trade balance through its aid programs and in the huge loans made by the international banking system, centered in U.S. banks, to these countries. The new international production system has been paralleled by this new world banking system to support industrial investments directly, and indirectly through loans to Third World governments committed to actions favoring export- and transnational-oriented production. (Socialist states such as Allende's Chile were boycotted). When the debt crisis appeared, the IMF and private banks imposed new austerity programs on governments in developing countries. These programs, as Walton demonstrates for twenty-two countries, have led to major strikes and food riots, urban protest which has forced most governments to rescind cuts in welfare provision. This community-based collective action has in turn forced the IMF and the international banks to renegotiate their loan schedules with the countries in turmoil. In most countries the state is the target of urban protests, since it is the most "visible" enemy of the poor. Much collective protest has targeted the state for providing poor public services, such as transport and water supply, and poor housing, and most protest has been based in working-class neighborhoods and squatter communities.

Conclusion

We have traced in this introductory chapter the impact that transnational corporate expansion, complementary state actions, and popular response by urban households have had on cities and communities around the globe. We have seen the many ways in which the world economy is indeed an integrated, worldwide, political-economic system laced together by transnational corporations and situated physically and geographically in those distinctive spatial places that we call cities. We have seen that, just as the activities of capital and the state constitute powerful constraints on the everyday activities of ordinary people, the key activities of households—immigration, informalization, and political mobilization—constitute household survival strategies which, in their turn, affect the accumulation strategies of global capital, the political management strategies of the state, and the character of urban life.

References

Anon. 1984. "Sweatshop renaissance." *Dollars and Sense,* no. 86 (April): 6–7.
———— 1985. "Carolinian finds a textile job, in Guatemala." *New York Times.* 14 April, 19.
———— 1986. "Militarism in America." *The Defense Monitor* 15:1–6.
Arkin, William M., and Richard W. Fieldhouse. 1985. *Nuclear Battlefields.* Cambridge: Ballinger.
Barnet, Richard L., and Ronald E. Muller. 1974. *Global Reach,* New York: Simon and Schuster.
Body-Gendrot, Sophie 1982. "Governmental responses to popular movements: France and the US." In *Urban Policy Under Capitalism,* edited by Norman I. Fainstein and Susan S. Fainstein 277–91. Beverly Hills: Sage.
Castells, Manuel. 1983. *The City and the Grassroots.* Berkeley: University of California Press.
Clairmonte, Frederick, and John Cavanagh. 1981. *The World in Their Web.* London: 2d Press.
Clarke, Susan. In press. "More autonomous policy orientations: An analytical framework." In *The Politics of Urban Development,* edited by Clarence N. Stone and Heywood T. Sanders. Lawrence: University Press of Kansas.
Cohen, R. B. 1981. "The new international division of labor, multinational

corporations and urban hierarchy." In *Urbanization and Urban Planning in Capitalist Society,* edited by Michael Dear and Allen J. Scott, 287–315. London: Methuen, 287–315.

Fainstein, Susan S., Norman I. Fainstein, Richard Child, Dennis R. Judd, and Michael Peter Smith. 1983. *Restructuring the City.* New York: Longman.

Feagin, Joe R. 1983. *The Urban Real Estate Game.* Englewood Cliffs, N.J.: Prentice-Hall.

———— 1985. "The social costs of Houston's growth. *"International Journal of Urban and Regional Research* 9:164–85.

———— 1987. "Local state response to economic decline." In *Urban Development in Britain and the U.S.* [provisional title], edited by Dennis Judd and Michael Parkinson. Manchester: University of Manchester Press.

Frobel, Folker, Jurgen Heinrichs, and Otto Kreye. 1980. *The New International Division of Labor.* Cambridge: Cambridge University Press.

Gottdiener, M. 1985. *The Social Production of Urban Space.* Austin: University of Texas Press.

Grunwald, Joseph, and Kenneth Flamm. 1985. *The Global Factory.* Washington, D.C.: The Brookings Institution.

Harvey, David. 1985. *The Urbanization of Capital.* Baltimore: Johns Hopkins University Press.

Lefebvre, Henri. 1970. *La Revolution urbaine.* Paris: Gallimard.

Macdonald, Michael C. D. 1984. *America's Cities.* New York: Simon and Schuster.

McGahey, R. 1983. "High tech, low hopes." *New York Times.* 15 May, 23.

Marx, Karl. 1967. *Capital.* vol. 1. New York: International Publishers.

Rodriguez, Nestor. 1986. Differential development of undocumented immigrant communities." Unpublished manuscript. University of Houston.

Rogers, Everett M., and Judith K. Larsen. 1984. *Silicon Valley Fever.* New York: Basic Books.

Sassen-Koob, Saskia. 1983. "Recomposition and peripheralization at the core." In *From Immigrant Labor to Transnational Working Class,* edited by Marlene Dixon and Susanne Jonas. San Francisco: Synthesis Publications.

Sivard, Ruth L. 1985. *World Military and Social Expenditures.* Washington, D.C.: World Priorities Organization.

Smith, Michael Peter. 1979. *The City and Social Theory.* New York: St. Martin's Press.

———— 1987. "Global capital restructuring and local political crises in U.S. cities." In *Global Restructuring and Territorial Development,* edited by Jeffrey Henderson and Manuel Castell. London: Sage.

Smith, Michael Peter, and Dennis R. Judd. 1984. "American cities: The production of ideology." In *Cities in Transformation,* edited by Michael Peter Smith, 173–96. Beverly Hills: Sage.

Smith, Michael Peter, and Marlene Keller. 1983. "Managed growth and the politics of uneven development in New Orleans." In *Restructuring the City,* Susan S. Fainstein et al. New York: Longman, 126–66.

Smith, Neil. 1984. *Uneven Development.* Oxford: Basil Blackwell.

2

The Global Context of Metropolitan Growth: Houston and the Oil Industry[1]

Joe R. Feagin

This paper examines in empirical detail the growth and development of Houston, the "capital of the Sunbelt," against the background of the changes in its economic and social base since the late 1800s. Houston's century-long sustained growth, unique centrality in Sunbelt expansion and in the world oil market, and commitment to an accentuated free enterprise philosophy make it an important urban case study in assessing the explanatory utility of mainstream and power-conflict theories of urban development, particularly those theories aimed at explaining the rise of Sunbelt cities. The global context of urban growth is accented in this analysis.

Recent analysis of city development has been characterized by a paradigmatic clash between a "mainstream" (order-market) approach and a "critical" (power-conflict) approach. The mainstream approach emphasizes demographic pat-

---

This chapter is reprinted with minor revisions from Feagin, Joe R. 1985. "The global context of metropolitan growth: Houston and the oil industry." *American Journal of Sociology,* 90 (May): 1204–30.

[1]I am indebted to the following colleagues for their critical comments on earlier drafts: Michael Harloe, Mark Gottdiener, Gideon Sjoberg, Walter Firey, Terry Sullivan, Nestor Rodriguez, Gerald Suttles, Bill Domhoff, Randy Hodson, Bill Tabb, and David Prindle. This project was partially supported by a University Research Institute grant, University of Texas (Austin), 1982–83.

59

terns of growth such as migration, metropolitan deconcentration, and descriptions of ecological distribution. Much current ecological research describes urban growth demographically, with little emphasis on interpretation. When conventional analyses move beyond description, they tend to accent migration and technological theories of urban growth. In contrast, a power-conflict approach is emerging from the work of scholars working in the neo-Weberian and neo-Marxist traditions. This approach emphasizes the broader politico-economic context of urban growth, structure, and decline. It is concerned with linking spatial growth to historical shifts in the capitalistic mode of production, with investments by the key economic interests that canalize growth, and with how the state cooperates with economic interests to shape settlement patterns (see Gottdiener 1983; McAdams 1980).

I will first specify the features of these paradigmatic approaches as they relate to Sunbelt growth and then examine their usefulness for evaluating the sociohistorical development of Houston, a city often described as the "capital of the Sunbelt" and the "oil capital of the United States." Houston's politico-economic development provides an important example of city growth, a major case that will enable me not only to evaluate the utility of the dominant paradigms but also to develop additional suggestive ideas about city growth in national and international contexts. In the 1920s and 1930s the Chicago school of urban sociology pioneered in the case-study methodological approach, an approach that develops and explores conceptions of cities by examining a particularly important case in great depth. As the major U.S. city least studied by social scientists, Houston, now the nation's fourth largest, would seem worth a thorough examination on the basis of its size alone. But its central role in the Sunbelt, its position in the global (oil-gas) market system, the accentuated free-enterprise philosophy of its leaders, and its thirteen decades of uninterrupted, rapid growth make it a particularly valuable case for analysis.

The Pattern of Houston's Growth

Population data (table 1) reveal that in every decade since 1850 the city of Houston's population has grown by at least 18 percent. Since the nineteenth century the growth rate has been high, in comparison with all other U.S. cities. In 1890 the city limits contained 27,557 people, making Houston the 112th largest city. By 1980 Houston had 1.6 million people and by 1983 had surpassed Philadelphia to become the fourth-largest city in the nation. Natural increase, migration, and annexation have contributed to this growth. Population growth has been accompanied by massive expansion of land area and of the built environment. Moreover, the incorporated city expanded by means of annexation from nine square miles in 1900 to 556 square miles in 1980.

Numerous analysts have emphasized Houston's rapid growth in the 1960s

Table 1 Houston's Population Growth: 1850–1990

Year	City (Incorporated Area)			Metropolitan Area		
	Population	Numerical Growth	% Growth	Population	Numerical Growth	% Growth
1850	2,396			18,632		
1860	4,845	2,449	102.0	35,441	16,809	90.2
1870	9,382	4,537	93.6	48,986	13,545	38.2
1880	16,513	7,131	76.0	71,316	22,330	45.6
1890	27,557	11,044	67.0	86,224	14,908	20.9
1900	44,633	17,076	61.9	134,600	48,376	56.1
1910	78,800	34,167	76.5	185,654	51,054	37.9
1920	138,276	59,476	75.5	272,475	86,821	46.8
1930	292,352	154,076	111.4	456,570	204,095	74.9
1940	384,514	92,162	31.5	646,869	190,299	41.7
1950	596,163	211,649	55.0	947,500	300,631	46.5
1960	938,219	342,056	57.4	1,430,394	482,894	51.0
1970	1,233,505	295,286	31.5	1,999,316	568,922	39.8
1980	1,594,086	360,581	29.2	2,905,350	906,034	45.3
1990	1,888,102	294,016	18.4	3,945,400	1,040,050	35.7

SOURCE: U.S. Bureau of the Census. Houston Chamber of Commerce. 1981. "Houston data sketch."

NOTE: Metropolitan data prior to 1950 and all data for 1990 are estimates.

and 1970s; the city gained about 30 percent in population in each of these decades. Yet to my knowledge no analyst has noted that the most rapid growth in the city's history occurred in the years 1920–30, during which period the city grew by more than 111 percent, from 138,000 to 292,000 people. The surprisingly dramatic growth in this distant decade is just one of the tantalizing demographic facts about Houston that begs for sociological explanation.

Convergence Theories of Urban Growth

In the literature on the growth of Sunbelt and Frostbelt cities, mainstream theories of development frequently are called "convergence" theories, whereas critical power-conflict theories are often termed "uneven development" theories.

Convergence Perspectives

Convergence theories often emphasize that Sunbelt cities are "catching up" economically with northern cities and that this convergence is part of an equilibrating tendency in U.S. society. Williamson, for example, has developed a thoroughgoing convergence theory; in his view a sharp and "increasing North-South dualism is typical of early development stages, while regional convergence is typical of the more mature stages of national growth and development" (1965, 44). Similarly, Rostow views Sunbelt cities as latecomers catching up with those that developed earlier, with regional disparities during the early stages and convergence later as the regions mature; the Sunbelt has prospered because it had "a larger backlog of technologies to bring to bear" (1977, 84).

Transportation technologies are accented as independent variables in mainstream urban ecology, which emphasizes regional equilibration as well. In a 1980 article, Kasarda views the rapid growth of Sunbelt cities substantially in terms of new technological developments such as highway systems, as well as in terms of the better business climate. In *Urban Society*, prominent ecologist Amos Hawley, in regarding the relocation of industry from the industrial heartland to the hinterland, explains decentralization substantially in terms of technological changes in transport and communication (1981, 174–77).

Key terms such as "filtering" and "trickle down" have been used by urban ecologists (e.g., Berry and Kasarda 1977, 279–80) to describe the diffusion of urban growth from one region to another. A key aspect involves labor markets, with the costlier markets in cities higher up in the urban hierarchy. This leads firms to migrate to cheaper markets in cities in other regions. The imagery is one of economic change being "transmitted in order from higher to lower centers in the urban hierarchy" (Berry and Kasarda 1977, 280). Following Thompson (1968), Berry and Kasarda discuss this heartland–hinterland filtering on a national scale and suggest that a threshold population of about 1 million is necessary for cities in peripheral regions to grow on their own, to be "self-generated metropolitan areas" (1977, 282).

Government

Mainstream analysts have given limited attention to government. Berry and Kasarda note that in market-directed societies such as the United States the role of the state has been primarily "limited to combating crises that threaten the societal mainstream," that state involvement tends to be incremental, and that government actions often follow rather than lead private enterprise (1977, 402). State actions aimed at dealing with the "social consequences of laissez-faire urbanization" are assessed as "ineffective in most cases" (Berry and Kasarda 1977, 353; cf. Berry 1973). Indeed, the "good business climate" of the Sunbelt (see Kasarda 1980) includes weak government intervention in the forms of low taxes and ineffectual regulation. Government usually is not an important subject to mainstream urban ecologists, as can be seen by the few pages Berry and Kasarda devote to the subject in *Contemporary Urban Ecol-*

ogy. In his revised edition of *Urban Society,* Hawley pays little attention to the state (1981, 228–29, 262–63). Largely dismissing the growth coalition literature, he argues that power is decentralized in families, churches, and industries and that the interplay of power in communities "approaches an equilibrium" (Hawley 1981, 225). In Hawley's view, power structure research has not demonstrated that business elites have dominant influence over urban development. A recent analysis of urban and regional trends by urban and other ecologists (Guest 1984; Poston 1984) includes little discussion of the role of government in urban development.

I should note that some mainstream theorists (e.g., Kasarda 1980) do allude briefly not only to the "good business climate" of Sunbelt cities but also the "bad business climate" of Frostbelt cities. Discussions of bad climates encompass the idea that state intervention—particularly in the form of high-quality services and tax programs—has had negative consequences for the health of Frostbelt cities. Moreover, because the good business climate in Houston has often been cited by order-market analysts as an example of the prosperity that can be accomplished in the absence of state intervention, it is important to examine the Houston case in detail.

The Uneven Development Perspective

Critical, power-conflict theorists have stressed uneven development as a normal aspect of cities embedded in a capitalistic system. Development in one set of cities comes at the expense of cities in other regions. For example, Hill (1977) has probed this uneven development conception and suggested its utility in explaining simultaneous growth and decay in Sunbelt and Frostbelt cities, respectively. Analysts Perry and Watkins take issue with convergence theories, arguing that "cities on disparate growth trajectories are not headed toward some common point but, on the contrary, are moving further away from each other" (1977, p. 22). They add that new corporate investment is not dispersed throughout the nation by an underlying equilibrating mechanism.

Perry and Watkins argue that Sunbelt cities have not prospered by a filtering process, by seducing low-wage industries from the North, but that the most rapid growth in the Sunbelt has been in certain relatively high-wage industries (1977, 45–48). Together with Sale (1976, 20–45), they assert that major "leading-edge" industries, including electronics, defense, and oil, have bypassed the North and located in the South. Northern cities have failed to capture these industries because of the commitment of investors to established industries, as well as because of other economic and social barriers.

Uneven development theorists have given more attention to the politico-economic context of technological development than have convergence theorists. Mainstream ecological analysis tends to view technological development as a broad, independent variable that shapes regional and urban development rather than as a dependent variable. Uneven development theorists have emphasized the dependent character of the technological developments, such as the role of General Motors in sabotaging mass-transit technologies and that of the private highway lobby in federal government decisions about highway technology (Snell 1979; Feagin 1983*a*).

Government

This development perspective also places much more emphasis on the role of government than does the mainstream view (Castells 1984; Fainstein and Fainstein 1983), and its proponents have been more attentive to the character and impact of governmental intervention. Perry and Watkins, for example, note that in the 1930s private investment in cities sank to new lows, and massive federal New Deal expenditures for infrastructure projects stimulated a new round of capital investment and thus of related urbanization in the Sunbelt (1977, 46–48). The federally subsidized infrastructure of the Sunbelt featured the automobile and the highway, but corporate executives (inside and outside of government) made the key decisions directing the development of these technologies. Moreover, after 1939 federal expenditures for defense facilities in the region generated the spin-off electronics technologies and industries.

In addition, the localized aspect of the relationships among governments, private capital, and cities has been emphasized by Harvey Molotch (1976) and G. William Domhoff (1983). Molotch has analyzed growth coalitions, that is, land-interested business leaders who operate through local government to foster growth (1976, 309–15). There is also an important linkage between land-interested capitalists operating at the local level and those operating at the top of national and international corporations, because the local business elite desires outside investment (Domhoff 1983, 160–87).

Cities in a Global Context

The key ideas in the convergence and uneven development theories provide useful frameworks for analyzing Houston's development, but each has certain distinctive weaknesses that will become apparent. One major weakness of both is an insufficient concern with the world context. Analyzing Sunbelt cities primarily against a backdrop of declining Frostbelt cities, which has been the focus of considerable debate between convergence and uneven development theorists, is not enough. One must go beyond the regional and national context to examine the international setting. Wallerstein (1979) has elaborated the conception of a capitalist world economy integrated by a global market of differentiated national economies, but world-economy analysis is just beginning to focus on the critical city nodes that anchor the global market network (see Chase-Dunn 1984).

This examination of Houston illustrates the central importance of studying the world contexts of U.S. cities in order to understand better the causes, character, and significance of urbanization. Historical data are critical to this task, because such empirical materials enable us to examine the changing character of economic bases and translocal ties over time and the ways in which earlier stages of urban economic and political growth become building blocks for later stages of growth or decline. Tracing the translocal linkages of Houston through several differentiated periods of development, I will show how this city's economic rhythm becomes ever more closely tied to events in the global (oil) market system than to national economic cycles. In-depth analysis of Houston highlights the following general arguments about the nature of cities:

1. The causes, character, and significance of city development can be understood best by analyzing cities in terms of their translocal linkages, especially their capitalistic world-economy context.
2. Evolving through historical stages of economic growth, with one stage often shaping the next, major cities in the world economy tend to specialize in particular aspects of raw materials, production, distribution, marketing, and finance activities.
3. Major cities, as the places where this politico-economic specialization is grounded physically, are the cotter pins holding the capitalistic world-economy system together.

The Economic Base and Houston's Development

Houston's development can be divided into four major periods:

1. a stage of commercial capitalism (1840–1900), in which agricultural marketing dominates;
2. a stage of competitive-industrial capitalism (1901–15), in which localized oil-related companies are characteristic;
3. a stage of oligopoly-industrial capitalism (1916–31), during which major oil companies come to dominate the area; and
4. a stage of state-assisted oligopoly capitalism (1932–present), in which the state plays an ever more substantial role in development.

Commercial Capitalism (1840–1900)

Houston began in a Gulf Coast swamp in the 1830s as a speculative real estate venture by two northern capitalists. In a few decades it had emerged as a regional marketing city dominated by a healthy commerce in agricultural products. Lumber, grain, and especially cotton generated an important commercial center of railroads, warehouses, cotton gins, and banks servicing the Texas agricultural economy. Houston was home for large cotton-brokerage companies; by 1901, with its base of agricultural commerce, it had become a major railroad center in the area west of New Orleans. By the end of this period Houston had grown to 44,633 people, and, including nearby counties, its population exceeded 130,000 (McComb 1981).

Competitive-Industrial Capitalism (1901–15)

The discovery of oil ninety miles east of Houston in 1901 and subsequent discoveries closer to the city from 1905 to 1919 set the stage for the city to become a major oil and gas production center. Three-quarters of Gulf Coast oil came from these fields. Houston's urban competitors in the region at the time, Galveston and Beaumont, confronted physical and infrastructural barriers to development. The devastation of Galveston's larger population and port by a hurricane in 1900 caused executives in oil-related companies to become concerned about its exposed coastal location. Beaumont, although closer to some oil fields, did not have the railroad and banking infrastructure that Houston had developed as an important agricultural commerce center (Pratt 1980, 53–56). Contrary to growth theories that see Sunbelt cities as bypassed by economic growth until postwar decades, by 1900 Houston had emerged as an important agricultural marketing center. Its basic commercial infrastructure laid the basis for subsequent dominance as an oil-industrial center from the 1930s to the present.

Soon after 1901 several oil companies that organized production in the Texas oil fields located in the greater Houston area. The new Texas Company (later Texaco) arrived in 1908. In 1916 the Gulf company, newly created in Houston-area oil fields, moved to Houston; the fact that this Texas firm was controlled by Mellon (Pittsburgh) interests signaled the rise of East Coast dominance. For a brief period many of the companies organizing production in the Texas oil fields were local, but the Gulf Coast oil industry moved quickly through this stage of competitive-industrial capitalism to that of oligopoly capitalism dominated by major companies.

In this 1901–15 period Houston's growth coalition played an important role in facilitating corporate location decisions. In spite of their professed free-enterprise philosophy, local bankers, real estate investors, and other leaders passed for governmental subsidies to improve Houston's port facilities. In 1902, under pressure from the local business coalition, the U.S. Congress appropriated about $1 million in public investment capital for port development. A few years later merchant capitalists met in the mayor's office to devise a plan for further aid. They proposed that a special navigation district be created to issue bonds, with the federal government matching local funding. Because the city had no authority to issue bonds for projects outside its city limits, Houston attorneys were sent to lobby the Texas legislature (successfully) to permit the new navigation districts (Sibley 1968, 133–35; McComb 1981, 65–67). Both the city lobbying effort and the new state form, the navigation district, were unprecedented in Texas (perhaps in the nation). The navigation district could issue taxpayer-backed bonds to pay for port expansion, but Congress had to be lobbied for matching funds. In 1910 Congress approved $1.25 million for deepening the Houston Ship Channel, the largest grant for local government purposes made by the federal government up until that time. From 1902 on, government played a crucial facilitating role in the rise of this "free enterprise" city; neither mainstream ecological theories nor extant uneven development theories prepare us for this early, essential state aid in a "lagging" region. The role of the local elite in securing federal aid is also significant in this example.

Oligopoly Capitalism (1916–31)

By 1916 the larger oil corporations were beginning to dominate many sectors of the Texas oil industry; over the next decade they consolidated their control. Events in Detroit, an industrial city more than a thousand miles away, spurred investment by major oil companies and helped transform Houston into an oil capital. This long-distance intercity relationship was not one of filtering growth down an urban hierarchy but rather of oscillating corporate investment (often drawn from outside both cities) linked by a manufacturing need for processed raw materials. The events in Detroit in the decade prior to Houston's major boom in the 1920s involved Henry Ford and his engineers, who perfected the mass production of the automobile.

Until auto production began in earnest in the period 1908–25, crude oil had been used for kerosene, fuel oil, and lubricants. In 1914 there were 1.8 million cars and trucks registered in the United States; a decade later the number had grown to 18 million. Fuel usage increased from 2.7 billion gallons in 1919 to 15.7 billion gallons in 1930 (U.S. Bureau of the Census 1961, 462). Coal had fueled the rise of U.S. industry in the nineteenth century, but by the 1910s and 1920s oil was beginning to replace it. Growing gasoline and oil sales generated much of the capital that corporations invested in Houston facilities. The raw materials factors emphasized by classical location theorists such as Lösch (1954) became important. In the 1916–31 period numerous refineries and other oil-related facilities were built in the Houston area for a number of reasons, including closeness to raw materials and to the state-subsidized port facilities. Jobs in the oil-related plants and offices attracted workers, stimulating the population explosion seen in table 1.

Executives in the headquarters buildings of major oil companies and allied back executives—mostly in northern cities—frequently made the broad, strategic decisions about putting capital into the oil industry, often basing these on the advice of operations' executives in Texas. In the oil industry the number of top decision makers in Texas declined as the industry became more centralized. Even though Standard Oil (now Exxon) had been split up in 1911, by the 1920s the former Standard companies, together with a handful of newer companies, dominated the oil-gas industry. By the late 1920s fully 70 percent of Texas production was in the hands of twenty companies, although there were 14,000 oil companies in the United States (Williamson et al. 1963, 330). Major companies expanded horizontally by buying other companies, moving into new fields, and driving smaller companies out of business; they expanded vertically by adding subsidiaries dealing with all aspects of the business from research to marketing. Broad strategic control over the Texas industry was often in the hands of East Coast companies and financial institutions (James 1953, 60–73).

Standard Oil began to expand horizontally into the Texas fields in 1918, when it began courting a Houston-based company. The web of ties among eastern finance capital, the major oil companies, and Houston's growth as an oil center can be seen in the trajectory of Houston's Humble Oil and Refining Company, which was formed by Texas oil men in 1917. Cash poor, these entrepreneurs needed capital, because their assets consisted of leases and equipment. They secured loans from local banks but soon sought out New York banks as well (Larson and Porter 1959, 72). Humble's independence—and its capital problems—did not last long. In 1919 Standard Oil bought a controlling share of Humble Oil. To circumvent Texas laws restricting its activities, Standard allowed Humble's board of directors to be mostly independent. Yet Standard executives controlled much of the flow of new capital to Humble and thus exerted influence over development. Between 1918 and 1929 the fixed assets of Humble increased from $13 million to $233 million, with much outside capital assistance. Soon the Humble Oil subsidiary became the largest producer of crude oil in the country (Larson and Porter 1959, 75–104).

The expansion of Standard and other major companies generated investment in allied oil companies. By the late 1920s oil services and manufactured products essential to the oil industry were being provided increasingly by local firms. Oil tools, well equipment, and services companies were financed substantially by Texas capital; most support companies had not been taken over by northern oil-gas corporations (McComb 1981, 80–81).

By 1930 the Houston area was a growing manufacturing center with 475 manufacturing plants, most of them oil related (Love n.d., 19). Still, manufacturing was not as dominant there as in other industrial cities. In this period Houston had a large cohort of clerical, managerial, and professional workers working in a growing number of major oil company subsidiaries and allied support firms (e.g., law and accounting).

State-assisted Oligopoly Capitalism: The 1930 and 1940s

New oil fields. The huge East Texas oil field was developed in the early 1930s; by 1939 it had twenty-six thousand wells. At first, 80 percent of the field was in the hands of the smaller oil companies, with just 20 percent in the hands of major ones. By 1940 these proportions were reversed. Much of the decision making about newly discovered oil fields was made by oil companies with major subsidiaries in Houston. In 1935 just under half of all Texas oil was shipped through the Port of Houston (McComb 1981, 127). Houston had more than twelve hundred oil companies and supply houses; oil facilities, from refineries to office skyscrapers, were the concrete embodiments of a continuing oil boom. A *Fortune* magazine feature article noted, "Without oil Houston would have been just another cotton town. Oil has transformed it into a concrete column soaring grotesquely from a productive substratum. . . . Take oil away and Houston's skyscrapers would be tenanted by ghosts" (1939, 81–85). At that time the oil industry accounted for over half the jobs in the area.

From the 1920s to the 1940s a series of much-sought-after technological innovations in refining (e.g., catalytic cracking) facilitated an increase in the quantity and quality of gasoline extracted from crude oil. By 1941 the Gulf Coast (Texas and Louisiana) was the dominant refining region, with more than one-third of the U.S. capacity. Pipelines carried oil and gas from Texas, Oklahoma, and Louisiana oil fields to Gulf Coast refineries and to tankers at the Port of Houston (Pratt 1980, 66–67). By the 1930s Houston was the nation's third-largest port in terms of exports and a major Sunbelt trading and shipping center. Cotton, lumber, and oil accounted for the rise in tonnage shipped from 1.3 million tons in 1919 to 27 million in 1941. Houston soon surpassed New Orleans as the dominant Gulf Coast port and southern metropolis. Population growth continued during the Great Depression, rising an unusual 32 percent over that troubled decade.

The role of government. The distinctive character of government intervention in Houston becomes clear when one considers the prevailing antistate, free-enterprise viewpoint advocated and advertised by the city's growth coalition since 1900. One observer has noted this traditional stance of Houston's leadership: "For many years, Houston politicians boasted that their city's growing economy allowed it to refuse federal aid while other cities pleaded for more and more help" (MacManus 1983, 1). Federal government grants for most urban uses have long been publicly cited as "socialistic" by local business groups and political candidates. An advertisement in *Fortune* by the growth coalition emphasized the business climate and lack of government interference that have been proclaimed since 1900: "Houston, by virtue of being in Texas, reaps the benefits of a state that has one of the best business climates in the nation. It is not just lukewarm to business, it is pro-business. It welcomes new ideas and people. There's little in the way of red tape. Free enterprise is still the gospel" (1980, 49). This advertisement goes on to portray Houston as having little government interference and the lowest tax per capita among large cities. Since the 1930s, the city's growth coalition has also waged a successful battle against local government interference with land use. The fact that Houston, unique among U.S. cities, has no city zoning laws is often cited as illustrating the predominance of the free enterprise ideology.

The accentuated enterprise ideology might lead to predictions that Houston would have received little, if any, direct federal aid. Yet we have already seen that the growth coalition contradicted its professed ideology in seeking aid for port expansion in the early 1900s. The infracture of Houston, moreover, was expanded during the 1930s with substantial federal assistance. The provision of large-scale aid was facilitated by close ties between the growth coalition in Houston (and Texas) and the federal government. Houstonian Jesse Jones, a banker in the Houston growth coalition, became head of the Reconstruction Finance Corporation (RFC) and later served as Roosevelt's secretary of commerce. Money from the RFC, the National Recovery Administration (NRA), the Public Works Administration (PWA), and the Works Progress Administration (WPA) rebuilt Houston businesses and built major public buildings, road, and utilities. For example, in 1934 the PWA gave Harris County $653,000 for road and sewer projects and the Post Office Department announced a major post office project for the city. Several million dollars were provided for improvements to the ship channel. From 1932 to 1941 a substantial infrastructure, its development guided by the growth coalition, was built, in part with the use of millions in federal funds (Writers' Project 1942, 120).

Oil companies demand intervention. Significant government intervention occurred in the East Texas oil fields, whose rapid development had brought Houston oil companies into vigorous competition with those based elsewhere. Oil prices dropped to extremely low levels; a considerable amount of oil was pumped out at illegal rates. Oil executives were urging federal officials to enforce pumping quotas in the East Texas fields. In 1933 President Roosevelt issued an order banning the shipment of oil pumped in violation of prorationing laws. Federal agents were sent to help the Texas Railroad Commission (the Texas oil agency) enforce order. This intervention, and continuing federal support for prorationing of oil pumping among big and little companies, operated from the 1930s to the 1970s to protect the petroleum industry. Houston-based companies prospered and Houston grew, protected from competition (Prindle 1981, 36–187).

Capitalizing petrochemicals. In the 1940s the federal government became a primary source of capital for oil-related development. Hundreds of millions of dollars were poured into private and joint private-public, oil-related enterprises in the Gulf Coast area. Federal capital flowed to Houston's petrochemical industry; aviation fuel and synthetic rubber were important to the war effort (Pratt 1980, 94). Five oil companies (Mobil, ARCO, Gulf, Texaco, and

Pure Oil) with refineries in southeastern Texas created a joint, nonprofit corporation to generate butylene for synthetic rubber. The corporation ran the plant, but the federal government paid for it, providing major capital for petrochemical research and development. This facilitated dramatic postwar growth in the petrochemical industry (James 1953, 78) as it began to produce commercial products.

Investment by the federal government also aided oil and gas distribution. In the early 1940s the Roosevelt administration built two major oil pipelines, called the "Big Inch" and the "Little Inch," to carry oil products from Texas to the East Coast, at a government cost of $142 million (James 1953, 77; Larson and Porter 1959, 566–87).

The range of federal government aid for development in a city dominated by a free-enterprise and anti-federal-government ideology has been remarkably broad, from aid for infrastructure projects, to capital for the petrochemical and oil pipeline companies, to regulation of oil field competition. A recognition of the extent, character, and significance of state aid in the Sunbelt is missing from mainstream urban ecological analysis; uneven development theorists have been more on the mark. As Mollenkopf's analysis has made clear, federal aid to recapitalize U.S. industry during World War II was massive and focused disproportionately on selected cities, with midsize Houston (population 384,514) ranking sixth nationally and first regionally in federal plant investment (1983, 106). Those federal capital decisions were made, or influenced greatly, by top corporate (e.g., auto and oil) executives in American industry, working through the federal war production agencies. These federal investments were by no means the only factor, for massive private capital flowed into Houston's oil and petrochemical industries in this period, but they were nonetheless critical.

State-assisted Oligopoly Capitalism: Houston since 1950

An expanding economy. After World War II Houston began a long boom based on the rising demand for oil products such as asphalt and plastics. State aid for the oil and petrochemical companies during the 1930s and 1940s helped place them in advantageous positions. A growing number of truck, pipeline, and shipping companies had grown up around greater Houston's oil and petrochemical complexes. There was continued growth in oil tools and services, metal, and construction companies. In the 1950s the city's population increased by 57 percent to nearly 1 million.

More state aid. The profitability of oil companies concentrating on U.S. production was enhanced by further state action. In 1959 President Eisenhower set quotas for imported oil, limiting imports to 12 percent of domestic production, a decision justified by the argument of national defense. This action raised prices, costing U.S. consumers an estimated $50 billion in the next

decade. Oil and gas price increases have had a regular stimulating effect on the
Houston economy since the 1950s (Cramer 1972, 575; Nash 1968, 201–8). In
the period 1960–80 there were other important examples of federal intervention. The National Aeronautics and Space Administration (NASA) complex
came to Houston in the 1960s. Federal intervention into Houston's economy
was won in major competition with other cities by Houston's growth coalition,
which included prominent local business leaders (e.g., the head of Brown &
Root) and politicians. Land for the NASA complex had been donated by Humble Oil (Exxon), whose nearby real estate projects increased in value.

Houston's government in the 1970s. Prior to 1970 the operating budget of
Houston's city government was not tied to federal monetary assistance. The
local growth coalition has been receptive to federal capital projects for many
decades, but its members, who viewed aid for operating budget and social service programs as illegitimate, had kept local government operating expenditures relatively low, permitting a low tax rate. By the mid-1970s some of the
city's leaders were partially abandoning their public antifederal position. During the 1970s city officials increased federal spending substantially. Various
pressures forced local business leaders to seek more aid. The social costs of
many decades of rapid growth under a "good business climate" became so critical that they could no longer be neglected. For example, half of Houston's
wastewater plants violated state discharge standards, and a sewer hookup (and
construction) moratorium covered three-quarters of prime development areas.
Flooding had become a serious problem, because of unrestrained real estate
development. Water pumping and development had created a subsidence
problem; some central city areas had subsided three to five feet since World
War II. Air pollution and toxic waste seepage into water systems had become
extremely serious. Traffic had become notorious. These and other social costs
of rapid capitalistic development (see Feagin 1983b) are neglected in mainstream urban ecological theories, which typically do not assess the negative
consequences of "good business climates."

During the mid-1970s a new mayor and council were elected with the help
of empowered minorities; for the first time in the twentieth century, city government became more desirous of federal support for people-oriented programs such as job training and youth employment. But because of the
continuing power of Houston's business leaders these new social (tagged "minority") programs were intentionally segregated from other city departments
(MacManus 1983, 45).

Recentralization. In the late 1960s and early 1970s, the top oil companies
shifted subsidiaries to or buttressed existing operations in Houston. Shell Oil
located its U.S. administrative headquarters there; Exxon concentrated more
administrative and research operations; Gulf, Texaco, and Conoco located or
expanded major national subsidiaries. As a result of shifts in the world oil sys-

tem, dispersed company operations around the United States were closed and consolidated in larger offices in a few key cities, including Houston.

Of the 35 largest oil companies, 34 have located major office and plant facilities in the Houston area. In addition, the city contains 400 major oil and gas companies, together with hundreds of geological firms, drilling contractors, supply companies, law firms, and other oil-related companies (Taylor 1983). Although so many top oil companies now have important domestic subsidiaries in Houston, most of these subsidiaries are dependent on northern headquarters' strategic investment and management decisions at the highest level. Concentration of control in the oil industry has persisted. In the late 1970s there were about 5,000 crude oil production companies in Texas; yet six large companies produced 37 percent of the oil. Most production was still in the hands of the top fifteen companies. The refineries of eight major companies processed two-thirds of the crude oil in Texas (Lamare 1981, 15–16).

Housing the oil industry. The expansion of Houston's oil industry since the 1960s has been obvious in the growth of its population—of people and of office buildings. Houston's population grew from just under 1 million in 1960 to an estimated 1.7 million in the early 1980s. Between 1970 and 1981 a total of 361 large (more than 100,000 square feet of floor space each) office buildings, more than 80 percent of all such existing buildings, were erected in the area (Houston Chamber of Commerce 1981*a*, 32–37).

Some oil-related operations are predominantly white collar and housed in office towers; others, housed in refineries and petrochemical plants, have large blue-collar work forces. In 1978 Houston was ranked the fourth-largest manufacturing center in the United States, behind Chicago, Detroit, and Los Angeles, but it was first in new capital expenditures in manufacturing (Houston Chamber of Commerce 1981*b*; Donahue et al. 1973, 48–50). Yet in 1980 about 57 percent of the Houston metropolitan work force was employed in white-collar jobs (managerial, professional, clerical, and sales), very close to the proportion of such workers in Philadelphia (58 percent) and above that in Pittsburgh (54 percent).

Houston and the world economy. By the 1960s and 1970s Houston had evolved into the oil-technology distribution center for the world's oil industries. After the discovery of major Middle Eastern oil fields in the 1960s, advanced oil technologies were needed there. By 1980 nearly $7 billion in engineering and related contracts were in effect between U.S. oil-support companies in Houston and elsewhere and Middle Eastern oil fields. Houston companies have been important in the development of other oil fields from the North Sea to Malaysia and Indonesia. By the late 1970s about 100 Houston companies were employed in the North Sea oil fields; by the early 1980s there were at least 100 Houston companies in the Malaysia–Indonesia oil fields (Taylor 1983). When the major oil companies began to develop international operations in the 1920s and 1930s, the city developed ties *outside* the U.S. economy. By the 1960s and 1970s, Houston had become an international city whose economic base was as much affected by international as by national events.

The relationship between Houston's prosperity and economic shifts in the larger world economy can be seen in the history of OPEC. In 1973 the OPEC countries gained control over their oil, and the once-dominant U.S. companies became primarily suppliers of technology and marketing agents for OPEC oil. U.S. company profits from Middle Eastern oil fell, but the sharp rise in world prices brought great increases in profits from oil controlled by U.S. companies elsewhere. Between 1973 and the early 1980s, the value of the oil and gas in Texas fields grew at the rate of 500 percent, although the amount produced declined 28 percent (Plaut 1982, 203). As a result, in the 1973–75 recession, employment in goods-producing industries dropped 6 percent in such cities as Dallas but grew by 18 percent in Houston, because its manufacturing firms produce for the oil world's industry. The rise in OPEC oil prices in 1973–74 gave a boost to oil exploration and drilling, thus stimulating the Houston economy during a national recession. Between 1968 and 1980 the percentage of Houston employment in oil exploration, drilling, and machinery increased (Brock 1981, 1–4).

The oil price rise had a major negative impact on one dimension of the Houston economy. Prior to the 1973–74 price rise there was a trend toward economic diversification, with growing investment in nonoil projects. With the sharp price rise, oil companies and allied bankers moved away from diversification to a heavier emphasis on investments in oil projects. In the late 1970s, yet another rise in the oil price further stimulated companies to overinvest and overproduce in oil.

The close ties between Houston and cities in Latin America, the Middle East, and the Far East can be seen in the substantial international trade passing through Houston. In 1981 more than $26 billion in exports and imports flowed through its customs district. By the 1980s Houston ranked as the nation's second port in total cargo tonnage and in foreign trade. The city's top foreign trading partners have been Mexico, Saudi Arabia, Japan, and West Germany. Crude oil is by far the number one commodity in dollar value that is imported at the Port of Houston; the next two major imports are steel products and automobiles. The primary recipient countries of exports from the Port of Houston are Mexico, Brazil, Saudi Arabia, and Venezuela. The number one export in dollar value is construction/mining/oil field machinery, although unmilled grain and organic chemicals also rank high (Texas Commerce Bancshares 1982, 24–25).

Houston and the world-market system: the 1980s. Houston's oil-gas economy buoyed the city during the Great Depression and most postwar recessions, but the 1980s were different. In 1982–83 economic activity declined and unemployment rose significantly there. The city's industrial production declined more rapidly than the national average. The downturn in oil prices caught companies with large inventories; for example, tool companies had overproduced such items as drilling bits. The recession of the 1980s resulted in oil companies' laying off people to cut costs and improve cash flow. The unemployment rate grew more rapidly in Houston than in the nation as a whole, hitting 9.7 percent in 1983, up sharply from 1981 (Plaut 1983, 16). Refinery use in Texas declined from 91 percent of capacity in the late 1970s to less than 70 percent in 1983 (Wright, 1982).

Until 1975 the growth in U.S. energy demand was similar to the growth in GNP. Since that time, in part because of higher oil prices, the growth in demand has been less than real GNP growth (Wright 1982). Gulf Coast oil and petrochemical industries have faced declining oil production as Texas oil reserves are being gradually exhausted; oil production peaked in the 1960s. By the early 1980s the fifty Texas refineries imported a third of the oil feedstocks they processed, a proportion that had been as high as 46 percent in the late 1970s. The comparable figure was 2 percent in 1972 (Wright 1982).

As a leading center for the operation, production, and technological diffusion of the U.S. and world oil industry, Houston is probably the largest metropolitan area directly and massively affected by investment and production shifts in the world oil-market system. The movement of major oil company operations to Houston in the late 1960s and early 1970s came at a time when oil production was beginning to decline. One oil expert has suggested that the recentralization and increased investment of oil companies in Houston would not have taken place if the Texas oil economy had been as troubled in the early 1970s as it has been in the 1980s (Taylor 1983). This suggests how critical any shift in the economic context can be for urban development—and how quickly the fortunes of a city tied to the capitalistic world-market system can change.

Houston and the world-market system: the future. Plaut (1983) forecasts Texas economic growth for up to the year 2000. His low-oil-price scenario, which assumes an oil glut and a lower price per barrel of $22, shows economic output increasing at 4.2 percent annually and population growth rising at only 1.7 percent. His high-oil-price scenario shows a growth rate of 5.3 percent and a population growth of 3.2 percent. By either scenario, the periodic oil-boom years of the 1920–80 period would be over. Moreover, because of the shifting price of oil, declining Texas oil reserves, and current excess capacity, many industry experts expect no new refinery construction in the Houston—Gulf Coast area.

The petrochemical industry faces similar problems. Third World countries such as Saudi Arabia, Mexico, and Nigeria are expanding their oil refining and petrochemical facilities in order to produce value-added products from their raw materials. Since the 1970s, large-capacity refineries have been started in these regions; much less capacity is being added in the United States. A large petrochemical complex is being built in Saudi Arabia that would sell products to Europe, reducing the market for Gulf Coast petrochemical products. The health of significant sectors of the U.S. oil economy depends currently on plastics and other petrochemical exports to numerous countries; yet some of these countries, including Mexico, are trying to decrease such imports and build up their own petrochemical industries (Hoffman 1983). These industry trends threaten Houston's growth and prosperity.

Reassessing Theories of Urban Growth

Mainstream Theories

Convergence theorists seem to be off the mark in their emphasis on the filtering down of urban growth from dominant northern cities to the Sunbelt hinterland cities. Cities such as Houston are not part of some inevitable catching-up process. Understanding Houston is not a question of discovering a recently developed urban economy with a primitive-economy past. It has had a developed economy since its days as a regional commercial (cotton) center in about 1900. The city does fit a growth-pole theory that emphasizes a distinctive export base attracting growth (see Thompson 1965), because development of the first oil companies and refineries in the area did attract much additional growth. But these mainstream theorists tend to believe that Sunbelt growth-pole areas emerge in regions bypassed by earlier urban growth. In Houston's case this is not accurate; even before the discovery of oil, it had not been bypassed by economic growth (Pratt 1980, 506). The discovery of oil and the expansion of the oil industry accelerated growth in a city already experiencing economic advance. Houston's oil economy did not suddenly emerge in the 1960s; it began on a large scale in the 1920s. This point underscores the tendency of much mainstream analysis to isolate urban dynamics from the long-term historical context.

Houston's economic history also suggests that theories of urban growth should specify carefully how earlier stages link to later ones. Urban social scientists need to modify theories to emphasize such historical linkages. Houston's development shows a linked series in which one epoch (cotton/railroad) builds a foundation for the next (competitive/oligopoly) oil epoch, which in turn link to the next (state-supported oligopoly) epoch. Most urban analysts have not dealt adequately with the cumulative character of development in the economic base of cities. Although stages in the history of cities have been delineated (see Gordon 1977), few analyses of cities have assessed systematically the linked character of a city's developmental stages. This building-block development can be seen not only in Houston but also in cities as diverse as Pittsburgh (Lubove 1969) and Cairo (Abu-Lughod 1971). Moreover, Houston's case suggests the extent to which initial site advantages, such as location near oil fields and an agricultural-commercial infrastructure, are utilized to attract additional economic developments that are partially dependent on those site advantages. The petrochemical industry is an example. Later, these cumulative advantages attract additional economic activities (e.g., NASA and a new medical-industrial complex), which are much less dependent on these site advantages but would not have developed without the economic and political networks of the historical base.

Mainline theories are weak in their treatment of the role of technology in the emergence of Sunbelt cities. The transportation and communication technologies emphasized by Hawley, Kasarda, and Berry have shaped the spatial layout of cities such as Houston, but these technologies did not drop as "sky hooks." The implementation and impact of auto-centered technologies (instead of, for example, a mixed system including much more mass transit) in such cities resulted from a decision-making process involving top corporate (auto/oil) executives and local business coalitions working outside and through the state. Moreover, mainstream theories seem to suggest that technological innovation with industrial implications filters down the urban hierarchy. Early on, in the case of the oil-gas industry, major technological innovations in the sphere of production "filtered up" from the oil refineries, research centers, and petrochemical complexes in the greater Houston area to oil complexes in the North and around the globe.

Mainline theories are underdeveloped in their view of the state, which they tend to see as either limited (in the case of Sunbelt growth) or as the villain in the bad business climates (in northern cities). We can see this issue more clearly if we look at key arguments made by uneven development theorists.

Uneven Development

Uneven development theories are frequently more useful than mainstream theories for understanding growth in a Sunbelt city such as Houston. Of particular importance is their conceptual emphasis on investment decisions by corporate actors who follow the accumulation logic and on the resultant oscillating waves of investment. The first important wave of oil-related corporate investments came to Houston in the period 1908–29 and gradually built up the city's oil-economy base. These investments came later than comparable investments in the iron-steel industries of Pittsburgh or the many industries of New York. Yet major oil-related investments were in place long before 1950–80, the period emphasized by most mainstream and uneven development analysts of Sunbelt cities.

The expansion of private investment in auto-centered Detroit helped to spur investment in the greater Houston area in the 1920s. The mainstream concept of an urban hierarchy within or between regions does not capture the relationship between Houston and Detroit. This linkage is not primarily a relationship of filtering but a functional one wherein economic development in the auto industry in Detroit fuels raw materials and industrial development a thousand miles away (development in Houston has a feedback effect on Detroit). Nor does this idea of hierarchy, of "lower" and "higher" centers, capture the empirical portrait of two cities that are world capitals in their own industries yet have had an interdependent development.

Houston is also firmly linked to New York City. Corporate investment decisions in the New York headquarters of international oil-gas companies and international banks have been central to Houston's growth for many decades. This dependence on New York for finance capital is not unusual in the U.S. urban system, but the point is missed by some analysts. Uneven development theorists such as Sale (1976) and Perry and Watkins (1977) portray the Sunbelt as prospering and as considerably independent from northern capital. Since the early twentieth century, however, much decision making about finance capital investment and top-level oil company strategies in the Sunbelt area has been made in the greater New York City area.

Urban analysts of both theoretical traditions portray northern cities as failing to capture the new post-World War II industries that lie at the heart of Sunbelt dynamism. This failure is attributed by convergence analysts to poor business climates and by uneven development analysts to the inertia of northern capitalists locked into existing investments. Yet Houston's dynamic oil and gas industry is not a new leading-edge industry of the postwar period. Oil and gas production and refining formed the industrial base of Houston at an early point in the twentieth century. Neither New York nor Pittsburgh nor any northern city had a chance to secure this important segment of the oil/petrochemical industry. One related problem with many explanations of Sunbelt growth is excessive attention to certain manufacturing industries, particularly the defense-related electronics and new high-tech industries located in a few Sunbelt cities. Older high-tech industries, such as oil refining and petrochemicals, are slighted.

Uneven development theories encourage us to look for the central role of the government in Sunbelt development. Vital throughout Houston's "free market" history has been the role of the federal government in fostering economic growth. At a remarkably early point, major federal subsidies facilitating capital accumulation went into making the ship channel a key transportation artery, whereas in the 1930s millions were spent to build government buildings, roads, and sewers. Much discussion of the state in cities (e.g., O'Connor 1973) neglects its regulatory function. It was in the East Texas oil fields that Houston-linked corporations learned the hard lesson that competition in oil capitalism can be irrational. The extent of state intervention in the Houston area since 1902 is important not only because these public investments built infrastructures and whole new industries, but also because this took place in the most "free enterprise"-oriented of American cities.

Houston's development illustrates empirically the role of local growth coalitions in development. The city has long had a successful growth coalition, which has included capitalist actors from real estate, oil, and other businesses, as well as top governmental officials. Often coordinated through the Chamber of Commerce, the coalition has worked effectively at all levels of government to bring public investment capital to Houston. Many uneven development theorists have targeted the role of the federal state. But they have neglected to specify its interrelated linkage to the local decision makers and the role of the growth coalition in shaping (as well as being shaped by) that federal role. Particularly in the cases of the Houston ship channel, the New Deal infrastructure, and intervention in the NASA decision, Houston's growth coalition utilized its business networks well and emphasized preexisting site advantages to attract federal involvement. Uneven development theories need to absorb the insights of Molotch (1976), Domhoff (1983), and Dear and Clark (1981) about the role of local government in urban decision making.

Conclusion: Houston and the World Economy

In the Houston case, a major weakness in both theoretical frameworks is graphically highlighted: the neglect of the world-economy context. Few studies of U.S. cities pay serious attention to their larger world context. Exceptions include the work of Hill (1977; 1984) and the recent project of Chase-Dunn (1984). Hill has emphasized the importance of the global economy in shaping Detroit's decline. One key aspect of this is auto company investment in global "sourcing" (dispersed auto production). The global sourcing strategy of automobile multinationals threatens Detroit with further disinvestment and unemployment. Hill (1984) links the internationalization of production to crises facing cities around the globe. Thus other international cities deserve similar contextual analysis. New York's economic base and labor shifts have been examined in detail (Tabb 1982; Sassen-Koeb 1984), but no one has published a systematic, in-depth analysis of their urban development against the larger international context. Soja, Morales, and Wolff (1983) have assessed the contemporary restructuring of Los Angeles and its rise as an international banking center. Implicit in their research is the suggestion that a U.S. city's economic and demographic growth or decline hinges far more than ever before on investment decisions made by top executives in multinational corporations who are regarding a global, spatial economy (see Tabb and Sawers 1984).

From 1900 to 1980 Houston went through several economic and population growth phases. In the first two, Houston's most important economic context was the southwestern United States, but by the 1920s the relevance of the national economy to Houston's growth was conspicuous. National oil companies moving into international operations began to dominate the city. World-market events had a major impact in the 1930s and the 1940s. The war with Japan, resulting in a cutoff of important raw materials from the Pacific basin, helped generate state aid for new petrochemical industries, which developed synthetic rubber and aviation fuel technologies critical to postwar petrochemical industry growth. It was also during the late 1930s and the 1940s that ties to Latin America became close and strong, with the establishment of major trading linkages to Mexico and South America and the beginnings of a flow of (often undocumented) labor from Latin America that provided cheap labor for local builders and other entrepreneurs.

Since the 1950s, billions of dollars' worth of oil tool, engineering, and other oil-gas service contracts have been made between Houston oil companies and oil fields from Malaysia and Saudi Arabia to the North Sea. Most large oil fields opened within the global economy have brought new growth to Houston. In addition, price-raising actions by OPEC nations affect the profits and investments of Houston companies; in 1973–74 the OPEC price increase brought rises in profits of oil companies and in exploration, boosting Houston's base. New world-economy conditions, such as the emergence of OPEC, have "forced multinational [oil] firms to shift investment from certain initial stage processes to final stage refining, and in many cases, to make the more controllable final stages greater centers for profit than before" (Cohen 1981, 289). Houston's refining and petrochemical plants have benefited from this shift. In the 1970s OPEC's actions brought an economic boom to Houston, part of which, the expansion in real estate, used undocumented Mexican aliens drawn from the world labor market, yet another linkage to the global economy. Changes in the world's oil economy have had negative effects as well. Economic diversification in Houston that had begun in the late 1960s was aborted by the rise in oil prices. The decline in oil prices in the early 1980s, by bringing the first major recession in recent memory to Houston, increased the growth coalition's concern with economic diversification.

In the past decade, Third World countries have not only taken back control over economic decisions once made only in U.S. multinational headquarters offices, but also have begun to progress from selling raw materials to developing value-added production facilities. Saudi Arabia, Mexico, and other countries are in the process of expanding petrochemical plants and oil refineries, often with the cooperation of U.S. oil companies. This global sourcing of the oil industry is likely to affect Houston's economic base and demographic growth significantly.

The research on Detroit and Los Angeles cited previously, together with this on Houston, points to the idea of city specialization in the capitalistic world-market system. In core countries, cities such as Houston and Detroit often specialize as centers for distinctive production, whereas other cities (e.g., New York) are centers for financial capital and multinational investment decision making. Cities such as Houston and Detroit are distinctive in that they specialize in particular types of industrial activity such as oil and automobiles. These cities have markets in both core countries and Third World countries, and they have a special industrial niche in the capitalistic world system. Specialization means more than a convenient location near raw materials; it is the outgrowth of capitalistic relational conditions that hold major cities, even countries, together. Cities, as places where specialization is grounded physically, are the cotter pins fastening the parts of the capitalistic world system.

Although uneven development theory seems to be useful in describing the development of cities such as Houston and Detroit, it, like mainstream theories, is unspecified regarding the world-economy context of urban development. In the future, substantial expansion of existing urban theories will require a much more careful examination of the international economy in relation to the growth, specialization, and decline of cities too long regarded only as national phenomena.

References

Abu-Lughod, Janet. 1971. *Cairo: One Thousand-One Years of the City Victorious*. Princeton, N.J.: Princeton University Press.

Berry, Brian J. L. 1973. *Growth Centers in the American Urban System*. Vol. 1. Cambridge, Mass.: Ballinger.

Berry, Brian J. L., and John D. Kasarda. 1977. *Contemporary Urban Ecology*. New York: Macmillan.

Brock, Bronwyn. 1981. "Houston less vulnerable than Dallas—Ft. Worth to impact of the recession." *Voice* (Dallas Federal Reserve Bank) (October), 1–5.

Castells, Manuel. 1984. "Class and power in American cities." *Contemporary Sociology* 13:270–73.

Chase-Dunn, Christopher. 1984. "Urbanization in the world system." In *Cities in Transformation,* edited by Michael P. Smith, 111–22. Beverly Hills, Calif.: Sage.

Cohen, Robert. 1981. "The new international division of labor, multinational corporations and urban hierarchy." In *Urbanization and Urban Planning in Capitalist Society,* edited by Michael Dear and Allen J. Scott, 287–318. London: Methuen.

Cramer, Clarence H. 1972. *American Enterprise*. Boston: Little, Brown.

Dear, Michael, and G. L. Clark. 1981. "Dimensions of local state economy." *Environment and Planning A* 13:1277–94.

Domhoff, G. William. 1983. *Who Rules America Now?* Englewood Cliffs, N.J.: Prentice-Hall.

Donahue, Jack, et al. 1973. *Big Town, Big Money*. Houston: Cordovan.

Fainstein, Susan S., and Norman S. Fainstein. 1983. "Economic change, national policy and the system of cities." In *Restructuring the City,* by Susan S. Fainstein, Norman I. Fainstein, Richard Child Hill, D. Judd, and Michael P. Smith, 1–26. New York: Longman.

Feagin, Joe R. 1983*a. The Urban Real Estate Game.* Englewood Cliffs, N.J.: Prentice-Hall.

————. 1983*b.* "The costs of growth: Houston reeaxamined." Paper presented at the Fifth Annual Conference of Urban Design, Washington, D.C., October.

Fortune editors. 1939. "Texas." *Fortune* 20 (December): 85–91, 162.

————. 1980. "Houston: The international city." *Fortune* 61 (July): 38–58.

Gordon, David M. 1977. "Class struggle and the stages of American urban development." In *The Rise of the Sunbelt Cities,* edited by David C. Perry and Alfred J. Watkins, 55–82. Beverly Hills: Sage.

Gottdiener, Mark. 1983. "Understanding metropolitan deconcentration: A clash of paradigms." *Social Science Quarterly* 64:227–45.

Guest, Avery M. 1984. "The city." In *Sociological Human Ecology,* edited by M. Micklin and H. M. Choldin, 277–322. Boulder, Colo.: Westview.

Hawley, Amos. 1981. *Urban Society: An Ecological Approach.* 2d ed. New York: Wiley.

Hill, Richard Child. 1977. "Capital accumulation and urbanization in the United States." *Comparative Urban Research* 4:39–60.

————. 1984. "Urban political economy. In *Cities in Transformation,* edited by Michael P. Smith, 123–38. Beverly Hills: Sage.

Hoffman, William. 1983. Personal Interview. Texas Department of Water Resources, Planning and Development Division.

Houston Chamber of Commerce. 1981*a.* "Buildings of 100,000 square feet or more." *Houston* 52 (February): 32–37.

————. 1981*b.* "Houston data sketch." Pamphlet.

James, Marquis. 1953. *The Texaco Story.* New York: Texas Co.

Kasarda, John D. 1980. "The implications of contemporary redistribution trends for national urban policy." *Social Science Quarterly* 61:373–400.

Lamare, James W. 1981. *Texas Politics: Economics, Power, and Policy.* St. Paul, Minn.: West.

Larson, Henrietta M., and Kenneth W. Porter. 1959. *History of Humble Oil and Refining Company.* New York: Harper and Row.

Lösch, August. 1954. *The Economics of Location.* New Haven, Conn.: Yale University Press.

Love, Ben F. N.d. *People and Profits: A Bank Case Study.* Booklet published in the 1970s. Houston: Texas Commerce Bank.

Lubove, Roy. 1969. *Twentieth Century Pittsburgh: Government, Business and Environmental Change.* New York: Wiley.

McAdams, D. Claire. 1980. "A power-conflict approach to urban land use." *Urban Anthropology* 9:295–318.

McComb, David. 1981. *Houston: A History.* Austin: University of Texas Press.

MacManus, Susan A. 1983. *Federal Aid to Houston.* Washington, D.C.: Brookings Institution.

Mollenkopf, John. 1983. *The Contested City.* Princeton, N.J.: Princeton University Press.

Molotch, Harvey. 1976. "The city as a growth machine: Toward a political economy of place." *American Journal of Sociology* 82:309–33.

Nash, Gerald D. 1968. *United States Oil Policy 1890–1964.* Pittsburgh: University of Pittsburgh Press.

O'Connor, James. 1973. *The Fiscal Crisis of the State.* New York: St. Martin's Press.

Perry, David C., and Alfred J. Watkins. 1977. "Regional change and the impact of uneven urban development." In *The Rise of the Sunbelt Cities,* edited by David C. Perry and Alfred J. Watkins, 19–54. Beverly Hills: Sage.

Plaut, Thomas. 1982. "Energy and the Texas economy: Past, present, and future." Research Report. Mimeographed. Austin: University of Texas, Bureau of Business Research.

———. 1983. "The Texas economy: Current status and short-term outlook." *Texas Business Review* (January–February), 15–20.

Poston, Dudley L. 1984. "Regional ecology." In *Sociological Human Ecology,* edited by M. Micklin and H. M. Choldin, 323–82. Boulder, Colo.: Westview.

Pratt, Joseph A. 1980. *The Growth of a Refining Region.* Greenwich, Conn.: JAI.

Prindle, David. 1981. *Petroleum Politics and the Texas Railroad Commission.* Austin: University of Texas Press.

Rostow, Walt W. 1977. "Regional change in the fifth Kondratieff upswing." In *The Rise of the Sunbelt Cities,* edited by David C. Perry and Alfred J. Watkins, 83–103. Beverly Hills: Sage.

Sale, Kirkpatrick. 1976. *Power Shift.* New York: Random House.

Sassen-Koeb, Saskia. 1984. "The new labor demand in global cities." In *Cities in Transformation,* edited by Michael P. Smith, 139–72. Beverly Hills: Sage.

Sibley, Marilyn McAdams. 1968. *The Port of Houston.* Austin: University of Texas Press.

Snell, Bradford. 1979. "American ground transport." In *The Urban Scene,* edited by Joe R. Feagin, 241–66. New York: Random House.

Soja, Edward, Rebecca Morales, and Goetz Wolff. In press. "Urban restructuring of social and spatial change in Los Angeles." *Economic Geography.*

Tabb, William K. 1982. *The Long Default.* New York: Monthly Review Press.

Tabb, William K., and Larry Sawers, eds. 1984. *Sunbelt/Snowbelt: Urban Development and Regional Restructuring.* New York: Oxford.

Taylor, J. L. 1983. Personal interview. Economic development officer, Houston Chamber of Commerce, July.

Texas Commerce Bancshares. 1982. "Texas facts and figures." Houston: Economics Division, Texas Commerce Bancshares.

Thompson, Wilbur R. 1965. *A Preface to Urban Economics*. Baltimore: Johns
    Hopkins University Press.
————. 1968. "Internal and external factors in the development of urban eco-
    nomics." In *Issues in Urban Economics,* edited by H. S. Perloff and L.
    Wingo, 43–62. Baltimore: Johns Hopkins University Press.
U.S. Bureau of the Census. 1961. *Historical Statistics of the United States*.
    Washington, D.C.: Government Printing Office.
Wallerstein, Immanuel. 1979. *The Capitalist World-Economy*. Cambridge:
    Cambridge University Press.
Williamson, Harold F., Ralph Andreano, Arnold Daum, and Gilbert Klose.
    1963. *The American Petroleum Industry: The Age of Energy 1899–1950*.
    Evanston, Ill.: Northwestern University Press.
Williamson, J. G. 1965. "Regional inequality and the process of national de-
    velopment: A description of the patterns." *Economic Development and
    Cultural Change* 13(4):3–84.
Wright, Mickey. 1982. "Texas industrial wateruse long-term projection."
    Draft report. Photocopied. Austin: Texas Department of Water Resources.
Writers' Project, Works Progress Administration. 1942. *Houston: A History
    and Guide*. Houston: Anson Jones.

3

Extractive Regions in Developed Countries: A Comparative Analysis of the *Oil Capitals*, Houston and Aberdeen

Joe R. Feagin

In this article extraction economies in less developed countries are compared to extraction economies in developed countries—to the Houston,
Texas, and Aberdeen, Scotland, petroleum regions. The following questions
are addressed: (1) What are the differences in Houston's and Aberdeen's development as petroleum regions? (2) How has their extractive development
differed from that in less developed countries? (3) What is the relationship
of early layers of development to later extractive investments? (4) How have
capital timing and scale shaped Houston's and Aberdeen's development as
urban regions? The historical timing of oil discoveries greatly affects the
way oil capital builds up and exfoliates relationally in urban regions.

Two principal regions in the world oil and gas system are the areas adjacent to
Houston, Texas, and Aberdeen, Scotland, urban regions called the *oil capitals* of
the United States and Western Europe. Aberdeen is the economic and political
center for the Grampian Region of northeastern Scotland, an area of 3,400 square
miles with a population of one-half million in the mid-1980s. Metropolitan
Houston, with a population of about three million in the 1980s, is the economic

This chapter is reprinted with minor revisions from Feagin, Joe R. 1990. "Extractive regions in developed countries: A comparative analysis of the oil capitals, Houston and Aberdeen," *Urban Affairs Quarterly,* 25 (June 1990): 591–619.

center for the western Gulf Coast. In this article I will first review the literature on development and extractive regions in underdeveloped countries and then examine the relevance of this and other research for assessing the development of extractive regions in core countries.

Extractive Economies and Underdevelopment

Advantages of Backwardness?

A number of ideas in the literature on underdeveloped countries can be weighed against the development of extractive regions in developed countries. Gerschenkron (1962) argued that there are major "advantages of backwardness," advantages that accrue to a "backward" country because of its late development. Belated industrialization often is promising because of the "backlog of technological innovations which the backward country could take over from the more advanced country" (p. 8). Moreover, mainstream stages-of-growth development theorists (for example, Friedmann 1966) have assumed that traditional economic sectors in less developed countries could be replaced by more dynamic industrial sectors through a beneficial integration into the capitalist world system.

Dependency theory has challenged this sanguine view. Working in the tradition of Andre Gunder Frank, Slater (1975, 168) demonstrated how integration into the world system has disintegrated Third World economies by putting key economic positions in the hands of foreign multinationals and forcing local urban growth where it facilitates multinational-dominated economies. Frank (1969) noted the use of foreign investment to create primary extraction oriented to supplying developed countries. Recently some scholars (Weede and Tieffenbach 1981) have argued that their data on countries show no relationship between a dependence on raw materials exports and economic underdevelopment, but others (Stokes and Jaffee 1982) have found underdevelopment linked to a dependence on unprocessed exports.

In his important work on extractive systems, Bunker (1984, 1017–25) distinguished clearly between *extraction* and *industrial* production, stating that the "economic models of industrial production neglect the physical dependence of industrial production on resource extraction" (p. 1017). Multinational location decisions involving extraction are limited severely by the geologically random distribution of resources. Extractive commodities are different from processed commodities in that they come "as they are" in terms of location and physical character. These commodities are extracted by multinationals, such as by mining in the Amazon, for immediate export to service manufacturing production in advanced countries. Bunker (1984, 1018) suggested that "the relative underdevelopment of regions from which matter and energy are extracted is best explained as a consequence of internal dynamics and the external trade relations of their economies." The extreme dependency of extractive regions and their nodal cities in developing countries is linked, among other things, to substantial external investment in materials extraction and in the removal infrastructure, which has meant heavy dependency on multinationals headquartered in the cities of core countries.

Jaffee and Stokes (1986, 533–46) corroborated earlier research on coal by demonstrating that multinational investment in the petroleum-extractive sector in underdeveloped countries has created trade dependence on core countries. Nemeth and Smith (1988) demonstrated that the international trade matrix has two dimension, the capital-intensity and extractive/processive dimensions. Moreover, unequal exchange between core and peripheral countries is usually discussed in terms of labor and capital intensity, but Nemeth and Smith (1988, 237) argued that it could as well be discussed in terms of the "environmental degradation, which results from economies dependent on extraction." They were elaborating a point that Bunker (1984) developed. He argued that the development of extractive economies involves the export of environmentally secured energy such as coal. This depletes the local ecosystem and undermines downstream economic developments. If the extractive capitalists are unwilling to put large investments back into the ecosystem, negative environmental effects can be so serious as to discourage diversified industrial development in the area.

Extractive Economies in the Core

Comparisons with Extraction in the Periphery

Although most development scholars have neglected extraction in core countries, the literature does provide concepts and theoretical suggestions useful in examining raw materials economies in core countries. Jacobs (1984) underscored the importance of downplaying nations and accenting urban regions — such as the extractive regions of Houston and Aberdeen — as the basic units for macroeconomic analysis. Gerschenkron (1962) suggested that backwardness should have benefited the late-developing extractive economy of the Aberdeen area, as compared with the earlier developing Houston area. Moreover, in his 1940s work on the early development of industrialized countries such as Canada, Innis (1940, 508) argued, in contrast to more recent dependency research, that the centrality of staples-exports development had been beneficial for a country's long-term development

Bunker (1984) and others have made it clear that corporate location decisions for extractive operations are different from those for manufacturing operations. The determinative character of extraction has been neglected in location theory. Theorists of corporate location have "always concentrated on manufacturing industry" (Chapman and Walker 1987: 2). Some scholars (such as Losch 1954; Greenhut 1956; Harvey 1985) skew the discussion of corporate location toward manufacturing operations and thus downplay geological and geographical factors in favor of labor (and other) costs and market-demand factors at a location, investment circuits, and managerial-interaction factors. Although extractive commodities are often in remote areas of core or underdeveloped countries, there are important examples of primary commodity discoveries near already-developed cities in the core.

The Multilayered Economy

Often in an underdeveloped country there is no preexisting industrial economy prior to the development of a new extractive region. In *The Spatial Division of Labor,* Massey (1984) suggested that the structure of a given local economy in a developed country is composed of economic layers representing successive rounds of investment within an international market. Extractive regions and their nodal cities in developed countries often have a multilayered economic system and have more socioeconomic depth than Third World extractive areas do.

However, even with layers of previous industrial or commercial development, the depletion of an extractive commodity can create serious problems, particularly when the primary resource has been depleted without significant generative investments in other sectors such as manufacturing (Corden and Neary 1982, 825–827). Some have termed such a condition the *Dutch disease* because of the situation in the Netherlands, a major North Sea producer of gas in the 1960s and 1970s. Dutch production was the first to peak among the North Sea producers; by 1977 new investment was low, unemployment was high, and manufacturing was falling. Major multinational firms had made substantial profits, and a temporary extractive boom had occurred. Yet there was no major spin-off of downstream gas-related industries and no modernization program for the nonpetroleum sector (Ellman 1977, 281–90). The problem was not necessarily the environmental degradation, which Bunker (1984) underscored as being the case in the less developed countries, but the multinationals' unwillingness to invest in downstream industries in this particular place.

Multinationals and Extraction Economies

The dependency literature demonstrates that the timing and character of multinational capital investment has been critical to extractive growth in the Third World. These findings in turn suggest questions about the timing and character of multinational intervention in core extractive development. Mandel (1978, 310–16) argued that the multinational company has become the central organizational form of capital in late capitalism, in both the core and the periphery. Most authors writing about multinationals (for example, Taylor and Thrift 1982) have neglected those engaged in the energy industry. Some authors have touched on multinational involvement in U.S. extraction, including Gaventa (1980) in his research on British multinational investment in Appalachian coal mining. In the literature on the oil and gas industry, scholars have explored a limited range of questions, such as price gouging (Sherrill 1983), country production, and monopolization (Chapman 1983), politics (Rand 1975; Odell and Vallenilla 1978), investment in developing countries (Jaffee and Stokes 1986), offshore boomtowns (Gramling and Brabant 1986), the Dutch gas decline (Ellman 1977; Corden and Neary 1982), and international oil politics (Odell 1963; Rees and Odell 1987).

Many of these authors target the oil and gas multinationals. Indeed, the development of ever-larger corporations with concentrated capital control has characterized the history of the petroleum industry in core and underdeveloped countries. Particularly after World War II, large oil firms produced so much with automated refining and petrochemical production that they required expanding worldwide markets for both raw materials and finished products, and this extractive/processive expansion drew the Houston and Aberdeen regions more deeply into global oil production relations. In turn, the fortunes of oil capital altered the material and spatial life conditions of Houston and Aberdeen, but not in even or homogeneous ways. In contrast to some extraction industries, the petroleum industry has become increasingly capital intensive, at least since the 1920s. By the 1940s, if not before, the increasing scale of capital required had become a major barrier to entry into petroleum production and marketing small- and middle-sized firms with local capital resources. In U.S. petroleum regions prior to the 1940s, it was easier to develop new oil and gas companies because of the lesser scale of capital required. Smaller firms and the modest scale of capital were sometimes compatible with the extraction of numerous onshore deposits. Within a few decades, however, large multinationals became necessary to provide the capital for much of the onshore drilling and most offshore drilling. The average cost of drilling a U.S. onshore well increased from $27,600 in 1936, to $49,000 in 1959, and to $231,912 in 1986; the average cost of an offshore well increased from $320,704 in 1959 to $3,126,096 in 1986 (Engineer Publishing Company 1947, D-72; American Petroleum Institute 1977, section 3, tables 8–9; American Petroleum Institute 1988, section 3, tables 9a and 10a). The timing of oil discoveries and the extant scale of capital also have been critical to the development of downstream processing industries, such as refining and petrochemicals, in particular oil regions.

Not only the size and global expansion of the petroleum multinationals but also their internal organizational structures have affected urban regions across the world system (see Chase-Dunn 1984). Hymer (1979, 157–63) probed the relationship of the internal structure of large corporations to the character and growth of particular cities. He developed a typology suggesting that large global companies locate their distinctive functional levels in three different levels of cities: top management functions in world-class cities, the field management functions in national cities, and day-to-day operations in lesser cities around the world. This worldwide organizational distribution across cities can be seen in the oil and gas industry. In addition, the dominance of large oil corporations with weak attachments to regional cities has affected location decisions; multinationals can abandon a city more easily than can local companies.

The important relationship between facilitating *governments* and extractive development by multinationals in Third World countries has been noted by development scholars (for example, Bunker 1984). In core countries the state also has developed an array of relationships with the oil and gas industry. In some cases, such as Norway, oil and gas development has been placed mostly under the direct control of the state in order to ensure, at least in theory, greater public control of, and benefits from, resource depletion. In other cases, such as Great Britain and the United States, governments have left oil and gas extraction primarily in the hands of the private sector; in these countries private oil interests have gained great economic and political power, including dramatic tax advantages. Moreover, although governments have been important in providing supportive subsidies for private extractive enterprises in Great Britain and in the United States, that support has varied with the timing of a region's oil-related developments.

Drawing on this diverse literature on development, extraction, and multinationals, I suggest as a guide through the case-study materials the following research questions: (1) What are the similarities and differences in development of the Houston and Aberdeen petroleum regions? (2) How has the development of extractive economies in the core countries differed from that in underdeveloped countries? (3) What is the relationship between early layers of economic development and later extractive investment? (4) How have the historical timing of oil development and the varying scale of capital influenced the emergence and character of the Houston and Aberdeen regions? A central thread running through the answers to these questions is that the historical timing of oil discoveries is of great significance in the way oil capital builds up and exfoliates relationally—economically and politically—in cities and surrounding extractive regions.

Incorporation of the Houston and Aberdeen Areas into the World Oil and Gas System

One of the most important primary commodity markets in the capitalist world system is centered on oil. The fugitive and hidden character of oil accounts for its pursuit being perhaps the "quintessential venture of risk-taking capitalism" (Solberg 1976, 4). Between 1901 and the present, major capital investments in oil-gas discovery, extraction, and processing were made in the Houston and Aberdeen regions. The chance discovery in 1901 of oil at Spindletop, 90 miles east of Houston, and in the North Sea east of Aberdeen in the late 1960s brought both cities into the world oil and gas system and introduced a new era of boom–bust economic development for both metropolitan areas. How was extraction-related development in Houston similar to, and different from, development in Aberdeen? Why were Houston and Aberdeen areas chosen as sites for the operations offices and manufacturing plants of oil and gas corporations?

The Timing and Character of Extractive Development: The Houston Area

A major difference between the Houston and Aberdeen regions lies in the timing of initial oil development. Houston had the earlier development. The discovery of onshore oil east of Houston in 1901 and subsequent discoveries closer to the city set the stage for this city to become a major oil center. By 1919 three quarters of Gulf Coast oil was coming from fields in the Houston area (Williamson et al. 1963, 22). By the mid-1930s Houstonians were proudly labeling their city the "oil capital of the world." Even in the months between January 1932 and March 1933, the nadir of the Great Depression, hundreds of companies reopened for business, including 113 oil-related firms (*Houston* 1933, 3). Half the world's oil production was then located within six hundred miles of Houston, a city with thousands of miles of pipeline linking it to hundreds of oil fields (Wharton, 1930: 9). Even during the Great Depression, Houston continued to grow because of its expanding oil base. By 1940 about three-quarters of the oil produced in the midcontinent area was controlled by companies tied to Houston. More than half of all U.S. oil flowed through the Houston-Gulf Coast economy. Texas had the nation's most productive oil field, that in East Texas, as well as 56 percent of proven oil reserves in the United States (Feagin 1988, 52–67).

Between the 1940s and the early 1980s prosperity continued in the greater Houston area. There was substantial development of downstream industries linked to oil exploration and production, including refineries, oil tools and services, and petrochemical plants. The value of foreign trade through the Port of Houston increased tenfold between 1970 and 1980. By the 1960s Houston had evolved into the oil-technology distribution center for many fields across the globe (Taylor 1983). In the early 1980s about 35 percent of the jobs in the area were connected directly to the oil and gas industry; another fifth were greatly dependent on the industry. Fully 70 percent of the large plants in Houston were part of the oil and gas industry.

The Multilayered Economy of Houston

Why and how did Houston become the oil capital of the Gulf Coast? Just before the petroleum discoveries, Houston, with an 1890 population of only 27,000, was the eighteenth-largest city in the South and was smaller than its sister city, Galveston, Texas. In contrast, the city's competitors, Galveston and Beaumont, confronted major barriers to becoming the oil and gas center. A hurricane destroyed Galveston in 1900; oil-related companies seeking an urban center began to avoid that exposed coastal location. Beaumont, a town closer to the first fields than was Houston, did not have the requisite infrastructure of banks, law firms, and railroads (Pratt 1980, 53–55).

Metropolitan Houston's economic structure is multilayered. Beginning with agricultural production and marketing, the region's economy expanded in the 1870s and 1880s and soon became the heart of a major railroad network in the Southwest. Large-scale cotton and other agricultural production created Houston as a commercial city serving a large agricultural hinterland, a city with a full range of transport, banking, and legal firms. By the 1910s the local ship channel had been dredged deeply enough for large ships, and the city was used as a center by seventeen railroads. Houston was becoming a major port. Texas was producing two-thirds of all cotton in the United States, much of which was shipped through Houston, which also had major cottonseed-processing mills. The local population, predominantly white but with a large and poor black minority, was heavily employed in agricultural processing and shipping activities.

With the discovery of oil and the location of firms in Houston in the 1910s and 1920s, a new economic sector was added to the local economy, substantially because of the infrastructure laid down during the agricultural commerce period (Sibley 1968, 133–35; McComb 1981, 65–67). The existing infrastructure served as a magnet in the logistical choices made by the petroleum firms in the selection of office and manufacturing locations. Houston had become the key metropolis on the Texas Gulf Coast just before the arrival of oil and gas. Moreover, by the late 1920s and 1930s the economic foundation of the upstream oil exploration and production activities attracted the development of an array of downstream oil-gas processing and manufacturing industries, including the oil-tool, refining, and petrochemical industries. By 1940 Houston had become a major port for the export of extracted crude oil, which attracted increasingly large shipping corporations to the port area. Three decades later, prior layers of infrastructure development again became significant. During the early 1970s several large oil corporations centralized major facilities in the city, shifting subsidiaries from elsewhere. Shell (U.S.) relocated its U.S. administrative headquarters from New York to Houston, and Texaco, Gulf, and Exxon consolidated principal domestic operations there. One reason for this relocation was the already thick palimpsest of infracture and oil-related facilities. In addition, the low oil price in this era encouraged multinational cost cutting and consolidation (Taylor 1983; Business Week 1970, 16).

Timing and Character of Extractive Development: Aberdeen

Oil-related development in the Aberdeen region began six decades later than in Houston. Although Houston was a growing agricultural center at the time of the oil discoveries in the late 1960s, Aberdeen was in a distressed economic condition. During the 1960s the Aberdeen economy was depressed compared to the rest of Scotland and Britain. Wage levels were lower than in other Scottish cities, which resulted in the highest rate of out-migration of any area in Britain. Even the fishing and textile industries were in decline. In 1964 the British government issued the first licenses authorizing firms to explore for North Sea oil and gas. An offshore oil boom resulted. The first offshore commercial find was the Montrose field in 1969; the first oil from the North Sea was brought by pipeline to the Scottish mainland in 1975. By the late 1970s many of the world's international oil corporations were involved in development of 16 fields in the U.K. sector of the North Sea, and by the late 1980s, 40 oil fields were·in production or being developed. Oil production increased from 12 million tonnes in 1976 to 110 million tonnes in 1983 (Grampian Regional Council 1981).

Offshore oil and gas discoveries spurred onshore development in the coastal towns and cities of northeast Scotland in the form of services and supply facilities, administrative offices, and, to a lesser extent, oil-related manufacturing. Transporting the oil involved the preparation of pipe systems, terminals, and storage tanks. Processing activities required facilities for the separation of oil and gas. The world's largest natural gas treatment plant was built by British Gas at St. Fergus, north of Aberdeen (Scottish Office 1987). By the early 1980s numerous major oil firms and oil service firms had set up operational offices in Aberdeen. The exploration and development of the oil and gas fields and the proliferation of associated service industries brought many jobs. In June 1984 about 64,000 people in Scotland were employed in firms wholly involved in the oil and gas industry (Scottish Office 1987). From 1970 until the decline in the oil price in 1985–1986, the number of oil-related jobs and population grew steadily in the Aberdeen area; oil-related employment grew from 1,000 in 1971 to 51,000 in 1985 (Grampian Regional Council 1986, 3). The oil boom lowered the unemployment rate in the Aberdeen area.

In the early 1980s many experts in northeast Scotland expected the oil and gas boom to bring unparalleled prosperity for at least the next two decades (Grampian Regional Council 1981). Optimistic projections by the director of physical planning for the Grampian Regional Council suggested that by 2001, 83 commercial fields would be under development, with 25,000 offshore employees and another 33,000 onshore employees in oil-related jobs in the northern North Sea area (Sprott 1986).

The Multilayered Economy of Aberdeen

In the Aberdeen case the commonly expressed reasons for the oil-gas multinationals' location choices have included weather permitting year-round operations, proximity to European markets, the Conservative party heading the
central government, and a location close to the North Sea fields. But a few
other Scottish cities in the northern North Sea area also had these features. Perhaps more fundamentally, as in the Houston case, the urban location choice
was affected by the preexisting infrastructure of the port, hotels, insurance
firms, and banks in Aberdeen, an infrastructure resulting from advanced agricultural, fishing, and other commercial operations. Of course, when oil came
to the Aberdeen area, it was a larger and more diverse urban region than Houston had been in the early 1900s. In the late 1960s the greater Aberdeen area had
a population of more than 400,000.

The first recorded reference to the port of Aberdeen, Scotland, dates from
A.D. 1136; by the 1600s much publicly subsidized work was being done to improve the harbor—improvements that in turn stimulated commerce throughout
the growing town. In the 1880s the steam-trawling industry came to Aberdeen,
establishing the basis for the development of a new and increasingly prosperous fishing industry. Although the city suffered some damage from German
bombing raids during World War II, after the war it prospered not only as a
fishing center but also as the regional center of governmental and financial services. Like the area of Texas near Houston, the hinterland of Aberdeen, called
the Grampian region, is a major agricultural region; it is the principal producer
of beef, pork, and barley in Scotland. More than half of the fish landed in Scotland and one-quarter of the timber produced in Scotland come from the region.
Aberdeen was prosperous early in its history from agriculture, forestry, and
fishing. Because of the agricultural and raw-materials economic layers, a small
manufacturing sector developed in textiles, paper, and shipping-related engineering. Food processing and shipbuilding, engineering, and other facilities
servicing the fishing industry contributed to its economic base (Bonney 1987).
Extractive commodities require commercial services somewhat different from
those for manufacturing, including port, banking, and legal services. Raw-
materials extraction was an economic layer on which were built large governmental services and commercial retailing and banking sectors. Prior to oil
development the region's economy was already a multilayered palimpsest. In
an early assessment of the impact of the oil and gas industry, MacKay and
Moir (1980) argued that the choice of Aberdeen as the headquarters for the
North Sea oil-gas industry was not inevitable but resulted from Aberdeen's superior infrastructure and active solicitation by local business and political authorities.

Thus both the Houston and Aberdeen cases demonstrate the importance of
economic layering in the evolution of regional and urban economies. Earlier

development grounded in developed agriculture and commerce had created a first-rate infrastructure that became the major reason for the location of the oil and gas multinationals in specific cities. There is rarely such an economic palimpsest in the Third World cases.

The Impact of Multinationals on Houston and Aberdeen

Houston and Aberdeen have multilayered economies now dominated by the oil and gas industry, but the character of these economies has varied because of the historical timing of oil development, the variation in scale of capital required, and the decision-making and organizational structure of the multinational oil corporations.

Small Firms and Multinationals: The Impact of Houston

Not long after the discovery of oil near Houston, several oil companies organizing production in the new fields opened headquarters in, or moved them to, the city. Between 1908 and 1916 the newly formed companies called the Texas Company (later Texaco) and the Gulf Company came to Houston. Moreover, the early timing of these oil discoveries and the accessibility of much of the oil meant that for the first few years a significant amount of exploration and production could be carried out by smaller firms. They were able to finance the limited research and development necessary, and much technological development came by trial and error. The relatively small amount of capital required enabled many local companies to participate in organizing production in the Texas oil fields. Gradually, however, the scale of the capital required increased; over the next two decades the increase in capital requirements, together with cutthroat competition, meant that large outside corporations would dominate many sectors of the Texas oil industry. By the 1930s fully 70 percent of Texas production was controlled by twenty big companies. The large firms moved into new oil fields and directly or indirectly drove smaller companies out of business; they expanded vertically by adding subsidiaries covering all aspects of the business from research to refining and marketing. The borrowing of outside capital by the southeast Texas oil firms came early. Historians Larson and Porter (1959, 72–104), noted that in the early decades of the 1900s, the larger companies of Texas origin developed "with the aid of capital from the Northeast," and in the next few decades, several placed their "headquarters in New York, Philadelphia, or Pittsburgh." By 1920 Standard Oil, formerly excluded by local government action from Texas fields, had bought a controlling share in Houston's local Humble Oil and Refining Company, which eventually became the largest producer of crude oil in the United States.

Building on the extractive base, the big oil corporations invested capital in a number of downstream processing facilities in Houston in the 1920s and 1930s. Numerous refineries and other oil-related facilities were built using the area's raw materials, not only oil and gas but also sulfur and salt water. By 1941 the Gulf Coast was the dominant refining region, with more than one-third of total U.S. capacity. The refineries became central to the anchoring of the integrated multinational companies in the area (Pratt 1980, 64–68; Ridley, 1930:18). The development of oil extraction and refinery capabilities in turn spurred massive capital investments in the petrochemical industry. By the late 1930s and 1940s a significant spurt in petrochemical industrialization had occurred that was linked substantially to World War II and to millions in federal government subsidies to the oil majors' and other large firms' petrochemical plants. Much private capital also flowed into chemical facilities; by the early 1980s large multinationals in the greater Houston-Gulf Coast area produced 40 percent of U.S.-produced petrochemicals (*Chase Manhattan Bank Petroleum Situation Newsletter* 1983, 1–3). During and after World War II, companies like Gulf, Mobile, Texaco, Exxon, and Shell solidified the domination of large multinational corporations in the Houston-Gulf Coast region by locating new facilities and subsidiaries there. Because they operate internationally, such companies have had greater sources of capital and labor than local firms, and the expanding market for their products has long been international (Pratt 1980, 8–9). By the 1960s and 1970s metropolitan Houston's role in the world oil economy had become central in research and operations in exploration, production, refining, and marketing. No fewer than thirty-four of the thirty-five largest oil companies had major office and plant facilities in the Houston region. At least four hundred other major oil-gas companies also were located in the metropolitan area, together with hundreds of geological firms, drilling contractors, tools and supply companies, law firms, and other oil-related service companies (Taylor 1983).

Interestingly, in the 1980s an article appeared in *Texas Monthly* in which the author (Burka 1983, 109) asserted that "Houston has shoved New York aside to become the center of the international oil business." This assertion is only partially accurate. Although the oil majors have important subsidiaries in Houston, most of these are dependent to some extent on the outside headquarters for highest-level management, planning, and investment decisions. Thus Exxon, the world's largest integrated oil company, has its international headquarters in New York. Yet this fact does not reveal the true significance of Houston: Exxon has four major division and subsidiary offices there.

Although the oil majors are not headquartered there, all but one of the chief industrial corporations with headquarters in the city are in the oil and gas business—and most are international leaders in the gas industry or oil tools and services. For example, in 1984 Houston was the site of the headquarters of several Fortune 500 industrial corporations: Shell-U.S. (ranked 13th nationally), Tenneco (19th), Coastal Corporation (55th), Pennzoil (147th), Cooper Industries (180th), Anderson Clayton (233rd), Mitchell Energy & Development (315th), Big Three Industries (360th), and Cameron Iron Works (457th) (Houston Chamber of Commerce, n.d., circa 1985). Oil tools and supply companies have been central to the international role of Houston. By the late 1970s there were about 100 Houston companies, mostly oil-gas tools and services firms, working in the North Sea fields, a sign of the major relationship between the two extraction areas (Taylor 1983). By 1980 nearly $7 billion in engineering and related contracts were in effect between Houston and other U.S. oil support companies and enterprises in the Middle Eastern oil fields. The important exceptions to East Coast corporate *headquarters* dominance of the Houston petroleum industry have been these international oil tools firms and the gas industry companies on the same list. Although much gas extraction has been controlled by the majors, a few Houston-based corporations on the list, including Tenneco and Coastal, as well as other large companies such as Transco and Texas Eastern, have played a major role in the gas extraction and gas transmission businesses (Moskowitz et al. 1980: 848–50).

Multinational Capital and Aberdeen

Aberdeen is considered the oil capital of Europe because there are more than 800 oil-related firms in the general area. Greater Aberdeen has become the focal region for the North Sea oil and gas industry in Britain and has the greatest concentration of the multinational oil business in Europe. The coming of the oil and gas industry changed the local economy from one dominated by a large number of locally owned firms to one dominated by large oil and gas multinationals headquartered in the United States, London, and elsewhere in Europe. Neither the production firms nor the offshore oil supply firms are headquartered in this oil capital. Decisions made in the London (and other) headquarters of multinational corporations and in OPEC offices have been determining forces: "Clearly the major influences determining the scale and scope of opportunities in the offshore oil industry lie far away from Aberdeen" (Bonney 1986, 5).

The offshore oil development has been carried out by large multinational corporations; those with operational centers in the area in the late 1980s included Amoco, British Petroleum (BP), Britoil, Chevron, Conoco, Marathon, Mobil, Occidental, Phillips, Shell Expo (with Exxon), Texaco, Total, and

Union Oil. The decision-making scope of the operations offices has for the most part been limited to the North Sea and Scotland. Subsidiaries and affiliates of non-Scottish firms are characteristic in the Aberdeen oil and gas industry. Deidre Hunt, researcher at Aberdeen's Gordon Institute, studied the local impact of the oil and gas industry; in a survey of 241 area firms she found that 70 percent were affiliates, subsidiaries, or branches of outside parent companies—that is, not locally owned. Among the affiliates and subsidiaries that were 100 percent oil related, half were owned by British parent corporations and half by overseas corporations—two-thirds of which were North American. Interestingly, the North American affiliates were the first to arrive in the area; some were Houston firms. Local papers celebrated the entry of Houston firms, accenting their "modernity and sophistication." Oil-related Houstonians were pictured as the first major immigrants "since the Vikings" (Hunt 1987). The dependence on Houston's tools and services corporations has persisted. Thus when, on July 6, 1988, a gas-fueled explosion on a North Sea oil platform owned by Occidental took 166 lives in the world's worst offshore disaster, the man called upon to cap and save the burning wells on the burned-out platform was Houston's Red Adair, whose company specializes in putting out oil field fires around the world (*Austin American-Statesman* 1988, A6).

The global dynamics of the oil supply industry "does not favor any permanent single supply base. Rather, the industry follows the oil majors as they locate and relocate in new offshore oil provinces" (Hallwood 1986, 6). The supply firms have delivered services on site as needed by the major production firms, and their supplies of machinery and tools have come from distant manufacturing sites mostly in the United States. Outside companies operating in the North Sea have come there to exploit the oil potential and to sell equipment made elsewhere. This ingress did increase employment significantly, but much of this is likely to be transitory. There have been few long-term career possibilities. Even most of the training and education were continued elsewhere, and few local personnel have been employed in research and development (Hunt 1987).

Aberdeen University researchers Lloyd and Newlands (1987, 12–13) have pointed out that although the involvement of the oil and gas multinationals brought 50,000 jobs, new investment and technology, and a major extractive industry, the multinationals' headquarters were located elsewhere; therefore, most profits from the oil and gas operations flow out of the Aberdeen area. Many affiliates in the area have been "relatively *unimportant* within their parent's ownership group (as measured by the affiliate's contribution to group employment and sales)" (Hallwood 1986, 5). This means that affiliates can be closed by parent companies without seriously endangering the performance of the parent group. Short-run exploitation of an extraction area can take place, not just in underdeveloped countries, but also in industrialized countries.

Contrasts in Investment and Firm Dominance

The Houston Case   Although the Houston and Aberdeen regions contrast dramatically with Third World extraction areas, particularly in the palimpsest aspect, there are major differences in these core cases. The two cities developed at different times during the growth of the capitalist world system and its oil- and gas-industry component. Barriers to generating sufficient capital for local company creation were not as great in southeast Texas in the 1910s and 1920s as in northeast Scotland in the 1970s and 1980s. In the earliest period the Texas oil industry was not as dominated by concentrated and centralized capital as later, so local oil entrepreneurs in production, tools, and services in the Houston-Gulf Coast area could sustain themselves in ways not possible later in Aberdeen. The oil discoveries near Houston preceded the establishment of a truly international oil and gas market system; the Houston area in effect grew up with and shaped, and was shaped by, that expanding system.

Another benefit flowing to extractive corporations operating in the Houston area was political. Unlike the Aberdeen extractive economy, the Houston economy grew up with the national government. That government supported the newly developing Sunbelt industry. Responding during World War I to the claims of small oil (and other raw materials) producers that they took great risks to extract a commodity that was rapidly depleted, in 1918 U.S. government officials created a huge tax benefit, called the oil depletion allowance, that permitted oil firms to shield about 28 percent of their gross income from taxes. This *tax expenditure* benefited not only the small wildcatters but also (primarily) the big oil corporations (Solberg 1976, 73–78). Beginning in the 1930s, Houston had a lot of powerful friends in Washington, D.C. John Nance Garner, as House member and vice president, had represented Texas for decades. A Texas senator was chair of the Senate Military Affairs Committee, and Texas House members chaired the judiciary, agriculture, and rivers and harbors committees. Between the 1930s and the 1960s there were many direct links between Houston's business leadership and the federal government. During the first decades of this period an important politician associated with the Houston business elite was House Majority Leader and Speaker of the House Sam Rayburn. During the 1930s and 1940s the powerful Houstonian Jesse Jones served President Roosevelt as head of the Reconstruction Finance Corporation (RFC), as Federal Loan Administrator, and as Secretary of Commerce. Under the guidance of this leading banker, the RFC became the state banker and stockpiler for war production, investing billions in industrial facilities. The Defense Plant Corporation (DPC), a subsidiary of the RFC, provided loans and leased, purchased, and built war production plants. Between 1940 and 1945 DPC financed 2,300 projects in 46 states, altogether about $9.2 billion in factories, mills, and machinery. Together with other Texas politicians in Washington, D.C., Jones saw to it that Houston got a very substantial share of the war production funds, which helped to stimulate the aviation fuel, synthetic rubber, and petrochemical industries in the Houston area (Jones 1951, 200–399). Because of these early political advantages, Houston's oil-gas development differed from Aberdeen's.

The Aberdeen Case   By the time of the discovery of oil and gas near Aberdeen, much more capital was required, especially for offshore development. I noted earlier the sharp increase in the cost of drilling U.S. onshore and offshore wells between the 1930s and the 1980s; the increase was particularly dramatic offshore, from about $320,000 per well in the late 1950s to more than $3 million per well in 1986. This increase was reflected in drilling wells in many offshore areas. Offshore development requires the kind of capital that the multinationals have, so offshore oil could not be developed so easily without them, particularly in difficult waters such as the North Sea. Aberdeen's development was centered around an offshore oil-gas industry, and the lateness of that development meant that the largest multinational corporations in the world dominated extraction there from the beginning. Mandel's (1978) argument about the scale of capital as an increasing barrier to entry in late capitalism applies to this lack of development of local exploration and production firms during the Aberdeen boom and explains the absence of major local oil tools and supply firms.

In addition, there are some significant differences in political linkages. Oil and gas development in the North Sea was facilitated through a favorable taxing regime provided by central government to stimulate oil and gas development in those difficult waters. Unlike the Houston case, however, it was the *foreign* multinational corporations, not the national (British) corporations, that mostly benefited from this governmental tax largess from the beginning. The government-owned British National Oil Corporation (BNOC) was not given much opportunity to participate in North Sea joint ventures, and the production subsidiary of BNOC was sold to private individuals. The British government left North Sea development largely in the hands of the subsidiaries of foreign multinational corporations (Harris et al., n.d., 30–31). Moreover, unlike Houston from the 1920s to the 1950s, Aberdeen and the Grampian region in the 1960s and 1970s were not represented by a coterie of powerful politicians in the national capital to guarantee that the local city and region would receive significant state capital investments or that local firms would receive a significant share of the state benefits. Of course, the divergent political systems and the effect of the historical timing of the acceleration of the flow of state capital investments during World War II in the Houston case should not be underestimated in contrasting the differences in political linkages.

Gerschenkron (1962) argued that there are advantages to later development. However, when compared to oil and gas development in Houston, late petroleum development was not an advantage in Aberdeen. Houston was better off economically, in terms of local firm development, because it developed early. Indeed, numerous world-class tools and services corporations came from Houston to Aberdeen to support the operations of the international oil corporations. The large multiplier effects of capital-intensive resource exploitation are apparent in both cities, but the breadth of the multiplier effects are different. The palimpsest layering has thickened more in the Houston case than in the Aberdeen case. Although some development of oil and gas separation facilities has occurred in the Aberdeen region, as yet there has been little investment of multinational capital in the more sophisticated technological layers of manufacturing, refining, and petrochemical plants. Aberdeen has developed only two local, medium-sized manufacturing firms linked to the new oil and gas industry (Hallwood 1986, 7–9). The historical timing of capital centralization and patterns of investment were critical. The discovery of oil near Houston coincided with increased automobile usage and industrial growth that amplified the demand for processed petroleum products in the United States and thus created a need for refining and petrochemical capacity, much of which was provided by large corporations in the Houston-Gulf Coast area. The North Sea bonanza developed late in the history of multinational development of worldwide refining and petrochemical facilities. Ironically, North Sea oil developments coincided with a decline in the relative significance of oil in the European energy economy, which had already adjusted to the post-1973 OPEC price increases with conservation and a reduction in the use of some oil and oil products. In these circumstances, refining capacity in the United Kingdom and western Europe has fallen since the discovery of North Sea oil; there has been no demand for new refining capacity to handle offshore production. For this and other reasons, and in contrast to the Houston case, there has been little national government aid for downstream petrochemical development in contemporary Britain.

The International Operations Subsidiary City

Hymer (1979) linked three corporate function levels to different types and levels of cities, with the top management function in world-class cities, the field management function in national cities, and the day-to-day operations in lesser cities. Cities like Houston and Aberdeen, in spite of their images as oil capitals, at first glance seem to fit into Hymer's category of field-office management because of their lack of headquarters facilities for major oil firms and because of the dominance of operations subsidiaries and affiliates. Aberdeen most clearly falls into the field management category. In regard to its passive extractive economy, Aberdeen responds to "forces unloosed in distant cities" (Jacobs 1984, 34).

Houston is more central to the world petroleum economy and more diversified than Aberdeen. Houston falls into a separate category missed by Hymer: the international operations subsidiary city. Houston is a specialized command city, without leading international oil firm headquarters but with substantial control over the oil industry beyond the regional or field-office level. Although the Houston metropolis does not house the executives who make the highest-level, companywide investment decisions for major integrated oil multinationals, more organizational units of oil- and gas-related corporations, from the largest multinationals to the smaller "independents," are concentrated there than in any other world city. The officers of the leading multinationals' operations subsidiaries are located in the metropolitan area. As previously mentioned in the example of Exxon, these are more than regionalized "field offices"—they often control oil operations across the United States and across portions of the globe. In addition to housing the subsidiary offices of the oil majors, Houston is the site of the headquarters (and subsidiary) offices and plants of (1) substantial international oil corporations (for example, Pennzoil), (2) the largest oil tools and services companies, and (3) major gas transmission companies. Thus Houston, as the more diversified oil-gas area, with more backward and forward linkages, has become the leading metropolitan area on the Gulf Coast, whereas Aberdeen in contrast, has remained less important as a metropolis in Scotland than Glasgow or Edinburgh.

Types of Decline after Extractive Booms

The cycles of economic boom and bust in extraction economies are somewhat different from those in industrial production economies. Several scholars (Bunker 1984; Jaffee and Stokes 1985, 533–46) have noted at least two types of economic crises for extraction systems in underdeveloped countries: the temporary downturn crises created by supply-and-demand factors (such as a sharp drop in the price of an extractive commodity) and the usually more serious crises created by the depletion of the extracted commodities. In contrast to most manufacturing sectors, increased productivity and efficiency in extraction economies accelerate depletion and the ultimate abandonment crisis. Moreover, each type of crisis affects extraction regions and cities within underdeveloped and developed countries.

Supply Crisis and Core Extraction Economies

In the 1980s global energy conservation and the substitution of non-oil-based fuels, as well the inability of OPEC and non-OPEC oil-producing countries to agree on enforceable production quotas, increased supply in relationship to demand and significantly reduced oil prices. The consequent changes in petroleum multinationals' investment strategies brought major recessions to the Houston and Aberdeen areas. Houston's oil-gas economy had buttressed the city against all twentieth-century recessions until the 1980s, but this unparalleled prosperity was followed by the most serious economic downturn in the city's history. Neither Houston's leaders nor its citizenry were prepared for the crisis with its high levels of unemployment, bankruptcies, and corporate restructuring. Between 1981 and 1986 Houston lost more than 100,000 energy-related industrial jobs. The unemployment rate grew more rapidly in Houston than in the nation, hitting 9.7 percent in 1983, up sharply from previous years. In 1985 there was a brief resurgence in Houston's economy, but late in 1986 the Chamber of Commerce estimated that the unemployment rate was nearly 11 percent; there were continuing and heavy job losses in manufacturing, oil mining, and construction (Eisenberg 1986, 5). However, the city's business leaders saw the downturn as temporary, and although they might have been too optimistic about the area's early recovery, it did seem probable that a decrease in world oil supplies eventually would bring a substantial Houston resurgence. The short-run problem lay not so much in this urban region's underlying extractive and processive realities but in the oversupply in the international oil market.

The Aberdeen area experienced an extractive boom for only fifteen years before a major downturn. The sharp drop in North Sea oil prices between 1980 ($40 a barrel) and 1986 ($9.50 barrel) paralleled that in the U.S. fields, except that the price at first declined more slowly in Europe. Initially the drop in oil prices did not slow production much but did sharply reduce exploration activity from 36 rigs in summer 1985 to 13 rigs a year later (Grampian Regional Council 1987). Heavy losses were taken in the offshore-drilling segment, as was indicated by the bankruptcy of Global Marine, the second-largest offshore-drilling participant. In 1986–87 alone major oil firms reduced their capital outlays for exploration by 50 percent (Standard and Poor's Corporation 1987, 75–99). Soon exploration and production cutbacks included those of major U.S. corporations, including Conoco, Phillips, Occidental, Exxon, Chevron, Texaco, and Mobil; there were also British cutbacks by Shell, Britoil, and BP. Oil firm profits fell from about £4 billion in the third quarter of 1985 to £1.5 billion a year later (Lloyd and Newlands 1987, 3–4). Cutbacks in the supply and service industries also occurred; fabrication yards and engineering firms laid off employees. By 1986 the Wood Group, a local supply firm, had laid off 500 of the 2,100 employees working in 1985 (Duncan 1987). The drop in price had a significant effect on workers, businesses, and real estate developers. Aberdeen's unemployment rate increased from 6.3 percent in April 1985 to 9 percent in April 1987. The region lost 12,500 of its 52,000 oil industry jobs between mid-1985 and 1987. By late 1987 optimistic observers were arguing that the oil and gas industry had hit bottom; they noted that only 50 of the 800 firms in the area had pulled out. Like Houston, the Aberdeen area was expected to recover in the short term (Cockhead 1987).

Although the Houston and the Aberdeen regions experienced serious job losses, housing foreclosures, increasing office vacancy rates, and out-migration in the 1980s recession, as of 1988 the comprehensive impact of this particular supply-driven decline appears to have been more severe in Houston than in Aberdeen. One important factor is the offshore, high-tech character of most of the oil and gas development off northeast Scotland. As Gramling and Brabant (1986, 177–201) have shown for Louisiana, offshore exploration and production allows workers to commute from a number of different urban areas, rather than having to relocate to one city, thereby reducing population growth in the principal city and the later negative costs of decline there. The lack of extensive downstream oil tools, refining, and petrochemical facilities in northeast Scotland also has meant fewer negative multiplier effects from the price decline. Another explanation for the difference in the recession's impact on the two regions lies in the local planning and other governmental restrictions that in Aberdeen slowed development in housing and office construction during the extractive boom period and thus reduced office vacancy rates and housing foreclosures in the downturn. Houston, in contrast, is the prototypical "free enterprise" city with no zoning and little planning; it experienced extraordinary growth in the built environment and the consequent effects of over-building. In addition, the British welfare state, though weakened by the Conservative party government, provided a more extensive safety net than that in Texas, one that relieved some negative effects of the decline.

The Dutch Disease: Depletion Problems in Extractive Economies

Longer-term environmental problems confront extractive sectors in core and Third World countries. I cited earlier the point that Bunker (1984) made about the degradation of the ecosystem caused by extraction such as strip mining. However, the environmental impact of oil and gas development in the Houston and Aberdeen areas has been somewhat different. Onshore oil drilling in the Houston area did not create ecosystem damage sufficient to drive off investors in downstream industries, investors who came in relatively soon after the discovery of oil. In addition, petrochemical and refining investment had greater support from the state than equivalent downstream industries have had in less developed countries. In the Aberdeen case the oil and gas development has been entirely offshore, and the potential environmental degradation, such as oil spills, has not been the major reason for the slow arrival of diversified economic activities.

In the core countries, however, there is still the problem of resource depletion—the problem of the *Dutch disease*. As noted earlier, multinational corporations were important in making the Netherlands a major producer of North Sea-area gas, but Dutch production was the first to peak. During the boom period multinational corporations saw a substantial increase in profits, and some knowledge was gained by a few firms in gas technology, but no major development of downstream gas-related industries and little capital spin-off into nongas industries occurred (Ellman 1977, 281–90). The boom in gas had come at a time when downstream industries were well developed, even overdeveloped, in Europe. So when the boom was over, the Netherlands' economy suffered a major setback. Will the Houston and Aberdeen regions face the same consequences when the extractive resources are depleted?

The Houston area and the rest of the Texas "oil province" face a probable long-term crisis because of the reduction in regional oil reserves. In the 1972–83 period approximately 6 billion barrels of oil reserves were discovered in Texas, but this was much less than the 10.6 billion barrels produced in those years. In the 1970s oil reserves declined 8 percent annually. During the 1980s recession that rate of decline slowed to 1 percent to 2 percent a year, but that loss rate has increased with the late-1980s economic recovery in the United States. By the mid-1980s Texas oil reserves were only half what they had been in 1952 (Jankowski 1986, 27–29). New reserves may be discovered, but the Houston-Gulf Coast area does face a probable long-run decline. Oil depletion already has had a severe impact on certain Gulf Coast areas of the adjacent state of Louisiana, which has been second to Texas in U.S. oil production. In an article in the *Wall Street Journal* (1984, 1) a reporter wrote that the Cajun communities dependent on oil extraction in southern Louisiana have faced severe economic and cultural problems because of the decline in the oil industry.

North Sea oil production may have peaked. When much of the North Sea oil is gone, probably in the first decades of the next century, the economic base in the greater Aberdeen area will decline rapidly. As one local scholar noted, "The first major recession in the industry after 15 years of growth and expansion marks the onset of a mature phase in the industry's development. The largest and most profitable fields have been developed, production and revenues have peaked but much activity remains" (Bonney 1986, 5). In the 1986 *Scottish Petroleum Annual* (p. 5) an author asserted that "it appears that UK North Sea oil production has peaked and started a long decline . . . already in some quarters there is pre-occupation with field abandonment costs." This industry assessment argued for expanded local education, training, and research as ways of reducing the negative consequences of the oil and gas decline. By 1987 a major issue for Great Britain (and adjacent Norway) was the dismantling of the 200-plus North Sea production platforms. When the oil and fields begin to peter out in the decades after the year 2000, this will become a $10 billion problem. The eventual decline of the oil industry in the North Sea also will mean a decline in the oil services and supply industry in metropolitan Aberdeen, because most British and multinational corporations have equivalent operations elsewhere (Harris et al., n.d., 32–35). Little local manufacturing spin-off has resulted from the extraction boom, and little of the profits and capital generated for local non-oil-manufacturing industries has been utilized. The potential for the Dutch disease to hit Scotland and the rest of Great Britain was anticipated as early as 1976. In a *Lloyds Bank Review* article, Kahn (1976, 12) stated that

> there is a danger that we shall export less and less, and import more and more, manufactured goods. The production and refining of oil, and the production of petrochemicals, provide little employment. As our industrics withcr away—as a result of our failure to be competitive—unemployment will become greater and greater. It will not be Keynesian unemployment, due to lack of demand. It will be unemployment which is the result of the lack of productive equipment. And when the flow of North Sea oil and gas begin to diminish, about the turn of the century, our island will become desolate.

Oil economist James McKie (1986, 9) has asked if Houston also is "in a danger zone of dependence, since there are really only two significant activities in Houston: energy and building Houston." A critical difference between Houston and Aberdeen exists. The Houston area has a far more extensive and diversified oil and gas industry, with more affiliates, divisions, headquarters, facilities, and operational facilities. With many downstream and upstream linkages, Houston is far more significant as an administrative center for worldwide operations and thus may be less affected by local resource depletion. In Aberdeen one sees extraction with short-run regional development; in Houston one views extraction with more sophisticated and longer-run development. Houston's hierarchical position in the world oil and gas system and its upstream and downstream economic layers give it greater potential for protection against local depletion shocks than Aberdeen, which is lower in the hierarchy of the world oil and gas system and which has fewer layers of industrial buffering. Houston is beginning to face the decline in regional petroleum reserves and also some worldwide restructuring in the world's refining and petrochemical industries. Nonetheless, Houston probably will remain significant globally as long as the multinational oil corporations that have headquarters and subsidiary operations offices there continue to be important.

Extractive Cities in Developed Countries

The importance of primary extractive systems, underscored in the work of a number of scholars researching underdeveloped countries, has been shown for the United States and Great Britain. I have explored research questions about these extractive economies, and the answers can now be summarized. In regard to the question about the differences between Third World extractive regions and core regions, certain locational similarities have been noted. In both underdeveloped and developed countries, extractive economic systems tend to be fixed in regional location because of linkage to natural resources. But in contrast to extractive regions in underdeveloped countries, extractive areas in core countries are more likely to have developed prior economic layers sufficiently advanced to provide the infrastructure facilitating later advanced industrial development. In the developed countries enclave extraction economies are more likely to generate downstream manufacturing sectors.

The question about similarities and differences in Houston and Aberdeen was answered as I explored the importance of the palimpsest and historical timing in each region's development (questions 3 and 4). Oil and gas firms chose Houston and Aberdeen as major command cities for the emerging oil and gas regions because in both coastal cities much infrastructure—such as the port, transport facilities, and banks—was substantially developed prior to the coming of the oil and gas industry. The historical differences in the scale of capital, in capital centralization, also have shaped the divergent characters of these core regions. Both Houston and Aberdeen have been greatly influenced by the investment decisions made by the multinational oil and gas corporations dominating the world oil and gas system. Expectations of continuing dominance are illustrated in a recent Exxon (1985, 32) report, which contained the statement that whatever happens in the governmental or OPEC spheres,

> by virtue of their financial resources, worldwide facilities and technical and managerial know-how, multinational energy companies like Exxon will continue to play a vital role in meeting world energy needs.

Yet Aberdeen's later development, oriented to an offshore industry, resulted in large-firm dominance from the beginning, whereas Houston's initial development was substantially dependent on smaller oil and oil tools and supply firms, some of which survived and grew. As a result, Houston developed considerably more oil- and gas-related firms with international scope than did Aberdeen. Early development, contra Gerschenkron (1962) and some other development analysts, was better. The metropolitan areas of Houston and Aberdeen now occupy different positions in the world oil and gas system. Aberdeen is an example of a field-office management city, whereas Houston is an international operations subsidiary city, one without the majors' headquarters but with operations control over the oil and gas industry beyond the regional office level. I also have documented the hierarchical linkage between dependent Aberdeen and Houston; numerous Houston oil tools and services corporations came to Aberdeen to support the operations of the international oil corporations.

Also important in differentiating the two regions is the early development in Houston of important downstream manufacturing and processing components of the oil and gas industry. Substantial downstream development has not occurred in Aberdeen. To paraphrase a University of Aberdeen sociologist (Moore 1987), the local people in Aberdeen did not understand what was going on. They did not understand that Aberdeen had become a branch plant of the international multinationals. Local people had big ideas about what would happen. People felt that bringing oil was bringing industrialization; they had the imagery of men hitting metal and of big manufacturing plants. The people of Scotland were aware that they were providing oil for Britain, but they did not understand that the multinational profits often would not benefit Scotland. Their "oil brings industry" view was wrong.

I have identified a number of reasons why this downstream development did not come to the Aberdeen area. Central here is the lateness of Aberdeen's development, because multinationals' refining and petrochemical capacities were overdeveloped around the globe when the North Sea fields came on line. The North Sea oil-gas boom developed late in the history of the world oil industry and of multinational centralization and concentration.

I also have demonstrated how the differing orientations of the American and British governments toward the oil firms has been important to the growth of the Houston and Aberdeen economies. Unlike Aberdeen, Houston and the oil-related firms located there developed along with the national state. At a relatively early period in the city's growth, powerful Texan politicians represented Houston in Washington, D.C. These oil politicians got huge concessions for the local and multinational oil and gas corporations, including the oil depletion allowance and the massive federal capital investments in the downstream development of the petrochemical industry. Men like Jesse Jones and Sam Rayburn were pivotal in these efforts. Sunbelt politicians linked to the oil companies have remained influential to the present day.

Aberdeen suffered the consequences of later development, politically as well as economically. Aberdeen has been more of a peripheral political area exploited by the national government; because of the differences in political systems and in historical timing, the local politicians have played a small role at the national government level in regard to oil development. In Britain the concessions to the oil multinationals came, but primarily because of oil firm power at the national level; a relatively favorable taxing regime was provided by the very southern (London-oriented) and conservative central government to stimulate North Sea production. However, unlike the Norwegian government, which controls the development in its eastern North Sea fields in the public interest and has become directly involved in extraction, the Conservative government in Britain left North Sea development largely under the dominance of foreign, multinational corporations.

References

American Petroleum Institute. 1977. *Basic Petroleum Data Book*. Washington, DC: Author.

American Petroleum Institute. 1988. *Basic Petroleum Data Book*. Washington, DC: Author.

Austin American-Statesman. 1988. "Adair surveys burned-out oil rig." 10 July: A6.

Bonney, N. 1986. "Explaining development in Scotland's North East: A working paper." Presented at Development Studies Association, Scottish Study Group, Stirling University, England, 6–7 June.

Bonney, N. 1987. "Personal communication." 12 June.

Bunker, S. G. 1984. "Modes of extraction, unequal exchange, and the progressive underdevelopment of an extreme periphery: The Brazilian Amazon, 1600–1980." *Amer. Journal of Sociology* 89 (March): 1017–64.

Burka, P. 1983. "The year everything changed." *Texas Monthly* 11 (February): 109.

Business Week. 1970. "Shell's $25-million trip to Houston." 19 September: 16.

Chapman, D. 1983. *Energy Resources and Energy Corporations*. Ithaca, NY: Cornell Univ. Press.

Chapman, K., and D. Walker. 1987. Industrial Location. London. Basil Blackwell.

Chase-Dunn, C. 1984. "Urbanization in the world-system," In *Cities in Transformation*, edited by M. P. Smith, 111–20. Beverly Hills: Sage.

Chase Manhattan Bank Petroleum Situation Newsletter. 1983. "Petrochemicals and petrochemical feedstocks." 1–3 March.

Cockhead, P. 1987. Personal communication. 16 June.

Corden, W. M. and J. P. Neary. 1982. "Booming sector and de-industrialization in a small open economy." *Econ. J*. 92 (December): 825–48.

Duncan, H. 1987. Personal communication. 17 June.

Eisenberg, N. 1986. "Economic newsletter." *Houston* 57 (August): 5.

Ellman, M. 1977. "Report from Holland: The economics of North Sea hydrocarbons." *Cambridge J. of Economics*. 1 September: 281–90.

Engineer Publishing Company. 1947. *Petroleum Data Book*. Dallas: Author.

Exxon Corporation. 1985. *This Is Exxon*. New York: Author.

Feagin, J. R. 1988. *Free Enterprise City: Houston in Political-Economic Perspective*. New Brunswick, N.J.: Rutgers University Press.

Frank, A. G. 1969. *Latin America: Underdevelopment or Revolution*. New York: Doubleday.

Friedmann, J. 1966. *Regional Development Policy: A Case Study of Development in Venezuela*. Cambridge: MIT Press.

Gaventa, J. 1980. *Power and Powerlessness: Quiescence and Rebellion in an Appalachian Valley*. Urbana: University of Illinois Press.

Gerschenkron, A. 1962. *Economic Backwardness in Historical Perspective*. Cambridge: Harvard University Press.

Gramling, B., and S. Brabant. 1986. "Boomtowns and offshore energy impact assessment." *Soc. Perspectives* 29 (April): 177–201.

Grampian Regional Council. 1981. *The Impact of Northern Oil in the Grampian Region.* Aberdeen: Author.

Grampian Regional Council. 1986. Report of Survey: Grampian Region Structure Plan, Aberdeen Area Review. Aberdeen: Author.

Grampian Regional Council. 1987. "Impact of lower oil prices since January 1986 upon Grampian Region." (unpublished)

Greenhut, M. 1956. *Plant Location in Theory and Practice.* Chapel Hill: University of North Carolina Press.

Hallwood, P. 1986. "The offshore oil supply industry in Aberdeen: the affiliates—their characteristics and importance." North Sea Study Occasional Paper no. 23. Aberdeen: University of Aberdeen.

Harris, T., G. Lloyd, A. McGuire, and D. Newlands (n.d.) "The management of change: Local government in Aberdeen." Department of Political Economy, University of Aberdeen. (unpublished)

Harvey, D. 1985. *The Urbanization of Capital.* Baltimore: Johns Hopkins University Press.

Houston 1933. "They still want to 'buy' Houston." Vol. 4 (March): 3.

Houston Chamber of Commerce (n.d. circa 1985) (untitled printed brochure.) Houston: Author.

Hunt, D. 1987. Personal communication. June.

Hymer, S. H. 1979. *The Multinational Corporation: A Radical Approach.* Cambridge: Cambridge University Press.

Innis, H. 1940. *The Cod Fisheries: The History of an International Economy.* New Haven, Conn.: Yale University Press.

Jacobs, J. 1984. *Cities and the Wealth of Nations.* New York: Random House.

Jaffee, D. and R. Stokes (1986) "Foreign investment and trade dependence." *Soc. Q.* 27 (4):533–46.

Jankowski, P. (1986) "What's the status of Texas' reserves." *Houston* 57 (April): 27–29.

Jones, J. 1951. *Fifty Billion Dollars: My Thirteen Years with the RFC (1932–1945).* New York: Macmillan.

Kahn, R. 1976. "Mr. Eltis and the Keynesians." *Lloyds Bank Rev.* 124:12.

Larson, H. M., and K. W. Porter. 1959. *History of Humble Oil and Refining Company.* New York: Harper and Row.

Lloyd, M. G., and D. Newlands. 1987. "Aberdeen." University of Aberdeen. (unpublished).

Losch, A. 1954. *The Economics of Location.* New Haven, Conn.: Yale University Press.

MacKay, G. A., and A. Moir. 1980. *North Sea Oil and the Aberdeen Economy.* London: Social Science Research Council.

Mandel, E. 1978. *Late Capitalism.* London: Verso.

Massey, D. 1984. *Spatial Divisions of Labor.* New York: Methuen.

McComb, D. 1981. *Houston: A History.* Austin: University of Texas Press.

McKie, J. 1986. "The impact of spindletop on Texas." University of Texas. (unpublished)

Moore, R. 1987. Personal communication. 12 June.

Moskowitz, M., M. Katz, and R. Levering, eds. 1980. "Tenneco," *In Everybody's Business: An Almanac*, 848–50. San Francisco: Harper and Row.

Nemeth, R. J., and D. A. Smith. 1988. "An empirical analysis of commodity exchange in the international economy: 1965–1980." *Int. Studies Q.* 32(2): 227–40.

Odell, P. R. 1963. *An Economic Geography of Oil*. Westport, Conn.: Greenwood.

Odell, P. R., and L. Vallenilla. 1978. *The Pressures of Oil*. New York: Harper and Row.

Pratt, J. A. 1980. *The Growth of a Refining Region*. Greenwich, Conn.: JAI Press.

Rand, C. T. (1975) *Making Democracy Safe for Oil*. Boston: Little, Brown.

Rees, J., and P. Odell, eds. 1987. *The International Oil Industry*. New York: St. Martin's Press.

Ridley, J. K. 1930. "Petroleum Refining." Houston 1 (June): 18.

Scottish Office. 1987. North Sea Oil and Gas [pamphlet]. Edinburgh, Scotland: Author.

Scottish Petroleum Annual. 1986. "Keys to the future—education, training research, imagination, courage, vision." Aberdeen: Aberdeen Petroleum Publishing, 5.

Sherrill, R. 1983. *The Oil Follies of 1970–1980*. Garden City, N.J.: Anchor.

Sibley, M. M. 1968. *The Port of Houston*. Austin: University of Texas Press.

Slater, D. 1975. "Underdevelopment and spatial inequality: Approaches to the problem of regional planning in the Third World." *Progress in Planning* 4 (Pt 2): 137–68.

Solberg, C. 1976. *Oil Power*. New York: Mason/Charter.

Sprott, T. F. n.d., circa 1986. "Impact of oil upon Grampian region: The first fifteen years." Grampian Regional Council, Aberdeen, Texas. (unpublished)

Standard and Poor's Corporation. 1987. *Industry Surveys: Oil-Gas Drilling and Services Basic Analysis*. New York: McGraw-Hill.

Stokes, R., and D. Jaffee. 1982. "The export of raw materials and export growth." Amer. Soc. Rev. 47 (June): 402–7.

Taylor, J. L. 1983. Personal communication. May.

Taylor, M., and N. Thrift, eds. 1982. *The Geography of Multinationals*. New York: St. Martin's Press.

Wall Street Journal. 1984. "In Louisiana oil rush, one thing depleted was culture of Cajuns." 25 October, 1, 22.

Weede, E., and H. Tieffenbach. 1981. "Three dependency explanations of economic growth. *European J. of Pol. Research* 9:391–406.

Wharton, C. R. 1930. "South Texas is resourceful." *Houston* 1 (June): 9.

Williamson, H. F., R. Andreano, A. Daum, and G. Close. 1963. *The American Petroleum Industry: The Age of Energy, 1899–1950*. Evanston, Ill.: Northwestern University Press.

II

POWERFUL ECONOMIC ACTORS IN CITY DEVELOPMENT

Section two provides three articles that examine the role of major economic actors and their political allies in the structuring, growth, and decline of cities under capitalism. The first article, chapter 4, is from my 1983 book *The Urban Real Estate Game* and provides a detailed look at the critical actors in the drama of urban real estate. Here I provide a nuanced typology of the private and government actors who have made critical decisions about city development in the past and the present. This book was perhaps the first contribution to the new political-economy paradigm that laid out who the major developmental actors are, and it was one of the first to examine in empirical detail the critical dimensions of the class conflict between development agents and citizens that lies at the heart of the formation of cities and their subcommunities. In addition to examples of powerful developers and other business actors, we see here an empirical discussion of how capital flows from one sector of urban capitalism, such as manufacturing or office towers, to another, such as land. Central to this chapter is the importance of the countervailing forces, the urban people's movements, that periodically challenge the powerful real estate interests.

In chapter 5, "Urban Real Estate Speculation: Implications for Social Science and Urban Planning," I examine one of the critical groups of development agents—the real estate speculators. This article challenges the traditional urban paradigm's image of cities as created by natural or impersonal forces. It shows how the mainstream conceptual tradition ignores everyday realities of land development and the role of class domination in urban structuring. Real

113

estate speculators, in particular, are seriously neglected in the social science literature. Speculation in land and buildings on that land involves a different type of capital investment than that of investment in machinery. It moves money into what Henri Lefebvre and others call the secondary circuit of capital, one with different characteristics from the circuit of manufacturing. Speculators have played a key role in picking what came to be the sites for many cities, and some of the largest and oldest fortunes in the U.S. stem, at least in part, from early speculative ventures. Speculators have been critical to the development of internal areas of cities, such as gentrified areas in central cities for the affluent, as well as to the development of suburban areas where the hopscotch pattern of speculative investment affects which land is developed, or not developed. The past and current evidence on speculators shows that a class-oriented theory of development is superior to conventional ecological and demographic models for making sense out of city development, as well as for democratic urban planning.

Chapter 6, "Irrationality in Real Estate Investment: The Case of Houston," shows why this is the case. Many dimensions of city expansion and decline are hard to explain without understanding both the system that is urban capitalism and the key actors who implement and reinforce that system. The real estate of U.S. cities has for many decades attracted an array of domestic and foreign investors seeking to profit as individual capitalists. In conventional economics, this is seen as "market rationality." Yet, in the real world of urban land and housing markets, individual investment actions are often collectively irrational, sometimes in the extreme. In the 1970s, for example, U.S. corporations asserted there was not enough office space in cities from Seattle and San Francisco, to Houston, to Chicago and New York. This spurred construction of office buildings and soon major economic "busts" came to these cities as vacancy rates soared and profits fell sharply. The boom–bust trends in major cities like Houston reveal that business decisions to invest are often made, not in terms of careful research, but rather in terms of very subjective perceptions of cities as "hot" or "cold" places in which to place large amounts of capital.

These chapters reveal the important role of powerful capitalists in building cities. We see their notions of profit and loss and the impact of those views on the creation of a range of projects in cities, including gentrified downtown areas, office parks, and large-scale suburban sprawl. Overaccumulation of capital and overproduction of commodities are chronic problems not only for profit making in a capitalist system but also for the ordinary residents of the cities. The latter must suffer the often severe consequences of urban irrationalities created by the dominant real estate and allied state interests.

4

Cities in Conflict

Introduction: Playing Monopoly with Real Money

Buying hotels. Mortgaging whole streets of houses. Buying and selling utilities. Paying taxes on a dozen houses. Buying entire blocks of urban land to secure a monopoly. Going bankrupt because of overextension in real estate. These actions are part of the real estate game played in every American city. How many Americans regularly play this game? Not many. The only place most Americans are able to play the urban real estate game is on the Monopoly board in living room encounters with their friends. The board game mimics the real world of real estate buying, selling, and development, but the parallels between Monopoly on the board and land monopoly in city streets are limited, for in the world of urban real estate there are real winners and real losers.

Class struggle is at the heart of the game of urban real estate. Recently the people of Santa Monica, California, voted out a city council long allied with developers, landlords, and corporate executives. They elected in their place a progressive council that seemed to be determined to break with the old business-oriented pattern of city politics. The new council rejected old policies favoring developers and took action to require development projects to meet community needs.

In U.S. cities the powerful elites that control urban development—the developers, bankers, industrial executives, and their political allies—have built

---

Source: This chapter is reprinted with minor revisions from Feagin, Joe R. 1983. "Cities in conflict." Chap. 1 in *The Urban Real Estate Game 1–19*. Englewood Cliffs, N.J.: Prentice-Hall.

In this chapter the term *corporation* will be used for the various organizational arrangements (including partnerships) capitalists utilize in profit making, whether or not they are legally incorporated.

large development projects, not just the hotels and houses of the Monopoly game, but also shopping malls, office towers, and the like—with little or no input from local community residents. Developers have typically been able to win a string of favorable concessions from city officials: cheap land, tax abatements, and utility services subsidized by the general taxpayer. In many cities developers have threatened to go elsewhere if these subsidies are not provided. Yet in the early 1980s the Santa Monica City Council was tying to change this way of doing city business and to force those seeking to build new office complexes and shopping centers to commit themselves to meeting certain important needs of local citizens. One city council agreement with a developer building a million-square-foot hotel-office complex specified that it must include landscaped park areas, a day-care center, major energy conservation measures, and a serious affirmative action plan for hiring and that it must also provide one hundred rental housing units in the project or in other buildings in return for city permits.[1]

Class conflict—developers and their allies versus citizens—has long been part of city dynamics. On the one side we have the progressive city councils and the urban grass-roots peoples' movements opposing unbridled growth and development. On the other side we have the class of profit-oriented developers, bankers, landowners, and industrial executives who buy, sell, and develop land and buildings in cities just like they do with other for-profit commodities.

Some powerful developers and bankers are becoming known to the public. There is, for example, Gerald D. Hines, a Houston engineer whose corporation is one of the nation's largest urban developers. Hines' company recently marked the laying of the foundation of a Republic Bank office complex in Houston with a lavish $35,000 reception for top business and government leaders; it included a brass ensemble playing fanfares, fine wine and cheeses, and other culinary delights. The massive building itself, red granite in a neo-Gothic style, is one of at least $2 billion worth of such office buildings, shopping malls, and other urban projects built by Hines' company in cities from New York to San Francisco. Older buildings may be leveled; new projects rise out of their ashes. Developers such as Hines have been a major force in making and remaking the face of American cities, particularly since World War II. Whether most local citizens desire such large-scale development, or in fact benefit from it, does not matter. The major U.S. developers often see their projects as the "cutting-edge of western civilization." Yet the sad irony is that these massive expenditures of capital for large-scale urban development, and such things as lavish towers and parties celebrating them, occur in cities like Houston with its severe urban problems (for instance, extreme poverty, subemployment, housing shortages, severe pollution), for whose solution little money allegedly can be found.[2]

Since the 1940s U.S. cities have exploded horizontally and vertically with thousands of large-scale developments built by developers and their associates. These projects dot the urban landscape—shopping centers, office towers, industrial parks, convention centers, and suburbs. The built environments of our cities have expanded to the point that their growing, and dying, pains have become serious national problems. Trillions of dollars have been invested in tearing down, constructing, and servicing the physical structures on urban landscapes.

Cities are human creations. They reflect human choices and decisions. But exactly who decides that our cities should be developed the way they are? Who decides that sprawling suburbs are the best way to house urbanities? Who decides to put workers in office towers that look like glassed-in cigar boxes standing on their sides? Who decides that shopping is best done in highly centralized shopping centers that look like upside-down ice cube trays? Who creates the mazes of buildings, highways, and open spaces? There is an old saying that "God made the country but man made the town." Cities are indeed manmade environments. But *which* men and women made the cities? And why? Do all the people residing in cities contribute equally to their growth, development, and decline?

Traditionally most urban analysts and scholars have argued that everybody makes cities, that first and foremost the choices and decisions by large groups of consumers demanding housing and buildings lead to the distinctive ways cities are built. But this is not accurate. Ordinary people often play "second fiddle." In the first instance, capitalist developers, bankers, industrial executives, and their business and political allies build cities, although they often run into conflict with rank-and-file urbanites over their actions. Cities under capitalism are structured and built to maximize the profits of real estate capitalists and industrial corporations, not necessarily to provide decent and livable environments for all urban residents. Today's cities are, as we will document in this book, growth-oriented machines substantially designed for private profit making. The desires and needs of ordinary working people are often a secondary matter.

In U.S. society there are fundamental social divisions between capitalists and top managers, on the one hand, and ordinary blue-collar and white-collar workers on the other. Capitalists include those powerful property and development actors, such as Gerald Hines, who own and control office buildings, industrial factories, shopping centers, and the like—the places where work and consumption occur in this society. The great class of ordinary workers, both blue collar and white collar, low paid and well paid, sell their labor to the capitalists in return for wages and salaries. The renters who elected the previously mentioned Santa Monica City Council are part of the class of rank-and-file working people. Between these major classes are managers, who have some control over the labor of others but do not make major investment decisions. These classes of Americans loom large in the ongoing drama of urban conflict.

Conventional Views of City Growth and Decline

Traditional analysts see urban space as a "neutral container" of buildings and streets designed to meet consumers' needs. In this view cities are impersonal creations generated by the actions of many more or less isolated individuals.

Government-supported conventionalism.   Recently a federal government report, *Urban America in the Eighties*, publicly articulated the traditional view, not only for President Jimmy Carter, for whom it was designed, but also for the general public. Its conclusions were hotly debated—particularly those suggesting that the federal government should leave dying northern cities alone and should at most intervene to facilitate the move of workers from them to the booming cities of the Sunbelt. Some northern mayors cursed the report's conclusions, but many southern mayors were enthusiastic. Many northern officials were concerned about the report's conclusions, and national controversy was generated. But few disputed the report's basic assumptions about how cities grow or die.[3]

Prepared under the direction of prominent business and academic leaders, this report articulates the view of cities found in many conventional arguments: that cities are "less conscious creations" than "accumulations—the products of ongoing change." Choices by hundreds of thousands of individual actors are emphasized as shaping urban landscapes. Changes in cities, such as the rising prosperity of Sunbelt cities, reflect "nothing more than an aggregate of countless choices by and actions of individuals, families, and firms."[4] Here cities are seen as the unconscious creations of a free-market system, a system with thousands of individuals and firms buying and selling land and buildings for many private uses.

This land and building market is viewed as self-regulating; supposedly it efficiently and rationally allocates land uses and thus maximizes the overall benefits for everyone living in the cities. The hidden hand of the market and the capitalist system's alleged lack of intentional design receive heavy emphasis in this conventional perspective. In their policy-oriented conclusions the authors of *Urban America* pursued this "market knows best" logic to its obvious conclusion: Those impersonal individuals and firms actively working in cities and shaping urban space know best, and government officials should thus not intervene when their impersonal decisions lead to the decline of cities in the North. Growth in, and migration to, booming cities such as those in the Sunbelt should simply be recognized, and, at most, governments should only encourage workers to move from dying cities to booming cities. Critics of the *Urban America* report resisted this do-nothing approach to urban decline; yet most did not reject the individuals-and-firms-freely-competing-in-market view of the city.[5]

Wrongheaded assumptions. Not only are the report's policy conclusions wrongheaded; the assumptions underlying this conventional perspective on cities are also wrong. One assumption here is that the interests of the individual and society are one. This view of land and job markets in cities is a version of neoclassical economic theory; it sees urban society as the "algebraic sum of the individuals . . . . the sum of the interests of individuals."[6] Given a free-market system, urban consumers and business firms will buy and sell. "If consumers want certain goods they will demand them. Businessmen will sense this demand through the marketplace and seek to satisfy the consumers' wishes. Everyone is happy."[7] There is a basic faith in the rightness and efficiency of buying and selling in markets, including the urban land market. The idealistic competitive market idea, Lewis Mumford suggested, was taken over from earlier theologians: "the belief that a divine providence ruled over economic activity and ensured, so long as man did not presumptuously interfere, the maximum public good through the dispersed and unregulated efforts of every private, self-seeking individual."[8] And this conventional view implies that whatever exists as the geography of the urban landscape is fundamentally good for all concerned if it results from competitive market activity.

Related to the market assumption is the idea that individual urbanites are really more important than business and corporate decision makers in shaping urban patterns, because business actors mostly react to the demands of consumers. Thus power is said to reside in the self-seeking consumer. A major study has noted the function of the American business creed: "One way of shedding awkward responsibility is to believe that the consumer is the real boss."[9] In this prevailing business creed individual workers are seen as "voting" in the marketplace with their consumer choices: Cities have been created by ordinary Americans whose demands for such things as autos and single-family houses have forced developers, builders, and manufacturing corporations to respond. Over the last few decades prominent business leaders have argued that through their consumption choices "the masses of Americans have elected Henry Ford. They have elected General Motors. They have elected the General Electric Company, and Woolworth's and all the other great industrial and business leaders of the day."[10] Moreover, the assumption that workers and consumers are by nature individualistic and selfish leads to the view that only some type of capitalism will work as the form of societal organization.

Consumers are often seen as kings and queens when it comes to urban land use and development. The conventional view sees land use and development, both in central cities and in suburbs, as resulting from individual self-maximizing behavior in a market context. It assumes that no one agent (group or individual) has a determinate influence on the urban land system. Land economists such as William Alonso and Richard Muth have argued that urban commercial and residential land markets are determined by free competitive bidding. In these theories thousands of consumers, and by extension thousands of firms, are pictured as autonomous atoms, largely without social relations and conventions, who have a "taste" for commodities, one of which is more space and housing. As their incomes grow, they will seek more space. Conventional analysts offer this as an explanation of why cities grow and expand. Actors in this competitive bidding are recognized as having different interests, even different incomes, which affect the bidding process. However, the fact that a small group of the most powerful actors can do far more to shape the land and building markets than simply outbid their competitors is not seriously analyzed.[11]

The urban land and building market is an important feature of our capitalistic system. Its operation does shape the built environment of cities. But it is not a "free" or "natural" market. It is a captive whose rules are determined by the most powerful players in the game — the array of land-interested industry, finance, development, and construction capitalists. Individual consumers and their families seeking jobs and housing do make important decisions that shape cities, but for the most part these personal decisions are of secondary importance when measured against the prior and determining actions of the capitalistic producers, whose decisions concern such things as the location development projects, mortgage rates, and types of housing construction.

Business leaders frequently see themselves as dependent, as following the lead of consumers in building cities, but occasionally even they admit their own overarching significance. One recent article in a major real estate industry journal, *Buildings*, candidly noted that "the building industry has always played a major role in determining quality of life and social groupings, whether it's in the work sector or in the provision of adequate housing."[12]

Moreover, for influential defenders of capitalism such as Edward Bernays, the founder of modern public relations, "democracy" in fact means that ordinary people should follow the lead of their "betters," such as business leaders. Bernays once commented that "the conscious and intelligent manipulation of the organized habits and opinions of the masses is an important element in a democratic society. . . . We are governed, our minds are molded, our tastes formed, our ideas suggested, largely by men we have never heard of."[13] And for him this mind-and-taste manipulation is a very good thing, because it avoids democratic participation by ordinary workers and consumers.

Powerful Actors Who Mold Cities

Limiting people's choices.   Powerful real estate actors such as D. M. Carothers, retired head of Allright Auto Parks, frequently seek what they call the "higher and better uses" for urban land, sometimes losing sight of older traditions of urban neighborhoods or the needs of smaller business tenants. For many the most important tradition to honor seems to be profit. As Carothers said to journalist Elizabeth Ashton recently: "In the growth of the city, you can't take care of old traditions." Long-term tenants, small-business people, or renters are only temporary tenants in this view. "They like to think of it as a heritage that has been passed on to them, but they're living in another century."[14] The city block Carothers had in mind is the site for one of the tallest office buildings west of the Mississippi, the Texas Commerce Tower in Houston. Small businesses were moved out in order to build the tower. Small businesses commonly lose out in the private urban renewal done by developers and their associates.

Allright Auto Parks has made money directly from fees off parking lots on cleared central-city land. In 1982 it had 1,600 parking lots in seventy cities; it owned 2.3 million square feet in thirty-nine downtown areas. But the parking lot revenues are not its only profitable aspect. "Banking" the land for "higher" uses is the goal, as Carothers has explained it:

> We were figuring how the property could, in effect, buy itself. If we could get the old buildings off it and begin to park the cars . . . would income be sufficient to meet the payments? And in the back of my mind was always this extra—this icing: the eventual control of real valuable property that could be turned for a higher and better use.[15]

Selling land has accounted for much of this parking lot company's income, as the parking lots are sold at good prices to developers and bankers who recycle the land. The plan is clear. Older buildings are cleared off, and the land is "banked" in the form of parking lots until a more profitable use is found for it. In central-city areas the more profitable use is usually an office tower, shopping mall, hotel, or high-rise parking garage.

A few hundred developers and financial institutions now construct and finance most major and many smaller urban development projects, from office parks and shopping malls to suburban subdivisions. Among the nation's dozen largest developers is Century Development Corporation, which, like Gerald D. Hines Interests, builds very large metropolitan projects. For example, Greenway Plaza, a major multiple-use development, involved the buying up of several hundred single-family houses in several large residential subdivisions not far from downtown Houston. Century had real estate agents buy houses from the local residents. Once the homes had been acquired, the houses were moved or razed. There was apparently no organized citizen protest to this destruction of residential neighborhoods in a city with a serious housing shortage. However, in other cities citizens have protested such large-scale destruction of much-needed residential housing in central-city areas. Moreover, Greenway Plaza is of such a scale that it required financing from large insurance companies. The scale of modern city developments is frequently staggering.[16]

Residential developers have shaped U.S. housing patterns in fundamental

ways. The famous Levitt and Sons firm is among the 2 percent of builders who
have constructed the lion's share of residential housing since World War II.
Using nonunion labor, Levitt and Sons pulled together in one corporation the
various aspects of the house manufacturing and marketing process, from controlling the source of nails and lumber to marketing the finished houses.[17]
Levittowns were built in cities on the East Coast. Levittown, New Jersey, was
carefully planned so that the acreage was within one political jurisdiction. According to Herbert Gans, the company executives had the boundaries of a
nearby township changed so that it was not part of the area in which Levittown
would be built, thus giving Levitt and Sons more political control. William
Levitt was the key figure in the firm by this time, and he reportedly built his
suburbs with little concern for the tastes of his potential customers. In a detailed analysis, Gans has noted that William Levitt was not especially "concerned about how to satisfy buyers and meet their aspirations. As the most
successful builder in the East . . . he felt he knew what they wanted."[18] Earlier
Levittowns had only one house type per neighborhood; in Levittown, New Jersey, three different models were provided, including pseudocolonial and
pseudo-Cape Cod styles. Profitability was the basic standard; community-
oriented features were accepted when they enhanced profit.

The shift to three models per neighborhood was apparently a reaction to critics who complained of the stifling homogeneity of the new suburban areas being created by developers. When this critique spread to the mass media, Levitt
reportedly became worried about sales and decided to market the new Levittown in New Jersey more aggressively. Gans points out that the choice of the
pseudocolonial design was made "not because of its popularity, but because
they would help them attract higher-income purchasers."[19] No surveys of potential buyers were made to determine consumer preferences, but a great deal
of attention was given to advertising, marketing, and selling the houses to consumers. Friendly salespeople were selected and trained by a professional
speech teacher. Buyers who were viewed as "disreputable" were excluded; and
blacks were excluded until the state government began to enforce a desegregation law. Moreover, once the developments were inhabited, Levitt executives were critical of local residents who complained about conditions.[20]

Corporations such as Allright Auto Parks, Gerald Hines Interests, Century
Development Corporation, and Levitt and Sons are the urban actors with the
power to shape the spread and decline of U.S. cities in fundamental ways.
They have indeed created their own Monopoly game, played out in the real
streets of urban America.

Efficient and rational for whom?   The choices made by top executives in
these and other powerful land-oriented companies are dominant, but they are
not necessarily efficient or desirable from the point of view of most city
dwellers. Ordinary citizens more or less have to accept what is in fact built and

available. James Lorimer has noted that in today's corporate cities "people may *feel* free to make their own decisions about how they will live, but in fact they are restricted by the limited number [of] choices offered by developers and planners."[21]

People are not coerced into using shopping centers, office towers, industrial parks, suburbs, high-rise apartment complexes; but so much of American life is centered in these places that it is hard for urbanites not to live out some, or much, of their lives in them. Often these developments provide the only realistic working, housing, and shopping choices. Other choices have disappeared (downtown shops run by small-business people) or are allowed to decay and disappear (older row-type housing). A major assumption of conventional theories is that the "most frequently chosen location is that which is most preferred." But what if an individual worker or family has no real choice? If there is only one option, or a limited range of options, no consumer preference is truly revealed. For example, if only a few housing (or working) facilities are in fact available, the lack of availability makes individual preferences less relevant. The "tastes" of individuals develop in a social context that is fundamentally shaped by a mode of production ruled by capitalists and top managers, one that involves not only the production of goods and services but also an intricate web of relations of unequal power and wealth.[22]

In this society the production of goods and services precedes consumption, but the two processes go hand in hand. The physical structure of production builds barriers and sets limits to individual choices. To a significant degree preferences are created and manipulated by powerful people working through advertising, public relations, and the mass media. The choices of those with moderate incomes are far more restricted than those of the rich. The inequality of money resources limits choices also. Small businesses are destroyed as real estate investors and developers shove them aside and build office towers. Much of the suburbanization literature argues that middle-income Americans express their free choice for more housing space by moving to suburbia. The implication is that the poor choose and prefer central-city locations. But this is not necessarily true. However they may be arrived at, everyone's reasonable needs and preferences are not met in this class-structured society of ours. The urban poor and the urban rich can live in central cities, but only the latter have the incomes to choose to live in central cities. Rank-and-file individual and family actions in cities do not necessarily reflect their fundamental needs or preferences.[23]

Land as Property

There is a limited supply of urban land. Unlike other commodities that are bought and sold, the amount of land cannot generally be increased by human action. And land is a commodity whose control and use are disproportionately in the hands of the powerful.

Creating profits.   Land is the explicit concern of the urban real estate industry. Profit accrues as land changes hands. A building is constructed. Land and improvements to land thus become an active part of the capital accumulation process. Urban land is used by some capitalists as area upon which to build profit-making offices, warehouses, and factories.

Profit from industrial and commercial enterprises can be "banked" directly in land. A major feature of modern land development is this banking aspect. Land and buildings are always important investments, but when economic growth slows in other industrial sectors, increased capital may flow to real estate. In this society both the land itself and the built environment on it become items just like other commodities, such as automobiles or refrigerators, which are developed and created with profitable sale as the objective. Yet there are differences. Real estate development at one point in time can become a barrier to real estate development later on. Buildings are relatively permanent commodities; they are fixed investments. New urban developments sometimes must be built at less valuable locations because the capital invested in already existing buildings cannot be easily abandoned.[24]

Private property.   The powerful people who buy, sell, and develop large blocks of urban land can do so because of a legal system which protects their propertied interests. Essential to the maintenance of inequality in land decision making is the legal protection of highly individualized property ownership. The rights of private property give owners a great deal of control over land and buildings. Within broad limits land can be developed, and buildings constructed, as owners see fit.

The unbridled use of private property has not always been predominant in the United States. The Puritans, for example, had highly planned towns from Maine to Long Island. For two generations Puritan towns were planned by pioneer folk whose strong religious values influenced the layout of urban areas. The private control of property was not central; communal and collective goals overrode private interests. But group-centered, folk-religious planning soon gave way to intensified private landholding, even in New England. Fee-simple (unrestricted transfer) ownership of land became central to the expanding capitalistic market system of eighteenth-century America. Early immigrants from Europe were generally hostile to landlords and vigorously sought to own their own land. Ownership of even a small piece of property was a sign of independence from landlords; many immigrants had come to the new American colonies to escape oppressive European landlords. Land was seen as a civil right in a nation with many small farmers.[25]

Yet this early and heavy commitment to the sacredness of privately held property had a major negative effect on development once the United States was no longer primarily a land of small farmers. By the early decades of the nineteenth century, there were fewer landlords and ever more tenants. In many cases, the growing number of Americans without property were seen as unworthy. Yet the heavy commitment to private property, on the part of both propertied and propertyless Americans, continued to legitimate the private disposal of property by powerful landowning factions. As a result, over the last two centuries control over urban land development has become concentrated in banks, insurance firms, development corporations, and industrial companies.[26]

There are major social costs for a system that gives owners of large amounts of land the right to use the land more or less as they see fit. Those who build large projects on central-city land have shown that they can shove certain social costs onto other people nearby. A good example is the modern skyscraper with its mirrored glass walls, which often generate heat problems for nearby buildings, and with its thousands of workers whose egress in the evenings can create massive traffic jams. These social costs of skyscraper development usually are not paid for by the developers and owners of the buildings. Private control of property, particularly of large blocks of land and development projects, can create enormous urban social problems that cannot be solved without violating the long-established right of private property owners to dispose of property as they see fit.   .

Naming the Corporate Producers

If ordinary individuals and families play a secondary or opposing part in the decisions shaping cities, who plays the primary part? The primary decision makers are the capitalistic producers, the key actors in the real estate industry. Today real estate capitalism is organized around a complicated network of entrepreneurs and corporations of varying sizes and functions.

Private and public decisions.   An approximation of the size and complexity of the urban development industry can be gauged from Exhibit 1, which lists real estate producers and associated government actors. The categories refer to sets of major decisions that are critical to urban development projects.[27]

Looking at the private sector, we see that Category 1 encompasses those corporations whose location decisions (for example, northern or Sunbelt city) often set the other actors into motion. Category 2 covers the developers, land speculators, and landowners who buy, package, and develop land for use by industrial corporations and others. Category 3 encompasses those financial corporations that make the loans for construction and land purchase. Category 4 includes the various design and construction actors who build urban projects. Category 5 covers a variety of supporting actors.

Exhibit 4.1 Urban Development: Decision Categories and Corporate Actors

---

Private Actors

---

1. Industrial and commercial location decisions
     Industrial companies (including service industries)
     Commercial companies
2. Development decisions
     Development companies (developers)
     Land speculators
     Landlords and landowners
3. Financial decisions
     Commercial banks (including trust and pension funds)
     Savings and loan associations
     Insurance companies
     Mortgage companies
     Real estate investment trusts
4. Construction decisions
     Architectural and engineering firms
     Construction companies (contractors)
5. Support decisions
     Chambers of commerce
     Real estate brokers
     Leasing and management companies

Governmental Actors

---

1. Utility services, building code, zoning, tax decisions
     City councils
     County officials
     Zoning and planning commissions
2. Subsidized housing and urban redevelopment decisions
     U.S. Department of Housing and Urban Development (HUD)
     Local and state government agencies

Such a listing can be somewhat misleading. In the first place, one modern corporation often includes within itself a development subdivision, which not only develops projects but also engages in land speculation; a real estate brokerage subsidiary; and an architectural subsidiary. Or a major insurance company may have a financial department as well as its own urban land development subsidiary. Large vertically integrated companies are involved in major decisions in more than one category in Exhibit 4.1.

Second, there is the issue of scale and region. Local developers, realtors, and bankers are critical decision makers in land development; studies of community decision makers show clearly the role and power of local business people in all types of cities in the North and South.[28] However, major real estate decisions are made not only by powerful local real estate companies but also by powerful regional and national companies, which also determine the shape of U.S. cities. There are complex interconnections between powerful interests external to cities and those that are part of the internal power structure of a particular city. An example would be a major insurance company, such as Prudential Life Insurance Company, which in connection with other local and national companies finances and owns real estate and development projects in many cities across the United States. There is indeed a complex urban puzzle lying behind the development and ownership of the modern city.

Close ties: Business and government.   There are the close ties between developers and government. Government plays a critical support role. For example, a Dallas mayor was recently quoted in the *Wall Street Journal:* "The system probably works better when a poor man is not in office." A major local developer, this mayor may have had in mind the working of the urban property and development system. When he was Dallas mayor, he was also a president, vice-president, partner, manager, or board member of many businesses. Many American cities have been directly governed by individuals with real estate or banking interests that are fostered by the decisions they make as government officials. Moreover, government officials without direct development connections make decisions supportive of the urban development industry.[29]

In the United States real estate capitalism has not been able to supply all the conditions for its profitable existence. Much government activity has developed substantially because of the continuing problems of capitalism, including the constant need for new capital and the persisting class conflict between capitalists and workers. Local and federal governments help provide an aid system (including urban renewal and special development loans) to facilitate profit making in urban development. Governments subsidize by means of taxes the services, such as roads, sewers, and utilities, critical to urban development. Urban land is valuable because it is usually not raw but "serviced." Human labor has been expended on it. Services are usually provided by governments out of ordinary people's taxes. Thus much urban land has taxpayer-subsidized features, which add to its value as a marketed commodity.

The U.S. market system often leads away from profitability in land use; early capitalist cities had a freer land market and little government regulation but also severe water, sanitation, garbage, utility, and related problems, which hurt land development. Supportive government intervention brought greater profitability back into urban real estate patterns. Inefficiency, pollution, and congestion in cities increase as capitalists and their minions seek the locations that maximize profits; so government, again and again, is pressured to intervene.[30]

Opposing Developers:
People's Movements

Unlike the game of Monopoly, the game of urban real estate has its counter-vailing forces—people's movements that periodically force developers and governments to make concessions and changes in their plans. Well-organized groups of workers and consumers can sometimes make a difference in patterns of urban development.

This chapter opened with the dramatic example of well-organized worker-renters in Santa Monica, California, who threw out a developer-oriented city council and replaced it with a council seeking to restrict developers to pro-jects meeting at least some community needs. Other people's movements have also pressed for changes in urban development projects. Portions of many major expressway projects in cities such as Boston, New York, Philadelphia, and Washington have generated organized citizen protest. In the early 1970s local and state governments in Massachusetts rejected cer-tain long-planned expressways in the Boston area and committed the state to spend $2 billion on mass transit because of organized citizen protest. Intense opposition to urban redevelopment projects has come from a variety of peo-ple's organizations in cities from Seattle to Boston. In Washington, D.C., the Capital East Community Organization and the Adams-Morgan Community Organization joined together to fight speculative real estate development; these citizens' groups pressured the city council to pass a bill called the Real Estate Transaction Tax, which would restrict speculative buying and selling.

There have been numerous attempts, and a few successes, by citizens' groups seeking to stop large mall developments. One was in Burlington, Vermont, where the citizens fought on environmental grounds against a nearby mall to be built by a major shopping center corporation. Citizens protested against the traffic congestion and accelerated decline of the down-town area that the new mall would bring. In Hadley, Massachusetts, another citizens' group took on a national mall development corporation. At issue were the questionable need for another mall in this small town and the air, water, soil, and traffic problems that a mall would create. In recent years renters' and tenants' movements have grown up, protesting condominium conversions by developers, the lack of development of moderate-rent hous-ing, and the ever-rising rents that the now short supply of housing seems to generate. Rapid growth in tenants' organizations can be seen in states like New Jersey, where they began in earnest in the 1960s. By the 1970s the New Jersey Tenants' Organization had organized many large-scale rent strikes. A majority of the strikes were effective in reducing rent levels and improving apartment conditions.

Conclusion: Public Balance Sheets?

In this chapter we have examined conventional perspectives on urban land use and development and have seen them to be substantially grounded in major assumptions of conventional (neoclassical) economics. These perspectives put heavy emphasis on a "free" land and property market, on private property, on efficient land use, and on the benefits that markets in land allegedly bring to all urbanites. But the realities are not what these perspectives suggest. There are no free competitive markets in cities, because land purchase and development is disproportionately controlled, if not monopolized, by powerful capitalistic agents and interests. Real estate capitalism shapes the major development projects in cities—the shopping centers, suburbs, industrial parks, office towers, and apartment complexes. Once the decisions of the powerful are made, smaller-scale builders often build around the larger-scale projects. Consumers choose within the limits provided. Worker-consumers must endure the many social costs of this capitalistic development system, which have been enormous.

But class struggle is also at the heart of capitalist cities. Some of those in people's movements have suggested new ways of looking closely at the *social* costs of private development. One of their tools is the *public balance sheet*, simply a way of tallying up, as David Smith puts it, the "tangible, measurable, quantifiable costs being imposed on citizens individually and collectively by the actions of the private sector."[31] The social costs, the social inefficiencies, of urban development take a variety of forms: a shortage of rental housing at reasonable rents, displaced families without suitable housing alternatives, racial segregation, added tax costs for rank-and-file taxpayers because of local development bonds, traffic congestion and air pollution, and highly constrained choices for consumers because of developer decisions about what housing will or will not be built. As we will see in detail in the last chapter, Smith and others have argued that these social costs of private enterprise should be calculated, and factored into the overall costs of urban development projects. Progressive people's movements in cities today are pressuring developers to compensate communities for the broader community costs that urban development creates.

Notes

1. This discussion is based on copies of developer-council agreements in author's files. See also Lindorff, Dave "About-face in Santa Monica," *Village Voice*, 2–8 December 1981, p. 20.

2. "The master builder." *Newsweek*. 31 August 1981, p. 45; Joe R. Feagin.

1983. "Sunbelt Metropolis and Development Capital." In *Sunbelt/Snowbelt: Urban Development and Regional Restructuring,* edited by Larry Sawers and William Tabb. Oxford University Press, 1984.

3. President's Commission for a National Agenda for the Eighties. Panel on Policies and Prospects. 1980. *Urban America in the Eighties: Perspectives and Prospects.* Washington, D.C.: U.S. Government Printing Office.

4. Ibid., 12, 104.

5. Roweis, Shoukry T. and Allen J. Scott. 1978. "The urban land question." In *Urbanization and Conflict in Market Societies,* edited by Kevin R. Cox. 46–47. Chicago: Maaroufa Press.

6. Quoted in Harris, Stephen E. 1977. *The Death of Capital.* New York: Pantheon Books, 64.

7. Ibid., 65.

8. Mumford, Lewis. 1961. *The City in History.* New York: Harcourt, Brace and World, 452.

9. Sutton, Francis X. et al. 1956. *The American Business Creed.* Cambridge: Harvard University Press, 361–62.

10. Filene, Edward A. *Successful Living in the Machine Age.* New York: Simon and Schuster, 98. This is quoted in Stuart Ewen, *Captains of Consciousness.* 1976. New York: McGraw-Hill, 92.

11. Alonso, William. 1964. *Location and Land Use.* Cambridge: Harvard University Press; Muth, Richard. 1969. *Cities and Housing.* Chicago: University of Chicago Press; Walker, Richard A. "The transformation of urban structure in the nineteenth century and the beginning of suburbanization." *Urbanization and Conflict in Market Societies,* Chicago: Maaroufa Press, 1978. 165–212.

12. Mikesell, Lillie. 1980. "Challenges of the New Community." *Buildings 74"* (January): 47.

13. Bernays, Edward L. 1928. In *Propaganda.* New York. This is quoted in Ewen, *Captains of Consciousness,* 93.

14. Ashton, Elizabeth. 1982. "Houston's doctor of urban decay." *Texas Business Review.* March, 53.

15. Ibid., 52.

16. Century Development Corporation, Greenway Plaza brochures and fact sheets. In author's files; interview with senior research official. Rice Center. Houston, Texas. May 1981.

17. Gans, Herbert. 1967. *The Levittowners.* New York: Random House.

18. Ibid., 6.

19. Ibid., 11.

20. Ibid., 5–13.

21. Lorimer, James. 1978. S. *The Developers.* Toronto: James Lorimer and Co., 220.

22. Sheppard, Eric S. 1980. "The ideology of spatial choice." In *Papers of the Regional Science Association,* edited by Morgan D. Thomas, 206. Vol. 45.

23. Ibid., 206–97.

24. Downie, Leonard. 1974. *Mortgage on America.* New York: Praeger, 6–7; Nofal, Maria B. 1981. "Fixed capital in the built environment," paper presented to Conference on New Perspectives on Urban Political Economy.

Washington, D.C., American University. May 6–7; cf. Bradford, C.P. and L.S. Rubinowitz. 1975. "The urban-suburban investment-divestment process: Consequences for older neighborhoods." *Annals of the American Academy of Political and Social Science 422* (November); 79.

25. Warner, Sam Bass. 1972. *The Urban Wilderness.* New York: Harper and Row, 16–17. See also 8–18.

26. Ibid., 18.

27. An earlier version of this exhibit appeared in D. Claire McAdams and Joe R. Feagin, 1980, "A power conflict approach to urban land use." Austin, Texas, University of Texas. Unpublished monograph. I have also been influenced here by D. Claire McAdams, "Powerful Actors in Public Land Use Decision Making Processes," 1979, unpublished Ph.D. dissertation, University of Texas, chaps. 1–3.

28. Walton, John. "A systematic survey of community power research." 1970. In *The Structure of Community Power,* edited by Michael Aiken and Paul Mott. 443–64. New York: Random House.

29. Fullinwider, John. 1980. "Dallas: The city with no limits." *In These Times.* 17–23, December, 13.

30. Roweis and Scott. "The urban land question." 57–63.

31. Smith, David. 1979. *The Public Balance Sheet: A New Tool for Evaluating Economic Choices.* Washington, D.C. Conference on Alternative State and Local Policies, 2.

5

Urban Real Estate Speculation in the United States: Implications for Social Science and Urban Planning

Joe R. Feagin

U.S. social scientists have written extensively about the city since the pioneering work of the Chicago school in the 1920s. With the research of U.S. sociologists like Park, Burgess, and McKenzie arose a research tradition with a central focus on urban land use and land patterning. Since the 1920s a considerable urban ecology literature has emerged. Yet, with brief exceptions, nowhere in this extensive U.S. literature on land use and urban patterning is there a serious concern with the ways in which the inequality of the urban structure of power or the class structure shapes the decisions which originate and arrange the physical face of cities.

It is the purpose of this paper to examine a central figure in urban land patterning decisions—the real estate and land speculator. Such a focus is linked to my concern to contribute to an alternative theory of urban ecology which accents the role of class structure, the role of powerful, land-oriented, capitalist actors in shaping the location, development and decline of American cities. A first step toward an alternative theoretical framework for urban ecology, as well as for urban planning, is an intensive focus on these powerful capitalistic land-interested actors.

This chapter is reprinted with minor revisions from Feagin, Joe R. 1982. "Urban real estate speculation: Implications for social science and urban planning," *International Journal of Urban and Regional Research*, 6 (March): 35–59.

I   Traditional Urban Ecology and Land Use

In their pioneering work Robert E. Park and E. W. Burgess (1925) saw the city as both a geographical and a cultural entity. Their papers in the famous *The City* volume fostered major traditions in urban ecology. In his contribution to *The City* Burgess outlines his view of the growth and development of cities, including the famous descriptive model of concentric zones. Burgess spoke of the city in organic terms, of urban land patterning in terms of a natural "urban metabolism." Yet Burgess did not develop an adequate explanation of why this natural distribution takes place. Burgess's deterministic view, as Firey (1947, 7) puts it, is based on "a denial that social values, ideals, or purposes can significantly influence the use of land." Though challenging Burgess's descriptive model of urban growth and land use, the subsequent sector and multiple-nuclei theories are similar in their nontheoretical descriptive emphasis and in their negligible emphasis on purposive action. Robert Park (1925, 4–5), in examining urban land use and physical structure, speaks of the "city plan" which "fixes in a general way the location and character of the city's constructions, and imposes an orderly arrangement." His language suggests a naturalness and inevitability to the layout of the cities, as when he speaks of the "inevitable processes of human nature" in shaping the "city plan." For Park, and many in this tradition, the dominant image is one of thousands of individuals pursuing their particular tastes and interests, so that "the city acquires an organization and a distribution of population which is neither designed nor controlled." No small group seems disproportionately to control the layout in urban space. Park also notes as important ecological forces such elements as transportation and communication, newspapers, elevators—that is, improvements in technology. Another still influential U.S. ecologist, R. D. McKenzie, argued in *The City* that general ecological forces shape the distribution of utilities, shops, factories, and offices in cities—his factors included climate, the organization of industries, and technical factors.

For many such theories the land-patterning process is impersonal and unconscious, even biotic or subcultural. Firey (1947, 17) accented their assumption of a "spontaneous, natural stability and order" in the layout of cities. This shows a commitment to the classical economics principle that utility for a part "coincides with the utility of the whole," that profit-seeking by individual units coincides with the "best," "most efficient" land-use pattern for the whole community. This seems to be a type of Adam Smith sociology, with the invisible hand operating so that an individual by seeking his or her own good benefits urban society. Given this premise, they logically deduced that the city is a natural, organic mechanism. Nowhere in this classical U.S. literature is serious attention paid to the role of powerful, land-oriented actors.

But what of more recent sociological analysis in the United States? A look at major textbooks in urban sociology signals that sociologists do not regard powerful capitalist actors as worth studying when it comes to urban land patterning. In the sixth edition of *Urban Society* (Gist and Fava 1974) virtually all of the attention given to land patterning is in the form of descriptive reporting, similar in nature to the descriptions by Burgess of the demographic distribution of urbanites across urban areas. The urban theories examined by Gist and Fava include the traditional ecological concepts of segregation, invasion, succession, centralization, and decentralization. For example, using the invasion-succession concept, cities are visualized as undergoing changes whereby one ethnic group inhabiting a given area is inevitably replaced by another in a series of invasions and successions. No discussion is given to the general role of developers, realtors, and speculators in determining urban patterning, apart from a few references to racial discrimination by realtors. The same is true of John Sirjamaki's *The Sociology of Cities* (1964) and Leonard Reissman's *The Urban Process* (1964). Moreover, the otherwise excellent readers by Charles Tilly (*The Urban World* 1974) and by Jeffrey Hadden, Louis Masotti, and Calvin Larson (*Metropolis in Crisis* 1967) offer no analysis of the role of such powerful actors as speculators and developers.

Since the 1940s interesting developments have taken place in ecological research. Some researchers have worked with the idealized descriptive schemes, suggesting corrections. Thus, Schnore's (1967) analysis of Latin American cities demonstrated a radically different (inverse) pattern from Burgess's concentric zone layout. Much urban-ecological analysis has been basically descriptive in its orientation. In recent decades there have been numerous studies looking at the distribution across cities of black populations, white populations, juvenile delinquents, and the like. Few of these studies examine the concrete mechanisms within cities which create the population effects being descriptively documented; this is clear, for example, in the studies associated with "social area analysis." A major recent book illustrating this continuing focus on a demographic-descriptive approach is that by Schwirian. Schwirian (1974, 7) sees urban ecological research as primarily "concerned with the distribution of population characteristics, organizations, activities, and behaviors across the urban terrain." Contemporary ecologists examine what spatial distributions are and how they are affected by such social processes as the division of labour. The concentric zone, sector, and multiple nucleii ideal-descriptive models are complementary and, when taken together with the statistical method of factorial ecology, provide "a very comprehensive approach to ecological phenomena."

In another important U.S. book on urban ecology, Berry and Kasarda (1977) are critical of demographic mapping; they accent the importance of how a population organizes itself, a theme originated by Amos Hawley in the 1940s and 1950s. They are not much concerned with urban land use and development, but rather with the organization of urban populations for survival. They also seem to accept the traditional view that urban structure has evolved largely through the spontaneous, unplanned competition of the market, "that even to-day, free-enterprise dynamics predominate in establishing urban order in the United States" (Berry and Kasarda, 1977, 353). Reporting on their own empirical work, Berry and Kasarda focus heavily on descriptive demographic analysis. They examine residential segregation, urban population size and densities, social areas of cities, demographic patterns of suburbanization, suburban growth as it relates to occupation, and the industrial structure of metropolitan areas. While the range of research issues is broader than traditional ecology, here too most of the data take the form of general population statistics and correlations among these statistics.

11 Urban Planning

The underlying philosophy of mainstream urban planning has a number of important parallels with urban ecology, as well as numerous points of cross-fertilization. Like Park and Burgess, traditional urban planners in the United States have seen the city as a natural, organic development, as a spatial and physical environment. But such planners have also held to a central belief in technical expertise, in the ability of scientific planners to intervene to enhance the rationality of an otherwise natural spatial and physical ecology. Originating in the "City Beautiful" plans around 1900, by the 1920s city planning had shifted to a greater emphasis on efficiency in the physical form of cities, on maintaining natural, homogeneous uses by means of such devices as zoning ordinances. In the 1940s and 1950s federal government involvement in urban renewal reinforced the planning orientation towards the efficient shaping of urban space (Burchell and Hughes 1978, xx). With an emphasis on technique (cost-benefit analysis, modeling, systems analysis, etc.) and a technical-expertise approach to urban development problems, traditional planners have generally operated as expert facilitators who did not research the actual structure of the capitalist market system whose goals they helped to pursue. As with traditional urban ecologists, there is a general acceptance of the capitalist principle of "rational" as the "best and most efficient" use of land.

In the 1960s Webber (1964, 84–93) articulated a major thrust in ecological planning when he asserted that the planner's major responsibility was technical planning of the location and physical layout of cities in order to improve the welfare of urbanites. Webber clearly recognizes the impact of physical-locational planning on the sociocultural character of urban communities. Commenting on what he explicitly terms "ecological planning," McHarg (1978, 14) has recently summed up the traditional role of the planner as a rational, apolitical expert who helps clients implement their values. Numerous U.S. planners have adopted a variant of this technical expert-client approach to urban redesign, sometimes with an added emphasis on the role of educating clients on what is good urban design (Hoppenfeld 1978, 18–19). A recent review of the planning profession puts it thus: "Planners have traditionally lacked access to the decision-making process . . . have tended to avoid political conflict, have been technique-oriented rather than goal-oriented, and are facilitators rather than initiators" (Burchell and Hughes 1978, xxvi).

One must recognize that many traditional urban planners have been concerned not only with technical expertise and a more rational use of land and the built environment but also with ideals of urban beauty and social justice. While a minority among planners, "advocacy planners," have recently given great emphasis to the social justice ideals (see Hartman 1974), for the most part the planning profession still tests its urban plans against its view of land use, location, and spatial distribution, which accepts the capitalist definition of land use rationality and efficiency. Missing in traditional planning theory is a serious concern with the character of the power-privilege structure of the urban environments within which planning takes place and with the ways in which neglect of that power-privilege structure leads to naive planning.

III   An Alternative Perspective

A close examination of the U.S. urban sociology literature revealed that there is only one brief paper which has developed the idea that the actions of specific, powerful land-use actors, an array of capitalist class actors, might be major factors shaping urban land use and development.[1] This unique, pioneering paper was prepared by William Form and appeared in the 1950s in *Social Forces*. Form (1954, 528) suggests there that the Adam Smith model of a free and unorganized urban land market must be discarded, for that market is very organized and that powerful actors operate in self-conscious and purposeful ways. Form notes four main groups: 1) the real estate and building business, 2) industries and utilities, 3) homeowners, and 4) local government agencies. After briefly sketching the important interrelationships between these groups, Form examines their impact on a few zoning decisions in Lansing, Michigan. The bottom line in Form's analysis is that social structure must be examined in order to understand land use and changes therein. He calls for a shift in urban ecological research which would place heavy emphasis on "isolating the important and powerful land-interested groupings in the city." This provocative suggestion has not been followed by most U.S. sociologists as yet.

However, clues for a thoroughgoing, class-based theoretical framework have been provided by a British urban geographer (David Harvey) and a few European Marxist social scientists, who have begun to criticize both conventional urban ecology and urban planning from a power-conflict perspective. Thus Manuel Castells (1976, 55) has argued that the Burgess concentric zone pattern is limited historically and geographically to certain types of cities; in a general analysis he demonstrates that modern capitalist cities are shaped by capitalist investment patterns. Another European, Lamarche (1976, 117), notes that the city is in the image of the larger capitalist society around it: "Subjectively, this means that urban advantages are appropriated by the same people who monopolize social wealth objectively, that the development of the city can only be determined by the development of capital." According to David Harvey (1973, 133) the power-class approach to urban zones in industrial cities taken by Engels in his *Condition of the Working Class in England* in 1844 is "far more consistent with hard economic and social realities than . . . the essentially cultural approach of Park and Burgess." The integration of the city, from Engels's point of view, was not the moral order of impersonal market equilibrium of ordinary consumers but rather the exploitative realities of a capitalist-dominated system of urban land development.

IV   The Producers of the Built Environment

If ordinary consumers play a secondary part in the shaping of cities, who is it that plays the primary part? The primary decision-makers who shape cities are the producers. Who are these producers? In the United States land-use and development decisions are governed by a capitalistic political-economic system. The conventional view sees urban land use and development as resulting from individual self-maximizing behaviour in a market context. Yet power and wealth inequality means that the decisions of some are far more important than those of others. Rank-and-file homeowners, or renters, often give way before the preferences of the powerful. Conventional thinking about cities assumes that there is a free market in land relatively unfettered by the actions of organized elite interests. Urban commercial and residential land markets are seen as determined by free competitive bidding. Actors in this competitive bidding for land are recognized as having different interests, even different incomes, which affect the bidding process. But the fact that the small group of most powerful and wealthy actors can do far more than simply outbid their competitors is not analyzed. Powerful actors such as wealthy speculators and industrial capitalists can and do shape the *rules* of the market system within which the ostensibly free land competition is taking place.

U.S. business leaders tend to see themselves as dependent, as following the lead of consumer values in building cities or as dependent on government action. Yet occasionally they admit their independence. Thus one recent analysis in a 1980 real estate journal, *Buildings*, candidly notes that "the building industry has always played a major role in determining quality of life and social groupings, whether it's in the work sector or in the provision of adequate housing." And profits are the major goal of this building industry. As Lorimer (1978, 79) put it, "The consequence of this arrangement, however, is that the corporate city and its interlocking pieces are designed not to provide a humane and livable city, but rather to maximize the profits to be made from urban land and to capture as much control over the process of urban growth as possible for the development of industry." The corporate capitalist city is a machine to make money.

V   Modern Real Estate Capitalism

Today real estate capitalism is organized around a complicated network of corporations and companies of varying sizes and functions. One way to list the critical corporate actors in urban development is in terms of the development decisions they take part in.[2] Such a listing can be misleading in a number of different ways. In the first place, one modern capitalist corporation can include within it a development subdivision (which not only develops projects but engages in land speculation), a real estate brokerage subsidiary, and an architectural department. Or a major insurance company may have a financial department as well as its own urban land development subsidiary. Thus the

Table 5.1

1   Industrial and commercial location decisions:
    Industrial companies (including service industries)
    Commercial companies
2   Development decisions:
    Development companies (developers)
    Land speculators
    Landlords and landowners
3   Financial decisions:
    Commercial banks (including trust and pension funds)
    Savings and loan associations
    Insurance companies
    Mortgage companies
    Real estate investment trusts
4   Construction decisions:
    Architectural firms
    Engineering firms
    Construction companies (contractors and builders)
    Building materials companies
5   Support decisions:
    Chamber of Commerce
    Business associations
    Real estate brokers
    Leasing companies

various decisions listed in Table 5.1 can be distributed among certain companies or concentrated within one large corporation. Second, there is the issue of scale and region. These land-use decisions are often made not just by local real estate companies but also by powerful regional and national companies. Powerful interests of regional and national scope now determine the shape of U.S. cities. There are complex interconnections between those powerful interests external to cities and those that are intricately interwoven into the internal structure of any particular city. An example of this would be Prudential Life Insurance Company which now finances and owns real estate projects and development projects in many cities across the United States. There is indeed a complex urban puzzle lying behind the development and ownership of the modern American city — involving development companies, banks and contractors, and supportive governmental agencies.

A third feature of this modern land development is its capital banking aspect. Land and buildings are always important investments, but when economic growth slows in other industrial sectors, capital will often flow in increased amounts to the real estate sector. Suburbanization has been linked closely to heavy capital flows into suburban land speculation and the construction of residential housing.

Thus the tabulation of powerful land-interested actors in Table 5.1 is only a first step towards identifying the critical decision makers whose land-use and development decisions disproportionately shape cities. In the rest of this paper I will focus primarily on the category of land speculation decisions and on closely related development decisions as they have affected U.S. cities.

VI   Land Speculation

A major figure in urban land use and development is the real estate speculator. Yet the central role of land speculation decisions has not been seriously discussed in the U.S. sociological literature centering on the patterning of cities. Form's pioneering article omits speculators, as does the work of the geographer Harvey and the social scientist Castells. One of the few theoretical discussions of these speculators in the American literature dealing with land use appears in the book *Progress and Poverty,* written by the nineteenth-century reformer, Henry George. This provocative analysis has been neglected by urban social scientists, yet it provides an excellent starting point for a new urban ecology, one directed towards those powerful land-interested actors that Form urged researchers to study. George argued that it is the work and effort of an entire community that brings a steady advance in land values. George (edn 1962, 264) notes that "this steady increase naturally leads to speculation in which future increase is anticipated." The land speculator thus secures, unjustly and without productive effort on the land, the increased value generated by community effort. By control of land, the speculator secures hard-earned dollars from working people who must rent or buy.

Speculation in real estate — including land and the buildings on that land — is a different sort of capital venture than investment in machinery. Real estate speculation is not productive, that is, it does not increase the goods and services available in the society. Yet great amounts of money are realized in land holding, buying, and selling. Land is a unique commodity, for it is finite. Occupying space is a fundamental requirement of existence; to live, to work, to be housed — human beings must occupy land. The "created value" of land is the explicit concern of the large-scale real estate industry, of bankers, speculators, developers, and builders. "Creation of value," often on paper, occurs as urban land changes hands many times in its life span. Land speculators are at the heart of this processing of land. A real estate speculator can be defined as an entrepreneur or corporate entity which purchases (or purchases and develops) real estate with the hope of a profit from rising land and property values. Major speculators are, broadly speaking, capitalists since they are investors who buy and sell for a profit in a capitalist market system. Such speculators can be individuals or corporations, but they are by definition owners seeking to become sellers for a profit. Of great interest in real estate speculation is the ability of these capitalists to shift capital not only from one real estate sector to another — as from slums to suburbs — but also to "bank" capital from commercial or industrial sources in the form of land holdings, banked wealth which is perhaps to be returned to commercial or industrial activities when future profitability dictates that shift.

I will now examine a number of activities which illustrate the central role of speculative land decisions in urban development:

1. the site selection of cities;
2. shaping the internal structure of cities, including slums and business districts;
3. suburban development.

1 Speculator and City Site Selection

In the urban sociological literature, geographical and communication factors are usually cited as major reasons for the original siting of cities. There is truth to this argument. Yet real estate speculators have had their hand in determining just which promising geographical locations actually become city sites.

Real estate speculation is an old enterprise in North America, coming into its own in the late eighteenth century. Many of the oldest fortunes in the United States have grown up out of land dealings. In the first centuries of development real estate speculators, especially men with wealth and means, launched city development from Washington to San Francisco, often setting the pattern for

future growth. Acting legally and illegally, they bought land, advertised to settlers, pressured legislatures, and bribed officials in their quest for land profits.
Colonial real estate speculators included the U.S. founding fathers. Indeed, the
large-scale real estate speculation of George Washington and Patrick Henry in
western lands brought them into direct conflict with King George III (Sakolski
1957; 53–55). After the American revolution, numerous cities, from Boston to
Yorktown, put in a bid for the site of the capital of the new nation. Thomas Jefferson's desire to have the capital near Virginia won out in the political struggle, and George Washington had Major Charles L'Enfant survey a large area
on the Potomac River. The land was then in the possession of wealthy speculators. Since the new government had no money, a deal was worked whereby
a large part of the surveyed area remained in the hands of the speculators. Part
of the tract was put up for sale to the public at a tavern auction in Georgetown
in 1791, presided over by Washington and Jefferson. But few people came to
buy lots in what was then considered a desolate area. Washington himself
bought a number of lots, for speculative purposes. Thus Washington's promotion of the city to American and European investors was not financially disin-
terested. Vigorous attempts were made to promote Washington, D.C., real
estate for European investment, and the President had his secretary work up a
pamphlet for London investors (Sakolski 1932).

Moreover, Cincinnati came to be located where it is because of an off-hand
decision of a trapper-turned-land-speculator. In pursuit of thieves, this trapper
traveled in the Northwest territory. Impressed by the fertility of the land and
the river location, he petitioned Congress to sell him millions of acres on the
Big Miami River. Soon, two real estate syndicates bought land in the region
because of this new activity, and on one of these tracts Cincinnati was located.
The location of Omaha, Nebraska, similarly reflected the profit-oriented activity of speculators. A financier, George Francis Train, had inside information
that a terminus of the Union Pacific railroad would be at a certain place (Omaha) in Kansas, so a real estate syndicate headed by Train bought up large
amounts of acreage. Another syndicate fought to locate the terminus 50 miles
to the south, but lost. According to Thomas (1977, 70–87) no less a figure than
President Abraham Lincoln was one of these competing speculators. In the development of western areas cheap government land meant, in numerous cases,
that wealthy agricultural, commercial and industrial capitalists could buy up
very large amounts of potentially valuable land; later, they could sell land and
lend money, sometimes at exorbitant rates, to the farmers and town dwellers
settling in the area. Thus "men in the East with surplus capital scanned maps
looking for likely spots to establish a town" (Wade 1959, 30). Some such city
speculators made no profit, but their speculative action shaped urban site locations nonetheless. Advertisements for these towns played an important role in
generating the migration west of the Appalachians.

Actions by U.S. railroad capitalists had a significant effect on land use and development, rural and urban, as the westward movement took place. Two major effects can be noted. Many railroad lines were extended into relatively unoccupied territory primarily for land speculation reasons. Railroad capitalists received huge government subsidies, the most significant of which, in the long run, were the large grants of government land along the railroads. These lands rose in value with the railroads and towns along the railroads, leading to large real estate profits. In addition, railroad capitalists sometimes shaped where and whether towns and cities grew and prospered. The growth of some midwestern and western cities was significantly accelerated or depressed by the actions of these men. Because the placement of railroads heavily shapes land values, many railroad companies sought private bribes from towns in return for putting the towns on a railroad line (George edn 1962, 192; Sakolski 1932; Sakolski 1957, 163–74). Towns and cities often had to pay or face serious economic troubles.

2 Speculation within and around Cities

Land speculation within and around U.S. cities has greatly shaped urban development. The practice of buying and holding land until nearby urban development pushes the price up has a long history in the United States. In the early 1800s land speculation within and around cities such as Louisville and St. Louis increased as real estate speculators drove up land prices. A considerable amount of the surplus commercial capital went into land speculation around cities, rather than into industrial development within these cities. In some nineteenth-century cities publicly chartered transit or utility companies secured considerable blocks of urban land, then held them off the market, driving land prices upwards to very high profit levels (Edel 1976, 114). Great fortunes were made in urban real estate, speculation which frequently charted the course for specific lines of urban growth. A German immigrant who first made money in the fur trade, John Jacob Astor, went on to found one of the great landed fortunes. Making his first million in commercial enterprises, Astor put his money into long-term real estate speculation. In the early 1800s Astor bought up large areas of farmland just outside central Manhattan, and lots in central Manhattan as well. His speculative actions generated a number of the developmental surges around Manhattan Island. By 1920 the Astor family real estate in New York made them the biggest landlords there, worth $1 billion (Sakolski 1957, 235–36; Thomas 1977, 40–46).

A good example of the influences of powerful real estate interests, including major speculators, in shaping the internal structure of cities can be seen in certain key units of urban space. The basic land unit selected was often the one best suited to business purposes in a capitalist system — individual lots set into a grid pattern of lot and block development. Lots narrow at the front and long at the side — such dimensions reflected land values calculated in terms of front

footage (Sakolski 1957). New towns and cities could be planned into standardized lots and blocks without any special surveying skills. Such lot-block
rectangularism was appropriate for division and sale of land for profit. Cities
would sprawl out along traffic arteries, and the gridiron plan forced utility lines
and streets to follow along (Mumford 1961, 422–23). In nineteenth-century
America the gridiron pattern was logically extended along the expanding
transportation lines. Traffic lines were sometimes laid out with speculative
profit specifically in mind. Thus engineers in New York's Public Service Commission in the early 1900s described the growing subway system this way.
"All lines must necessarily be laid to the objective point — Manhattan. Every
transit line that brings people to Manhattan adds to its real estate value"
(quoted in Mumford 1961, 425). A few government reports have recognized
the role of land speculators. In England, for example, one government reported
noted that "the artificial causes of the extension of the town are the specula-
tions of builders encouraged and promoted by merchants dealing in the material of building, and attorneys with monied clients, facilitating, and indeed
putting into motion, the whole system" (quoted in Mumford 1961, 428).

Some land-oriented capitalists have been so powerful that they have actually shifted the business center of cities, profiting on the side from the rising
real estate values this shift resulted in. Take for example the two powerful
landed capitalists, Marshall Field and Potter Palmer, whose real estate operations remade the face of Chicago. At the end of the civil war, the Lake Street
area there was the central retail and financial district. A single powerful capitalist, Potter Palmer, rechanneled this business growth to another section of
Chicago. The area he chose, the State Street area, was a rundown area then
viewed as a slum. Palmer quietly bought up much of the property in the area,
pushed for and got a wide street heading into the area, and then built a plush
hotel to entice other businesses there. He eventually succeeded in relocating
the center of Chicago business activity, a result signaled by the rise of property
values from $300 a front foot in 1860 to $2000 a front foot in 1869. This speculative venture was dramatically successful. Moreover, after the great Chicago
fire in 1871, Marshall Field made decisions that relocated substantial business
activity in Chicago. As with Palmer, Field avoided former business centers and
chose another dilapidated area inhabited by the poor. Field rebuilt his large retail store in a poor Irish area. Numerous major businesses followed his lead, a
clear indication of the importance of one powerful capitalist in reshaping urban areas. Together with a partner, Field became the largest real estate speculator and landowner in Chicago; his speculation came to be more profitable
than the retail business operations (Thomas 1977, 145).

Speculation in central city areas remains of great importance today. Central
city land in major cities, particularly that useful for office buildings, is very expensive, in part because of land speculation. One survey found that average
acre values for prime office space ran in the $2 million to $9 million range,

with figures up to $17 million in New York City (Meyer 1979, 52). Much of the land in central areas already has older built structures on it. Many powerful speculators have gone into land buying for new building construction. Old buildings, including those in good condition, are torn down and replaced with new construction, since there is more profit to be made, given the high depreciation allowed, in new buildings. Freeways, parking lots, and high-rise buildings come to dominate areas where such speculators operate in conjunction with other powerful actors. The diversity of housing and life there previously disappears; cities increasingly look alike. Note that skyscrapers have emerged with monopoly capitalism, the domination of industries by a few firms. Earlier, competitive capitalism did not require such highly concentrated office facilities (Sawers 1975, 65). With the rise of monopoly capitalism major administrative centers were necessary in order to control these economic empires. Numerous central districts became administrative centers. Government-funded urban renewal has been used to facilitate these developments.

Speculators play an important role in pulling together smaller parcels, hoping that the large land package can be used, for example, by a big corporation interested in an office building. Once speculators have finished their packaging of land, sometimes with the aid of urban renewal, profitable insurance companies and real estate syndicates have been used to generate the money to put up office skyscrapers, the depreciation on which attracts highly paid professionals (such as, doctors and lawyers) and other outside investors seeking tax shelters. Downie (1974) notes that in 1972 these real estate syndicates were one-tenth of new security arrangements on Wall Street. Two results frequently follow from this office-oriented speculation — too much unrented office space and cheaply built office buildings which may become the slums of tomorrow. This process has become common in some European cities as well (Downie 1974, 72, 211).

In addition, speculative real estate operations create or contribute significantly to contemporary slums in central cities. Ghettos and slums with slowly or rapidly deteriorating housing are sometimes seen by urban sociologists as the result of 1) disorganized poor people without the means to keep up the property or 2) the inevitable invasion and succession process whereby as one group of people becomes more affluent, another moves in behind them. Yet there is another view of this slum-making process: that this degradation of central cities is the natural result of intentional profit-making on the part of those who invest in slum real estate, and that for most such speculative investors the investments are very profitable. While most slumlords are small-scale operators (Sternlieb 1966, 123), there is a significant minority engaged in buying slum property for depreciation and speculation purposes, which activity helps create dilapidated, later even abandoned, residential areas. There are profits to be made in this speculation. Thus one Washington, D.C., savings and loan association grew from $30,000 in assets in 1952 to $57 million in 1967 in part by loaning money to speculators working Washington slums (Downie 1974, 32). Slum speculation can involve outside speculators by means of real estate syndicates. Doctors, lawyers, and business executives buy into a slum investment scheme because the very large depreciation allowed on such buildings can sharply reduce their income taxes. Slums are created by this profit-centered activity, as upkeep on the purchased buildings is kept low to keep profits high. As Downie notes, "far from being the pitiful victims of unavoidable deterioration of inner-city housing, as they so often represent themselves to be, the slum speculators are cunning actors in a sophisticated real estate industry conspiracy aided and abetted by large, respected financial institutions and agencies of the federal government" (Downie 1974, 39–40). The quality of the housing can be irrelevant to this speculation. Rundown poverty area tenements can bring in as much profit, because of depreciation and mortgage advantages, as better-quality housing elsewhere.

3 Gentrification

In the last decade or so a considerable amount of urban revitalization has occurred in the central cities of the United States. One type of revitalization has involved the displacement of lower-income urbanites by higher-income urbanites, often returning to the central city from outlying city areas, or from suburban backgrounds, or, in the case of young people, opting for the central city instead of the suburbs. Often called "renaissance," this process has taken two major forms: 1) incumbent upgrading, where local residents together with newcomers of the same socioeconomic background upgrade a central city area; and 2) speculator-developer upgrading, where land speculators and developers buy up low-income housing, rebuild or replace it, and then sell it to white, affluent, often young, families with professional, technical, or managerial workers (gentrification). Poorer, local residents are pushed out. Displacement resulting from private urban renewal has been documented in various U.S. cities, including Atlanta, Baltimore, Boston, and Houston, to name just a few.

4 Gentrification and Capitalism

Gentrification is associated with two aspects of modern capitalism. One aspect is continuing and constant; the other is cyclical. The continuing aspect is the importance of cities as headquarters for large corporations. The city is the symbolic center of American capitalism. It is the center for political, cultural, and economic dominance by the ruling class. Decline there has a tremendous negative symbolism for the ruling class. So decline can be tolerated for a period, but then new pressures arise from the cyclical aspect, the investment aspect. Capitalists must decide whether to abandon the capital already in built environments or to rehabilitate that investment.

There is today an urban renaissance in many U.S. cities. The new hotels, exclusive neighbourhoods of historic houses, marinas, and specialty shops signal the return of well-off people to central cities. But this is only the superficial face. Beneath is the long-term urban process of uneven development. Cities under capitalism grow and decline as part of this process of uneven development. The spatial seesawing of capital, from central cities to suburbs, then from suburbs to central cities, is to be expected. It is rational in terms of profit seeking by land-oriented capitalists. Gentrification is only a small part of the larger economic restructuring going on in the society. But it does signal the fact that central cities are now the locations for a new round of capital accumulation in residential housing. Once central city housing and land prices have declined sharply as a result of the earlier withdrawal of capital, as in the undermaintenance of older rented buildings by landlords, then there is a renewed opportunity for redevelopment and a new round of profit-making in central cities (Smith 1981, 20–21).

Absentee investment is often a part of the gentrification process. Speculators buy property, often in large amounts, in areas potentially attractive to better-off white-collar families. Existing tenants are forced out by eviction or rising rents. "These properties are purchased at a low price, and may be sold quickly at a substantial profit (sometimes after renovation but often without any additional investment)" (U.S. Department of Housing and Urban Development 1979, 23). Many speculators look at the gentrifying and nearby areas in terms of their investment potential.

A recent National Urban Coalition report found significant speculative activity in the forty-four U.S. cities surveyed. The more extensive the citywide rehabilitation, the more speculation was reported as a threat to existing neighbourhoods. The threat occurs because "speculative activity is impersonal; monied forces appear to manipulate the lives of those with little money who have lived in the neighbourhood and yet have no control over their future there" (National Urban Coalition 1978, 21). Speculators and developers usually play a critical role in the gentrification process as it proceeds. One study in Washington, D.C., found speculators combing "neighbourhoods on foot and by telephone just ahead of the restoration movement, making attractive cash offers to owners" (Richards and Rowe 1972, 54–61). If owners do not wish to sell, building inspectors may be called in; and they may order expensive repairs, forcing a sale. Between 1972 and 1974 a fifth of all recorded sales in Washington, D.C., involved two or more sales of the same property; most of these were located in five neighbourhoods (Richards and Rowe 1977).

Gentrification has been important in the District of Columbia, in both the Georgetown and in the Capitol Hill areas. Zeitz (1979) has documented the role of speculators and developers, who have bought up blocks of rental housing for conversion to owner occupation. In one block houses selling for $7,000 to $15,000 in 1973 were bought up and resold for $100,000 in 1978. Zeitz further notes a typical transaction in the Adams-Morgan area: "A row of houses on one particular block were sold fully tenanted and unremodeled for $26,000 per house. These houses were sold only weeks later for $65,000 per house. Remodelers are now working on these houses and sales are expected to be in excess of $125,000" (Zeitz 1979, 78). Clearly, the displaced black renters cannot afford the new housing, and the amount of available, livable housing for working-class renters in a low-vacancy-rate area such as D.C. is gradually reduced. White middle-income and upper-income families replace the poorer black families. Political discontent in D.C.'s black areas facing gentrification has even led to the passage of a city ordinance, called the 1975 "Speculator's Bill," designed to limit speculation and tenant evictions for the purpose of gentrification. Watered down considerably, it became law in the summer of 1978; several loopholes protected most real estate speculation and gentrification development (Zeitz 1979, 82). Well-organized speculators and developers had successfully lobbied the city council.

In her research on a half dozen areas in D.C., Zeitz (1979, 101–12) noted several steps in the gentrification renewal process:

1. Pioneers call attention to a new area.
2. Real estate agents become interested in sales there.
3. Speculators and builders move in, with the assistance of banking institutions.

This research suggests one common pattern of powerful actors' intervention: realtors follow a few (white) pioneer families and publicize the virtues of a new area. Speculators and builders expand the area beyond the pioneers and make much more housing available for higher-income families, usually at prices even the pioneers could not afford. Realtors, speculators, and developers require lending institutions, with which they usually have close ties from previous land projects.

In their research, Pattison (1977) and Clay (1979) found two somewhat different patterns in many gentrifying neighbourhoods. Clay's study of 105 neighbourhoods in 30 cities found 57 examples of gentrification and 48 examples of incumbent upgrading (Clay 1979, 17–21, 105). In many cases of gentrification the first stage involved the "sweat equity" and personal savings of pioneer families, who were followed at first by small then by larger speculators and developer-speculators. In other cases, a few capitalist speculators or developer-speculators (usually small companies) were found to have actually begun the gentrification in some central city areas without pioneer families showing them the way. Most of the neighbourhoods had previously housed the elderly poor, nonwhite families, or poor white (blue-collar) families prior to gentrification. Afterwards, more than 80 percent of the gentrified neighbourhoods were dominated by whites, mostly by professional and other white-collar families. Most gentrified neighbourhoods possessed attractive city features such as "high elevation and proximity to water public spaces, parks, landmarks" (Clay 1979, 21). Because of professional whites' demand and speculation, most gentrified housing has sold for relatively high prices, often over $100,000 by the late 1970s.

Clay (1979, 26) found neighbourhood observers complaining that developer-speculators frequently did not carefully restore the housing, but rather modernized it. They "butcher" fine old buildings, as some local critics have phrased it. Developer-speculators often have not been sensitive to the distinctive architectural features of an area and have ignored the negative effects of their actions on incumbent residents. Yet many of these have been small or new developers whose speculative interest in seeing risky investments pay off in substantial profits was coupled with the courage and imagination to work in older central city areas without massive bulldozing. Clay also got complaints that the actions of speculators and developers were uncontrolled, that they cut too many corners to make a profit. In most gentrifying areas concerned officials and incumbent residents were at the mercy of a capitalist housing market. Thus Clay (1979, 27) notes that "in almost all cities developers who have access to capital and who can identify a market for their products can operate at will."

Realtors also play a role in gentrification, sometimes as brokers and sometimes as land and housing speculators themselves. In addition, city governments have frequently cooperated with the capitalist actors by improving local facilities in gentrifying areas, such as parks and streets, by subsidizing gentrification with below-market interest-rate loans, and by selling government-owned structures at low cost, and even by helping to market and actively publicize the gentrified areas with home tours, fairs, and media campaigns (Clay 1979, 26–29).

This cooperative action by developers, speculators, realtors, government and banks has displaced low-income and moderate-income families in most gentrified areas. These families, often black or other nonwhite families, must move to other areas and there compete with other families of modest incomes in what is usually a declining number of decent housing areas in the central city. Here we see a small group of powerful capitalist actors again rearranging the face of cities for private profit, with little input into the process from those most directly affected, the incumbent residents. By seeking profit, they can shift poor areas and change the racial composition of large neighbourhoods, a type of "reverse blockbusting."

5 Condominium Conversions

Condominium conversions may or may not involve housing renovation, but they are often similar to gentrification in the housing problems they create. For example, a Denver study (Flahive and Gordon 1979, 6–10) found that in the 1973–78 period 5,500 apartments and multifamily structures were converted to condominiums, most of which were sold to affluent households. A significant number of low- and moderate-income households were thus displaced. Looking at 85,000 households in a large, U.S. central-city area for 1978, the Denver study estimated that 2,000 households were displaced in that year alone, with demolitions, condo conversions, and houses going from renter to owner accounting for most of the displacement.

In recent years a number of corporations have become involved in conversion of existing apartment buildings into condominiums. Large, if not huge, speculative profits are being made in this process. In a typical case in Philadelphia an apartment building worth only $25 million was sold to a development corporation for $50 million.[3] The development corporation then, with little renovation, converted the rental apartments into condominium apartments for sale. Reportedly, a typical rental charge was about $560 a month prior to conversion, but after conversion the total payment (for mortgage and interest, etc.) was $1,200 a month, plus several thousand dollars in a down payment on the unit. As a result, most existing households had to leave such a building because they could not afford the greatly increased cost for the same housing unit. And in most cases low-income and low-middle-income families will never be able to afford housing in such apartment buildings, forcing them to look elsewhere, often for less than adequate housing.

6 Suburban Speculation

Obvious gridiron-block extensions in the twentieth century can be seen in the suburban patchwork quilt sprawling out from the edges of central areas in American cities. So far the great suburban migration has involved more than 50 million people. The area currently used for urban use in the United States is over 10 million acres, although twice as much land is withdrawn from other uses because of the leapfrogging which characterizes much suburban growth. Such idled land, one land-use report notes, is "ripening for active urban use" (Ackerman et al., 1962, 9). By 2000 AD, perhaps 40 million acres of U.S. land will be withdrawn from other use for urban development, mostly for suburban growth. Clawon (1971) has estimated that as of 1970 the rise in land prices each year, for land moved from rural to suburban use, is about $14 billion. Like cities, suburbs are usually seen by urban sociologists as spontaneous, disorganized developments, the result of an unpredictable free-wheeling market system. This is part of the usual explanation of suburbanization, which touches on other explanations such as rising affluence leading to demand for single-family housing and government-subsidization of mortgages and utilities. But in reality the growth has involved considerably more planning and purpose than the traditional view suggests. Here too the role of profit making on the part of real estate speculators and their partners, developers and bankers, has radically shaped urban development. This applies as well to suburban growth.

Suburban real estate speculators often have been seen in the real estate literature as a critical group of capitalists who fill the ownership gap between agricultural users who sell out, usually to speculators willing to hold the land for later development (Lindeman 1976). In urban fringes land will often go through a series of speculators before it becomes a suburban development. A number of studies have illustrated the profits made by speculators buying up such farmland. In areas like California land speculators have bought out farmers by offering $200 to $6,000 more an acre than they paid for it. Such sales push up the property taxes on surrounding farmlands not yet sold to speculators. Tax pressures, coupled with the water runoff and pollution problems of suburban development, eventually force even the most obstinate farmer to sell out to speculators. As a result, residential land prices, particularly in suburban areas, have risen 200–400 percent faster than the price of housing in the same areas (Downie 1974, 88). In some areas, such as Los Angeles, the price of residential land went up at the rate of 40 percent a year in the late 1970s, in part as the result of speculative activity.

In some cases, suburban development at the rim of major cities had been generated by the profit objectives of only one or two real estate speculators, as can be seen in the operations of two brothers in Cleveland after the First World War. Using speculative options and large-scale leveraging, they generated a surge of suburban development in the Shaker Heights area of Cleveland. Then to reinforce their highly influential suburban real estate activities they got into trolley line operations as well (Thomas 1977, 255–56). In other cities, a number of speculators triggered suburban development. Downie has shown that real estate people in Los Angeles admit that sprawl development there was heavily shaped by the quest for private profit, that the sprawl pattern was "merely the easiest, fastest, most lucrative way to cash in on the motor-age California land rush: buy a tract of vacant land, wait a short time for the population and roads to move toward it, subdivide it into lots for cheaply built single-family homes, and sell them to builders at prices that total several times the land's original cost" (Downie 1974, 10). This drive towards profit created the sprawling freeway system as well.

Speculation is regarded in the conventional literature as a positive bridging force, as a brokerage operation between the farmer and the builder, but as we have seen it has numerous negative effects. There are others yet to mention. Illegal and unethical activity is, according to one researcher, commonplace among speculators, developers, and their financiers. Downie notes that "land speculators push farmers off their land and employ deceit and bribery to rezone and subdivide it" (Downie 1974, 6). Moreover, Lindeman (1976, 150–51) argues that real estate speculation activities actually alter the nature of the land commodity primarily by restricting the supply of available land and by forcing prices up above what they would have been without the speculative activity. Higher-than-necessary prices come in part from the expensive, usually highly leveraged, financial arrangements that speculators get into, as well as from the speculative pricing process itself. Both costs are passed on in the form of higher prices for actual land users. Restrictions on land supply sometimes arise because of the complex legal arrangements a series of speculators bring to a parcel of land, legalities which can later hamper the sale of land to builders; encumbered by mortgages, land changes its character as a commodity. One result of this is an acceleration of sprawl, as builders try to leapfrog land which is too tied up or held by speculators holding out for very high profits. The characteristic pattern of urban sprawl is often defined by the flight of speculators and developers to cheaper land farther out.

7 Financing Speculation

A complex social structure is woven around the operations of city and suburban speculators, including government officials (as in the case of urban renewal) and banking organizations. Speculators nearly always rely on lenders for their leveraging operations. Leverage is the mechanism which allows the pyramiding of a large investment operation on a small initial investment. Since the property bought serves as collateral, real estate speculators need far less of their own money to get into the real estate business. They can borrow far more (80–90 percent) of the purchasing price from banking institutions than if they purchase industrial equipment. And for those who buy land and older buildings, build new apartment and commercial buildings, and rent them out, there are several ways to profit. "For here there is not only the prospect of leverage at a high ratio but also of shielding the resultant profits through the liberal tax shelter permitted to owners of income-producing property in the form of depreciation allowances, as well as other expense deductions associated with development and ownership" (Goodkin 1974, 6).

8 Large-Scale Corporate Intervention in Speculation

In the last two decades very large multinational corporations have moved into real estate banking speculation, construction, and development. Until the 1950s, the land and housing industries were dominated by relatively small capitalist entrepreneurs, some of whom were only involved in real estate operations. When there are distinct landowning and industrial capital groups within the top capitalist class, there can be conflict. Excessive land costs may mean increased worker demands for higher wages, which can generate industrial capitalist support for holding down land and housing costs. However, the growing corporate and conglomerate involvement in land and housing development makes this distinction among capitalists less significant. Corporate intervention, into a real estate industry once dominated by relatively smaller capitalists, has developed rapidly. In the 1960–75 period 300 of the top 1,000 corporations developed real estate departments; particularly active in this area have been the oil, food, chemical, paper, and machinery industries. Profit making ("equity participation and diversification") was the major reason given for land activities by corporations in a 1971 survey by the Society of Real Estate Appraisers (Goodkin 1974, xv). The 250 corporations replying to that survey held $25 billion in real estate in 1971. While the recessions of the 1970s forced some companies to get out of real estate, many still remain.

Certain rationalizations for the activities of monopoly or oligopoly-oriented corporations have appeared to defend the growing domination of fewer and fewer corporations in most major American industries. Now these rationalizations are being extended to oligopoly trends in the housing industry and land markets. One capitalist rationalization of monopoly-corporate involvement in real estate operations in cities is that corporations provide larger-scale planned developments. Thus Goodkin (1974, 20) notes that the smaller "entrepreneurial builder, short on bankroll and long on leverage" has to follow a hedgehopping pattern of suburban development, so large-scale development can mean less hedgehopping and less sprawl. Large corporations have now built a number of major suburbs, including many in California. The now-troubled Chrysler Corporation set up a real estate department in 1967, with holdings of over $300 million by 1970. Chrysler was into "a whole string of projects around the country, including townhouses, office buildings, student housing in California and Arizona, shopping centers, condominiums, and a ski resort in Montana headed by the late TV newsman Chet Huntley" (Goodkin 1974, 22). Aerospace companies (e.g., McDonnell-Douglas), major utility companies (e.g., Mississippi Power and Light), timber corporations (e.g., Weyerhaeuser) and oil companies (e.g., Exxon) have expanded into the land, residential, and recreation development business. Today the trend in the land and housing industry is in the direction of accelerated monopoly control. Inflation creates tighter profit margins, forcing smaller developers and builders out of business. Soon two hundred major developers may be in control of a majority of the U.S. housing business; one informed estimate sees that figure as dwindling to 25 large firms by the year 2000.

VII Conclusion

The purpose of this chapter has been twofold. First, I have illuminated the role of real estate speculation in shaping urban and suburban land and building development. At best shadowy in the existing social science literature, real estate speculation has not been systematically studied by urban analysts in the United States. The materials presented here show that real estate speculators are in fact powerful land-interested actors, as individual entrepreneurs or as corporations, who buy, bank, and sell land in a quest for forever renewed profit.

Real estate speculators have shaped the sites for numerous American cities, using legal and illegal means to secure their goals. Powerful land-interested capitalists have contributed substantially to the internal physical structure and patterning of cities themselves. The central areas of cities such as San Francisco have been intentionally remade, in the name of private profit, by combinations of speculators and other capitalists, such as developers.

Slums too have often seen the intervening hand of the real estate speculator. The theories which focus on the values of the poor or the inevitable invasion-succession process — fairly common in conventional urban sociological treatments of slums—need to be supplemented with a theory of real estate speculation. In this process, speculators can create or accelerate increased dilapidation in central cities. They can help create that area Burgess called the "zone of transition." Later, they can help gentrify such areas. Burgess's commuter zone emerges in part because of the activities of land speculators. The hedgehopping look to suburbia reflects in part the planned profit of real estate speculators and their associates.

Tracking speculators through site selection, central-city decisions, and suburban sprawl, we see the planned, organized activities of these powerful land-interested actors — which brings us to the second purpose of this paper. It is very important for urban analysts in the United States and Europe to develop an alternative framework to deal with urban land use and land patterning, topics which have been at the heart of both urban ecological theory and urban planning theory for more than half a century. I have here emphasized that a class-oriented theory of urban land use provides significant insight into the internal dynamics of urban land use, development, and change, which traditional ecological and planning theories do not offer. In this paper I have illustrated this point by cataloguing major groups of capitalist actors which deserve systematic, detailed research on how and where they operate in shaping and reshaping the land uses and built environments of cities. Even the challenging theoretical discussions of Europeans such as Harvey and Castells tend to be vague when it comes to identifying the exact role of specific capitalist land-use actors. Here I have gathered together scattered data to document in specific detail one major category of land-use decision making by capitalist actors. If urban ecologists are to understand the how, when, and where of urban land-use change and development, they must begin with a systematic analysis not only of complex demographic patterns but also of the character and operations of powerful land-interested actors.

Moreover, the practical field of urban planning has traditionally operated with a theoretical framework closely allied to that of traditional urban ecology. Both have assumed a free market in land, without much analysis of that market. Indeed, in recent years both urban ecology and urban planning have placed emphasis on demographic analyses, computerized analytical techniques, and cost-benefit procedures. Sophisticated technical analysis of data for the clients at hand often seems to have replaced a concern for a broader theoretical understanding of urban structure and process. This is not to say that both fields have totally ignored the need for new urban theory, but they have neglected such a task. Careful analysis of all categories of powerful land-interested actors would provide a more realistic framework not only for understanding how cities actually work but also for understanding why idealistic urban planning often ends in problems and frustration.

Planning which attempts to meet idealistic goals such as the "decent home for every American family" proposed in the 1949 U.S. Housing Act or environmental quality often founders on the day-to-day realities of adapting planning to the needs of capitalist actors. Thus in a recent study of a massive commercial mall development in a southwestern city McAdams (1979) found that urban planners entered into the development process in two ways, as private consultants for the developer and as staff planners for the city's Planning Commission. The first phase of development was hidden from the general public and a private planner helped the developer prepare a profitable development plan in secret. When the city's staff planners finally saw the plan, several raised idealistic objections to the plan's environmental impact. In spite of their misgivings, however, and surrounded by pressure to improve the "business climate" of the city, the planners recommended approval of zoning changes with a plea that the "applicant continue to recognize" the environmental impact of the project. A start towards coping with this planning dilemma would be to develop a class-based planning theory coupled with power structure research which would clearly explicate the way planners relate to and serve the powerful land-interested actors.

A move towards more democratic urban planning in the United States requires more than new developments in planning theory. It requires implementation of theory in actual planner-aided efforts on behalf of working-class people in cities to help them express their values in their struggles with speculators and developers. A few "advocacy" planners have already made attempts to provide planning skills for "have-nots" in the urban revitalization process. One prominent planner, Chester Hartman, provided aid to the residents in San Francisco's South-of-the-Market area, where a tenants' association successfully forced capitalist leaders, including developers, speculators, and builders, to revise their commercial plans for the area to include a significant number of low-income residential units (Hartman 1974). In this case the advocacy planner and tenants' association came in too late to stop the revitalization process, but they did force significant changes in the original project. In two more recent struggles in San Francisco social advocacy planners have developed the information and financial plans for incumbent residents attempting to fight the bulldozing of two major buildings in areas developer-speculators wish to develop (Hartman 1980, 78–79).

Hartman (1980, 76–77) has suggested to a planners' conference that planning from the bottom up will require recognition of the skewed power structure shaping urban land use and the development of mechanisms that provide for democratic control over land-use decisions. With regard to speculators and developer-speculators, in 1974 one community-based group in Washington, D.C., the Capital East Community Organization, made an aggressive attempt to halt gentrification and the displacement of low-income renters. Trying to stem the tide of what they termed "reverse blockbusting" in D.C., they pressured the city council to pass a bill called the "Real Estate Transaction Tax," which would have restricted speculative buying and selling by imposing a stiff transaction tax. Yet developers and speculators organized to resist what was popularly called the "Speculator's Bill." They succeeded first in delaying the bill's passage until 1978 and then in watering it down so that developer-speculators were effectively exempt from the law. In this case, in part because of a lack of effective planning assistance and of adequate resources, a community-based group was not ultimately successful in its attempt to bring developers and speculators under democratic popular control. Still, increasingly, speculators, developer-speculators, and bankers seem to be targeted by community groups for more democratic control. A class-based planning theory and expanded advocacy planning might assist such community groups to be more successful in their struggles with powerful capitalist land-orientedactors.

Notes

1. A partial exception to this statement is the work of Henry Molotch (see Molotch 1976).

2. An earlier version of this typology appeared in a joint paper (McAdams and Feagin 1980) with D. Claire McAdams. McAdams has done pioneering work on shopping center development in the United States.

3. This discussion is based on information presented in a "60 Minutes" news report, CBS News, 29 March 1981.

References

Ackerman, J., M. Clawson, and M. Harris, eds. 1962. *Land Economics Research*. Baltimore: Johns Hopkins University Press.

Berry, B. J. L, and J. D. Kasarda. 1977. *Contemporary Urban Ecology*. New York: Macmillan.

Burchell, R. W. and J. W. Hughes. 1978. "Introduction: planning theory in the 1980s—a search for future directions." In *Planning Theory in the 1980s,* edited by R. W. Burchell and G. Sternlieb. New Brunswick, N.J.: Rutgers Center for Urban Policy Research, xv + liii.

Castells, M. 1976. "Is there an urban sociology?" In *Urban Sociology,* edited by C. G. Pickvance, 33–59. London: Tavistock.

Clawson, M. 1971. *Suburban Land Conversion in the United States.* Baltimore: Johns Hopkins University Press.

Clay, L. 1979. *Neighbourhood Renewal.* Lexington, Mass.: D.C. Heath.

Downie, L. 1974. *Mortgage on America.* New York: Praeger.

Edel, M. 1976. "Marx's theory of rent: Urban applications." *Kapitalistate* 4–5:100–24.

Firey, W. 1947. *Land Use in Central Boston.* Westport, Conn.: Greenwood Press.

Flahive, M., and S. Gordon. 1979. *Residential Displacement in Denver.* Denver, Colo.: Council Committee on Housing.

Form, W. 1954. "The place of social structure in the determination of land use." *Social Forces* 32:317–23.

George, H. edn 1962. *Progress and Poverty.* New York: Robert Schalkenbach Foundation.

Gist, N. P., and S. F. Fava. 1974. *Urban Society.* New York: Thomas Y. Crowell.

Goodkin, M. 1974. *When Real Estate and Home Building Become Big Business: Mergers, Acquisitions, and Joint Ventures.* Boston: Cahners Books.

Hadden, J. K., L. H. Masotti, and C. J. Larson. 1967. *Metropolis in Crisis.* Itasca, Ill.: F. E. Peacock.

Hartman, C. 1974. *Yerba Buena.* San Francisco: Glide Publications. 1980: "Social planning and the political planner." In Burchell, R.W. and Sternlieb, G., editors, *Planning Theory in the 1980s,* edited by R. W. Burchell and G. Sternlieb, 73–82. New Brunswick, N.J.: Rutgers Center for Urban Policy Research.

Harvey, D. 1973. *Social Justice and the City.* London: Edward Arnold; Baltimore: Johns Hopkins University Press.

Hoppenfeld, M. 1978. "Planners as architects of the built environment—or vice versa." In *Planning Theory in the 1980s,* edited by R. W. Burchell and G. Sternlieb, 17–27. New Brunswick, N.J.: Rutgers Center for Urban Research.

Lamarche, F. 1976. "Property development and the economic foundations of the urban question." In *Urban Sociology,* edited by C. G. Pickvance, 85–118. London: Tavistock.

Lindeman, B. 1976. "Anatomy of land speculation." *Journal of the American Institute of Planners* (April) 142–52.

Lorimer, J. 1978. *The Developers.* James Lorimer Ltd.

McAdams, D. "Powerful actors in public land use decision-making processes." University of Texas, Doctoral Dissertation.

McAdams, D., and J. R. Feagin. 1980. "A power-conflict approach to urban land use." Austin, Texas, unpublished monograph.

McHarg, I. 1978. "Ecological planning: the planner as catalyst." In *Planning Theory in the 1980s,* edited by R. W. Burchell and G. Steinlieb, 13–15. New Brunswick, N.J.: Rutgers Center for Urban Policy Research.

Meyer, P. 1979. Land rush. *Harper's* 258 (January): 45–60.

Molotch, H. 1976. "The city as a growth machine." *American Journal of Sociology* 82 (September): 309–22.

Mumford, L. 1961. *The City in History*. New York: Harcourt, Brace and World.

National Urban Coalition. 1978. *Displacement: City Neighbourhoods in Transition*. Washington, D.C.: National Urban Coalition.

Park, R., E. W. Burgess, and R. D. McKenzie. 1925. *The City*. Chicago: University of Chicago Press.

Pattison, T. 1977. "The process of neighborhood upgrading and gentrification." MIT, Department of City Planning, Master's Thesis.

Reissman, L. 1964. *The Urban Process*. Glencoe: Free Press.

Richards, C., and J. Rowe. 1977. "Restoring a city." *Working Papers for a New Society* (Winter): 54–61.

Sakolski, A. M. 1932. *The Great American Land Bubble*. New York: Harper and Brothers.

Sakolski, A.M. 1957. *Land Tenure and Land Taxation in America*. New York: Robert Schalkenbach Foundation.

Sawers, L. 1975. "Urban form and the mode of production." *Review of Radical Political Economy* 7 (Spring): 52–68.

Schnore, L. F. 1967. "One the spatial structure of cities in the two Americas." In P. M. Hauser, and L. F. Schnore, *The Study of Urbanization*. New York: John Wiley, 347–98.

Schwirian, K. P. 1974. "Some recent trends and methodological problems in urban ecological research." In *Comparative Urban Structure,* edited by K. P. Schwirian, 7–18. Lexington, Massachusetts: D.C. Heath.

Sirjamaki, J. 1964. *The Sociology of Cities*. New York: Random House.

Smith, N. 1981. "Gentrification and uneven development." Baltimore: Johns Hopkins University, unpublished paper.

Sternlieb, G. 1966; *The Tenement Landlord*. New Brunswick, N.J.: Rutgers University Press.

Thomas, D. L. 1977. *Lords of the Land*. New York: G. P. Putnam's Sons.

Tilly, C. 1974. *An Urban World*. Boston: Little, Brown & Co.

U.S. Department of Housing and Urban Development. 1979. *Displacement Report*. Washington, D.C.: U.S. Government Printing Office.

Wade, R. C. 1959. *The Urban Frontier*. Chicago: University of Chicago Press.

Webber, M. M. 1964: The urban place and the nonplace urban realm. In M. M. Webber et al., *Explorations into Urban Structure*. Philadelphia: University of Pennsylvania Press, 79–153.

Zeitz, E. 1979. *Private Urban Renewal*. Lexington, Mass.: D.C. Heath.

6

Irrationality in Real Estate Investment:
The Case of Houston

Joe R. Feagin

Numerous Marxist theorists have written about the irrationality of accumulation and investment processes under capitalism. Overaccumulation of capital in certain enterprises and business sectors leads to a quest for new outlets for investment of surplus capital. But where should that surplus capital be invested for the best possible return? The urban real estate sector has in recent decades been a major part of the answer. Real estate in the United States has attracted foreign as well as domestic investors, because overaccumulation is a worldwide problem. Latin American, Asian, and European investors have poured large amounts of money into an array of land and building projects in cities from Boston to Houston to Los Angeles and San Francisco. While it makes sense for individual capitalists to seek the best return on their money in this fashion, the result is often highly irrational investment behavior considered from a collective capitalist or general public welfare point of view. And given the *fixed* character of such investments, these irrationalities are literally enshrined in concrete.

The overbuilding of Houston in the last two decades is a striking example of how overaccumulation leads to irrational investment behavior. The excessive investment in buildings in Houston has exaggerated the up-and-down swings in the local business cycle. This exaggeration of cycles is not new, of

---

This chapter is reprinted with minor revisions from Feagin, Joe R. 1987. "Irrationality in real estate investment: The case of Houston," *The Monthly Review,* 38 (March 1987): 18–27.

course, since it has been observed in a number of cities since the Great Depression. But it is certainly new to Houston, which *Fortune* magazine in 1939
called the "city the depression missed."

Office Building Boom and Bust in the Cities

The dominance of skyscrapers and smaller office buildings is new in all but
a few American cities, most tall glass-and-steel boxes having been built
since the Second World War. In building industry handbooks, office buildings are described as structures where business services are provided or
where information is processed. But they are more than that. The largest
buildings reflect the shift from an older competitive capitalism of smaller
firms to the modern monopoly capitalism of huge firms described by Baran
and Sweezy in their classic 1966 book *Monopoly Capital*. A huge U.S. real
estate industry—composed of developers, builders, bankers, and realtors—
has grown up to meet the perceived needs of giant industrial and commercial
corporations.

Between the 1960s and the early 1980s there was a heavy demand from corporations for space. In the 1975–81 period major cities—including Seattle,
San Francisco, Los Angeles, Phoenix, Dallas, Houston, Denver, Atlanta, Miami, Washington, Chicago, and New York—were experiencing shortages of
downtown office space. According to one major business survey, the average
vacancy rate in buildings in the United States and Canada declined throughout
the 1970s. But by 1982–87 the office construction boom gave way to a bust in
numerous cities. This time real estate developers and investors were caught in
the general economic downturn of the early 80s. Many industrial companies
were forced to cancel plans to expand, to occupy new offices, or to move to
new areas of the country. Those that could still move began seriously consid-
ering office space outside the expensive downtown areas. These decisions
meant less demand for the formerly soaring office building construction and
leasing. Journals such as *Newsweek* and *Business Week* were reporting a long-
term "office glut."

Houston, now the nation's fourth-largest city, and the one with the longest
uninterrupted record of economic growth, was the nation's premier boom
town, in both population growth and building construction, until the dramatic
post-1982 bust. Houston began in the 1830s as a speculative real estate venture by two Yankee capitalists seeking to make their fortunes by selling
marshy land to unwary investors and settlers. From 1850 to 1980 the average
increase in population per decade for the city of Houston was 60 percent: from
1910 to 1980 the total increase was from 78,800 to 1.6 million.

Houston has been called the "oil capital of the world." Beginning in the
1920s, investment in oil, gas, and petrochemical companies grew to the point

where now 34 of the nation's 35 largest oil companies have major administrative, research, and production facilities in the Houston area, as do hundreds of smaller oil and gas companies and thousands of support firms. One quarter of U.S. oil refining capacity is centered in this Gulf Coast area, together with half of U.S. petrochemical production.

The rapidly expanding oil-petrochemical economy not only has attracted non-oil companies but also has motivated banks and insurance firms to invest in major development projects, including office towers, industrial parks, shopping centers, and residential subdivisions.

Perhaps the most dramatic aspect of this explosive growth is in office buildings. During the present century more than 470 major office buildings have been constructed, with most (401) of those built in the years 1971–85. The accompanying table provides some basic information on this remarkable flow of capital into these major real estate investments.[1] The recent pattern is one of an oscillating number of buildings completed each year. There is a general increase from 1971 to 1983, followed by a precipitous decline. In 1971, 19 large office buildings were completed; this figure drops to a low of 7 and 8 in 1974 and 1975, respectively, then begins to climb more or less regularly to a peak of 79 in 1982. Since 1982 a drastic decline has occurred, to a low point of two buildings expected to be completed in 1987.

The total square footage of office space has increased dramatically over time: 1949—6.9 million, 1969—28.6 million, 1986—163.5 million. Houston's present 163.5 million square feet places it near the top of all U.S. cities. When compared to Philadelphia, with only 41.8 million square feet, or Boston, with 58.4 million square feet, the immensity of Houston's office construction becomes clear.

The three million people in Houston's Standard Metropolitan Area are distributed over nearly 600 square miles, a decentralized sprawl city. There are eighteen definable business areas with a concentration of major office buildings, most of which are located in northwest and southwest corridors, in the airport area, and downtown. This highly decentralized pattern is distinctive. While other major cities have a few large buildings outside the downtown area, Houston has many. This is the result of a number of factors, including the huge volume of real estate investment activity in the 1970s and early 1980s, the absence of zoning laws, the significant amount of cheap land, and the early development of a massive freeway system.

Among these 18 major business centers, the downtown area is the largest, with 34 million square feet of office space in 1982. The tallest building west of the Mississippi river is located in this downtown area, the seventy-five-story Texas Commerce Bank building, whose developer/owners are Gerald P. Hines Interests, one of the nation's two largest real estate developers, and the Texas Commerce Bank, one of the nation's largest banks and a recent merger candidate for Chemical Bank.

Table 6.1. Major Office Buildings and Crude Oil Prices (Houston Metropolitan Area)

Date	Large Office Bldgs	Crude Oil Price (Bbl)
1971	19	$ 3.39
1972	11	3.39
1973	13	3.89
1974	7	6.87
1975	8	7.67
1976	11	8.19
1977	21	8.57
1978	16	9.00
1979	21	12.64
1980	32	21.59
1981	46	31.77
1982	79	28.52
1983	75	26.19
1984	27	25.91 (Oct.)
1985	15	24.00
1986	7*	17.00 (March)
1987	2*	—

Single-tenant buildings not included.
*Expected date of completion

Oil and gas companies of all sizes, together with allied service firms, require large amounts of space for their management, financial, exploration, research, marketing, and accounting operations. In the early 1980s, about 61 percent of the office space in the central business district was occupied by energy firms, with related banks, law firms, and accounting firms occupying another 30 percent. In 1982, thirty-three corporations with offices in downtown Houston each employed more than 1,000 people.

An Overburdened Office Market

The boom and bust in office building since 1978 is a classic example of speculative investment run amok. Thus, the percentage of vacant office space in Houston soared from 2.5 percent in 1978 to 24 percent in 1985. Vacancy rates above 6 to 10 percent are generally considered unprofitable; hence, with one quarter of its office space empty, many of Houston's building owners are losing money.

Houston, it is important to note, is not the only city with excess office space. The average vacancy rate of offices in U.S. cities was 20 percent in 1985. Only

Manhattan and the Los Angeles downtown area had profitable occupancy rates. The lowest occupancy rates in the United States are now in the formerly prosperous Sunbelt cities, not only the oil-linked cities of Dallas, New Orleans, Denver, and Houston, but also Miami and suburban San Francisco.

In cities like Houston a game of "musical buildings" has been created, in which many completed before 1982 have high vacancy rates, while newer buildings have lower vacancy rates, often by taking tenants away from older buildings. This has resulted in a citywide chessboard of occupied and unoccupied space. Another consequence of overbuilding has been a sharp increase in concessions to tenants. One recent survey of corporate tenants in six downtown buildings in Houston found that 86 percent had received some type of rent concession. Half had received free rent for six to twelve months, and some benefited from lower rent payments, old-lease buyouts, or moving expenses. Numerous companies were leasing more office space than they currently needed, causing the real vacancy rate to be higher than the official rate. Courting tenants with concessions has become commonplace in cities across the United States. Even in San Francisco, where in the early 1980s tenants were paying whatever office developers asked, tenants can now routinely get eighteen months free rent on a ten-year lease.

Another response to the overbuilding has been an increase in aggressive courting of real estate brokers and potential tenants by developer-owners. Note, for example, the actions of a developer of an eleven-story building a great distance from downtown Houston. Although his building is in a depressed office market area, it is 85 percent leased. This development firm threw a lavish opening party for its new building, replete with a safari theme, a wild-game dinner, and champagne. No fewer than 1,200 people drove, many a long distance, to the party. The firm had also distributed Tiffany brass clocks to brokers, lenders, and others when it announced the plan to construct the building.

Another aspect of the present situation is that much vacant space is in lower quality or less desirable buildings. The office building boom created millions of square footage in poorly constructed buildings. In recent years developers have built many brand-new, but second-rate, office buildings, with construction so poor that they are unlikely to be able to overcome their high vacancy rates any time soon.

One suggested explanation for the rampant Houston building boom is that it involved the direct recycling of petrodollars gained from the nearly tenfold rise in the price of a barrel of crude oil in the 1970s. As can be seen in the preceding table, that price increased from $3.39 a barrel in 1971 to $31.77 a barrel in 1981. It would seem logical that the city often called the "oil capital of the world" would prosper physically, as well as in economic terms, as the profusion of petrodollars sought out new investments. Yet knowledgeable lending officials in Houston point out that this explanation is not accurate. Petrodollars have been involved in some real estate projects, but most of the money capital, they say, has come from a variety of other nonoil investors and lenders. The effect of the oil boom was indirect; it created an image of oil-driven prosperity which attracted outside investors.

Basically, the office glut was created by financial capital, which is said in the nation's business newspapers to have "poured too much money into the real estate market." In particular, outside lenders—including S&Ls, banks, and insurance companies—channeled much money into the greater Houston area, accepting what the local developers told them about the viability of what were often questionable projects. The situation was one of "too many dollars chasing too few deals." During the building expansion at least sixty major outside lenders were active in Houston. Speaking about the behavior of finance capital during the boom, a prominent broker explained that

> when there is money to build buildings, developers will arise to relieve the banks of those monies. . . . The source of this funding did not come from [Texas banks]. . . . It came from outside lenders . . . basically responding not to any market place, but to a need to lend funds, and to the fact that certain parties had a need to buy a product.[2]

In the same vein, a former Citibank executive pointed out that finance capital often has a herd mentality; lenders move to "hot" cities. Houston, he said, became a money center with "plenty of money available at the best possible world rates."[3]

Another factor is that in Houston, as in all U.S. cities, much commercial construction is "tax-driven." The tax advantages in office towers come from the eighteen-year or less rapid depreciation allowed under current U.S. tax laws. Changes in tax laws between 1969 and 1981 reduced the depreciation period for real property. Investors in a high tax bracket can receive large depreciation deductions (giving large tax savings) for investments in office buildings; developers consequently seek out well-off people willing to invest in office buildings. The new 1987 tax law significantly reduces the number of real estate tax shelters, which should have a depressing effect on the movement of spare capital into office construction.

Houston is part of a world market: European and Middle Eastern firms and individuals have also invested substantially in Houston real estate. In the late 1970s and early 1980s, this city was second only to New York as a place for foreign capital to invest in real estate, including office buildings. By 1980 U.S. real estate accounted for one-third of all foreign investment in the United States. In the early 1980s foreign investors said to their brokers, according to one expert, "if it's in Houston, I want it."

Hot and Cold Cities

It might be expected that decisions to invest in major office building projects would involve careful research by well-heeled investors into the market situation to assess the need for more office space in a particular urban setting, as well as careful analysis of what other development capitalists are doing. Yet discussion with numerous real estate operators and experts has revealed to me that much depends on the kind of reputation particular cities have for being "hot" or "cold" for investments. It appears that cities gain "hot" images based on how aggressively and successfully they are advertised and marketed by the local business elites ("growth coalitions") and how they are assessed by major corporate location firms or by the business media such as the *Wall Street Journal* or *Business Week*. As a result, development and finance capitalists in U.S. cities frequently make decisions about urban development projects which are indeed very irrational from a tough cost-accounting approach. As they themselves have noted in the business press, many development decisions are made on the basis of seat-of-the-pants "feel" and "image." There is thus a social psychological dimension to capital investments flowing into the "secondary circuit" of real estate. One expert in Houston recently noted in the *Houston Business Journal* that "for what would seem to be sophisticated business, real estate is awfully unsophisticated. It's done by feel or by stomach. Buildings go up and are financed and designed without a lot of research." Real estate investment is to a substantial degree based on a type of herd psychology and on speculative guesses about what inflation and leasing rates will be over a period of three to thirty years.

Conclusion

This flow of worldwide surplus into the real estate investment circuit is an illustration of a concept first delineated by the maverick French Marxist Henri Lefebvre and recently developed by British geographer David Harvey in his 1985 book *The Urbanization of Capital*.[4] Harvey's discussion of the "secondary circuit of capital" encompasses capital flows into the built environments essential to production (e.g., factories) and to consumption (e.g., houses). In Harvey's view there must be a surplus of capital in the primary circuit of commodity production in order for capital to flow into these investments in the built environment. Overproduction of commodities and overaccumulation of money capital are chronic problems in a capitalist system. Surplus money capital is typically recirculated through a variety of financial institutions. A major aspect of Harvey's argument about the secondary circuit is that investment in real estate is undertaken not only for corporate use-value reasons, but also for purely financial reasons, that is, solely in a quest for the highest rate of return on investment. The Houston experience strongly supports Harvey's argument.

By 1980, if not before, the behavior of capitalists investing in Houston and other metropolitan real estate markets was often irrational from the point of view of business requirements for office space, as well as from the point of view of the "human needs" of the general public. Yet investors continued pouring money capital into highly questionable projects. The resulting intense competition led to a huge oversupply of office space, a recurring feature of urban capitalism. This process is driven by a number of factors, including the availability of surplus capital and its search for maximum returns, development capitalists aggressively seeking financing for projects to keep their firms in operation, tax laws encouraging the proliferation of office buildings created as tax shelters, and a particularly volatile type of "herd psychology."

Notes

1. Data in the table are drawn from the following: Department of Energy, Energy Information Administration. 1985. *Monthly Energy Review*. January; "1986 guide to office space." 1986 *Houston 57* (February): 5–54; Research Division, Houston Chamber of Commerce. 1984. "A year-by-year survey of Houston office building development: 1949–1985. *Houston Business Journal*. 30 July, 26c.

2. "Forget the gloom and doom, opportunities still abound." 1985. *Houston Business Journal*, 11 February.

3. Ibid.

4. Lefebvre, Henri. 1970. *La revolution urbaine*. Paris: Gallimard; Harvey, David. 1985. *The Urbanization of Capital*. Baltimore: Johns Hopkins University Press. For an incisive theoretical critique of Harvey's broad theoretical analysis, see the following: Mark Gottdiener. 1985. *The Social Production of Space*. Austin: University of Texas Press, 96–100.

III

THE POLITICAL DIMENSION
OF CITY DEVELOPMENT

In this section I offer three assessments of the role of government actors and agents in the creation of cities under capitalism. Chapter 7, "The Corporate Center Strategy: The State in Central Cities," is a book review essay in which I develop some ideas about what is sometimes called "the corporate center strategy" in the urban literature. This refers to the strategy of rebuilding downtown areas in the interest of corporate elites and their government allies. Drawing heavily on the work of the Fainsteins, Richard Hill, Dennis Judd, Michael Smith, Roger Friedland, John Mollenkopf, and Todd Swanstrom, I show how recent work on the national government's involvement in shaping modern capitalism needs to be brought down to the city level. The reviewed research shows that powerful economic elites draw heavily on local governments to build and rebuild centers of cities, more or less as they desire. For example, these business coalitions have used government urban renewal programs to displace residents of color and to bring white-run businesses and white residents back into central cities. This article calls for a comprehensive theory of local government (yet to be completed) that recognizes the different levels of government, as well as the economic factions, involved in corporate center strategies of urban development.

Chapter 8 is a contribution to a deeper understanding of the ways in which specific governmental programs and actions, such as land-use zoning, have been shaped in the interest of the dominant real estate groups imbedded in the urban-capitalist system. In this contribution to the new political-economy paradigm I explore how the exchange-value concerns of developers and specula-

167

tors come into conflict with the use-value concerns of citizens interested more in the utility of urban spaces than in profitability. Here I update my critique of the ecological paradigm and show in detail how, and how fast, capital from the primary circuit is "valorized" in urban spaces. The bulk of the article is concerned with land-control measures such as zoning laws now found in virtually all U.S. cities. Central city merchants, suburban developers, and real estate brokers have played critical roles in the emergence of zoning and planning regulations. The data here provide a corrective to the notion that state intervention and the "free market" are in opposition. Indeed, most zoning and planning regulations—including exclusionary racial zoning—were initially proposed or substantially created by those representing dominant real estate interests in the cities, although there have been conflicts between the smaller builders and the larger land-development interests over the character of this zoning and planning. The concluding section of this article explores ideas for democratization of land-use controls that would accent the use-value interests (for example, concern with home and families) of ordinary urbanites and their communities.

Chapter 9 revisits the comparative study of Houston and Aberdeen, this time with a close look at the impact of oil-related economic and real estate development in the two regions. I show in some detail the range and severity of the many social costs that have stemmed from overinvestment and the associated boom town growth in the two metropolitan areas. These problems have included severely overburdened sewer and water systems, overcrowded schools, underdeveloped roads, and many insufficient public services, such as too few or inadequate schools and recreational facilities. Houston, the much larger city, has had the more severe social costs. One reason for this has been the lack of any zoning laws and the much weaker urban planning system in the Houston area, compared to the more extensive planning system in Aberdeen.

Ironically, for some years Houston has been held up by political and capitalistic elites in cities across the globe as an example of how urban development should be done under the free-market values currently in vogue among elites. A closer look at Houston, however, will show the long-term catastrophe that such capitalistic values can bring for the ordinary residents of cities.

7

The Corporate Center Strategy: The State in Central Cities

Joe R. Feagin

Fainstein, Susan S., Norman I. Fainstein, Richard Child Hill, Dennis Judd, and Michael Peter Smith, *Restructuring the City: The Political Economy of Urban Redevelopment* (New York: Longman, 1983), 296 pp.

Friedland, Roger, *Power and Crisis in the City: Corporations, Unions, and Urban Policy* (New York: Schocken Books, 1983), 248 pp.

Mollenkopf, John, *The Contested City* (Princeton: Princeton University Press, 1983), 328 pp.

Swanstrom, Todd, *The Crisis of Growth Politics: Cleveland, Kucinich, and the Challenge of Urban Populism* (Philadelphia: Temple University Press, 1985), 307 pp.

These four important books contribute to the development of a more adequate view of the state and urban redevelopment. While there has recently been an explosion of theoretical work on the state and capitalism, very little of that theorizing has targeted the city or the local state. This theoretical neglect of the local state can be corrected by drawing on the rich empirical analyses presented by the eight authors of the books listed above. All of these authors deal with the redevelopment of central cities, with the "corporate center strategy" and the large-scale state assistance required to implement and to ameliorate the consequences of that major urban restructuring strategy. While each of the

This chapter is reprinted with minor revisions from Feagin, Joe R. 1986. "The corporate center strategy: The state in central cities," *Urban Affairs Quarterly,* 21 (June): 617–28.

books overlaps to some extent with at least one of the others, each contributes a different piece of the state-urban economy puzzle. The list below provides a summary of these contributions.

The State and the Central City: An Overview

Key Dimensions	*Relevant Authors*
(1) The state responds to the needs of capital (the "corporate center" strategy).	the Fainsteins, Hill, Judd, Smith, Friedland
(2) Capital responds to political entrepreneurs.	Mollenkopf, the Fainsteins
(3) Unions collaborate with capital.	Friedland, Mollenkopf
(4) Minority displacement.	the Fainsteins, Hill, Judd, Smith, Friedland
(5) Minority resistance and riots.	the Fainsteins, Hill, Judd, Smith, Friedland
(6) The local state and the national state.	the Fainsteins, Hill, Judd, Smith, Friedland
(7) State redistributive policies.	Friedland, the Fainsteins, Swanstrom
(8) Organizing populist resistance to the corporate center strategy.	Swanstrom
(9) The global context shapes capital flight.	Hill

It is clear from this listing that a *comprehensive* analysis of the "corporate center" strategy of central city restructuring would include not only the way in which this state strategy was a response to the needs of capital, but also such dimensions as political entrepreneurs, minority displacement and resistance, unions, state levels, the global context, populist resistance, and state redistributive policy. Cities have become arenas of struggle between different levels of the state, different worker groups, and different fractions of capital.

Pluralist theories of urban politics take a beating in these four parallel but distinctive analyses of urban development. In the pluralist paradigm, individual voters and an array of interest groups compete for influence in urban politics within a social system in which there is a general value consensus. Government is seen as a mosaic of agencies which are readily accessible to democratic influence. The structure of political power results from contention among an array of private individuals and interest groups with their own resources and power. Yet these four books show how the pluralist view is contradicted by the empirical realities of urban redevelopment.

In this review essay I will show how the pluralist view is called into question in each case. I will accent the corporate center strategy.

In *The Contested City* John Mollenkopf looks at data on urban programs and urban redevelopment, particularly for Boston and San Francisco. Mollenkopf argues that neo-Marxist analysis and pluralist analysis are wrong: "This study rejects the two dominant traditions for explaining the structure of political power: the notion that some controlling 'power structure' or capitalist elite intervenes to determine what decisions are made, or, alternatively, that they result from the contention among private interest groups" (p. 9). Mollenkopf, in contrast with all the other authors reviewed here, views politics and government as "independent driving forces" which can override economic interests and diverse interest groups. Economic factors are mediated through and influenced by the political system. Particularly important are the "political entrepreneurs" at the federal and local levels. Democratic presidents have led the progrowth coalition at the national level, since urban development and other social programs have been used by the Democratic party to cement various groups together (e.g., minorities, unions, city machines) to build that modern party. Republican presidents, as a result, have resisted various urban development programs. Democratic leaders also played a critical role as political entrepreneurs building growth coalitions at the local city level. At the city level, no single elite is in control; public actors take the *initiative* in creating the growth-oriented urban programs. Mollenkopf notes that while political entrepreneurs may be dependent on business interests for campaign contributions, they frequently act *against* the interests of business elites.

To document his political entrepreneur theory, Mollenkopf reviews the cases of Boston and San Francisco, where, he argues, four mayors and two prominent urban renewal administrators used their expert political skills, together with help from national political entrepreneurs, to build huge redevelopment programs. The political entrepreneurs were not "class-conscious," but were seeking concrete solutions to the general societal problem of decaying cities. Mollenkopf traces the decline of large-scale urban redevelopment programs both to the Republican opposition in the Eisenhower, Nixon, and Ford years and to the opposition from the central-city poor and working-class elements of the Democratic coalition which did not benefit from urban renewal.

In my judgment, the most valuable part of the *The Contested City* is not the discussion of political entrepreneurs, which, as I will show below, is flawed, but rather the brilliant discussion of certain trends in U.S. cities since the 1930s. Mollenkopf tracks the huge array of governmental programs which were developed during the Roosevelt, Truman, and Johnson years and shows how programs such as the 1930 Public Works Administration rebuilt urban areas, including billions of dollars for bridges, roads, airports, and sewer projects. Mollenkopf is the first to emphasize the massive recapitalization of U.S.

industry in cities under the War Production Board and allied wartime agencies. Additions to the U.S. physical plants in 1942–44 amounted to about $37 billion, only a little less than the *total* value of U.S. manufacturing facilities in 1939! About $14 billion went to build military facilities and housing, while $23 billion went for new manufacturing facilities. These plant investments disproportionately favored certain cities, with Detroit, Chicago, New York, and Pittsburgh among the top cities, as one might expect, but with Sunbelt cities like Houston, Dallas, and Los Angeles also receiving huge per capita infusions of federal investment capital. My own research on wartime expenditures in the greater Houston area indicates that a substantial portion of that city's industrial base—particularly the petrochemical industry—was laid during World War II with huge infusions of federal investment capital. Yet this infusion of capital was directed and influenced by corporate executives and elites working behind and through federal war production agencies. This wartime operation of business elites through national-level government agencies presents some problems for Mollenkopf's excessively political analysis.

The empirical data on U.S. cities and governmental agencies do not support an "independent state" view of the state under capitalism, both at the national and at the local level. Even in Mollenkopf's two major examples, Boston and San Francisco, there is substantial evidence of small business elites *initiating* and *guiding* urban development. Political entrepreneurs are important and should not be neglected, but they are not independent forces. In Boston a group of banking, retail, and industrial capitalists, called "The Vault," played a major role in shaping the city government's fiscal and redevelopment activities. The mayor of the city (Collins) implemented their advice and was a broker who worked with union groups, but he was hardly an example of an independent political entrepreneur who initiated the idea of downtown redevelopment. In San Francisco a number of capitalist elite groups, including the 1946 Bay Area Council, formulated the basic ideas about redevelopment and guided later development. An "independent state" theory, at the very least, does not fit Boston and San Francisco very well; and in many Sunbelt cities, such as Dallas, Houston, and Los Angeles, downtown redevelopment programs fit an orthodox "instrumentalist" state theory, since local capitalists working through agencies such as the Chamber of Commerce or the (Dallas) Citizens' Council have directed government in the area of redevelopment and in many other spheres. Independent political entrepreneurs are of modest importance at the local level in these latter cities.

The other three books recognize the importance of the state and political entrepreneurs, but they also point up the dominant power of capitalist elites in urban development. One of the best theoretical assessments of urban redevelopment programs can be found in the concluding chapter of *Restructuring the City*. Susan and Norman Fainstein track the historical development of urban renewal; they note the shift from an early concern for housing working-class families (a labor-business coalition backed the 1949–54 urban renewal legislation) to the reality of massive clearance followed by high-rise commercial, governmental, and luxury apartment construction. As the renewal programs evolved in cities across the nations, they were used by local white authorities to displace minority residents and to bring whites back into central city areas. The heavy redevelopment emphasis on expanding office and luxury retail facilities in downtown areas to attract corporations and suburbanites illustrates this point.

However, the availability of federal funds for redevelopment was only a necessary condition. Local business action was necessary to bring programs to particular cities. In virtually every case, urban growth coalitions, involving close cooperation between local government officials and a business elite, have been behind central city redevelopment programs. In San Francisco, Boston, and Detroit business groups were dominant, while in New Haven and New Orleans mayors helped to organize business coalitions.

Local governments depend heavily on taxes paid by affluent urbanites, so they try to attract and keep affluent whites. Since private enterprises provide most jobs, city governments must attract new private investment using subsidies and tax concession. Business elites finance and dominate the political system as well as the mass media. Given these conditions, local governments facing central city decline have tried to bring corporations and the affluent back, to displace and remove low-income and minority households, and to maintain residential segregation. Attempts to restructure central cities along these lines regularly bring local growth coalitions into conflict with their poor and working-class residents. There may be conflict over construction of manufacturing plants (with blue-collar jobs) and of office towers (with white-collar jobs). Since local governments are composed of and mostly represent business elites and affluent urbanites, they "significantly advance lower-class and working-class interests in redevelopment only when compelled to do so by political movements, protest, and social disorder" (p. 257). Such mobilization did eventually force changes in the massive clearance approach to urban renewal. But citizen protest is resisted. In response, capital mobilizes its own agents to influence local governments. Millions have been spent to stop rent-control movements in numerous cities, to promote elite projects (such as BART in San Francisco and the Superdome in New Orleans), and to overthrow populist and progressive elected governments, as happened with the Kucinich government in Cleveland.

The Fainsteins suggest that we have seen three types of local governments since the 1950s: In the 1950s, *directive* governments planned large-scale redevelopment in the interest of upper- and middle-income groups, with no real opposition; from the mid-1960s to the mid-1970s, many urban governments were *concessionary*, forced by protests of the era to consider the needs of their low-income populations; from the mid-1970s to the 1980s, the *conserving* governments in cities paid more attention to low-income needs than in the 1950s, but also paid more attention to facilitating private enterprise. This typology fits certain northern cities with protest movements, but does not fit the histories of numerous other cities, particularly cities in the Sunbelt.

In an opening essay the Fainsteins frame a set of questions originating from the case studies:

1. What conditions give rise to state-sponsored redevelopment action?
2. What class and political conflict conditions shape that redevelopment action?
3. Who wins and who loses in that action?

An article on New Haven by the Fainsteins raises these basic issues. An old manufacturing city in decline, in the 1950s and 1960s New Haven became the leader in state-assisted redevelopment programs. Working-class neighborhoods and old business areas were demolished and replaced with highways, office buildings, garages, and a hotel. Government and university leaders initially took the lead, with substantial support from some (but not all) local capitalists. The government-university-business coalition projects were challenged in the 1960s. Pressures from black communities brought some reforms, including jobs for black professionals and social service contracts for advocacy organizations. Low-income groups had forced some changes, but they were not able to translate their protests into a dominating political position.

Hill's essay on Detroit is one of the best in *Restructuring the City*, in part because it is the only piece that sets the decline of a major city within a *global* context—in this case, the global reorganization of the auto industry. One of the major needs in the area of urban political economy is for more attention to be given to the impact of shifts in the capitalist world system on cities. In the Detroit area, capital and job losses between 1968 and 1977 were colossal; about 200,000 jobs were lost. The response to decline was a downtown redevelopment plan, as in New Haven, but with a significant difference. Business and government leaders worked together "to transform this aging industrial city into a modern corporate image," with a financial and professional services center for auto and related firms, a research and development center, and a luxury shopping complex. A coalition of industrial, commercial, financial, and real estate capitalists was the basic force behind this corporate-center strategy. One result of their actions is the now-ailing Renaissance Center complex. Substantial public aid was provided for a range of business-oriented redevelopment projects. Yet the price to citizens was austerity in the form of reduced social consumption services (so as to lower taxes). Hill's assessment of this restructuring strategy is essentially negative, because it is a *local* strategy for a city that is primarily whipsawed by the national and international reorganization of the auto manufacturing industry.

The article on New Orleans by Michael Peter Smith and Marlene Keller deals with an older southern city which has also seen a business-government growth coalition trying to rebuild a city with severe poverty and race problems. After attempts at massive urban redevelopment (e.g., a riverfront expressway) failed, the growth coalition decided to pursue revitalization projects in selected areas of the city, such as office towers in the central business district. Projects aimed at tourists, such as the 1984 World's Fair buildings, were also subsidized from public funds. Because of the huge population of poor people, government officials had sought out and secured hundreds of millions of dollars in federal monies to keep the city afloat. Reagan cutbacks then had a severe impact on social service and other programs in the city. The huge investments in office construction, in a World's Fair, and in other business-oriented projects did not bring the jobs that the growth coalition had promised. Again urban redevelopment had many losers, with life becoming even harder for low-income residents. Smith and Keller accent the major social costs of redevelopment schemes. Similarly, Judd's analysis of Denver points up major conflicts over urban growth.

In 1955 several dozen downtown business leaders began developing a coordinated strategy for downtown redevelopment. Early projects were traditional slum clearance projects. In 1961–78, the Skyline redevelopment project involved $.6 billion and a dozen new office and hotel buildings in the downtown area. As in most other central cities, these were office, commercial, and hotel projects. In his analysis, Judd also accents the social costs and uneven benefits of Denver's growth, not only the urban sprawl, water problems, and air pollution, but also the racial segregation, poverty, and poor housing. Judd notes the conflict between neighborhoods, including minority neighborhoods, and downtown business interests. A part of a corporate center strategy, central city housing has, as in other urban areas, displaced minority residents.

Taken together, these essays in *Restructuring the City* highlight several of the key dimensions cited in the list above, most notably the local and national states responding to the needs of capital (the corporate center strategy) and the conflict generated by minority displacement and "rewhiteizing" of central city neighborhoods. It is also very clear in these case studies that Mollenkopf's political entrepreneurs are generally not independent driving forces, but rather are one group of local actors typically drawn from, or dependent upon, local business elites. Together they make up the local growth coalitions emphasized by Harvey Molotch.

In *Power and Crisis in the City* Roger Friedland gives particular attention to the role of large multinational corporations and major unions in shaping urban policies. In his view "corporate and union powers shaped local policy responses to local constraints on local economic growth and social control" (p. 207). Friedland shows how the corporate center redevelopment strategy works in cities with powerful corporations; massive slum clearance facilitated office development. Friedland argues that national corporate elites dominated the origins of urban growth programs, with unions playing "second fiddle." Urban renewal programs were conceived by a coalition of liberal and business groups, yet they soon became programs serving office-centered downtown redevelopment. A broad array of capitalistic organizations dominated national urban policy formation, including the National Association of Real Estate Boards and its Urban Land Institute, the Chambers of Commerce, and numerous local corporate organizations from San Francisco to Boston.

Looking at the local level, Friedland quotes the classic conservative analysis of urban renewal of Banfield and Wilson, which notes that "the business elite of the city met privately, agreed upon more or less comprehensive plans for the redevelopment of the central city, and presented the plans to the press, the politicians and the public."

In some cities, corporate executives have participated in these growth coalitions. In others, they have not been active. It is not so much the participation of particular corporate executives that reflects the power of large corporations, but rather is these organizations' broad control over economic and mobilization resources. Powerful corporations not only shape particular local government policies but also shape the structure of the policymaking process itself by shaping economic conditions. Among these are economic growth (new office towers, garages, apartment complexes) and the public costs of economic transformation (loss of industrial jobs, damage to neighborhoods). City governments were used to change the face, the infrastructure, of central cities to facilitate private (office-centered) growth. Friedland points out major differences in corporate and union power to shape local policies and policy-making processes. Unions have power in cities primarily because they can mobilize voters, but corporations control the economic resources which can severely constrain the policy and fiscal successes of local governments. If corporations feel unions are too active in influencing government, for example, they can disinvest and leave a community with fewer jobs.

Among the four books, Friedland gives the most attention to the black ghetto revolts, which threatened the policies of urban economic growth and the strategy of corporations. The redistributive (state) response to the black revolts varied: In cities dominated by corporations, blacks got substantial federal War on Poverty funds, but less local public employment expenditures than in cities where unions were more powerful. In cities with significant union strength, public sector expansion helped unions sustain the electoral support of black constituencies. Those excluded from the growth process, including blacks engaging in rioting, forced governments to respond with state employment and other redistributive services. The growth coalition's central city growth program, with its huge governmental subsidies, had failed to create the forecasted benefits for central city residents. The hostile response of excluded citizens forced federal and local governments to spend large amounts on public services. Friedland makes the important point that urban renewal agencies hurt people, but rarely faced the victims directly. It was other government agencies, the police, public housing, and social service agencies, which had to deal with the casualties of redevelopment. The police and social service agencies are more visible and politicized, while the renewal agencies were generally hidden from the city electorates and worked in close relationship with private investors. Public spending, particularly federal aid to cities, helped to purchase political peace for a while, but eventually cities suffered the heavy fiscal strain of expenditures for policing and social services and of expenditures to aid investors and developers. Friedland's analysis thus accents both the importance of large corporations in the corporate center strategy and also the state redistributive policies highlighted in the list above.

Swanstrom's book, *The Crisis of Growth Politics*, is a case study of "growth politics" in one troubled northern city, Cleveland, Ohio. By "growth politics" Swanstrom means the efforts by local governments to enhance the economic attractiveness of cities for capitalist investors with mobile wealth. In *conservative* growth politics the planning and implementation of growth are left primarily to the private sector; this type of politics rejects redistributive policies benefiting urban folk below the upper-income level. *Liberal* growth politics, in contrast, is a balancing act, providing incentives for wealthy investors interested in growth and also providing some redistributive action for the non-wealthy. Liberal growth politics can be seen in the mayoral regimes of Stokes in Cleveland and of Lindsay in New York. More recently, the swing toward conservative growth politics, with an emphasis on cutting back social and welfare programs, can be seen in the Koch regime in New York. Examining Cleveland in lush detail, Swanstrom shows how, in the 1950s and 1960s, the federal urban renewal program was used to benefit downtown corporate interests at the expense of neighborhoods and minorities. In the 1960s and 1970s, Cleveland's private utility used its monopoly over the production of electricity to try to destroy the local public utility. In the 1970s, the city government gave large tax abatements to assist local developers. And in the 1970s, the populist Kucinich fought against business interests.

Swanstrom profiles the rise and fall of Cleveland's populist mayor, Dennis Kucinich, a man who *rejected* the politics of growth, who abandoned costly urban development policies aimed at attracting corporations downtown, and who, instead, pressed for distributing the limited resources of city government to the people in the form of redistributive government services. Kucinich implemented his populist rhetoric by *killing* state aid for downtown redevelopment. He axed $41 million in federal aid for a downtown "people mover" and a $153.5 million government subsidy for a Republic Steel dock project. He also killed a tax abatement program, which he demonstrated provided little benefit to city residents but good profits for developers. Kucinich also got involved in protecting Cleveland's money-saving public utility (Muny Light) against an orchestrated attack on it by a local private utility and allied local banks. However, Kucinich's aggressive populism was not an alternative political program of well-thought-out economic democracy backed by organization; Kucinich was unable to develop a political organization that could give him control of the city council or public bureaucracy. He was inept at coalition politics and even got into conflict with his natural allies, the neighborhood groups.

In December 1978, the local banks "precipitated the city's default for political reasons: to facilitate the sale of the public utility and help defeat a radical populist mayor" (p. 228). The city government did not go into default for economic reasons; it was forced into default by local banks for *political* reasons. The city was still a good investment for local banks, but local bankers were so upset over Kucinich's actions, particularly in regard to Muny Light, that they gave him the ultimatum of selling Muny or city default. Kucinich refused, and the banks retaliated. A key aspect here, in contrast to European cities, is that local governments in the United States are heavily dependent for credit on private banking firms. Thus, city governments can be manipulated by finance capitalists.

A couple of other contributions by Swanstrom are worth noting here. He makes a useful distinction between two factions with local growth coalitions. Growth coalitions are viewed as alliances between mobile wealth (large industrial corporations) and immobile wealth (real estate interests, banks, utilities, newspapers). The immobile fraction, in particular, seeks to make money off of rising land prices (an "externality") which come from large corporations locating in an area. In addition, he makes the important point that the federal government's important role in shaping cities is often more indirect than direct; that, for example, accelerated depreciation laws render "older buildings in central cities relatively less attractive for investment" and accelerate "the decentralization of jobs and the flight of industry out of central cities" (p. 28). Most prominently, however, Swanstrom adds dimension 8 to the list above; that is, he provides a clear example of people organizing successfully (for a time) to fight a corporate center development strategy.

In conclusion, I would like to emphasize that each of these books accents certain dimensions of the state and local economy drama, key dimensions that need to be integrated into a comprehensive theory of the local state. That task will require a recognition of the relevant structural conditions, such as the need of large corporations for office buildings, for the state-linked corporate center strategy. And it will require a recognition of the different levels (local, regional, national) of the state, as well as of factions (Democratic Party entrepreneurs, multinational corporations, unions) within the national growth coalition, and factions (mobile wealth, immobile wealth) within the local growth coalition. In addition, the dimension of community (class, race, territorial) struggles is accentuated here, particularly in the discussions of minority displacement and protest, and of Dennis Kucinich's populism. Government re-distributive policy, thus, was in part a response to government investment and urban redevelopment policy. And we must not forget the global context in which state development program responses to the needs of capital take place. That context involves a high velocity of investment flows in and out of particular places, a velocity which makes many local growth coalition efforts to get mobile wealth to locate in a place ephemeral, as Hill's discussion of Henry Ford's Renaissance Center redevelopment ("white elephant") project makes very clear.

8

Arenas of Conflict:
Zoning and Land-Use Reform
in Critical Political-Economic Perspective

Joe R. Feagin

An adequate understanding of zoning and related land-use regulation issues requires an assessment of their historical and political-economic contexts. Many
land-use controversies can be viewed as part of a century-long struggle in U.S.
society over conflicting land use interests: "exchange value" interests versus
"use value" interests. Pursuit of divergent land-use goals is imbedded in a capitalistic system with distinctive historical features. That political-economic
system has unrestrained growth as its internal combustion engine. Individual
and corporate investors aggressively pursue their capital investments across
rural and urban space, across national and international space, and even into
outer space.

Land is a unique type of commodity in this expansive investment process.
In terms of the new urban political economy perspective discussed in this
chapter, "exchange value" is often the dominant value in land-related decisions under capitalism. This can be seen in the investment actions of developers and speculators seeking to profit from the sale of and construction on
land itself. But exchange-value decisions often come into conflict with use-

This chapter is reprinted with minor revisions from Feagin, Joe R. 1989. "Arenas of conflict: Zoning and land use reform in critical political-economic perspective," Chap. 3 in *Zoning and The
American Dream*. Chicago: Planners Press.

value concerns emphasizing the utility rather than profitability of space. Such use-value concerns, for example, motivate the decisions and actions of neighborhood residents seeking to keep large-scale urban development projects from intruding on their "home space." Often reflecting use-value concerns, homeowner-supported zoning and similar land-use controls throw up barriers to the unrestrained expansion of capitalistic investment across urban space. Historically, much pressure for such land-use regulation has come from worker-homeowners concerned with protecting family spaces and neighborhoods against economic, social, and racial incursions. Their commitment to the land is primarily to its use value as a place to live and raise a family. Other pressures for land-use controls have stemmed from local capitalists, such as New York merchants concerned with protecting certain Manhattan spaces for profitable marketing uses. In this case the commitment to the land is primarily to its use value as a place to make a manufacturing or commercial profit. Thus, we have three basic interests in land: (1) in the exchange value of the land itself; (2) in the use value of the land for living, family, and neighborhood; and (3) in the use value of the land for commercial or industrial profit making.

The history of successful and unsuccessful attempts at implementing land-use regulations in the United States is one of conflict, which has taken various forms, including racial conflict, interclass conflict, and intraclass conflict. Often the language of struggle is technical and abstract-legal, but the technical terms are sometimes little more than obfuscating euphemisms for the aforementioned land-related interests. Much discussion in the planning, law, and policy literatures on land use emphasizes the need to seek the "public good." Indeed, in the *Euclid* case Ambler Realty viewed the zoning ordinance to be in conflict with the general "public interest," which meant in reality its exchange-value interest. Under capitalism, what is called the public good or the generalized public interest usually is a parochial interest; because of the major and fundamental class (capitalist/worker) and race divisions there can be *no* general consensus on most issues of urban development, environmental degradation, and land-use controls. Conflict of interests is the common condition.

This chapter examines the struggle over land-use controls, particularly zoning, in the light of a critical political-economic perspective. After reviewing the replacement of the now-in-decline urban ecological paradigm with the new urban political-economy paradigm, the chapter examines the development of zoning laws in the early decades and assesses certain conflicts over zoning and land-use controls in recent decades with the aid of insights from the new urban paradigm. The next section provides a critical review of land-use reform proposals in the 1960s and 1970s; a concluding section discusses an alternative slate of reforms with land-use relevance, as seen from a progressive-democratic perspective.

The New Urban Paradigm in the Social Sciences

Mainstream Urban Ecology

In the last decade, the dominance of an urban sociology rooted in the ideas of Herbert Spencer has been challenged by a more critical power-conflict paradigm substantially influenced by a sophisticated reading of Marx, Weber and recent European theorists such as Henri Lefebvre, David Harvey, and Manuel Castells. The first major burst of energy in urban sociology in the United States occurred in the 1920s and 1930s at the University of Chicago. There, researchers such as Robert Park and Ernest W. Burgess drew on nineteenth-century theorists, especially Herbert Spencer, in crafting an ecological framework for viewing urban life. Park and Burgess derived their concept of competitive relations between human groups from the Spencer tradition; competition "invariably tends to create an impersonal social order in which each individual, being free to pursue his own profit . . . invariably contributes . . . to the common welfare" (Park and Burgess 1924, 507). Together with geographers, these urban sociologists viewed this market competition as resulting in unplanned regularities in urban land-use patterns and thus as generative of a social map of concentric *zones* moving out in waves from a central business district. These zones were considered to be naturally segregated areas of location for a diverse human population. Segregation of these zones was viewed as ensuring the "common welfare," another term for the generalized "public interest."

In the decades that followed, most mainstream ecologists have been more interested in broad demographic trends (e.g., the statistical analysis of metropolitan deconcentration) than in the zonal mapping of Burgess; yet for mainstream ecologists today competition, conflict, and accommodation still take place within a "framework of rules approximately the same as those advocated by Herbert Spencer—with room for social evolution, enterprise, and the survival of those most fit to survive" (Greer 1962, 8). A string of important books and articles from the 1950s to the 1970s (Hawley 1950; Berry and Kasarda 1977) established the dominance of this ecology paradigm in the urban social sciences. The basic assumptions of this framework include an uncritical acceptance of a self-regulation market system (viewed as operating for the public good), a pervasive technological determinism, a downplaying of inequality, and a structuralist approach deemphasizing human actors and classes of actors. While there were some early critics (Form 1954), since the 1950s ecologists have dominated much discussion of U.S. cities. In Hawley's theoretically oriented analysis, as well as that of other less theoretical ecologists, the central problem of inquiry is usually how a population organizes itself in adapting to a changing environment ("sustenance organization"). There is a strong concern with (societal) balance and equilibration. This equilibrium-seeking ecological view is an example of what passes for mainstream urban science today, namely, the use of mystifying abstraction and an emphasis on a noncontentious process of adjustment and functional integration to hide the important concrete issues of everyday life arising from the unequal distribution of resources, which both Weber and Marx recognized as a principal driving force of social history. [Gottdiener 1985, 39]

Mainstream ecologists frequently view the functional complexity of cities as determined by transportation and communication technologies. Changes in urban form are explained in terms of some type of technological transformation, particularly in terms of shifts in rail and automotive transport systems. The political-economic history and decision-making context that resulted in the dominance of one type of transport over another is largely ignored. Thus, the role of government (e.g., federal highway programs or the FHA) is often left out of mainstream discussions of such topics as metropolitan deconcentration and suburbanization. However, federal intervention in the form of subsidies of home mortgages, highways, oil production, and decentralized airports significantly encouraged urban deconcentration by reducing the cost of decentralized suburban development. Urban processes such as suburbanization are not simply the natural result of market forces, but rather the result of intentional actions by powerful economic and political actors. Mainstream ecologists have little interest in corporate capitalists or urban residents as actors, preferring instead to emphasize self-regulating markets and market-determined equilibria (cf. Logan and Molotch 1986, 8–9).

Mainstream ecological analysis tends to be conservative in social-justice terms; that is, mainstream analysis tends to see city patterns as inevitable, even as efficient and neutral. The actual patterns of city development are not neutral; they reflect social inequality. The work of mainstream ecologists in sociology, as well as in geography and economics, has on occasion been used to buttress the existing urban system with its built-in social injustices. Thus a 1980 report sponsored by the Carter administration suggested that the federal government should look with favor on corporate growth in Sunbelt cities, to the point of letting northern cities die. Prepared by the President's Commission for a National Agenda for the Eighties (1980), the report called on the federal government to refrain from assisting the declining cities of the north. This market-knows-best view of the Frostbelt-Sunbelt shift in capital investment drew on the work of such ecologists as John Kasarda (1980) and Brian Berry (1982). In some of Kasarda's work, profit-seeking by capitalist entrepreneurs appears to be the intelligent directive force in metropolitan expansion and contraction: "An Urban Policy apropos northern cities should be well informed by the favorable business climate that has fostered so much recent economic development in the South" (1980, 389). Profit is also described as an innate sense that drives entrepreneurs to avoid the "negative externalities" of inner-city locations. The controllers of capital follow the "beneficent" logic of a capitalistic system, which creates good business climates in the Sunbelt cities and which dictates that the needs of working people in northern cities for adequate jobs be sidestepped in the quest for profit. Mainstream ecological analysis has not dealt adequately with such critical factors in urban development as inequality, class conflict, vested capitalist interests operating in space, and government subsidy programs that are pro real estate. In an overview book, *Sociological Human Ecology* (Micklin and Choldin 1984), numerous urban ecologists and demographers review the question of how humans survive in a changing environment, including cities, but with no significant discussion of inequality, conflict, or poverty.

In addition, mainstream ecologists generally neglect the role of the state in urban and regional development. Not one of the dozen authors in the aforementioned Micklin and Choldin collection discusses issues of government or politics. Earlier books by Hawley (1950) and Berry and Kasarda (1977) give brief attention to such topics as the effect of population shifts on local governments or government housing policies, but no serious attention to the growing and extensive role of government intervention in shaping urban economies. There is an interesting contrast between contemporary ecologists and earlier ecologists such as Park and Burgess. The latter go beyond a strict laissez-faire view to argue that the growth of people, communication, and organizations in cities has so increased mutual interdependence that some state intervention is necessary. Park and Burgess had a Darwinist view of the urban scene, but a "reform Darwinism" or a "corporate-liberal" view which accepted the necessity of an independent state adjudicating conflict and protecting essential values such as private property (Park and Burgess 1924; 512, 558–559). The reason for this emphasis is that Park and Burgess argued that in periods of rapid population growth competition is converted into conflict; the expansion of judicial and other governmental institutions are necessary to mediate this conflict. Many contemporary ecologists, in contrast, seem to have moved away from this corporate-liberal framework back to the neo-individualist framework of the nineteenth century.

The New Urban Political Economy

By the mid-1970s, a number of European social scientists had published critical assessments of the ecology paradigm (Harvey 1973; Castells 1977). The winds of paradigmatic change had blown across the Atlantic; by the 1980s this European influence was one of several important ingredients in the maturing of the new urban paradigm. Over the past decade much published work in urban social science has directly challenged the fundamental assumptions and explanatory schemes of the mainstream ecological paradigm. To take one important example, Gottdiener (1985) develops a new sociological framework following the lead of Henry Lefebvre, a French urbanist who has accented space as a central feature of modern capitalism and who has portrayed the users of urban space as caught in a web of economic, political, and cultural forces. Gottdiener argues that spatial production is the material manifestation of complex political and economic processes associated with phases of capitalist development. Sociospatial patterns are the outcome of the many complex contradictions in capitalistic development, but not always the direct result of a particular capitalist's actions. What is crucial here is that the "valorization of capital" requires a spatial complex and that class conflict and capital accumulation do not occur in space, but rather they are about space.

The new urban analysts examine the processes and contradictions of capital accumulation in direct relation to urban spatial development. Prototypically, accumulation by a small capitalist elite involves mobilizing and transforming the inputs for production and then selling the output of that production, with the profit from the sale cycled back into production. Investment and concern for exchange value are the guiding forces behind this forever-expansive accumulation process. Since even in this contemporary period of oligopoly capitalism there are usually at least a few corporations in competition in most industrial and other sectors, capitalists are action-oriented and seek investments and profits by transforming labor processes, generating supplies of labor, increasing capital goods, and transforming rural and urban space. The constant renewal of profits is at the heart of this process; profits are invested and reinvested, thus generating change. Late capitalism is not a post-industrial society, as analysts such as Daniel Bell have suggested. Rather, the modern U.S. economy is one which for the first time in history has a condition of generalized industrialization, an economy characterized by the generalization and expansion of mechanization, standardization, overspecialization of labor, and the concentration of capital in virtually all sectors (Mandel 1978). Indeed, the extension of these industrialization, mechanization, and concentration processes to previously neglected areas such as agriculture and urban real estate development is a major characteristic of the current period.

Central in shaping the sociospatial patterns of cities is the development sector of capital (McAdams 1980; Feagin 1983; Gottdiener 1985). Since the 1940s, the development process has involved at least five major categories of development-related decisions — corporate location, land ownership, land development, building construction, and land and construction financing. Some land-oriented entrepreneurs and companies specialize in one area, such as land ownership, but most such companies are multifaceted. Numerous industrial corporations, such as Exxon, have added real estate development subsidiaries in recent decades. Many land-use actors operate in dozens of cities across regional and international boundaries. For example, as of the early 1980s,

Canada's Cadillac-Fairview Corporation, one of the ten largest firms operating in the United States, had eight divisions, including a financing division, a shopping center division, and a construction division. Since the 1940s large firms have increasingly dominated commercial construction in cities (and, to a growing extent, residential development). Some firms started after World War II as local firms tied into a local growth coalition, but they later became complex bureaucracies developing projects in numerous cities and engaging in a variety of financial, landowning, construction, and marketing operations.

The capitalist system of investment, production, and marketing is a powerful engine for the social and physical transformation of cities. Growth in capitalist cities typically hinges on the decisions made by industrialists, bankers, and real estate entrepreneurs calculating profit at the firm level. Social costs have been defined as the negative consequences of for-profit production, as costs that are not paid for by an individual firm but which are shifted into third parties, onto individuals, and onto communities (Kapp 1950). Urban real estate investment decisions commonly create social costs because the decisions are calculated at the microeconomic level of the individual company in terms of its exchange-value concerns: profits, future net revenues, and share of the market. Many problems in cities are generated because decision making affecting the use-value concerns of neighborhoods and communities is done at the level of the individual firm. As a result, much traditional analysis of urban economies has had trouble dealing with the broader social costs linked to private investments. The economist Kapp (1950) has surveyed the literature and suggested that many traditional accounts emphasize Alfred Marshall's concept of social problems as externalities, of problems as more or less isolated cases of market failure, or they accent outside factors such as rapid technological change or large population shifts stressed by mainstream ecologists. While these latter factors can be important, they themselves are often dependent on more fundamental factors central to the decision-making process of a capitalist system.

Cities are in the first instance physical and geographical environments into which human action has intruded. The physical environment has its own regularities and laws—for example, ground and surface water flows. If these givens are ignored when investment and production decisions are made, then the negative consequences of such decisions may well be substantial. In addition, the high velocity of contemporary investment capital affects social costs. Bluestone and Harrison (1982, 106) have noted that the impact of city growth is greatly shaped by capital velocity:

> How much expansion can be absorbed, and how quickly, depends on the dynamics of the people and the environment of the community involved. . . . With suitable planning and reasonable forecasts, new schools can be built, teachers hired, roadways, water, and sewage systems constructed,

and job training. . . . But when the capital influx is totally unrestrained, the absorptive capacity of the social system can be quickly overwhelmed.

The absorptive capacity of a particular city varies not only with the dynamics of its environment but also with the role of government in that context. When governments operate to facilitate profit making by pollution-causing firms or when they retreat from the planning and intervention to deal with the problems created by private profit making, they cooperate in inflicting social costs on the citizenry. The new urban political-economists give particular attention to the role of government (the state) in modern capitalism, drawing in part on the work of James O'Connor (1973) and Jurgen Habermas (1973). The state in late capitalism, according to O'Connor, has had to cope directly with the social crises of capitalism. Government under capitalism must try to meet certain obligations: (1) enhancing capital accumulation and (2) maintaining the legitimacy of the system in the eyes of the public. Capital accumulation is fostered by local and federal government action that increases productivity of labor and the rate of profit, such as government-subsidized industrial development parks, urban renewal projects, airports, and large-scale utility projects. Feagin (1985) has added to O'Connor's list a third type of state intervention: regulation. Many types of government regulation, including land-use controls, have been implemented under homeowners' or capitalists' pressures for government to rationalize a too-irrational capitalism.

While there is still much diversity among the scholars adhering to this new perspective, there is a growing consensus on certain basic concepts and assumptions:

1. Societies are fundamentally shaped by their means of production. Societies are more than demographic assortments of people; rather, they are socially organized along class lines and are fundamentally shaped by the logics of production and reproduction.

2. In this historical period, U.S. and Western European countries are organized around and structured by the capital accumulation process; they are shaped by a class system rooted in that process.

3. This capital accumulation process is centered in firms calculating profit at the firm level and thus results in irresolvable contradictions, such as major social costs not figured into firm accounts, capital flight, and periodic overaccumulation and underaccumulation crises. Capital accumulation involves an ever-expanding exploitation of labor (inequality) on a national and an international scale.

4. This capitalistic class structure and accumulation process articulates with space (place) to generate patterns of urban structure, growth, and decline.

5. The state in modern capitalistic societies, usually under the control of capital, plays a crucial role in fostering capital accumulation, in groping with market contradictions, in mediating struggles between classes and fractions of

classes, and in enhancing the legitimacy of the established political-economic system in the eyes of its inhabitants (Gottdiener and Feagin 1988).

The contrast with mainstream Spencerian ecology is clear. From this critical perspective, society is characterized by antagonistic class relations that generate change; change is not simply generated, as the mainstream ecologists would have it, by a biotic integration and equilibrium upset only by outside social influences such as the incursion of new technologies (e.g., the automobile). Much change flows out of the conflict-ridden capitalistic system and its mode of production. U.S. and West European societies have seen the emergence of strong capitalism-conditioned states, which attempt to intervene to solve crises in market functioning and capital accumulation, as well as to mediate intra- and interclass conflict. The inequality of power, of control over economic and political resources, is a central feature of capitalistic societies, and thus of their cities, and *not* an inevitable consequence of societal organization as the mainstream ecologists would have it (Hawley 1981, 224). In addition, the new urban approach emphasizes the point that no society is an island in time or space; it must be analyzed in light of its political-economic history and its position in an increasingly globalized capitalistic system.

Zoning in Political-Economic Perspective

The new urban paradigm points to the import of broader historical and political-economic frameworks for a deeper understanding of developments in governmental land-use policy such as zoning and similar regulations. Let us now turn to the early decades of zoning in the United States.

Investment Expansion and City Growth

Between 1916 and the late 1920s, zoning and related land-use laws became dominant governmental policy in U.S. cities. This state intervention in economic matters did not take place within an economic or social vacuum. Indeed, it was the direct result of efforts to alleviate some of the negative effects (so-called externalities) of rapid capitalistic expansion—of the accelerating capital flows moving into industries in numerous U.S. cities between 1870 and 1930. Industrial capitalists usually sought out cities for labor supply reasons. There were already workers in many towns and cities from the commercial capitalist period prior to the 1870s. Labor migration and population growth also followed capital investment. The concentration of the new industries in many cities stemmed from decisions of top corporate executives or free-wheeling entrepreneurs establishing dominant major industries. As plants and factories became situated in certain cities in this national investment process, the new urban workplaces attracted workers from rural areas, from the South,

and from Europe. In this 1870–1930 period, cities were booming and industries of a dozen major varieties were locating hundreds of plants in them. Professional, managerial, technical, and skilled blue-collar workers increased to
significant numbers, opening up by the 1920s a new market for consumer
goods, including mass-produced automobiles and houses in central cities and
the suburban rings. By 1922 there were 135,000 homes in the suburbs of sixty
cities that were dependent on an auto-centered transport network (Flink 1975,
164). Without the significant increase in a relatively affluent group of white-
collar and skilled blue-collar workers, there probably would have been no suburban expansion and thus no zoning litigation.

This suburban expansion slowed dramatically in the 1930s because of an
overproduction crisis in U.S. capitalism. Overproduction in the automobile industry during the mid-1920s triggered huge layoffs in all auto-related industries, thus precipitating the general economic crisis called the Great
Depression (Flink 1975). Sharply expanded state investments during and after
World War II bailed the nation out of that major crisis and further accelerated
the growth of suburban development and zoning regulations.

The Interventionist State

Ecologists and other urban analysts have often neglected the critical role of the
capitalist-conditioned *state* in shaping U.S. cities. The history of cities in the
last century is not only a history of boom–bust capitalism, of capital investments and capital strikes, but also a history of gradually increasing *state* intervention, at several levels of government, into the national and urban
economies, in large part to deal with market-generated pressures, crises, and
contradictions.

This state role in urban structuring and restructuring has taken a number of
different forms. There are numerous state subsidies to foster accumulation in
favored industries. Both the federal and local governments, for example, have
played a central role in subsidizing the growth of the auto-truck industry. By
the 1910s and 1920s, state subsidies for transport systems were shifted away
from interurban rail systems and intraurban mass transit to highway systems
and other infrastructural facilities necessary for the auto-truck industry to expand production and sales. This "socialized" infrastructure facilitated the dominance of and profit making in the auto and truck firms, a situation unique
among major capitalistic countries. One result of this state action was the fostering of a distinctive expansion of suburbia in U.S. conurbations. Moreover,
after World War II suburban expansion continued to be related to an expansion
of an auto-centered highway system. This socialized highway system cost local, state, and federal governments no less than $249 billion between 1947 and
1970. The nationalized, auto-centered system and its accompanying car culture occurred "less because of consumer demand in a competitive market than

because of the government's massive indirect subsidization of the automobile and oil industries, especially through the Interstate Highway Act of 1956" (Flink 1975, 213). Rail transit, utilized for people transport, was a major casualty of this state bias toward the automobile. O'Connor's theory of the role of the state in modern capitalism, particularly his emphasis on the role of the state in facilitating capital accumulation—and thus in this case facilitating urban deconcentration and zoning segregation—can be seen in these historical events.

Local and federal support of capital accumulation in this period was accompanied by growth in the number and significance of local governmental units. From the 1890s to the 1930s, and again after World War II, there was a major increase in the incorporation of municipalities around cities. By 1920, Cook County (Chicago) had 109 such municipalities walled off from the central city. Pittsburgh had 107 and New York City had 204. During the decade of the 1920s, new suburban areas were created by the dozens around U.S. cities (Judd 1984, 173). After World War II, moreover, the numbers of walled-off suburban municipalities continued to increase. This balkanization of cities reflected a growing concern for the externalities of expansionist investment, a concern among those managers, professionals, and affluent blue-collar workers able to decentralize their residences. These suburban areas (and protosuburban areas, e.g., the village of Euclid) sought to protect their families, homes, and neighborhoods from the noise, pollution, congestion, and other negative consequences of industrial expansion, as well as from white immigrant and nonwhite workers drawn to cities by the new industries. In their origin, zoning and related regulations represent an attempt to use government to solve the negative problems created by the aggressive exchange-value expansionism of industrial and commercial capitalism. The willingness to give up a laissez-faire approach to government for increased intervention appears by the 1920s, not only in regard to zoning but also in regard to the regulation of many aspects of the American economy.

The zoning regulations used in suburban municipalities had first emerged in central cities, with New York City being the most important of these. By 1910, the New York Real Estate Board had advocated limiting the height of buildings. Reportedly, real estate values in the retail section of Manhattan had decreased by half in the decade prior to 1916; in particular, Fifth Avenue retail merchants were worried about the encroachment of the Jewish garment merchants, their new buildings, and their immigrant workers. The 1916 New York zoning law resulted from pressure from these central Manhattan merchants, rather than from homeowners. In this case, the concern was primarily with the commercial use value of the land, a concern for retail marketing and profit making by merchant capitalists concerned with maintaining a presence in a particular urban land space. Yet this New York law was influential in broadcasting the concept of zoning to cities across the country. By 1920 there were

904 zoning ordinances, according to a survey of the U.S. Bureau of Standards. Altogether, 82 of the 93 largest cities, those over 100,000 in population, had zoning laws. By April 1932 there were 766 comprehensive zoning ordinances (Davies 1958, 146). Under the zoning acts of the 1920s state governments delegated land use planning and controls to local governments, which in turn provided zoning ordinances.

Central city merchants and suburbanites played an important role in the emergence of zoning and allied planning regulations, but there were other powerful actors as well. There were those actors whose principal concern in real estate transactions was with the exchange value of land, particularly builders, developers, and real estate brokers. Before there were large developers engaged in residential and commercial construction in central cities and suburbs, there were smaller developers often called "builders." Initially, some business leaders representing these builders were opposed to zoning. In 1911, one leader argued at a National Planning Conference that the "German policy" of city zoning may come in the future, but "it is as yet undemocratic" and "savors too much of class-consciousness, to be popular in America" (Davies 1958, 78). Soon, however, the views of the leadership of the National Association of Real Estate Boards reflected the fact that local boards were strong supporters of zoning (Davies 1958, 78). According to Davies (1958, 146), these U.S. real estate boards played an important role in framing the model zoning enabling act in 1925.

Zoning Validated

In *Village of Euclid v. Ambler Realty Co.*[1] the Supreme Court dealt with a zoning statute passed by the village of Euclid, an area adjacent to Cleveland and just beginning to be a suburb. By 1920, the village of Euclid had 3,363 inhabitants and was still mostly farmland. Some areas of the village were being developed for residences, but much was still undeveloped. In 1922, the village adopted an ordinance establishing comprehensive zoning of all land. The intent of the ordinance was to reserve much of the village land for residential development and to segregate industrial plants near the major rail lines. When much of the land owned by Ambler Realty was designated for nonindustrial use, Ambler pursued its lawsuit. Ambler Realty argued that zoning regulations will "throttle the great metropolises with a multitude of local regulations, in conflict with the general public interest" (Fluck 1986, 326). As with many real estate corporations, special pleading for profit was couched in terms of the general public interest. As the new urban political economy has demonstrated, in a class-stratified capitalistic society there is often no general consensus on land-use matters. There is the interest of corporate investors, and there is the interest of worker-homeowners in suburban areas. Indeed, arguing for Ambler, attorney Newton Baker pointed out that *no* village or suburb could anticipate in its planning the freewheeling expansionism of capitalistic investors: "the surging and receding tides by which business evolves and grows" (Baker, 653).

Reportedly, the author of *Euclid*, Mr. Justice George Sutherland, initially viewed the ordinance in a negative light, but he was convinced to alter his view. Influenced by the thought of Herbert Spencer, the prominent nineteenth-century sociologist who influenced mainstream urban analysis, Sutherland was a foremost advocate of laissez-faire. Sutherland was similar to many early and contemporary urban ecologists in his respect for Spencer's thought, which apotheosized the public benefits of a market system free from government interference. Like the ecologists, Sutherland was "so immersed in the Spencerian philosophy that he had no power to criticize it judiciously . . . no vantage point from which to see how much of Spencer was merely the expression of an age" (Paschal 1951, 242). In Spencer's view, government resulted from such an increase in population that people came into conflict with one another. But government was not neutral and should be limited to settling disputes and preserving order in the face of overcrowding (Paschal 1951, 9–15). Going beyond Spencer a step or two, both ecologists such as Park and Burgess and jurists such as Sutherland accepted *some* governmental intervention into the complex workings of a capitalistic economy. Thus, in *Euclid,* Sutherland argued that growth in population meant growth in social complexity; and that growth in complexity required the intervention of the state to protect private property. Zoning was not a taking of property, but in fact a protection of property. Common law permitted the abolition of nuisances; the Euclid zoning law protected residential property (residential-use values) from the nuisance of the industrial development sought by the Ambler firm. Since in Sutherland's view the problem was created by significant demographic growth and overcrowding, the zoning ordinance was beneficial in that it protected private property from divergent land-use incursions (Paschal 1951, 26–27).

Conflict over Zoning

Early Criticisms

Zoning regulations had become the target of much criticism by the 1930s. In that decade, questions already were being raised about the large number of zoning variances being granted in various cities. City councils and boards of adjustment were accused of destroying zoning maps and thus of breaking down the integrity of the zoning districts (Toll 1969, 281). Zoning variances had become "marketable commodities, with investors subverting the law." This problem has persisted since the 1930s. For one example, in the 1960s the executive director of the American Society of Planning Officials cited with approval the statement of a city planner: "You can buy with money any kind of zoning you want in half the communities of the United States" (quoted in Toll 1969, 301). The complaint here seems to be with the way in which local developers and land entrepreneurs gain concessions. Because the governments in cities and municipalities historically have depended on taxes from development to survive, they often have gone out of their way to provide zoning concessions to local developers. Not unexpectedly, bribery scandals have been common in the history of zoning. In recent decades there have been pay-off scandals in New Jersey, California, New York, and Chicago (Popper 1981, 52).

While residential use-value concerns seem to underlie some of the criticism of zoning variances, there have also been many criticisms from those real estate actors preoccupied with the exchange value of land. By the 1930s, some leaders in the real estate industry were criticizing certain failures of zoning laws. Walter Schmidt, then NAREB president, called for replanning and rezoning because "in the average American city many times as much property as can ever be used has been allocated for apartments, business, manufacturing, and industrial purposes, crowding out and destroying home neighborhoods" (quoted in Davies 1958, 184–85). He acknowledged that real estate people were "the most aggressive group in the organized planning movement" and were partially responsible for "blunders made." An early advocate of zoning reform and streamlining, Schmidt anticipated the reformers of the 1970s when he called for state housing and planning acts to coordinate and simplify local codes.

Challenges to and Conflicts over Land-Use Restrictions

There was no real challenge to zoning at the Supreme Court level until the early 1970s. Yet in the decades before and after the early 1970s there has been conflict over land use and land-use controls. Much of this has centered on three areas of dispute: (1) low-income and minority apartment buildings; (2) environmental quality and no-growth issues; and (3) community attempts to restrict expansion by big developers. Each of these areas of dispute has involved zoning and related land-use ordinances, but each also has encompassed different sets of actors. Thus the issue of low-income apartments has often been a struggle between low-income minority families and civil rights advocates on the one hand and white suburban families on the other. The struggle over the environment has often pitted environmentalists and local residents against developers and their allies. And the third struggle has been suburbanites and residents in other residential subdivisions struggling to keep out large-scale urban development projects such as the shopping malls, power plants, and highways desired by large development firms.

The Civil Rights Challenge to Exclusionary Zoning

Racial and ethnic separation and exclusion have been at the heart of urban land-use regulation since the 1880s. Indeed, the first zoning actions were taken in San Francisco in the 1880s in order to stop the spread of Chinese laundries. The 1916 New York City ordinance originated from Protestant and German Jewish merchants on Fifth Avenue pressing for zoning to protect their marketing area from the garment factories of southern and eastern European Jewish industrialists and workers. Popper (1981, 55) calls this "racism with a progressive, technocratic veneer."

This technocratic racism has persisted in suburban zoning laws used to exclude minority families. In this case, the dubious use-value concerns of *affluent* suburban homeowners have been enshrined in land law, but the use-value concerns of less-well-off Americans have not been recognized in this fashion. Many suburban areas ringing U.S. cities are self-governing; most such areas are controlled by whites, with no blacks participating in the establishment of local government regulations. "Exclusionary zoning" in suburbia usually includes such things as prohibition of multi-family units and mobile homes and minimum lot-size restrictions. Suburban zoning laws have been successful in excluding not only low-cost housing, but also many minority families.

Moreover, the location of publicly subsidized housing in city and suburban areas has provoked considerable discussion of exclusionary zoning laws. Local governments control the sites for public housing, while the federal government provides most of the money. But federal agencies have provided little protection for minorities against discrimination by local governments. Instead, federal agencies have played an important role in perpetuating the encapsulation of minorities in ghetto areas by allowing federally subsidized housing projects to be concentrated by local governments in segregated areas. Although the federal government has the authority to cut off funding to local agencies that do not comply with fair housing laws, it has shown a preference for local wishes. White fear has prompted suburban governments to turn down federal funds in order to retain local control and exclude public housing, and thereby minority families.

In the mid-1960s, the Chicago Housing Authority (CHA) presented a proposal to the city council to construct low-rent public housing projects throughout the city. At that time virtually all of the public projects already built were located in ghettos. The CHA proposal was rejected by the city council; the CHA then made an unsuccessful appeal to federal officials in Washington, following which the CHA retreated to the segregated policy the city council desired. A group of black tenants and applicants filed suit in 1966 against the CHA, charging it with selecting its public housing sites to keep blacks out of white neighborhoods. The federal government was charged with financially supporting these discriminatory practices. Three years later in *Gautreaux v.*

CHA,[2] the federal district court found CHA guilty of violating the constitutional rights of black tenants by its discriminatory site selections and tenant assignments and ordered the CHA to disperse future housing in all-white neighborhoods, discontinue its discriminatory assignment procedures, and move rapidly to increase the supply of nonsegregated units. In a subsequent case, the federal housing agency was also found guilty of helping to perpetuate "a racially discriminatory housing system in Chicago." The CHA's refusal to comply with the order prompted a maze of further litigation (Feagin and Feagin 1978, 108–10).

In *Hills v. Gautreaux,*[3] the Supreme Court held that the federal housing agency must provide low-income housing in the Chicago suburbs. But the Court allowed local municipalities to retain their zoning powers. The white mayor of a Chicago suburb said, "I really don't think the federal government will go charging out to the suburbs to put in housing where it's not wanted. If you don't have local cooperation, you'll have a hell of a situation." Alexander Polikoff, an attorney who has been involved with the public housing debate for a long time, argued that the Court's decision to uphold local zoning powers would limit the effectiveness of the low-income housing dispersal order: "Any community that wants to oppose subsidized housing can use its land use powers just as it always has" (Feagin and Feagin 1978, 110–11).

Arlington Heights, an affluent Chicago suburb, resisted the building of low- and moderate-income multifamily housing units by using its zoning regulations. The publicly expressed concern did not explicitly touch on race, but rather on the way in which local property values in this single-family area would be affected by multifamily housing units. However, the real concern was keeping neighborhoods exclusive. After the local zoning board voted nine to two against the necessary rezoning proposition, the case went to the federal courts. Because there was no evidence of racially exclusionary action on intentional grounds, the Supreme Court upheld this zoning decision in an important case, *Village of Arlington Heights v. Metropolitan Housing Development Corp.*[4] The Supreme Court had retreated to the position that racial discrimination must be proven by complainants to be intentional in order for it to be ruled illegal (Feagin and Feagin 1978, 111).

With the Supreme Court showing a reluctance to deal with the obvious discrimination institutionalized in zoning in the suburbs, it has been left to the New Jersey Supreme Court to order change in segregated housing patterns. In a celebrated case, *Southern Burlington County NAACP vs. Mount Laurel,*[5] the New Jersey justices unanimously reaffirmed an earlier *Mount Laurel* decision and ordered Mount Laurel and similar suburban communities to develop inclusionary zoning practices; in effect, "every municipality's land-use regulations . . . must provide a realistic opportunity for decent housing for its indigenous poor" (Babcock and Siemon 1985, 212). The New Jersey court had in effect suggested that 20 percent of any new housing development be set aside for low- and moderate-income families. The exact figures for particular communities have been the source of much debate, but the radical implications of this New Jersey decision are quite clear: Towns and cities must allow for the housing of people of all income levels. The Republican governor of New Jersey even went so far as to say that the decision was "communistic" (Babcock and Siemon 1985, 215). The New Jersey Builders Association, made up primarily of smaller developers, expressed opposition to this government intrusion into the free-market economy. As in other cases of state action, some larger developers, in contrast, have seen the new situation as an opportunity, for they have the greater resources to comply with the development regulations. For them, at least, it is helpful that these particular land-use regulations are consistent across the state of New Jersey (Babcock and Siemon 1985, 220). Nonetheless, New Jersey stands virtually alone as the state which has sought to recognize as legitimate the use-value interests of the bottom third of the U.S. population, the concerns of moderate-income tenants for decent living space.

The No-Growth Restrictions: Zoning for Use Values

Zoning and related land-use laws have been used for a variety of purposes. One purpose has been to exclude minorities. Yet another purpose has been to try to maintain a certain quality of life. In the last two decades, numerous cities and towns have become greatly concerned about the social costs of urban growth; some have passed growth-control ordinances. Many of these costs have stemmed from the decisions of commercial, industrial, and real estate capitalists calculating company profits at a microeconomic level. As the urban political economy perspective would suggest, because corporations do not figure social costs into their balance sheets, the costs are not charged against the profits the firms make from producing and marketing products. As Bluestone and Harrison (1982) noted in the passage above, unrestrained capital influx, whether in the form of large subdivisions or rapid industrial expansion, can overwhelm local government capacity to cope with the capital flow.

It is not surprising then that cities and towns in the growing areas of the United States, such as the Sunbelt, have been the most likely to regulate growth. The no-growth movements in many towns and cities have increased the number of local laws with which developers must cope. In the last decade the no-growth movement from Florida to California has resulted in laws specifying large-lot zoning, restrictions on the number of sewer and water taps, limits on housing permits, and delayed service provision for large projects. This has sometimes created a war between development interests and local citizen groups and their governments. The expansion of local zoning and planning ordinances to regulate growth runs directly counter to the interests of most development capitalists. Moreover, it is of interest that communities of various income levels, from moderate to very rich, have barricaded themselves against the intrusion of development interests and fought growth with new controls (Babcock and Siemon 1985).

Environmental Restrictions on Land Use

A related land-use conflict has grown up around land-use restrictions aimed at reducing environmental problems. In the 1960s, a number of activists working in the environmental movement began to target the negative impact of development on the urban and rural landscapes. Since most local zoning and other land-use ordinances seemed inadequate to the task of environmental protection, many pressed for regulation at the higher levels of government. By the early 1970s, numerous environmental laws had been passed into law. Indeed, the 1970s have been called a "decade of quiet federalization." Laws coming out of Congress attempted to regulate air pollution, water pollution, utility siting, land conservation, strip mining, and wilderness lands (Mayer 1979, 55). The new laws have covered large projects such as power plants and strip mines, as well as coastal and mountain areas. State governments have taken back some of the police powers delegated to local governments. Thus, the 1972 Coastal Zone Management Act gives thirty seacoast and Great Lakes states federal dollars to regulate coastal developments (Popper 1981, 16–17). Toward the end of the decade, Representative Morris Udall estimated that there were about 140 federal programs that shaped local government land-use decisions, ranging from direct regulation to federal funding of state regulation, and from broad guidelines to detailed stipulations. In addition to federal laws, state governments have passed hundreds of land-use laws since the early 1970s (Meyer 1979, 56).

This wave of environmental regulation has been strongly opposed by some powerful real estate actors, particularly developers. Often arrayed against environmentalists have been development corporations and their local government allies, although there have been temporary coalitions between environmentalists and some big development firms. As Popper (1981, 6) notes, "this opposition has not succeeded in stopping land use reform legislation, but it has imposed a variety of prodeveloper concessions and compromises on what began as strictly environmentalist bills." This major struggle has often involved local homeowners and environmentalists primarily interested in use values on the one hand and certain factions of capital, such as real estate developers interested in exchange values, on the other. But the picture is often complex; some communities with unemployed residents have preferred the social costs of corporate investment to what they have regarded as the "purism" of environmentalists. The logic of capitalism, as it is currently structured, often forces a Hobson's choice between a clean environment and jobs.

Conflict over Large-Scale Development Projects

In recent decades, localized zoning and other land-use regulations have been increasingly attacked by big developers and their allies among land-use reformers. Prior to the 1940s, most urban development projects were carried out by small builders and developers. Beginning in the 1940s and 1950s, large developers such as Levitt and Sons began to build very large suburban development projects. By the 1960s there were numerous big developers constructing large shopping malls, office buildings, warehouses, and residential subdivisions. In the late 1960s and early 1970s, many large firms put together or acquired their own development subsidiaries, such as ITT taking over Levitt, and Exxon creating the Friendswood Development Corporation. At the peak of corporate involvement in the 1970s, many top executives expected to reap new profits from shifting investments into large-scale urban development projects. With much surplus capital to expend, large industrial firms moved capital into real estate investment circuits, including large planned unit developments (PUDs), such as Kaiser Aluminum in Rancho, California; Gulf Oil in Reston, Virginia; and Exxon in developments in Clear Lake City, Texas. Independent real estate development corporations grew ever larger as capital became more centralized and concentrated in firms like Cadillac-Fairview, Gerald Hines Interests, and Olympia and York, Ltd.

As the scale of urban development projects increased, local regulations became problematical for the big developers: "Traditional zoning and subdivision regulations with their piecemeal approval, density limits, and fixed-use districts were not in accordance with the new scale and design of major projects" (Walker and Heiman 1981, 71). The Urban Land Institute (ULI), the research arm of big developers, took an active part in pressing for land-use reform. One ULI publication notes that "broadening the concept of zoning to meet the needs of large new communities and redevelopment projects" is a goal of "planning bodies, redevelopment authorities, large corporations and foundations and those qualified to engage in large-scale developments" (ULI 1961, 59).

Shopping malls are one major type of large-scale development project. Existing zoning maps map the locations for commercial projects, but in the view of large developers the "prezoned, mapped commercial strips are usually not suitable locations for shopping centers" (McKeever, Griffin, and Spink 1977, 51). This quote is from the *Shopping Center Development Handbook* of the Urban Land Institute. The *Handbook* continues by noting that in numerous communities zoning laws have not been "revised to automatically provide for the planned unit concept (and the shopping center *is* a planned unit)." The *Handbook* calls for the updating of ordinances so that existing building height, lot size, and setback regulations will not prevent large shopping mall projects. The shopping mall project is said to be in the public interest because of the increased taxes accruing to the local community and because the community is relieved of the need to provide parking facilities (McKeever, Griffin, and Spink 1977, 53).

In the 1960s and 1970s, large-scale infrastructure projects using public money also ran into local land-use barriers. Local communities used land-use controls to keep out power plants, highways, and airports. Plotkin (1987) cites cases of successful citizen mobilization: the Tocks Island dam in New Jersey, the Miami-Dade Jetport, and the North Expressway project in San Antonio. Backed by large-scale development interests, these projects were attempts to improve the local transport-energy infrastructure using federal government funds. Such land-use conflicts have been viewed as "the result of poor planning" or a "lack of coordination," to quote Senator Henry Jackson (quoted in Plotkin 1987, 183). But they represent something far more fundamental, again the use-value concerns of urban and suburban residents versus the exchange-value concerns of, to use the ULI language above, "those qualified to engage in large-scale developments."

Proponents of large-scale development projects have seen themselves as positive forces for social change. Thus Berry (1973, 24) notes that the "planning commission in a social sense and the zoning ordinance in a real estate sense . . . are holding operations against the forces of social change." The defenders see local opponents of growth as opposed to progress. It has often been asserted that large-scale development projects can better meet the goals of racial desegregation, can lower housing costs, and can better protect the environment than the disorganized and fragmented projects of smaller developers. However, Walker and Heiman (1981, 79–81) have demonstrated that for the most part such assertions cannot be supported from the existing data on large developments.

The Strange Career of Land-Use Reform

Regulation versus Profit?

Land-use reform has been on the nation's agenda since the late 1960s. Land-use reformers have been committed strongly to race and income desegregation of the suburbs, rational planning and control of the environment, and greater efficiency in the location of large-scale development and infrastructure projects. Popper (1981, 212) portrays the land-use battles as between those who view land as "a resource that was subject to stringent centralized regulation" and those who see land as a "loosely and locally regulated commodity on which its owners could make a profit." But Popper misses the complex reality of the class backgrounds and interests of many of the reformers. Indeed, the struggles over land use have involved a diverse array of competitors and actors, some concerned with the use value of land as living space, some concerned with the use value of land for commercial profit making, others with the exchange value of land. Worker–homeowners have often pressed for territorial separation; mall developers, for investment expansion. But the picture can be complex; land-use politics often brings together strange bedfellows.

The 1960s and 1970s were a period of great debate over zoning and other land-use ordinances. Because of the problem of land-use localism, big business interests worked through private planning groups such as the Regional Plan Association of New York, the Bay Area Council of San Francisco, and the Committee for Economic Development in order to press for metropolitan reorganization and planning. In the 1960s there were numerous foundation-funded critiques of local political and zoning fragmentation. Particularly important have been the Ford and Rockefeller Brothers foundations. The Ford Foundation funded a study on this subject by the Regional Plan Association of New York. In 1961, the Ford Foundation gave a grant to the American Society of Planning Officials to review zoning laws, with Richard F. Babcock as the key evaluator. Two years later, Ford also gave a half-million-dollar grant to the American Law Institute to study zoning laws and to propose a model law. Out of this latter project came draft proposals for a Model Land Development Code that would bring up to date the Standard Zoning and Planning Acts of the 1920s. In *The Zoning Game* (1966), Babcock argued that the patchwork quilt of such local laws should be transformed into a set of development controls operated by higher levels of government. He argued that existing zoning practice deifies municipal plans and "enshrines the municipality at a moment in our history when every social and economic consideration demands that past emphasis on the municipality as the repository of 'general welfare' be rejected" (Babcock 1966, 123). For Babcock, as for many reformers, the public good (of big developers?) can be better preserved at a level of government beyond the local level.

Major government-funded reports took up the cause of land-use reform in the late 1960s. One major reform issue grew out of the civil rights protests. One response to the intense black ghetto riots was the 1968 Kerner Riot Commission's strong critique of exclusionary zoning by suburbs as a cause of the central-city racial crisis. The report of the 1968 National Commission on Urban Problems also argued vigorously against the use of land-use controls to segregate housing. That report argued that the right of minority individuals to achieve their housing choices must be given priority over the desire of white neighbors to exclude them: "The principle, of course, is well established in such matters as the invalidity of racial zoning . . . there are many gray areas, however, in which a regulation with a purported 'physical' objective (e.g., a minimum house or lot size) may have a dominant motive of exclusion" (National Commission on Urban Problems 1968, 241). The commission recommended that state governments amend zoning acts to include as a legitimate zoning purpose the inclusion of housing sites for persons of all income levels.

The report of the 1973 Rockefeller Brothers Fund Task Force on land use and urban growth, called *The Use of Land*, was a major step in the struggle for national land-use reform. It also called for removal of exclusionary zoning laws to keep minorities out of suburban areas. Moreover, this report pressed vigorously for new governmental action to facilitate capital accumulation by big developers frustrated by local zoning and planning regulations. In its attacks on small-scale development, the report reflects the interests of big developers:

> The small scale of most development remains a major obstacle to quality development. Although an increase in scale does not guarantee high quality, it significantly increases the developer's opportunity to achieve quality [Reilly 1973, 28].

The Use of Land is aggressive in proposing large-scale developments as a solution to urban development problems and in arguing for the abolition of local planning and zoning barriers that interfere with large projects. It proposes state government entities, such as New York's pioneering Urban Development Corporation, with the "power of eminent domain, the power to override local land-use regulations, and the power to control the provision of public utilities, when necessary, to overcome the barriers that now prevent most developers from operating at the larger scales that the public interest requires" (Reilly 1973, 29). The report further calls for depriving "local governments of the power to establish" various land uses in excess of state government statutes and for a remolding of the regulation process so as to reduce the control of governments over land-use regulation "that significantly affects people in more than one locality" (Reilly 1973, 27–28).

Major Federal Legislation

A centerpiece of the reform movement was the National Land Use Policy Act introduced in various incarnations by Arizona Rep. Morris Udall and Washington Senator Henry Jackson between 1968 and 1976. This bill would have given state government dollars "to devise comprehensive land use programs to regulate large developments and other building in environmentally fragile areas" (Popper 1981, 17). It passed the Senate easily in 1974, but was defeated by four votes in the House. While Senator Jackson claimed his land reform was "the best possible protection for basic property rights" and that the $100 million provided under the act would not allow the "federal government to substitute its own policies for those of the states," it was clear that the law would require that states to set up detailed land-use planning requirements and agencies as a condition of eligibility. House supporters such as Udall saw the bill as a national land-use planning policy, one needed because there was "no real order, no overall policy to cope with future land development and the struggle between speculators and preservationists" (quoted in Meyer 1979, 57). The Jackson bill was presented as "policy neutral" and as oriented toward greater efficiency in land-use planning. But the bill actually shifted power away from local governments to the federal and state governments.

Classes and Class Factions in the Land-Use Reform Struggle

The new urban political economy perspective would suggest an in-depth investigation of the relationship of the land-use reform commissions and bills to the larger class and political-economic context, in particular to oligopoly capitalism and attempts to rationalize the chaos of a profit-centered market system. Because of the class-structured character of capitalism and of state intervention, there is typically no consensus on land-use goals. Reformers have included not only environmentalists and civil rights advocates, but also those representing the interests of big developers and those planners committed to rationalizing the problems of cities under advanced capitalism. Some large-scale development interests have worked for land-use reform, particularly major developmental and industrial companies that see centralized policy-making as neutralizing local regulations and reducing local no-growth barriers to development.

Environmentalists testified for the Jackson bill, together with big corporations and their real estate and banking allies: the National Wildlife Federation, Exxon, Bank of America, the National Association of Realtors, and the Conservation Foundation. Energy and utility companies have sometimes been supportive of a certain type of national land-use policy. The environmentalists wanted a law that would protect the U.S. environment against rape from local interests. But the large corporations "preferred a system that would minimize the risks inherent in an uncoordinated and decentralized approach to land use planning" (Meyer 1979, 57–58). Not surprising, thus, was the testimony by an Exxon executive before a Senate committee that emphasized that "we believe the time has come for a more orderly, disciplined way of planning for and managing for future growth of the nation" (Meyer 1979, 58).

Zoning reformers have noted the problems that local zoning laws create for large firms interested in urban development. Thus Babcock notes that these "sophisticated advocates are chagrined to discover that village codes often are a major barrier to marketing their dwelling-related products. . . . In short, there are powerful and conservative forces that would welcome an erosion of local land use control" (Babcock 1966, 59–64). The point is that localism in land-use regulations is a major headache for large development firms. Thus a national land-use law is in order to rationalize local "irrationalities" in land-use regulations.

The 1920s *Euclid* zoning debate was centered on getting what was seen as a *reform* past the judiciary of that era. In the 1960s and 1970s, reformers such as Babcock wanted to remake that reform. Babcock seems to fear that the "one-man, one-vote" concept increases the power of the suburbs in state legislatures and thus makes zoning reform difficult. In this sense, his corporate-liberal view is basically antidemocratic. He and other reformers prefer state and federal legislatures to reform the laws in spite of what voters might want (Toll 1969, 306). Big firms and their advocates seem to prefer centralized planning because they more easily can influence decisions at these state and federal levels of government than smaller developers and the general public can. Large developers need standardized zoning and planning regulations to facilitate huge development projects over large geographical areas. Moreover, the participation of federal and state authorities can help steer development projects away from the most resistant and assertive local communities.

Corporate land-use reformers and their professional allies had the value commitments and practical wisdom to try to build a coalition with civil rights advocates who find exclusionary zoning repulsive and environmentalists who find certain traditional state practices as degrading of the environment. In a review of the literature of the late 1960s and early 1970s, Walker and Heiman (1981, 73) found numerous calls "for alliance between developers and proponents of environmental quality, social equity, and growth control." The major land-use commission studies pressed hard (1) for streamlined regulations for large-scale development and (2) for restrictions on exclusionary zoning, goals supported by divergent factions in the reform coalition. However, from the beginning there were major tensions in any coalition of this type. The benefits of large-scale projects have been exaggerated, and environmentalists often disagreed with big developers on such matters. Many minority activists have also been ambivalent about land-use reform. While they recognize its potential for reducing racial zoning, they also fear that new environmental rules will create the possibility of new types of exclusionary zoning. For example, one group of middle-income whites in Newark was able to block a low-income housing project by questioning the environmental impact of the project, using the environmental impact law (Popper 1981, 70, 258).

Another set of allies for the national land-use reformers were the environmentalists who had succeeded in getting Congress to pass laws regulating water and air pollution. Many environmentalists supported the use of state police powers to regulate the environment, and they supported the national land-use planning legislation in the 1970s. But this love affair did not last long. The environmentalists' concern with pollution controls ultimately "stood in opposition to developer interests . . . The latter disapproved of protecting critical environmental areas without balancing this with the power to override local restraints on development elsewhere" (Walker and Heiman 1981, 75).

Localized Opposition to Land-Use Reform Bills

The most effective opposition to national land-use planning legislation came from local forces. When they lost, some reformers saw their opponents as right-wingers who conducted a "campaign of strident sloganeering" (Meyer 1979, 58). But the opposition was more substantial than this implies. Local business and government officials, small farmers, and local developers opposed the National Land Use Policy Act. For example, Chicago Democrats, controlled by Mayor Richard Daley, provided crucial votes to defeat the act. Popper (1981, 62) suggests that the reason for this opposition was a concern that higher levels of government would get the power to regulate land use; local government officials wanted that power, as well as the political contributions given by local builders and developers to those politicians in control. But Popper gives too much weight to the political officials. The land-use struggle was between a national and rationalized land-use system of the corporate-liberal, land-use reformers and a localized land-use system of suburban homeowners and local real estate actors.

Plotkin (1987) notes that the nationally oriented land-use elite pressing for the rationalization of development ran into the basic problem that few local people wanted land-use law changes. For these local officials land-use decision making was a stabilized and routinized activity, with routine access for the powerful actors at the community and city level. In some areas, the application of zoning and other ordinances favored growth, but in other areas decisions favored zoning and no-growth. In any event, most local real estate actors had little reason to support federal government intervention.

The defeat of the comprehensive land-use law has led some reformers to target more restricted goals such as expanding regional action. Some large developers and allied reformer-lawyers have tried to participate on regional environmental bodies, in order to influence regional land-use policies. Others have tried to piggyback onto the conservative (laissez-faire) deregulation movement of the 1980s, arguing that streamlined land use is necessary in order to deal with the "dramatic increase" in local regulations.

Alternative Strategies for Dealing with Urban Development

Large-scale Organizations and Corporate Liberalism

Large-scale industrial, real estate, and development organizations increasingly have come to dominate American urban landscapes. Corporations often have annexed the power of the state to help them in private profit-making. At the core of the struggle over a streamlined national land-use policy has been a corporate-liberal approach to the problems of modern capitalism. The corporate-liberals long have disagreed with their laissez-faire conservative brethren and have pressed for more government involvement in dealing with the irrationalities of the capitalist system. Urban protest movements, such as that in Santa Monica (see below), have raised fundamental questions about capitalist cities including questions about the quality of life, the pervasive profit criterion of investment, and the dominating influence of capitalist elites. While recognizing the significance of these urban movements, those adhering to the corporate-liberal ideology remain committed to a capitalist system and see the solution to many problems in more centralized regulation and in coopting certain elements of popular protest. But the corporate-liberal solutions are illusions, since the real issue is not the "obsolescence of zoning and small-scale development" but the "obsolescence of organizing social life around class inequality and the accumulation of capital" (Walker and Heiman 1981, 83).

Corporate liberalism appears to be a reform effort. Yet in reality corporate-liberalism offers "equality of opportunity" for real equality; bureaucratic regularity and rationalization for expanded citizen participation; and consumer goods for democratic control of workplaces (Lustig 1982, 248). The problem with corporate liberalism is that it encompasses a strong faith in a profit-oriented capitalism, albeit a state-administered and rationalized capitalism. But profit-oriented production and development frequently do not respond to basic human needs very well, either in the short run or in the long run. And a concern with making city development more rational and efficient is not the same as ridding cities of deepening injustices. If we are to meet the needs of all city dwellers, we must move beyond the choice of twentieth-century corporate liberalism and the choice of a renewed nineteenth-century individualism and Social Darwinism.

Democratizing Land-Use Controls: Accenting Home-Use Values

Henry George (1962, 264) long ago argued that it is the work and effort of all the people in communities that create land values and bring whatever advances in land prices that do occur. In his view, land dealers and real estate speculators secure, unjustly and without much effort, the increased prices generated by community labor. Extending this insight, George argued that the inequality of property holding and property control was a major source of the extreme imbalances in wealth and poverty in the United States. Real estate capital—and other land-interested capital, one might add—often is concerned only with the exchange value of urban space itself or the use value of space for money making, whereas most ordinary worker-renters and worker-homeowners view their residential urban spaces in terms of family-use values, as "home." When capital becomes highly expansive and mobile, great tensions can occur. Critical to the health and progress of U.S. society have been certain basic social and cultural arrangements—stable neighborhoods and communities, dependable social relationships, and a sense of the limits to destructive capital investments. Yet these family-home arrangements are being destroyed by the world-oriented operation of modern corporate capitalism. A capitalism that has always operated as though "community, tradition, family, and morality made no difference, now finds them disappearing in fact" (Lustig 1982, 256).

A major problem with the national land-use reform proposals of the corporate-liberal reformers is that they would reduce citizen input, input that has been expanding at the local level in recent years. Certain land-use reforms may be appropriate, but they should be set in a context of human concern with use values and citizen participation.

Major class and income inequalities, major imbalances in political power, racial exclusion in matters of housing, struggles over air and water pollution, conflict over siting of large development and utility projects—all these reflect the "normal" problems of the elitist system we call capitalism. As long as that elitist system is in place, reforms will be biased in favor of the exchange value interests of the powers that be. The existing social relations of capitalistic production set significant limits on reform, so in the end capitalism will have to be replaced. But there is still a need for reforms "in the meantime." Urban land-use reforms can be related to more progressive and democratic goals rather than the corporate-liberal or reactionary Social Darwinist goals. What progressive reforms might be, or have been, attempted?

Plotkin's Proposal

In a provocative analysis, Plotkin (1987, 241) has suggested the need for a National Community Security Act bringing together five basic goals often considered separately by progressive analysts:

1. To achieve full employment;
2. To control prices in oligopoly sectors;
3. To eliminate speculation and to control housing prices;
4. To restrict corporate flight from communities;
5. To establish integrated planning and investment controls.

The first step here would be to provide the breadwinners in every family with a decent income and a guaranteed job and thereby to reduce the residential isolation of poor minorities now suffering job and racial discrimination. Adequate incomes would be corrosive of exclusionary zoning. Controlling prices for primary commodities (e.g., food and energy) would involve regulation of only a few major firms and would control inflation. Housing could be treated as a basic necessity and valued for its home-use value, rather than its speculative exchange value. For example, Congress could pass legislation controlling the prices of all houses built with federal aid or federal tax subsidies. A heavy tax on undeveloped land could be used to reduce speculation, as Henry George proposed. Racial exclusion might be reduced because there would be less of an income and housing cost differential between city neighborhoods. Plant-closing legislation is necessary to reduce the negative impact of capital flight. Without control of job-creating investments, cities are without control of their futures. Plotkin suggests the further step of actual contracts between companies and cities such as those made by professional sports teams. The new law would require that a corporation that violates its written contract by leaving would be liable for the costs of abandonment.

"Contracts" between Communities and Corporations

The idea of a contract between communities and corporations has been broached by other analysts of the urban scene. David Smith (1979), for example, has argued that the "reliance" doctrine can be linked to a conception of "implied contracts." There is in the common law a "reliance" doctrine. If a local government promises to build a sewer and water system for an area, and a builder constructs houses on that promise, and if the government fails to deliver, the builder has a legal right to sue for breach of contract. There was no written contract, but there was an implied contract on which the builder took action. Smith (1979, 7) has suggested that this principle should be applied to decisions by private companies as well. When a company locates a major plant or office facility in an area, it not only attracts people to work there but also encourages people to settle in for the long term with their families, to build schools and city buildings, and to take out long-term mortgages on their homes. Tax breaks are granted to the company by the local community. Workers and their families develop strong social ties to the community. There is an implied contract between the company and the people; the company implicitly has agreed that it is there for the long term. But, if a company leaves after a short time or with a few weeks' notice, it has clearly violated that implied contract. Yet in such a case there is as yet no way for citizens to sue a company for damages or to force compliance with community needs. Today, a basic community necessity is to build into American law such contracts in order to hold corporations accountable for the broader community costs for investment and disinvestment.

In Europe, pressures from organized workers have resulted in some laws restricting corporate flight. A company in Great Britain desiring to close or relocate must get an industrial development certificate from the government's Department of Trade and Industry. Corporations are thereby discouraged from leaving a troubled area and are encouraged to enter high unemployment cities. In cases where firms must close, workers are required to be given training, relocation, or job severance pay benefits. Similar laws are in operation in France and West Germany.

But what is the relevance of this to urban land-use debates? There are two points here that are relevant to an alternative progressive perspective. One central point is that capital flight is indeed a *land-use issue*. When companies abruptly leave a community, they destroy the viable context for securing home- and neighborhood-use values, and they take capital with them that has been created by the collective efforts of the workers in the community. In many apologies for capitalism, capital itself is viewed as a *privately* generated resource, and thus as legitimately beyond the control of citizens and local communities. But companies frequently borrow money from banks and other lenders, or they draw on past profits. Where does that money come from? Smith (1979, 7) has put this well:

> Capital is a social resource. The people created it collectively, by their labor, savings, and their presence in a community which creates markets. It is absurd to say that once this money moves into the hands of some financial intermediary, it ceases to be theirs and is no longer accountable to public concerns.

Capitalists often borrow from the savings of workers in banks, insurance companies, and pension funds. Or they draw on the past profits generated by the labor of their workers. It is ironic that capital created by people's sweat and savings in a particular locality is used to create unemployment there as companies abandon that place for lower-wage labor markets around the globe.

A second point is that Smith's conception of an implied contract and of much capital as a resource created collectively by people's labor and savings can be extended to land-development corporations and their relationships to communities. The latter come into communities seeking profits; they too can be viewed as making an "implied contract" with the community residents whose labor and efforts there give land a price—and a rising price. And they, too—for example, in hit-and-run developments or in environmentally disastrous projects—can create major social costs for community residents to pay. Moreover, real estate firms draw on lenders' capital whose source is, partially at least, collective in the sense that Smith eloquently describes above.

Forging Contracts with Developers

Progressive policies regarding land use have been implemented in a number of U.S. cities in the last decade (cf. Clavel 1986); but Santa Monica seems to have moved the most substantial distance in the direction of forging major agreements and contracts with real estate development firms. Santa Monica, a beachfront city of 90,000 surrounded by Los Angeles, has been the site of major conflict over the use value of land. In the 1970s, housing in Santa Monica became a critical issue, particularly for senior citizens. Housing price increases outran incomes by eight to one in the late 1970s (Clavel 1986). Speculative sales of residential units increased tenfold; between 1970 and 1978 landlords increased rents twice as fast as landlords elsewhere in Southern California. While moderate-rent apartments were being razed in large numbers for larger-scale development projects, expensive condominiums and homes accounted for most new units being privately developed (Capek 1985; Feagin and Capek 1986).

The business-dominated city council repeatedly suggested that moderate-income residents were "second-class citizens." In response, a group of senior citizens in 1978 spontaneously organized to put a rent-control initiative on the ballot. It lost, but Proposition 13 won. Proposition 13 was a property tax measure publicly linked to promises of rental savings for tenants. When landlords instead increased rents, opposition formed against this "exchange value" solution. This time voters passed a strict rent-control law. Two years later, the successful grass-roots electoral coalition targeted the destruction of the city by landlords and developers and elected a slate of progressive candidates to the city council.

The new city council took some dramatic steps, including a moratorium on all real estate development. Unlike most cities, which typically vie with each other to capture footloose investments, Santa Monica's democratically elected progressive council forced developers to negotiate givebacks to the community in exchange for the right to make a profit there. Santa Monica exacted a whole new category of social goods: low- and moderate-income housing, day-care centers, public parks, energy-saving features, and affirmative action hiring. The projects themselves were made to conform to a "human scale" construction. For example, one developer came to the Santa Monica council for permission to build a multistory office complex. The council agreed, but only after the developer committed himself to meeting major community needs as part of the project: an affirmative action program of hiring, a public park, thirty units of low- and moderate-income housing, a 1,500-square-foot community room, and a day-care center. In addition, an agreement between the city of Santa Monica and another real estate firm specified that a significant portion of a proposed commercial-office project be constructed to house low- and moderate-income citizens, including units for senior citizens and families with children. In another agreement with a real estate developer, Welton Becket Associates, the Santa Monica City Council reportedly reshaped a 900,000-square-foot commercial-office-hotel complex to include the following: 100 rental units in new (or existing) buildings for low- and moderate-income renters (including the aged and handicapped); three acres of landscaped park areas with athletic sport facilities; a day-care center, promotion of car pool, bicycling, and flex-time arrangements to reduce traffic programs; and an arts and social services fee (Feagin 1983, 203–5).

Reviewing the Santa Monica proceedings, Lindorff (1981, 20) noted the extraordinary character of such negotiations between a city council and important developers. These are rare written contracts because in big cities, such as New York, "developers routinely threaten to drop projects if the city doesn't give them something (usually a height exemption and a giant tax abatement)." The usual procedure is for city councils and other government officials to rush to the aid of developers with subsidies and to require no negotiations with developers for contributions to community needs or meeting social costs. The new council, not dependent on development interests for its campaign financing, argued that developers should pay for some social costs they create, including housing destruction and increased city service expenditures. Other city council innovations stressing democracy and local control included city funding of neighborhood organizations, the creation of citizen task forces, development policies encouraging open space and public amenities, a housing policy to preserve the income and racial mix of the city, an innovative anticrime program, toxic disclosure regulations, and farmers' markets (Shearer 1982; Feagin and Capek 1986).

Democratization of decisions about urban land use is a central feature of the reforms in Santa Monica and a number of other towns and cities across the United States. But the expansion of democratic input does not come easily. The progressive politicians in Santa Monica faced a host of problems. While they had laid down some new people's rules governing their city, they could not control the regional economy and investment flows into and out of that region. Landlords besieged the city with expensive lawsuits. Progressive city council members often faced hostile community groups and found that democracy was limited by the existing hierarchical (antidemocratic) structure of city hall and by constant pressures on the city by the larger political-economic system in which it was embedded. Organizing a routinized government and regulating real estate development resulted in the city council members compromising their ideals in order to take effective action in a capitalistic economy. Even the aforementioned developer agreements signal the compromises made by progressive council members who were initially opposed to all private development in the city. At the same time, the Santa Monica People's Movement raised democratic participation in the city significantly and rewrote the traditional urban script on land-use decision making in a way that favored non-elite actors (Feagin and Capek 1986).

Conclusion: Lessons for Land-Use Decision Making

The democratic reform impulse has not been limited to a few city councils. We have noted the progressive elements of the New Jersey (*Mt. Laurel*) court decisions concerning the income and racial desegregation of housing in that state's suburbs and cities. The negative consequences of exclusionary zoning practices there slowly became evident to judges who were in no sense "radicals," although their actions were taken, accurately, by conservatives as fundamentally radicalizing for traditional land-use practices. The judges recognized that "freedom and equality for all U.S. citizens," an American ideal since at least 1776, has a force of its own which in the long run is difficult to resist. People of all income levels and racial backgrounds have a right to secure home and neighborhood use values. This principle of the right to a life-space is one that could well become a guide to future planning and court decisions in regard to U.S. cities. The essential ideal has two parts. First, maximize the resources available to all citizens, even if that requires redistribution of income or housing rights down the status ladder (cf. Rawls 1971). Secondly, maximize the participatory rights of the entire citizenry, even if that entails the sacrifice of the tradition of elitist decision making on behalf of that citizenry. This democratization ideal can be seen as encompassing both the political and the economic spheres—and thus as challenging the maldistributions of rights and of wealth which are grounded fundamentally in a capitalistic political-economy.

It has been pointed out that in order to exist, capitalism must continuously convert life-space into commodity-space in order to sustain profits. Whole communities created by a large developer—or organized around a particular industry—may be defined as commodity-space; particular neighborhoods may be singled out to be converted into investment space, as in gentrified areas from New York to San Francisco. In the process of expansive capital investment, life-space often is rendered abstract economic space and separated from the fact that it is a place where people carry on their lives. It is in this sense that capitalism must swallow the "roots" of people to stay alive. Such a process raises basic questions of fairness. It does not take place without a struggle, as Santa Monica illustrates. And by enshrining the private property principle, capitalism creates its own nemesis—people want to defend their life spaces, their use-value concerns, and thus stand in the way of capitalism's restless appropriation of urban space.

Notes

1. *Village of Euclid v. Ambler Realty Co., 272 U.S. 365 (1926).*
2. *Gautreaux v. CHA,* 304 F. Supp. 736 (1969).

3. *Hills v. Gautreaux,* 96 S. Ct. 1538, 1549 (1976).
4. *Village of Arlington Heights v. Metropolitan Housing Development Corp.,* 429 U.S. 252 (1977).
5. *Southern Burlington County NAACP v. Mount Laurel,* 456 A. 2d 390, 410 (1983).

References

Babcock, Richard F. 1966. *The Zoning Game.* Madison: University of Wisconsin Press.

Babcock, Richard F. and Charles L. Siemon. 1985. *The Zoning Game Revisited.* Boston: Oelgeschlager, Gunn & Hain.

Baker, Newton D. 1975. "Brief and argument." *Landmark Briefs and Arguments of the Supreme Court of the U.S.* Vol. 24. Edited by P. Kurland and G. Casper. Arlington, VA.: University Publications of America, Inc.

Berry, Brian J. L. 1982. "Islands of renewal — seas of decay." Paper presented at Urban Policy Conference, University of Chicago, 18–19 June. In *The New Urban Reality,* edited by P. Peterson, 69–98. Washington, D.C.: Brookings, 1985.

Berry, Brian J. L. 1973. *The Human Consequences of Urbanization.* New York: St. Martin's Press.

Berry, Brian J. L., and John Kasarda. 1977. *Contemporary Human Ecology.* New York: Macmillan.

Bluestone, Barry, and Bennett Harrison. 1982. *The Deindustrialization of America.* New York: Basic Books.

Capek, Stella. 1985. "Progressive urban movements: The case of Santa Monica." Ph.D. dissertation, University of Texas.

Castells, Manuel. 1977. *The Urban Question.* Cambridge, Mass.: MIT Press.

Castells, Manuel. 1983.*The City and the Grassroots.* Berkeley: University of California Press.

Clavel, Pierre. 1985. *The Progressive City.* New Brunswick, N.J.: Rutgers University Press.

Davies, Pearl J. 1958. *Real Estate in American History.* New York: Public Affairs Press.

Feagin, Joe R. 1983. *The Urban Real Estate Game.* Englewood Cliffs, N.J.: Prentice-Hall.

Feagin, Joe R. 1985. "The Social Costs of Houston's Growth." *International Journal of Urban and Regional Research.* 9 (June): 164–85.

Feagin, Joe R., and Clairece Booher Feagin. 1978. *Discrimination American Style.* Englewood Cliffs, N.J.: Prentice-Hall.

Feagin, Joe R., and Stella Capek, 1986. "Grassroots movements in a class perspective." Paper presented at annual meetings of Society for the Study of Social Problems, New York, August.

Flink, James J. 1975. *The Car Culture.* Cambridge, Mass.: MIT Press.

Form, William H. 1954. "The place of social structure in the determination of land use: Some implications for a theory of urban ecology." *Social Forces* 32:317–24.

Fluck, Timothy A. 1986. *Euclid v. Ambler:* A retrospective." *American Planning Association Journal.* Summer.

George, Henry. 1962. *Progress and Poverty.* New York: Robert Schalkenbach.

Gottdiener, Mark. 1985. *The Social Production of Urban Space.* Austin: University of Texas Press.

Gottdiener, Mark, and Joe R. Feagin, 1988. "The paradigm shift in urban sociology." *Urban Affairs Quarterly* 24:163–87.

Greer, Scott. 1962. *The Emerging City.* New York: Free Press.

Habermas, Jurgen. 1973. *The Fiscal Crisis of the State.* New York: St. Martin's Press.

Harvey, David. 1973. *Social Justice and the City.* Baltimore: Johns Hopkins University Press.

Hawley, Amos. 1950. *Human Ecology.* New York: Ronald Press.

Hawley, Amos. 1981. *Urban Society.* 2d ed. New York: Wiley.

Judd, Dennis R. 1984. *The Politics of American Cities.* 2d ed. Boston: Little, Brown.

Kapp, Karl. 1950. *The Social Costs of Private Enterprise.* New York: Schocken Books.

Kasarda, John. 1980. "The implications of contemporary redistribution trends for national urban policy." *Social Science Quarterly* 61:373–400.

Lindorff, David. 1981. "About-face in Santa Monica." *Village Voice.* 2–8 December.

Logan, John, and Harvey Molotch. 1986. *Urban Fortunes.* Berkeley: University of California Press.

Lustig, R. Jeffrey. 1982. *Corporate Liberalism.* Berkeley: University of California Press.

Mandel, Ernest. 1978. *Late Capitalism.* Trans. J. De Bres. London: NLB-Verso.

McAdams, D. Claire. 1980. "A power-conflict approach to urban land use," *Urban Anthropology* 9:292–318.

McKeever, J. Ross, Nathaniel M. Griffin, and Frank H. Spink. 1977. *Shopping Center Development Handbook.* Washington, D.C.: Urban Land Institute.

Meyer, Peter. 1979. "Land Rush." *Harper's.* January, 258:45–60.

Micklin, Michael, and Harvey Choldin, eds. 1984. *Sociological Human Ecology: Contemporary Issues and Applications.* Boulder: Westview Press.

National Commission on Urban Problems. 1968. *Building the American City.* Washington, D.C.: U.S. Government Printing Office.

O'Connor, James. 1973. *The Fiscal Crisis of the State.* New York: St. Martin's Press.

Park, Robert E. and Ernest W. Burgess. 1924. *Introduction to the Science of Society.* Chicago: University of Chicago Press.

Paschal, Joel F. 1951. *Mr. Justice Sutherland.* Princeton, N.J.: Princeton University Press.

Plotkin, Sidney. 1987. *Keep Out: The Struggle for Land Use Control.* Berkeley: University of California Press.

Popper, Frank J. 1981. *The Politics of Land-Use Reform.* Madison: University of Wisconsin Press.

President's Commission for a National Agenda for the Eighties, Panel on Policies and Prospects. 1980. *Urban America in the Eighties: Perspectives and Prospects.* Washington, D.C.: U.S. Government Printing Office.

Rawls, John. 1971. *A Theory of Justice.* Cambridge: Harvard University Press.

Reilly, William K., ed. 1973. *The Use of Land: A Citizen's Guide to Urban Growth.* New York: Crowell.

Smith, David. 1979. *The Public Balance Sheet.* Washington, D.C.: Conference on Alternative State and Local Policies.

Shearer, Derek. 1982. "How the progressives won in Santa Monica." *Social Policy.* Winter, 7–14.

Toll, Seymour. 1969. *Zoned American.* New York: Grossman Publishers.

Urban Land Institute. 1961. *New Approaches to Residential Land Development.* Technical Bulletin 10. Washington, D.C.: Urban Land Institute.

Walker, Richard A., and Michael K. Heiman. 1981. "Quiet revolution for whom?" Annals of the Association of American Geographers. March, 71:67–83.

9

Are Planners Collective Capitalists?
The Cases of Aberdeen and Houston

Joe R. Feagin

I Introduction

For more than a century petroleum firms have poured capital into widely scattered regions and cities, gradually developing a worldwide oil and gas extraction and processing system. Two of the most important extractive areas are
centered around Aberdeen, Scotland, and Houston, Texas, often called the "oil
capitals" of their respective regions. Aberdeen and Houston have been greatly
shaped economically, politically, and spatially by the investment decisions
made by multinational oil and gas executives at the top of the world oil and gas
system. The character and timing of petroleum discoveries and investments
have led to differing relationships between these extractive regions and the
state, including state planning. In the U.K. and the U.S., governments have
generally left oil and gas extraction, whether early in this century or more recently, in the hands of the private sector, but these governments have nonetheless maintained, to a varying degree, surveillance over growth and
development costs. The discovery of petroleum in a region where a local and

This chapter is reprinted with minor revisions from Feagin, Joe R. 1990. "Are planners collective
capitalists? The cases of Aberdeen and Houston," *International Journal of Urban and Regional
Research,* 14 (N. 2): 249–73.

I am indebted to the following for their comments and suggestions on an earlier version of this
chapter: Bob Beauregard, Mark Gottiener, James McKie, Roger Olien, Keith Chapman, Norman
Bonney, Patsy Healey, and Bryan Roberts.

national planning system is extensively developed can mean a different relationship between oil-related investors and government agencies—and a different orchestrated response to growth costs—than in a region where there is a weaker system of governmental planning.

II   The Costs of Growth

Social economist Karl Kapp (1950, 13–25) has defined the "social costs" of private enterprise as the negative consequences of profit-centered capitalistic investment and production, as costs created by business expansion and production that are not paid for by an individual firm, but rather are shifted onto third parties. Decision making by this criterion will seek to reduce business costs and, if possible, to ignore the community costs of business-linked growth. Indeed, mainstream economics treats these costs as "externalities," as costs not processed through the market and therefore irrelevant to conventional economic analysis. Yet many urban growth problems are regularly created, and remain partially or totally uncompensated, because corporate investment and decision making does not entail corporate compensation for the community costs created by such actions.

Much of the cost of investment-generated growth is paid for (if it is paid for) by what Leipert (1985, 14) has called governmental "defensive expenditures," including the external costs of actual production, such as the cost of dealing with environmental pollution and toxic waste, as well as the "external costs of spatial concentration, centralization of production and associated urbanization," including infrastructural planning, roads, and waste-water systems (Leipert 1985, 14). Without the appropriate governmental planning and action, the costs of a rapid infusion of capital investment can be dramatic:

> How much expansion can be absorbed, and how quickly, depends on the dynamics of the people and the environment of the community involved
> . . . With suitable planning and reasonable forecasts, new schools can be built, teachers hired, roadways, water and sewage systems constructed
> . . . But when the capital influx is totally unrestrained, the absorptive capacity of the social system can be quickly overwhelmed (Bluestone and Harrison 1982, 106).

III   Does Planning Matter?

A major issue here is that concerning the role of planning in protecting against, and coping with, these social costs of growth, as well as with problems of urban decline. Theoretically, planning matters because the character and design of urban space matters. Some theoretical analysis has accented the role of space as a constituent part of the forces of production (Lefebvre 1972; Gottdiener 1985). Spatial configuration is a force of production together with technology, capital, and labour. This configuration can be viewed as encompassing the locational and design features of space, including land and privately and publicly constructed environments. More specifically, spatial configuration and design include the capital-shaped built environment, the state-shaped physical and infrastructural environment, the spatial patterns arising from unplanned deconcentration of metropolitan area and the mixed spatial outcomes that result from political struggles over urban space (Gottdiener 1987, 415). Space is involved in both the realization and valorization processes of capital accumulation. The character of spatial design can limit or speed capital circulation and thus affect the realization of surplus value. Yet much of the urban spatial configuration of modern capitalism is shaped by the aforementioned firm-level calculations about profit. While such calculations can provide for jobs and economic prosperity, they can also generate broader social and spatial side effects, such as traffic congestion on inadequate road systems, environmental degradation, and harmful land-use mixes. Individualized investment decisions create a chaos in urban space accompanying the economic prosperity. Urban planning has developed in part to cope with this chaos of urban sociospatial development. Since space is a force in production, then the character and shaping of space, the intentional and unintentional sociospatial design, are important for understanding modern capitalism.

As a rule, government planning about space is top-down and elitist. In the U.S. and the U.K. the élitism of planning has been targeted in the critiques of advocacy planners, who have called for its democratization. Assessing the U.S., Goodman (1971) has suggested that most urban planners today do not represent those who are affected by their plans; they are "soft cops"—experts who use what they view as "scientific" methods to buttress a class-stratified, inegalitarian system of urban development. The advocacy critique suggests the need for a broader array of interests in planning and points up the significance of sociospatial configurations as reflective of use values as well as exchange values. Urban spatial development is more than a matter of the exchange-value considerations of oil firms and development corporations; it is also a matter of the use-value concerns of families and neighbourhoods.

Even with regard to the elitist facilitating of the exchange-value interests of industrial firms and developers, however, planning systems and planners have different roles to play in a capitalist society. In the U.K. and the U.S., planners often respond to the needs and pressures of individual industrial and development capitalists; in this role they operate as "middlemen" negotiating regulations. But in other ways governmental planners have played a "collective capitalist" role. For example, the development of broad comprehensive planning and trend research is in the *collective* interest of capitalists, but subsidizing such activity is often not seen as being in the interest of individual entrepreneurs and firms. Since the collective interests of industrial and real estate investors are best promoted through the state, state-managerial planning has been critical of urban capitalism in this and other ways. Planners *qua* state managers have often pursued the general interests of capitalists, including actions stabilizing and rationalizing investments in the primary and secondary circuits. Professional planning can and does rationalize capital accumulation.

David Harvey (1985, 2–11), writing cogently about the primary and secondary circuits, suggests that there must be a surplus of capital in the primary circuit of production for capital to flow into the built environment, the secondary circuit. An activist government becomes involved because individual capitalists have difficulty in switching capital from one circuit to another without government-backed banking institutions. With this state-banking aid, capital flows relatively smoothly between the primary and secondary circuits. But frequently capital does not move smoothly between the primary and secondary circuits or within the secondary circuit itself. There can be extremely irrational swings in investment in real estate projects in the secondary circuit. For that reason, governmental actions beyond the sphere of banking have dealt with the anarchy of private investments in both circuits. In some cases, substantial economic and land-use planning can even out the capital flows between and within investment circuits. Planning can help rationalize the accumulation process in a society that goes through major business crises and cycles.

1 Planning in the U.K.

Generally speaking, cities in the U.K. are subject to more urban planning in the public interest than U.S. cities. Substantial town and country planning, which came to the U.K. during the 1940s, was held out as a morale-boosting version of better housing, schools, and communities after the war. According to Ambrose, planning legislation in the U.K. reflected the need of successive governments for legitimization in the eyes of the public and, on paper at least, "would have severely inhibited the rate of capital accumulation via land development" (Ambrose 1986, 23). Postwar planning was initially established under the assumption that most urban construction would be undertaken by government authorities. However, in reality much development was commanded by private interests and developers, as in U.S. cities. As a result, U.K. planning agencies found themselves riding herd on private developers (Hall 1987, 151). In contrast to the U.S., in the U.K. governmental planning has been viewed by most as a positive force in the economy. The benefits of governmental planning in the U.K. have been important. Extensive land-use planning at the local and regional levels has encompassed a large number of economic, environmental, and land-use regulations significantly limiting the operation of the "free market" in land decision making. Even according to one critic of U.K. planning there has not been as much piecemeal expansion, and the peripheries of cities and adjacent agricultural land around cities have not been gobbled up rapidly, as in U.S. cities. "Manhattan-type tower blocks" have not submerged historic central cities (Ambrose 1986, 258). The zoning of land-uses in cities has reduced the number of unpleasant and dangerously polluted environments.

In the United Kingdom a long succession of welfare-state governments at the national level has made a difference in the U.K. orientation to planning. These governments have been run by civil servants sensitive both to the use-value demands of organized workers and to the exchange-value demands of industrial and development investors. The relative autonomy of civil servants in the United Kingdom contrasts with civil servants in the United States, and probably accounts for the ability of U.K. planners and other officials to act, as the occasion warrants, as middlemen, collective capitalists, or citizen advocates. In the U.S. there has been more of an ongoing debate over the legitimacy of citizen advocacy and collective capitalist goals. There has also been stronger support for planning at the local government level in the United Kingdom, in part because of the substantial ties of local authorities (as in Aberdeen) to the Labour Party. At the local level in the United States, there is much weaker party organization around ideological issues and generally weaker support for multifaceted planning. As a result, in the U.K. planning and planners are taken more seriously and planning has attracted talented professionals. In the United States talented professionals leave planning because there is a weaker public-regarding stance. Because of the greater organization and political power of workers in the United Kingdom, and their greater influence on local and national governments, planning has been more likely to take into account the use-value concerns and needs of the local citizenry than in most U.S. cities. Because of the organized working class, urban planners, and the government officials to which they report, do not listen only to investors. Zoning of land use benefits investors by protecting land prices, but it also protects residents from harmful adjacent land uses and thus makes the quality of life better in many neighbourhoods. Planning in the public interest can provide for a more pleasing living environment, such as by developing an adequate park system.

Moreover, with greater rationality in the movement of capital into the primary and secondary circuits, there can also be more measured and rational governmental investments in the public infrastructure. Fewer surges in infrastructure are required. Savings can be achieved and many growth costs can be tempered.

2 Planning in the United States

In the United States, urban planning originated in the "City Beautiful" plans prominent around 1900, but by the 1920s urban planning had shifted its emphasis from aesthetic qualities to one of efficiency in the physical form of cities and to maintaining homogeneous land uses and the value of private property by governmental zoning. Larger U.S. developers were concerned with developing the suburban rings of residential areas "properly" and thus worked with the leading planning association (American City Planning Institute) to issue a joint statement that became the nucleus of the federal government's model planning act, which in turn became the basis of the decentralized system of planning. The Standard State Enabling Act (1924) was adopted by forty-four states and provided that zoning should be "in accordance with a comprehensive plan." Although few comprehensive plans were implemented, by the 1940s, 1,360 cities had zoning ordinances and 517 had subdivision regulations. However, in contrast to the United Kingdom, substantial local option is possible in the United States, so business and governmental elites in a few cities, including Houston, have refused to adopt zoning and comprehensive planning (Weiss 1987), With their business-oriented, technical-expertise approach, mainstream planners have operated as "expert" facilitators for the projects sought by developers and industrialists, and thus as hired guns who rarely analyse or respond to the social justice problems created by the profit-oriented city development they have helped to implement (Burchell and Hughes 1978, xx). Influential planners have accented this technical expert-client approach to urban redesign, sometimes with an added emphasis on the role of educating clients on what constitutes "good" design. As a review of the urban planning profession has expressed it, planners have traditionally "lacked access to the decision-making process . . . have tended to avoid political conflict, have been technique-oriented rather than goal-oriented, and are facilitators rather than initiators" (Burchell and Hughes 1978, xxvi). This has meant that U.S. planners, especially in the Sunbelt, are more likely to function as servicing middlemen than as collective capitalists.

In the remainder of this article I will first examine the development of the social and community costs of the extraction economies in the Aberdeen and Houston areas: then I will analyse governmental planning and allied responses to costs. Aberdeen and Houston have different regulatory systems, but they have confronted broadly similar patterns of oil-related boom–bust development. A central question is whether a developed planning system such as that in Aberdeen has provided relief from the major social costs of urban development in comparison with a much weaker planning system such as that in Houston.

IV   Oil-Gas Development in Aberdeen and Houston: A Brief History

1   Aberdeen

Located on the North Sea, Aberdeen is the economic and political center for northeastern Scotland. An agricultural and fishing center, Aberdeen has become a central *entrepot* before the discovery of petroleum. In 1964 the U.K.

government issued licenses authorizing multinational firms to explore for North Sea oil and gas; by the late 1970s many international oil firms were involved in the North Sea. In the late 1980s forty offshore oil fields were in production or being developed. Before the hydrocarbon discoveries, in the two decades after the Second World War, the greater Aberdeen area was relatively depressed, and there was substantial outmigration. According to David McIntosh (1987), who served in, and as head of, the Aberdeen planning department from 1959 to 1984, before oil the Aberdeen area was in "a rather depressed period" and was losing population; "something like 2,000" people were leaving annually. There were few job opportunities for young people, and wage levels were low (Lloyd and Newlands 1987, I-1; Bentley 1987). However, from 1970 to the OPEC-related oil price decline beginning in the early 1980s, the exploration and development of oil and gas fields brought many well-paid jobs to northeast Scotland; oil-related employment grew from 1,000 in 1971 to 51,000 in 1985. The general population also grew steadily. There was a major onshore construction boom, as sites were chosen for pipelines, terminals, plants, and administrative headquarters. By the early 1980s numerous major oil firms and oil service firms had set up operational offices in Aberdeen (Scottish Office 1987). There was major expansion of investment in the secondary circuit, in real estate, mostly by outside developers from London and Holland. As one real estate official has put it, "one of the sad facts of life was that in the late seventies, the Monday morning plane from London was fifty-percent developers" (Young 1987). However, the declining price of oil over the 1980s, and the sharp drop in 1986, reversed Aberdeen's movement to economic prosperity. There were major business retrenchments and job losses.

2   Houston

A major diference between the Houston and Aberdeen regions lies in the timing of initial oil development in the subsequent layering of downstream industries. Houston had the earlier development. The discovery of oil ninety miles east of Houston in 1901 and subsequent discoveries closer to the city in the next three decades set the stage for Houston to become an international oil center. By 1940 about three-quarters of the oil produced in the midcontinent area was controlled by companies tied to Houston. Texas had the nation's most productive oil field, that in east Texas, as well as 56 percent of proven oil reserves in the United States. Between the 1940s and the early 1980s there was a continuation of oil-driven prosperity in the greater Houston area. There was a general construction boom—plants, houses, office buildings and stores—from the 1910s to the 1930s and then again from the 1940s to the early 1980s. After the Second World War Houston evolved into the oil-technology distribution center for oil fields around the globe. By the 1970s there were 100 Houston companies working in the North Sea fields, a sign of the developing relationship. Between the 1960s and the 1980s there was a dramatic increase in oil-related employment; more than one-third of Houston's jobs were directly connected to oil and gas, with another fifth dependent on the industry. Thirty-four of the thirty-five nation's largest oil companies had facilities in the Houston area, and there were 400 major oil and gas companies in the area (Feagin 1988, 52–67). A major economic downturn began in 1982; and since then Houston, like Aberdeen, has experienced a significant oil-related decline.

V   Boomtown Growth: A Sampling of Social Costs

1   Social Costs in Aberdeen

The oil booms have imposed many infrastructural and other costs on the residents of northeast Scotland and southeast Texas. The offshore oil discoveries in the North Sea brought much onshore activity to Aberdeen and the surrounding Grampian region. There were long-term effects on onshore resources, community structure, service infrastructure, population growth, local labour markets, and housing supply. There was a sharply increased need for a more adequate infrastructure to service the new industries and workers coming in. The social costs of growth for the Aberdeen area included an overburdened sewer and water system, underdeveloped roads, a housing shortage coupled with a housing affordability crisis, insufficient schools and crowded recreational facilities. For example, a Grampian Regional Plan prepared by local planners concluded that the growing population did not have adequate urban recreational facilities (Grampian Regional Council 1986, 29). There was a negative impact on nearby areas, such as the Gordon District just north of Aberdeen. As in Aberdeen, heavy immigration there brought a sharp increase in population; land and housing prices increased; recreational and other facilities were swamped; and there was a significant increase in the untreated sewage dumped into the North Sea.

To take a major example of the consequences of growth, the oil-related economic developments and associated population increases brought a sharp increase in inflation, particularly in hotel and restaurant prices, land prices and housing prices and rents. David McIntosh, former head of the Aberdeen planning department, has described the situation during the first part of the oil boom in the 1970s:

Now when oil came along, that changed the structure completely because only those connected [with oil] got big increases, but that was more or less a small proportion of the population. And the effect that had was that many people jumped on the bandwagon, including the local hotels, restaurants, and so on, and all the prices went up. . . . It was getting fairly desperate that way, just the imbalance. (1987 McIntosh)

For homebuyers there was a substantial increase in the price of housing; by the mid-1980s housing prices were nearly 50 percent higher than the national average (Grampian Regional Council 1986, 29). A house bought in 1971 for £5000 sold for £10 000 a few years later, and by 1981 was worth £40 000. Contributing to the high prices was speculation in land; this became commonplace for various types of land development, as speculators participated in land flipping. Land prices rose to astronomical sums; sometimes land sold for U.S. $160,000 an acre just outside Aberdeen (Kennedy 1987).

2 Social Costs in Houston

The extended hydrocarbon boom imposed many infrasructural and other social costs on the people of Houston. Many costs have been similar in type to those in Aberdeen, such as serious deficiencies in sewer and water systems. From 1900 to the late 1980s a central watercourse, called Buffalo Bayou, has been an open sewer for disposing of wastewater from city and private sewage plants. By the 1970s the city had a massive deficiency in sewage facilities, and by the early 1980s the city of Houston's forty-four treatment plants regularly violated Texas wastewater standards. In addition, rapid industrial growth from the 1940s to the 1980s seriously depleted the local water supply, and the city had to change from deep-water wells to surface-water sources, including Lake Houston; because of residential development in the lake area, inadequately treated sewage has flowed through numerous small treatment plants into the now polluted lake.

Traffic congestion has been a major Houston problem for decades. A survey of freeways found that in peak traffic periods the average distance one could drive from the downtown area had been reduced by one-third between 1969 and 1979. The number of autos had increased at a rate twice that of population increase (Rice Center 1981, 27–28). In addition, such public amenities as recreational parkland have been lacking; in 1977 a U.S. Interior Department study ranked Houston 140th among U.S. cities in *per capita* parkland (Carreau 1982, A1). In addition, Houston has long had a housing crisis. In 1987 Houston had an estimated 10,000–15,000 homeless persons, 18,000 persons waiting to get into public housing, half a million low- and moderate-income persons paying unaffordable housing payments and a quarter of its low-income citizens in overcrowded houses. Moreover, Houston has only 3,000 public housing units, down from 4,000 just a few years ago, which compares with New York's 207,000 units (Feagin, Gilderbloom, and Rodrigeuz, 1989).

VI   Relying on the Planning System:
The Defense against Social Costs in Aberdeen

1   Planning in Aberdeen

In the U.K. and the U.S., planning agency action has been a major example of state intervention designed, at least in part, to cope with the costs of economic and related population growth. Comparing Aberdeen and Houston reveals that the planning system has been much more comprehensive (for example, including substantial economic planning) and considerably more interventionist in the former city. For decades the greater Aberdeen metropolitan area has had a much more developed planning system than most U.S. cities, including Houston; and from the beginning of the oil boom to the present there have been considerably more professional planners *per capita* in northeast Scotland area than in the Houston metropolitan area. For example, in the late 1980s the Grampian Regional Council, the regional governmental authority for northeast Scotland, had a staff of forty professional planners, with a total of perhaps 100 professional planners in the entire region around Aberdeen, an area with a half million people (Cockhead 1987).

In comparison to the Houston situation, the Aberdeen planning system has provided greater protection for northeast Scotland from numerous negative costs of secondary circuit growth because planning permission must be secured before any significant development project can begin. Local authorities have the right to reject any development project, subject to review by the Secretary of State for Scotland (the Scottish Office), the representative of the central government in Scotland (Baldwin and Baldwin 1975, 132–35). In 1974 the planning organization was restructured: the Aberdeen District Council replaced the old Town Council and in the process lost some planning functions to a newly created Grampian Regional Council, which took over educational, social work, and certain health-care services and planning for northeast Scotland, leaving local Aberdeen planners with responsibility for housing, environmental health, recreation, tourism, and industrial development. Under the 1972 Town and Country Planning (Scotland) Act the Grampian Regional Council and its planners have prepared a detailed "structure plan" and the Aberdeen District Council and its planners have been developing a "local plan" with more specific recommendations and land allocations within the regional council's structure plan framework. By the late 1980s the Aberdeen District Council had begun the preparation of, but had not adopted, a formal local plan; it has used instead informal policy statements generally in line with the structure plan to channel development (Grampian Regional Council 1986, 6). The Regional Council planners have the responsibility for strategic planning and implementing the structure plan, which involves public investments in such spatial configuration items as sewers, water, schools, and roads. This structure plan lays out the strategy for at least a ten-year period. Preparing and enforcing the local plans and other development control are the basic functions of the Aberdeen district planners, who are responsible for such spatial configuration items as council housing, recreational facilities, and industrial estates (Healey 1983, 91–104; Bentley and Campbell 1987).

One major contrast between planning in the cities of Aberdeen and Houston can be seen in the regulation of investors in the secondary circuit of real estate. In Scotland, at the local and regional levels, the planning system tries to regulate real estate developers and to control numerous social costs of development with planning and zoning regulations and by assessing charges on developers. Land-use regulation is one form of existing development control that has been used to cope with the costs of boom-town growth. The 1972 act requires that developers get planning permission for the development of land; developers are also regulated under the 1984 Roads Act and Building Acts of 1959 and 1970 (Scottish Office 1987). Aberdeen and Grampian Region planners are supposed to approve only projects that are in accord with the locational stipulations of the structure plan and the local plan. The plans provide templates for urban development with which developers must for the most part comply. In addition to the structure plan and the local plan there are other development control procedures. A developer makes a planning application for a development. When someone wants to develop, even if the development accords with the land-use plan, he or she must make a planning application, which is passed on by the district council, for there is no right to develop even in accordance with the land-use plan. The developer can still put in an application if the proposal is not in accordance with the plan. The local authority may then decide that there are various factors which lead them to regard it as acceptable (Cockhead 1987). Unlike Houston, the planning permission process significantly slows down the pace of real estate development. Under the 1972 act developers have the right to appeal planning decisions to the Secretary of State for Scotland, but few do, in part because of the appeal costs and in part because they do not want to disturb their relationship to local planning authorities.

2   Coping with Growth Costs: Collective Capitalists?

The oil boom presented major challenges for local planners. A report by the Grampian Regional Council expressed this conclusion: the "sudden expansion of the oil industry in Grampian Region brought unprecedented problems for the local authorities who had previously been more pre-occupied with the problems of declining population rather than dynamic industrial and commercial activity" (Public Relations Section 1981). Prior to the late 1960s, when an Industrial Development Committee was created, the Aberdeen Town Council had devoted most of its attention to the provision of "social goods such as health care, education, and housing" (Harris, *et al.* no date, 4). The oil discoveries brought unprecedented growth and strained the local planning agencies. The total planning agency expenditures for infrastructural improvement in the path of the boom have been high. For instance, by 1981 the total capital expenditure by the Grampian Regional Council alone, for infrastructure and other projects linked to the North Sea oil and gas industry, had totalled £38 million (Public Relations Section, no date).

In an in-depth interview Aberdeen planner McIntosh (1987) has described the early pressures for quick planning decisions to aid the oil industry. Discussing the arrival of a French oil multinational in the 1970s, McIntosh (1987) noted that they approached him with what they wanted:

> They eventually ended up in an industrial estate. Naturally, we were trying to stop the drift in population, we obviously bent over backwards to help them. We were more or less processing the plans when almost overnight I noticed people saying that TOTAL's got a gas claim or an oil claim in the North Sea. And, within about a week they came in and said scrap these plans, we're doubling in size. So, it was that sort of urgency of the time, quick change.

We can see here the heavy dependence of even the well-developed U.K. planning system on the engine of profit maximization for the creation of jobs. In addition, it is clear that planning was taking place on the slippery slope of rapid changes in the offshore petroleum industry.

The oil firm executives seemed more interested in their individual firm's problems than in larger questions of trend data and infrastructural planning. For example, during the boom period Aberdeen area planners were involved in estimating the amount of infrastructure and industrial acreage that would be needed by the oil and oil services firms. In an interview Allan Kennedy (1987), former chief executive officer of the Gordon District north of Aberdeen, noted that in the late 1960s local planners did meet with the oil firms, but the oil executives were not prepared to participate in cost-related public planning or to indicate what would be needed. Similarly, McIntosh (1987) discussed attempts by local planners and other public officials to meet with representatives of major oil companies to find out "what is required to service this industry . . . [but] we got nothing from the oil companies, and we had to decide ourselves." Here is a conspicuous example of how local planners found little interest among oil executives for dealing with essentially collective capitalist needs. Much of the state economic planning signalled that planners were operating as collective capitalists.

3   The Dilemma of Housing

According to planner McIntosh (1987), the oil firms were also of little help in planning for housing expansion and development: "then when it came to housing, and for housing, the oil companies were not willing to give us much information. Again, we just had to take a stab in the dark." Planners again acted as collective capitalists and laid out detailed plans for housing and related public infrastructural projects. During the boom period this planning was significantly influenced by what the building developers and land speculators were doing, by what they thought should be provided for land and housing. Many land speculators came into the Aberdeen area and took advantage of the oil boom; they bought or took options on much private land. They would buy the land later "and sell it off immediately to the developer" (McIntosh, 1987). This almost anarchic speculation on and flipping of land often created unanticipated planning problems. Aberdeen planners have tried, often successfully, to control development. They went through a period in the early 1980s when they received many applications from developers to develop retail, industrial, and housing areas unacceptable to the district council. Attempts to reject applications brought numerous appeals to the secretary of state. There were two large housing areas which the city council opposed for development. One was approved anyway by the regional council against city officials' wishes. Another application was for 1,400 houses on a greenbelt site. The district council had blocked several applications in such critical areas before, but on this occasion, the builders made such a strong case to the secretary of state that the decision went against the advice of both the Aberdeen Council and the Regional Council (Bentley and Campbell 1987). Most development proposals have eventually been approved; in 1983, for example, Aberdeen planners rejected only 11 percent of the 2,014 planning applications submitted to them. Applications for large development projects, such as office block projects, have gone through the planning department and district council relatively easily (Bonney 1987). However, many of these approved applications have been made subject to major restrictions and conditions; and most projects have been slowed by the review process, far more so than they would have been in U.S. cities such as Houston.

In contrast to the heavy development of huge new office buildings in downtown Houston, most office block construction in Aberdeen has been decentralized by planning regulations limiting central-city construction. There has been a split between the Grampian planners, who have pressed for office block decentralization, and the Aberdeen planners, who have permitted somewhat more central-city construction. However, when this is compared to U.S. cities, there has been much less in the way of concentration in the downtown area of new office buildings. For the most part, the advocates of decentralized office construction prevailed. "What has tended to happen, though, and I think it's probably been for the best, is that the oil companies have been encouraged to cite on the periphery"; few companies have their offices in the city center; the "general rule has been that they move from the center to the periphery" (Cockhead 1987). In the Aberdeen case we can see the dramatic impact of planning interfering with the bulldozing of older buildings and the concentration of office development downtown.

4   Shopping and Industrial Facilities

The planners at the Grampian Regional Council have allowed a fair amount of decentralized shopping facility construction in the outlying portions of metropolitan Aberdeen (McIntish 1987); and these decentralized stores have had an effect on businesses in the downtown area. However, for proposed outlying store developments local planners have required an impact assessment on other stores, particularly in the city center. And, unlike comparable situations in Houston, Aberdeen area planners have successfully slowed or restricted outlying development, thereby insuring the viability of most central city retail stores. In striking contrast to the Houston situation, outside development firms have not always been allowed to locate wherever the market criteria might dictate (Cockhead 1987).

An important local authority response to the oil boom was the support of corporate needs by provision of industrial land. With the oil-fueled growth, private industrial land prices skyrocketed in the Aberdeen area, rising from about £2500 an acre in 1971 to about £50 000 an acre in 1980 (Public Relations Section 1981). The Aberdeen District Council and its planners took action to provide industrial areas. The industrial development committee of the council promoted economic development, purchased land for industrial estates and leased land to private firms. For a time the local authority did very well financially from leasing industrial land; and it did not have to reduce local rates to attract these oil/gas corporations, as is the custom in most U.S. cities (Bonney 1987). In addition, the Grampian Regional Council spent a considerable sum of money to service industrial sites linked to the oil and gas industry. While the procorporate boosterism is evident, there is an important difference between Aberdeen and Houston in this regard. While the political leadership in both areas sought job-generating investments, the Aberdeen officials were able to use governmental control over land and land use planning to bring greater benefits to the community, including substantial leasing returns to the city government.

In Aberdeen there has also been planning regulation of private industrial development projects. Specific locations have been set aside for industry in the structure plan. More industrial land development was actually permitted than specified under the original structure plan, in part because of planning permissions granted on appeal to higher governmental levels by private developers. Thus when the economic downturn came in the mid-1980s the local land market had too much industrial land and prices fell. The location of industrial land was an issue with some corporations. The 1986 Grampian Council review of the 1979 structure plan noted:

> the overall performance of the structure plan has been generally success-
> ful in ensuring an adequate supply of development land but not always at

the detailed locations anticipated, thus contributing to some of the problems which have been experienced in phasing the provision of infrastructure and services (Grampian Regional Council 1986, 33).

5   Water, Sewage, and Road Subsidies

The major infrastructural problems faced by local planning authorities have included inadequate water and drainage systems. The Aberdeen Planning Department has supervised not only the location of developers' projects but also the provision of infrastructure such as sewage and water systems. Unlike Houston the local planning system had some built-in spare capacity. According to a regional planning official (Cockhead 1987), the water system required some improvements to deal with the economic boom, but there were no major problems in expanding it to meet industrial and housing needs. In his view infrastructural projects were for the most part financed and constructed in parallel with growth. In contrast to Houston, Aberdeen area planners were usually able to slow down much private industrial and housing development until the construction of adequate infrastructure, including water facilities, sewerage systems and roads, by public authorities was at least well underway. Moreover, planning controls embodied in river purification boards have not permitted the construction of inferior sewage plants, and the severe water pollution, such as has been permitted in the outlying suburban areas of Houston. The relevant planning regulations set down strict requirements for such sewage plants (Cockhead 1987). Some infrastructure building has come slowly; not until 1987 was a new sewage outfall south of the city completed (Moore 1987). Moreover, when the recession hit in the mid-1980s, the city officials found that they had some government-serviced land on which there was no housing development. When the land was allocated for housing, the infrastructure was put in, at major cost to the city and regional governments, but the housing was not developed because of lack of demand (McIntosh 1987).

Traffic problems have plagued the Aberdeen area. Between 1975 and 1984 the traffic flow in the inner core of Aberdeen grew by 21 percent and in the outer corridor by 40 percent. The percentage of households owning a car increased from 48 percent in 1971 to 59 percent in 1981, the latter near the national figure. At the same time there was a downward trend in the passengers carried by the local bus services (Grampian Regional Council 1986, 15). There was also an increase in the numbers of heavy trucks on the narrow roads. The road infrastructure, including highways linking Aberdeen to the north and the south, was overloaded. At an early point, the head of the Aberdeen Planning Department wrote to the secretary of state for Scotland about the new roads needed from Aberdeen south to Edinburgh, but that office was not yet sensitive to what would be required to meet the costs of the boom. The regional government in Scotland initially did not place emphasis on the road problem around relatively prosperous Aberdeen, but instead accented in the 1970s the needs of less prosperous areas such as Glasgow. Much requisite road construction seems to have come slowly. Conflict among governmental levels over priorities was important. By the mid-1980s the priorities of the Scottish government shifted and more attention was given to roads.

In addition, the central government limited how much the local government could spend for local road improvements (McIntosh 1987). A 1986 Grampian Council review of the 1979 structure plan concluded that most of the badly needed road improvements had at least been started, even though central government financial restrictions had not allowed all of the road projects to be implemented. The 1986 regional review also noted a failure in the local governmental implementation of certain road construction: "It is also perhaps too early to judge the extent to which the partial failure of Inner Area policies and their implications for traffic and transportation will eventually affect the environment of that part of the City" (Grampian Regional Council 1986, 33). Central government subsidies later increased, and the roads were improved by the late 1980s (Cockhead 1987).

6 Regulating Housing

One substantial cost of the boom and the influx of workers was the enormous increase in the cost of housing for owners and renters. As I noted previously, house prices rose rapidly in the greater Aberdeen area; for a time they were the highest in the country outside London and many workers had difficulty in purchasing them. Unlike Houston, local Aberdeen planning and other public authorities have been substantially involved in the regulation of new housing construction and the subsidization of council (public) housing; the 1979 structure plan of the Grampian Regional Council laid out the expected level of planning permissions for new housing developments (Public Relations Section, no date). It should also be noted that one of the consequences of planners' slowing construction to parallel infrastructure development, mentioned above, was a decreased supply of housing and probable price inflation.

In the late 1970s about 4,000 homes a year were constructed, with just over half in the public sector. Priority for renters in this housing was given to new workers from outside the region. The Aberdeen District Council controls much council (public) housing and has tried to keep rents low to protect the extant lower-income population from oil-generated inflation. Because of heavy immigration and the Conservative central government's policy to discourage public housing, there was a shortage and the waiting list for council housing grew longer (Bonney 1986, 3, 12). Central government restrictions on council housing, including its financing, made the local task of building new houses complicated. As a result, the public sector proportion of the housing stock in the Aberdeen area fell from 44 percent to 34 percent from 1979 to 1986. This had a negative impact on the availability of housing for moderate-income groups (Grampian Regional Council 1986, 11–12). However, in contrast to U.S. cities like Houston, the low-income residents of Aberdeen have generally not faced the options of severe overcrowding or homelessness.

VII   The Planning System in Houston: A Weak Defense against Social Costs

1   Planning in Houston

A major zoning ordinance and a street and park plan were presented to the Houston city council in the late 1920s, but real estate interests organized the Property Owners League, which in 1930 brought out 350 people to protest successfully proposed zoning legislation at city council hearings. After this failure to secure zoning laws, supportive groups unsuccessfully tried several times between 1930 and 1962 to convince the city council or the voters to accept zoning ordinances. The ideological attack on zoning involved the equation of governmental zoning with the violation of personal property rights. Moreover, in 1924 Houston's Mayor Oscar Holcombe appointed the first permanent City Planning Commission. Subsequently abolished and recreated several times, in 1940 the City Planning Commission and a City Planning Department were permanently reestablished, the latter with a budget of only U.S. $10,000 and a staff of three employees for a city of 384,000 (Feagin 1988).

By 1980 the planning department budget was U.S. $920,301 and the staff was made up of sixty employees. This would appear to be a significant increase, but only twenty-nine of the employees were professional planners, in a city that then exceeded 1.6 million. A recent study of thirty planning departments in the Sunbelt found that Houston's planning budget (U.S. $1.86 million) was the smallest of the large cities reporting. Dallas, for example, had a 1986–87 budget of U.S. $3.4 million. Among the thirty Sunbelt cities Houston's *per capita* expenditure for planning ranked 28th, at U.S. $1.08 per capita. Houston's ranking on the proposed 1987–88 budget was similar, a *per capita* projection of U.S. $1.13. In constant dollars, the budget for the Houston Planning Department did not increase over the 1980s. This same report found that in 1986–87 Houston had received no state or federal planning funds, while half the other cities had received such funding (Short 1987).

Houston ranked 24th in total planning staff per 100,000 population and only 29th among the thirty cities in number of planners per 100,000 population; Houston's 1.6 planners per 100,000 compared with 4.2 in Dallas, 11.4 in Richmond and 3.0 in San Diego. In 1986–87 Houston reported twenty-eight professional planners, 27 technical people, and 27 secretarial and clerical staff. In addition, only 29 percent of the planners had a master's degree, ranking the

city next to last among the twenty-seven cities reporting (Short 1987). However, in a 1988 interview one Houston planner estimated that the Houston
Planning and Development Department then had thirty-nine professional planners working on plat supervision (12), economic development (10) and comprehensive planning and data systems analysis (17) (Siaweleski 1988). However,
these figures appear to include planning technicians and data analysts as well
as professional planners. In any event, Houston's planning department is mi-
nuscule by metropolitan Aberdeen standards, even though it has responsibility
for more than 500 square miles of developments in the city, 1,500 square miles
of extraterritorial jurisdiction, and more than 1.8 million people.

In the early 1980s a top official in Houston's planning department commented to the author that "we plan for Houston's future like weathermen for
the next weekend; we do short-range planning." Long-range planning is missing. According to this planner large development projects were planned by developers with little input from city departments and agencies. "In Houston the
project just happens" (Chou 1981). As a result, effective government planning
has been difficult. The head of the planning department from 1964 to 1983,
Roscoe H. Jones, restricted the department to the relatively modest role of research, record keeping and plat checking during these decades of extraordi-
narily vigorous growth. Beyond record keeping, the city planners did little
more than approve subdivision plats for such basic items as street design and
provide modest supervision of the extraterritorial jurisdiction. In the 1970s
there were at first only informal platting guidelines for developers, and few enforceable standards. In 1976 the "Land platting policy manual" was developed
with formal guidelines for developers; this formalized the informal policy and
resulted in more extensive subdivision platting activity, but provided no en-
forcement of most standards. Prior to 1982 the planning department regulated
land-use development by policy rather than by ordinance (Siaweleski 1988).
One result of this general lack of planning is that outside governmental agencies (e.g., the Harris County Flood Control District) have sometimes inter-
vened to undertake long-range planning and infrastructural construction.

2 Modest New Controls

By the 1980s the city council was taking modest steps to deal with the city's
development problems. A 1982 ordinance expanded platting activities. And in
1985 the *Houston Business Journal* ran a scare headline: "Look Out Houston,
here comes zoning." The spectre of zoning was alleged to be haunting the business community. The headline referred to proposed ordinances to restrict land
use in limited ways. The city planning commission recommended modest ordinances to the city council: restrictions on location of pornography shops, off-
street parking requirements, mobile home restrictions, and a limited building

setback ordinance—moderate recommendations described as "backdoor zoning" by real estate interests. The council passed several ordinances, including a requirement that commercial structures outside the downtown area be built at twenty-five feet from thoroughfares and that city blocks be certain lengths. These very modest restrictions were a first step towards more intervention by city planners into rationalizing anarchic developers' activities (Feagin 1988).

In 1986–87 the city council debated and approved the drafting of a comprehensive study of, and plan for, development in and around the city. The new land-use plan generated fierce opposition from some local real estate interests. However, the private Chamber of Commerce, as a local newspaper noted, gave the plan its "blessing." In effect, after a four-year study the "comprehensive plan" for the city would emphasize governmental projects, the private sector recommendations would be *nonbinding* and developers and business groups would play a *central* role in all recommendations (Gravois 1986, 10A).

3   Planning Action in the mid-1980s

By the mid-1980s the Houston Planning and Development Department was doing more extensive plat reviewing but was still not involved in zoning or substantive location controls. Under the 1982 Development Ordinance, planners review plats for new residential and commercial developments for compliance with far more mandatory provisions than in the 1970s, particularly street systems, building setbacks and block lengths. Compliance with the building code is also checked. The Public Works Department checks on the adequacy of the utilities proposed. However, in the Houston region, and unlike in the Aberdeen region, these modest land use controls have not been extended to the large portions of the metropolitan area beyond the city's control. Thus, planning restrictions are still negligible in Harris County, the primary county surrounding the city. There is not even a building code there: and no building permit is required. By the late 1980s the planning department was working on the aforementioned comprehensive plan, an informal guide to development. No land-use restrictions or zoning laws will be in the plan. As one senior planner noted to the author, even local Houston planners harbour a "free market" approach and do not feel their city would benefit from the extensive zoning and other planning controls such as those in the Aberdeen region or even the moderate zoning controls in many other U.S. cities (Siaweleski 1988). In part because of a lack of expertise in the planning department, in the mid-1970s Mayor Fred Hofheinz created divisions of "economic development" and "community development" in his office. It was not until 1983 that the divisions were placed in the Department of Planning and Development. In many U.S. and U.K. cities these have long been functions of the planning department. Most of Houston's economic planning has traditionally been done by the Chamber of Commerce.

4   Coping with Growth: Sewage and Water

Sewage planning has been inadequate in Houston's planning and public works departments. The sewerage crisis noted earlier brought a sewer connection moratorium on new construction. In the mid-1970s the Texas Water Quality Board ordered the city to improve its underdeveloped sewage system. A sewer moratorium covering three-quarters of the city was implemented, in order to reduce significantly the raw sewage being processed at many treatment plants. Large tracts of land could not be sold or developed because of a lack of sewer capacity. This sewer connection moratorium cramped the activities of developers in many areas, but not in the downtown district. No restrictions on sewer hookups were placed on the city's powerful downtown developers. Moreover, in March 1987 the Water Commission fined the city government U.S. $500,000 for what they regarded as the worst municipal sewage disposal problem in Texas; and local officials agreed to a compliance order with required sewage improvements at an estimated cost of nearly U.S. $2 billion (Feagin, 1988). The head of the city's wastewater division has explained his dependence on the whims of local developers:

> And in many cases a developer would first build a warehouse structure that had low-income sewage needs and then, after the city had built lines to serve it, would change the use of the land to high-rise condominiums or other buildings that need much larger sewer lines. (Bryant 1983, A1)

The absence of government zoning and the weak character of local government planning are revealed in these comments.

Water planning by the various Houston city agencies has also been inadequate. While the amount of water available for the Houston metropolitan area is considered adequate until the late 1990s, the pumping stations and treatment facilities necessary to maintaining adequate pressure during periods of drought have not been constructed. Indeed, in 1984 the Texas Health Department withdrew its special "state approved" designation for Houston's water systems because the city did not have adequate water storage facilities, particularly for a time of crisis such as a major drought. A city planning commission report noted that Houston's water distribution facilities would not be able to handle Houston's (then) expected growth after 1992 (Houston City Council 1984, 6).

5   The Response to Traffic

In Houston planning for traffic and road problems has been less than adequate. Most substantive planning for the area's major road systems has either been left to the Texas Highway Department or has been planned privately by the Chamber of Commerce. For example, in 1985 the Texas Highway Department commissioned a major study of severe traffic problems on the city's major east-west highway. State of Texas outlays on fixing up Houston's state-maintained roads had become very expensive by the late 1980s—$1 billion a year. Revealingly, in 1980 the city's planning department made a move away from its traditional activities by considering the problem of traffic snarls in the Galleria/Post Oak area, but the business-oriented, antiplanning mayor cut money for that purpose out of the budget (Feagin 1988).

6   The Lack of Recreational Facilities

There has been little planning for, or provision of, recreational facilities in Houston. In 1910 Houston had the lowest per capita parkland acreage of any major U.S. city; and the situation did not improve much in succeeding decades. In 1977 a federal government study ranked Houston 140th among cities in parkland per capita. Then the fifth largest city in terms of poulation, Houston had more than 500 square miles of territory but only 6,200 acres of parkland. By the mid-1980s city government planning and expenditures had increased the parkland, but the city still ranked very low. Houston had far less parkland than most comparable Sunbelt cities (see Carreau 1982, A1).

7   An Unexpected Fiscal Crisis

Although Houston has often been cited as a model for other urban development, both in the U.S. and in the U.K., in fact it is at the extreme end of an urban growth problems continuum. In a context with relatively little planning in local governmental agencies and no zoning, the high velocity of investment into, and later out of, Houston has accentuated or created major infrastructural problems, including dramatic sewage crises, water pollution, and traffic congestion. By the 1980s, however, the lack of planning could no longer be ignored. A spring 1983 issue of the *Houston Business Journal* heralded: "City in the Red: Houston Feels the Heat of Fiscal Crisis." The lead sentence in the front page article asked "Is Boomtown going bust? Is Bayou City sailing into the straits of New York City?" Since Houston's leaders and citizens have traditionally seen their city as different from those of their counterparts in the north, these questions would have been unthinkable before 1983. Now metropolitan newspapers were dramatizing the unprecedented fiscal crisis in this "shining buckle of the Sunbelt." Annual city government budgets were running multimillion dollar deficits. The reasons are closely tied to the postponed costs of the industrial and population growth, coupled with poor planning and low taxes. In the early 1980s even Houston's city controller noted in a speech that there was a gloomy fiscal picture facing Houston, a retrenchment period with the possibility of service cutbacks. He attributed the problem to required increases in spending for local services and to the persisting lack of planning by government officials, noting a bit too optimistically that the "ill-planned

days of the past are over in Houston" (Snyder 1982, Section 1, 10). Even leading business leaders were coming to see that the lack of planning and zoning
was having a severe impact on the current and future livability of the city. Another important aspect of the fiscal crisis was the tax structure. The fiscal-
conservatism philosophy guiding Houston has resulted in a modest tax base
for government. Property taxes, set at a relatively low level, have been a major source of revenue. In cities such as Houston the local business elite demands a good business climate with relatively low taxes; it follows that public
planning and defensive infrastructural expenditures must be kept at the minimal level consistent with low taxes. With a laissez faire government approach,
Houston has been unable to absorb its high velocity of investment and population growth without much social cost and many infrastructural crises.

VIII   Conclusion

1   Reading the Planning Actions and Consequences

At one level, the Aberdeen-Houston contrast can be seen as a planning success
story in which the Aberdeen planners attempted to modulate the negative externalities of growth and to adapt the public infrastructure to that growth and
to channel private investment, at least to some extent, even against a number
of barriers including, since 1979, a Conservative central governmental thrust
reorienting planning to the needs of developers. Unlike Houston, planning was
not weak or delegitimated. Attempts to define the public interest, and implement that, were to some extent successful. Structure plans did provide restrictions on growth and did protect some use-value concerns of the citizenry from
the more severe aspects of unrestrained growth seen in the Houston case. For
the most part, growth was not allowed to outrun the infrastructure, at least once
the initial shock of the boom was felt. And the infrastructure was more adequately funded than in the Houston case, so that no service-centered fiscal crisis has resulted for Aberdeen.

However, the Aberdeen story can also be read at another level. The planners
remained prisoners of capitalism. The public officials and planners in Aberdeen have had to support the engine of private enterprise in order to secure
jobs and increased economic prosperity. There has been an aggressive attempt
to court the oil and gas industry. Given the previous decline, the Aberdeen local government and planning authorities were "beguiled by the oil developments" and became boosters of the oil industry (Lloyd and Newlands 1987,
16). When it came to industrial planning there was much initial inclination to
give the oil and gas industry much of what it wanted. There was "never any attempt to prevent or delay developments while a local government strategy was
formulated" (Harris et al., no date, 41). Facilitation of the oil and gas industry

became the conscious choice of the local authorities, not as some have suggested something forced upon them or something they were naively aware of (Bonney 1986, 21). From its creation in the 1970s the Grampian Regional Council was also very promotional as regards the oil and gas industry. The public officials and planners were generally more strict in regard to developers and real estate development. Particularly at the peak of the boom, Aberdeen planners were stronger versus the developers and pressed for more concessions than they did after the decline in the oil and gas industry beginning in 1984, when local authorities became more willing to make concessions to businesses and to cover even more infrastructural costs (McIntosh 1987).

2 Collective Capitalists?

In dealing with investors, Aberdeen area planners have sometimes operated, like Houston planners, as brokers negotiating with individual oil firms and developers seeking to shape space for their profit-maximization goals. Yet, given the greater independence of the U.K. civil servants, the Aberdeen area planners have also operated as collective capitalists. In a number of specific ways, the planners' attempts to research and modulate the social costs of growth have rationalized primary-circuit and secondary-circuit (real estate) investments. The planners at the Aberdeen District Council and the Grampian Regional Council have done a lot of planning for the oil companies, planning very useful for primary-circuit investments. For example, the Grampian planners have undertaken much detailed analysis of oil and gas exploration and development trends, utilizing data collected from the individual oil firms, in order to forecast the impact on local infrastructure and housing. One surprise to these planners was that the major oil companies had not done this research, but instead made substantial use of the governmental statistics and forecasting, because of the quality and commercial realism of the forecasts. As one chief planner put it, the oil firms operating "tend to view the North Sea through their own blinkered eyes"; and the data thus provide a broader view and a "base for the service companies in respect to their own planning for the future as to what the capacity of the offshore industry's going to be" (Cockhead 1987).

State planning has also been beneficial to U.K. and other European investors who came into Aberdeen to invest in secondary-circuit estate projects. One Aberdeen real estate company official (Young 1987), while critical of the Labour-controlled district council, was nonetheless pleased to have a city department of physical planning that tried to forecast industrial growth and industrial support requirements. Knowing the likely industry trends greatly improves the rationality of investment in real estate. Planners have provided careful and detailed land use maps and have planned infrastructural development. Developers with access to this planning can more rationally calculate their future investments. Planning regulations have fostered opportunities for additional growth-oriented profit making, including land speculation taking into consideration the planning regulations setting up land-use zones. "Structure Plans may not arouse much general interest, but they are usually carefully examined by land investors and developers" (Ambrose 1986, 259). Land-use planning and regulation have also helped U.K. real estate investors by slowing down secondary-circuit investment and rationalizing cycles of investment. From the 1970s to the early 1980s the expectation of many in northeast Scotland was that the oil boom would bring prosperity for many decades. Investors flocked to the area, and there was a sharp increase in real estate investments. One local real estate official (Young 1987) has argued that in the 1970s the Aberdeen planners played a major role in creating artificial scarcity in office construction by their restrictive rules. In the mid-1970s government planners put a moratorium on new planning permissions, waiting for infrastructure planning and construction and thereby contributing to an undersupply of office space. Once the moratorium was lifted, however, there was an overreaction by the private sector, and overinvestment created some oversupply of buildings for the downturn in the 1980s. However, even this oversupply was quite modest by Houston standards. The planners had slowed development to the point that in the recession of the mid-1980s developers and estate agents were not saddled with a built environment as overpopulated with office buildings and suburban housing developments as was the case in U.S. Sunbelt cities. Ironically, it was the public sector in Aberdeen that had an oversupply of constructed infrastructure, once the recession hit. Such an oversupply of publicly supplied infrastructure has not been much of a problem in service-starved Houston.

3   Needed Changes

In spite of the obvious advantages to both workers and capitalists, in comparison to the Houston planning system, the Aberdeen and U.K. planning systems are viewed by critics as not going far enough and as losing too much force in actual implementation. Ambrose (1986, 61) has argued that the structure plans required by the Town and Country Planning Acts are theoretically a sound planning idea, but in reality the plans have been "little more than a set of well-intentioned statements" about infrastructure needs. While this may be too pessimistic, given the Aberdeen example, it does point up a problem. Although planning came to the United Kingdom as, in part, a concession to public demands for dealing with postwar destruction and unbridled development by developers, by the Thatcherism of the 1970s the accumulation function of development regulation seemed to be gaining ground in relation to the public interest function. Healey (1983, 62) has noted that, especially since the Conservative government took over in 1979, many local authorities have given greater attention to industrial and property interests in decisions on land-use plans.

Yet some local officials in the Aberdeen area have called for more direct regulation of the multinational investors. Allan Kennedy (1987), former chief executive officer of the Gordon District, has argued that, if he had it to do over again, he would insist that oil firms be welcomed *only* if they would help pay for the public infrastructure they require and the major social costs that they create. Kennedy has also suggested that much stronger planning control should have been exercised over the developers and speculators who invested in secondary-circuit projects during the oil boom (Kennedy 1987).

References

Aberdeen Beyond 2000 Group. 1987. *Aberdeen Beyond 2000.* Aberdeen, Scotland.

Ambrose, P. 1986. *Whatever Happened to Planning?* London: Methuen.

Anonymous. 1986. Keys to the future—education, training research . . . imagination, courage, vision. In *Scottish Petroleum Annual.* Aberdeen, Scotland: Aberdeen Petroleum Publishing Limited.

Baldwin, P., and Baldwin, M. 1975. *Onshore Planning for Offshore Oil.* Washington, D.C.: The Conservation Foundation.

Beauregard, R. 1988. Correspondence with author. 16 August.

Bentley, C., and Campbell M. 1987. Interview with author. Department of Planning, Aberdeen District Council. Aberdeen, Scotland.

Bluestone, B., and Harrison B. 1982. *The Deindustrialization of America.* New York: Basic Books.

Bonney, N. 1986. Explaining Development in Scotland's North East: A Working Paper. Paper presented to Development Studies Association, Scottish Study Group, Stirling University, 6–7 June.

———. 1987: Interview with author. Department of Sociology, University of Aberdeen, Aberdeen, Scotland.

Bryant, D. 1983. "Inner City Ready to Grow as Sewer Moratorium Ends." *Houston Business Journal* 5, (December): Section A, 1.

Burchell, R. W., and Hughes, J. W. 1978. "Introduction: planning theory in the 1980s—a search for future directions." In R. W. Burchell, and G. Sternlieb, editors, *Planning Theory in the 1980s.* New Brunswick, N.J.: Center for Urban Policy Research, Rutgers University.

Carreau, M. 1982. "Houston's park system could be at its most critical juncture ever." *Houston Post.* 8 November, Section A, 1.

Cockhead, P. 1987. Interview with author. Grampian Regional Council. Aberdeen, Scotland.

Feagin, J. R. 1988. Free enterprise city: Houston in political-economic perspective. New Brunswick, N.J.: Rutgers University Press.

Feagin, J. R., Gilderbloom, J., and Rodriguez, N. 1989. Private-public partnerships: the Houston experience. In G. Squires, editor, *Unequal partnerships,* 240–59. New Brunswick, N.J.: Rutgers University Press.

Goodman, R. 1971. *After the planners.* New York: Simon and Schuster.

Gottdiener, M. 1985. *The Social Production of Urban Space.* Austin: University of Texas Press.

Gottdiener, M. 1987. "Space as a force of production." *International Journal of Urban and Regional Research* 11, 405–12.

Grampian Regional Council. 1981. The Impact of North Sea Oil in the Grampian Region. Aberdeen, Scotland: Grampian Regional Council.

Grampian Regional Council. 1986. Report of survey. Grampian Region structure plan. Aberdeen area review. Aberdeen, Scotland: Grampian Regional Council.

Gravois, J. 1986. "Chamber of Commerce Backs Form of Zoning." *Houston Post.* 8 September, 10A.

Hall, P. 1987. *Urban and Regional Planning.* 2d ed. London: Allen and Unwin.

Harris, T., Lloyd G., McGuire A. and Newlands, D. no date. The management of change: local government in Aberdeen: Scotland. Typescript. Aberdeen: University of Aberdeen.

Harvey, D. 1985. *The Urbanization of Capital.* Baltimore: Johns Hopkins University Press.

Healey, P. 1983. *Local plans in British Land Use Planning.* Oxford: Pergamon Press.

Houston City Council. 1986. Report of the City Council Committee on Lake Houston. Houston: Houston City Council.

Hurley, M. 1966: *Decisive Years for Houston.* Houston: Houston Magazine Press.

Kapp, K. 1950. *The Social Costs of Private Enterprise.* New York: Schocken Books.

Kennedy, A. 1987. Interview with author. Aberdeen, Scotland.

Lefebvre, H. 1972. *Le pensée marxiste de la ville.* Paris: Casterman.

Leipert, C. 1985. Social costs of economic growth as a growth stimulus. Paper presented at the Conference for a New Economics. The Other Economic Summit, Bedford College, London. 16–19 April.

Lloyd, M. G. 1987. Interview with author. Aberdeen, Scotland.

Lloyd, M. G., and Newlands, D. 1987. *Aberdeen.* Typescript, Aberdeen, Scotland: University of Aberdeen.

Lloyd, M. G., and Rowan-Robinson, J. 1987. The social costs of land development: a report of the Scottish Development Agency. Transcript. Aberdeen, Scotland: University of Aberdeen.

McIntosh, D. 1987. Interview with author. Aberdeen, Scotland.

Moore, R. 1987. Interview with author. Aberdeen, Scotland.

Rice Center. 1981. *Houston initiatives: phase one report.* Houston: Rice Center.

Scottish Office. 1987. *North Sea Oil and Gas.* Pamphlet. Edinburgh: Scottish Office.

Short, R. N. 1987: Planning Agency Survey Results. Typescript Hillsborough County City-County Planning Commission, Tampa, Florida.

Siaweleski, T. 1988. Letter to author.

Smith, M. P. 1988: *City, State, and Market: The Political Economy of Urban Society*. Oxford: Basil Blackwell.

Snyder, M. 1982. "Labor says city facing 'retrenchment'." *Houston Chronicle*. 23 February, Section 1, 10.

Weiss, M. A. 1987. *The Rise of the Community Builders: The American Real Estate Industry and Urban Land Planning*. New York: Columbia University Press.

Young, D. 1987. Interview with author. Aberdeen, Scotland.

IV

RACE, RACISM, AND
CITY DEVELOPMENT

This section includes articles illustrating the concern of those working in the new urban paradigm for racial domination as a central factor in the lives of many people residing in the cities of North America. In the introduction to this volume I discussed how racial domination is central to creating the racial apartheid characteristic of cities, in their spatial forms and social relations. In chapter 10, "Slavery Unwilling to Die: The Background of Black Oppression in the 1980s," I spell out the utility of a racial-domination (internal colonialism) model for understanding the conditions inflicted on African Americans by white elites and rank-and-file whites. The present system of urban apartheid is rooted in early American history—in the development of African-American slavery in the 1650–1865 period.

The system of informal segregation central to urban racism today was set in place in northern cities in the form of Jim Crow laws in such areas as public accommodations and housing and in informal practices not set out in laws. These practices developed in northern cities well before the end of slavery in the South. The last part of this article challenges the undue optimism of some scholars writing on U.S. racial relations, such as that of William Julius Wilson in his famous book, *The Declining Significance of Race*. This article draws on data showing significant racial inequalities in a major 1984 research report, *Falling Behind: A Report on How Blacks Have Fared under the Reagan Policies*. More recent 1990s data on school, housing, and job conditions faced by African Americans in cities show little improvement.

The current situation still reveals a "slavery unwilling to die." This contention is documented in chapters 11 and 12. Both chapters provide detailed accounts of everyday experiences of African Americans with whites in urban areas and institutions. While the 1960s civil rights acts theoretically abolished most discrimination, they have been very weakly enforced. In spite of denials by white commentators of the persistence of racism, antiblack discrimination remains common in public accommodations, business, education, housing, and jobs (see also Feagin and Sikes 1994; Feagin and Vera 1995). In both chapters we see that contemporary racial domination in urban areas is not just a matter of isolated incidents over one black person's lifetime but rather of a steady "acid rain" of racist incidents over that lifetime. In one person's experience and memory individual encounters with racism are coupled with accounts of the accumulated incidents of racial oppression faced by friends and relatives.

The individual and collective cost of racism is very great. It can be seen in the social and spatial apartheid that characterizes all U.S. cities, and it can be seen in the day-to-day lives of African Americans, and other Americans of color. The life expectancy for black newborns is today nearly seven years less than that for white newborns. In a mid-1990s focus group conducted for the author we encountered comments such as this from a successful black engineer: "The stress does make a difference. I think it probably takes five years off your life, to tell you the truth, if you let it get to you."

Chapter 13 is a brief reaction by the author to two articles by leading social researchers working in the area of racial relations. An article by Jomills H. Braddock and James M. McPartland reported on a large survey of employers in which they examine patterns of networking and job discrimination. Another by Thomas F. Pettigrew and Joanne Martin assessed the role of prejudice in occupational attainment for African Americans. They developed the idea called the "ultimate attribution error," which is seen in the tendency of whites to opt for stereotyped explanations of black behavior considered "bad" rather than reasonable situational explanations. In my evaluation of this important research I suggest where research on racial inequality, as it affects cities, needs to go in the future. I underscore the need to look at the ways in which a capitalist system interrelates with racism in both its structural and attitudinal forms and call for a new holistic approach integrating both structural and sociopsychological models of human behavior.

Bibliography

Feagin, Joe R., and Melvin P. Sikes. 1994. *Living with Racism: The Black Middle Class Experience*. Boston: Beacon.

Feagin, Joe R., and Hernan Vera. 1995. *White Racism: The Basics*. New York: Routledge.

10

Slavery Unwilling to Die: The Background of Black Oppression in the 1980s

Joe R. Feagin

Of all the races and varieties of men which have suffered from this feeling, the colored people in this country have endured most. They can resort to no disguises which will enable them to escape its deadly aim. They carry in front the evidence which marks them for persecution. They stand at the extreme point of difference from the Caucasian race, and their African origin can be instantly recognized, though they may be several removes from the typical African race. . . . They are Negroes—and that is enough, in the eye of this unreasoning prejudice, to justify indignity and violence. In nearly every department of American life they are confronted by this insidious influence. It fills the air. It meets them at the workshop and factory, when they apply for work. It meets them at the church, at the hotel, at the ballot-box, and worst of all, it meets them in the jury-box. . . . He has ceased to be a slave of an individual, but has in some sense become the slave of society. [Douglass 1881]

The great black leader, Frederick Douglass, wrote these penetrating words more than one hundred years ago in assessing the widespread racial discrimination that filled the air during the late nineteenth century. The badges and dis-

This chapter is reprinted with minor revisions from Feagin, Joe R. 1986. "Slavery unwilling to die: The background of black oppression in the 1980s," *Journal of Black Studies*. 17 (December): 173–200.

abilities of slavery were still pinned to ostensibly "free" black Americans. While blacks ceased to be slaves of individuals they, nonetheless, were still "slaves of society." I will argue in this article that this "slaves of society" analysis by Douglass is still useful to assess the Center of Budget and Policy Priorities (1984) "Falling Behind" report, since today, racial discrimination remains a "spectacle of slavery unwilling to die" (Douglas 1968, 445).

Slaves of Society: A Theoretical Perspective

Internal Colonialism Updated

A number of scholars apply the term *internal colonialism* in developing a model of intergroup adaptation in the United States. The internal-colonialism framework owes a debt to the analysts of "external" colonialism. Covering hundreds of millions of individuals, external (white) European colonialism extended into Africa, Asia, and the islands of the oceans. Raw materials from these external colonies sustained the technological development of the mother countries in Europe. External colonialism becomes internal colonialism when the control and exploitation of the labor and/or land of subordinate groups passes to dominant groups within the newly independent society, when the white colonists "run the show" themselves. Internal colonialism emerged out of European colonialism and imperialism, yet it takes on a life of its own. It is a system grounded in the sharp differentiation of white and nonwhite labor. In *Racial Oppression in America* (1972, 57–58), Blauner argues that black Americans are in a type of internal colonization. Forced labor for blacks has been at the heart of this colonial system. Capitalist development reserved free labor for white workers. European-American whites created forced (precapitalist) labor systems within the framework of a larger capitalistic system. The internal-colonial dynamic was most thoroughgoing for the United States, because it was here that the correlation between (white/black) race and (free/slave) work status was nearly perfect.

The internal colonialism theory has been utilized by a number of analysts of black-white relations since the late 1960s. It is much more accurate than the more conventional assimilation theories that have been applied to black Americans. Internal colonialism theories accent force, the expropriation of labor, segregation in the extreme, and ideological rationalization; the image is one of blacks being subordinated to certain European-American requirements for the purpose of gaining *labor*. The structure of racial subordination was already well established when non-English whites began to arrive in significant numbers.

In this article I will utilize an updated version of the internal colonialism model to assess the 1984 Center on Budget and Policy Priorities reported entitled "Falling Behind: A Report on How Blacks Have Fared Under the Rea-

gan Policies" (hereafter cited as the "Falling Behind" report). But before probing the data, I will first update the theoretical discussion of internal colonialism by drawing from recent research on the slavery and semislavery systems
encompassing black Americans from the 1600s to the 1980s. In order to inter-
pret the data in "Falling Behind" it is very important to understand the historical background of a "slavery unwilling to die."

Slavery's Essential Features: Persistence and Continuity

Table 10.1 highlights many of the essential features of slavery in the
1640–1865 period. Black slaves were not citizens with rights. They were the
only racial or ethnic group explicitly signaled out in the U.S. Constitution for
subordination and enslavement. About 90 percent of Afro-Americans were the
property of white people. Even in the North many were slaves until the 1850s.
The threat of violence in the form of whipping and brutality was high. Residential and job segregation were very extensive. There were few schools for
blacks. Intermarriage was all but impossible, North and South. The badge of
color was critical for distinguishing slave and nonslave. A well-developed system of ideological rationalization emphasized the biological and civil inferiority of black slaves as well as of free blacks.

   In the next century (1865–1960) the white ruling class introduced certain
changes. Constitutional amendments freed blacks from legal ownership as
commodities and gave them certain citizenship rights; many of these rights
were, however, effectively denied by Supreme Court and executive action
from the 1880s to the 1950s and 1960s. Violence and the threat of violence by
whites increased as part of the process of reinstituting control over freed
slaves. Residential, school, and job segregation remained high. After a brief
period of political enfranchisement, blacks were denied electoral influence
from the 1890s to the 1960s, particularly in the South where most resided in
this period. Intermarriage was generally prohibited. Discrimination on the basis of color coding was very high; the ideological justification was similar to
that of the earlier period. It is quite clear that from the 1860s to the early 1960s,
a century after slavery was legally abolished, that black Americans suffered
terribly from the badges and disabilities of a slavery unwilling to die.

   Since the early 1960s some additional changes have been made in the semislave system chaining blacks to U.S. society. Again, these alterations have
been incomplete, falling far short of dismantling that system. While blacks enjoy more civil rights, there is still, mainly from white police officers in the
cities, a serious threat of violence. Residential segregation remains very high,
as does school segregation in most non-southern cities. Job segregation is still
substantial, with a majority of black men still experiencing unemployment and
underemployment conditions or confinement to traditional service jobs and
occupations servicing black communities. Black women are also concentrated

in traditional "Negro jobs," in professional/managerial jobs serving black communities, or in moderate-wage clerical jobs in central business districts encircled by black populations. Color coding remains widespread and critical to persisting discrimination, however subtle and covert, and to the low inter-marriage rate. The ideological rationalization for black inferiority has become more sophisticated and is clearly reflected by the adamant white opposition to any *nationwide* government program aimed at aggressively desegregating jobs, housing, and schools.

The overall impression one gets from Table 10.1 is of persistence and con-tinuity in the basic conditions faced by black Americans since 1640. Certainly there have been important changes, yet black Americans continue to be "slaves of society" on many of the ten dimensions. At least half the changes so essen-tial to effect full liberation for black Americans remain to be made for most categories. We will now review this critical developmental history of slavery and semislavery in some detail.

Slavery from 1650 to 1865

The Legal System

The North American slave system involved the forcible importation virtually of all the ancestors of black Americans today. Historically speaking, slavery is a form of involuntary servitude in which slaves are owned by others and are deprived of most rights and freedoms. But black slavery was considerably more extreme than slavery in ancient Rome, because black slaves were for-bidden by law to get an education or to earn an income for themselves. An es-sential feature of North American slavery was the denial of basic citizenship and fundamental human liberties. As Du Bois (1935, 10) put it, slaves were not considered human beings, "for they could own nothing; they could make no contracts; they could hold no property; nor traffic in property; they could not hire out; they could not legally marry . . . they could not appeal from their mas-ter; they could be punished at will." The number of slaves in the colonies in-creased from 59,000 in 1714 to 263,000 in 1754; by 1860 there were 4.4 million black slaves in the United States.

The slave owner class extracted its profit from the forced labor of African and Afro-American slaves, whose labor in agriculture built up capital not only for planter investments but also for the merchants, shippers, and industrialists of the North. The Civil War represented the culmination of a growing conflict between the northern capitalist class and the planter oligarchy. Between the 1790s and the 1840s the slaveholding oligarchy dominated the U.S. political and economic system. That ruling class controlled much of the wealth in the United States, in-cluding billions of dollars in slaves, prime agricultural land, crops, warehouses,

Table 10.1

Basic Features of Slavery and Semislavery: 1640–1986

Basic Features	Eras		
	Slavery *1640–1865*	*Semislavery* *1865–1960*	*Semislavery* *1960–1986*
1. Citizenship (Constitution)	No	Yes	Yes
2. Legal Ownership	Yes	No	No
3. Violence and Threat of Violence	High	Very high	High
4. Job Segregation (Subordinated labor)	High	High ("Negro jobs")	High, decrease 1960s–1970s, then increase in 1980s
5. Residential segregation	High	High	High
6. School segregation	Extreme (few schools for blacks)	High	High, then reduction in South until 1980s
7. Political enfranchisement	None	Low, greater in North	Moderate, stalls in 1980s
8. Intermarriage rate	Extremely low	Low	Low
9. Color coding	High	High	High
10. Ideological rationalization for Black Condition	Overt (biological) racism	Overt (biological) racism	Covert (biological) racism; overt anti-government intervention

and other facilities. Most U.S. presidents were slaveholders or sympathetic to slavery. That ruling class also controlled the U.S. Supreme Court, as was made clear in the 1857 *Dred Scott v. John F. A. Stanford* decision, which ruled that the black person had no rights that whites need respect. The emerging industrial capitalists of the northeast, however, relied upon free, waged labor. Conflicts, therefore, were inevitable as the planter/industrialist engaged in battles over western lands, over tariffs, and splits over control of the Democratic Party, which in 1860, permitted Abraham Lincoln to become president. The position of black slaves in this situation is instructive. Conservative members of the Republican Party negotiated with representatives of the southern planter class and proposed a Thirteenth Amendment of the Constitution that would *guarantee* slavery forever in the South. Lincoln himself was willing to accept this amendment. But the planter oligarchy rejected this "compromise" proposal (Aptheker 1984). Ironically, the Thirteenth Amendment added to the Constitution in 1865 legally abolished the slave system.

Slavery to the North

Recent research has made it clear why many northern Republicans were willing to perpetuate slavery. In the North as well as in the South slavery had long been seen by the majority of whites as legitimate. Significant numbers of slaves could be found in most northern states. The North was built in part on forced labor and, as Ringer (1983, 533) puts it, "despite the early emancipation of slaves in the North it remained there, not merely as fossilized remains but as a *deeply engrained coding for the future.*"

Take Massachusetts, for example. In 1641, three years after slaves were brought in, slavery was made a part of the law. Massachusetts merchants and shippers played a central role in the North American slave trade. An attempt to abolish slavery failed in the Massachusetts House of Representatives in 1767. In was not until the 1780s that public opinion and court cases came together to abolish slavery effectively in New England. Even then, it was *not* a recognition of the rights of blacks, but pressure from the growing number of white working people who objected to having to compete with cheap slave labor that won the day (Higginbotham 1978, 63–65). By the mid-1600s there were strict slave codes in the North. In 1712 there was a major slave revolt in New York City; fifteen slaves were hanged, starved, or roasted to death. In New York there was great fear of slave revolts. By 1786 slaves made up 7 percent of that state's population. It was not until 1799 that a partial emancipation statute was passed. However, the statute only freed the children of slaves born after July 4, 1799, and then only when they became 25–28 years of age. All slaves did not become free until the 1860s. But even this emancipation of slaves was linked explicitly to the extreme subordination of free blacks politically and economically (Higginbotham 1978, 144–49).

An understanding of this entrenched slavery so embedded in the North's legal system is vital for understanding today's internal colonialism. Slave colonialism in the U.S. is not just a southern phenomenon, but an extensive national system of oppression. This is a crucial point for understanding the "Falling Behind" report's findings.

Semislavery from 1865 to 1960

From 1865 to 1900

The end of slavery as a legal condition did not end the subordination of black Americans. While legal ownership no longer ruled after 1865, subordination nonetheless persists in an ever-changing succession of white yokes. From 1865 to the 1960s legalized segregation became the yoke of control for most southern blacks in the form of the semislavery institution of debt peonage. For the North, the yoke of control involved a similar pattern of segregation effected by informal rather than legal means. The Thirteenth Amendment abolished the legal institution of slavery, but it did not abolish the "badges and incidents" of slavery. After 1865, the essential economic conditions of slavery persisted for blacks, most of whom remained in agriculture. A key problem for blacks was the denial of land by whites. After, just as before, the Civil War blacks were largely excluded from landownership in the South. And white leaders in the North generally did not support a redistribution of slave plantation land to blacks. As Harris (1982, 30) puts it, this blatant discrimination "locked blacks into a system of perpetual poverty, the inevitable status of people unable to acquire land in an agriculture dominated society." Most blacks, unlike most white immigrant groups, found themselves in an agricultural society with no access to the sources of wealth.

During Reconstruction newly freed slaves found themselves slipping into new forms of subjugation ranging from tenant farming and sharecropping to debt peonage. In the 1880s, Booker T. Washington described the conditions the theoretically free blacks face on the plantations as "a kind of slavery that is in one sense as bad as the slavery of antebellum days" (Daniel 1973, ix). The superexploitation of black tenants and sharecroppers was commonplace in the South. In theory the poor black farmer could sell his or her share of the crops, pay off his or her debts, and buy his or her own land. But most were not able to make enough to escape the cycle of debt and to think of becoming landowners. The next step down from sharecropping was debt peonage, where the planter would by force not allow a cropper to leave. Debt peonage involved the creation of laws to keep black laborers from leaving their "employment." They had limited choices: Suffer quietly under the burden of debt and semislave working conditions or "run away and be pursued, shot, or beaten; or kill the employer and risk lynching" (Daniel 1973, ix).

Moreover, when industrialization finally came to the South in the 1890s, blacks there were virtually excluded, except for janitorial-type jobs. Outside agriculture, blacks in towns and cities were largely in the domestic and service jobs so close in lineage to house-slave jobs of the earlier period.

The World War I Period

In 1910, about 83 percent of black Americans lived in twelve southern states; more than two-thirds of all blacks lived on farms in the South. In the decades just before and after 1910, they began to migrate to the North in significant numbers. There black workers were regularly displaced by the new white immigrant groups, who forced blacks out of job after job (for example, construction) and into marginal, low-paying pursuits. Without this race discrimination associated with waves of white immigrants, "the Harlems and South Chicagos might have become solid working-class and middle-class communities with the economic and social resources to absorb and aid incoming masses of Southerners" (Blauner 1972, 64).

Rex (1983, 81–91) analyzes the movement of nonwhite peoples from the colonies in the British and other European empires to the great metropolitan cities in the imperial countries. There, the colonial immigrants get the most inferior and marginal industrial jobs, the highest unemployment, and the poorest working conditions. Rex notes that the social immigrants become a "structurally distinct element from the established native working class." They are clearly viewed as an *outcast* group of *aliens*. Ringer (1983, 536–37) has applied Rex's view to the migration of black southerners to cities. Blacks migrated from an economically backward region similar to the colonies of the empires. As in the case of colonial migrants to London, they got the most marginal industrial jobs and were viewed as aliens. Yet unlike the colonial immigrants to Britain, black southerners also migrated into a region with a long history of subordinating black Americans—of slavery and Jim Crow laws.

In the North as well as in the South blacks remained in an internal colonial situation; many were concentrated in occupations tied closely to their prior situation as slaves, especially domestic and service positions. Other evidence of strong internal colonialism can be seen in the rapid displacement of black workers from good occupational niches by white immigrants. A third aspect was the almost total exclusion of blacks from better-paying jobs in the expanding industrial settings. When the white immigration was cut off in the late 1910s and 1920s, blacks finally penetrated the industrial sector, but through the bottom rungs (Ringer 1983, 535).

A New Deal?

In the 1930s two-thirds of black Americans still lived in the South and in Washington, D.C. Most could not vote. Most black agricultural workers in the South were still wage laborers or sharecroppers; only 13 percent were owners or managers. As Myrdal phrased it, the background of slavery meant that black people did not enjoy "much of that kind of legal security which is a necessary condition for successful entrepreneurship. . . . The best security has been to become associated with a white person of some status in the community" (Myrdal 1964, vol. 1, 240).

North and South, blacks remained in low-wage jobs as menials, unskilled workers, domestics, croppers, and agricultural laborers. The Great Depression demonstrated their marginal position. Unemployed whites pushed for menial "Negro jobs," such as cleaners and domestic workers; white women took the blacks' restaurant and hotel jobs. Whites in Atlanta organized the Black Shirts under the slogan "No Jobs for Niggers until Every White Man Has a Job." By 1932, half of all urban blacks, most of whom resided in the South, were unemployed. Starvation was often their lot, because less than a fifth received relief aid from southern governments. Private organizations refused to allow blacks in the soup lines. In 1935, in "liberal" Manhattan, two-thirds of the hotels refused to employ blacks, and major insurance companies and retail stores also excluded blacks (Sitkoff 1978, 37–38).

However, there was one very important change in the 1930s. As public employment programs began to put a million blacks back to work and provided some economic support, however minimal, black voters shifted from a solid Republican vote in 1932 to a solid Democratic vote in 1936. As blacks moved North, their votes counted more. And the Roosevelt campaigns paid some attention. Moreover, the growth of the federal government in the 1930s helped to create a new black middle class. The number of black federal employees increased from 50,000 to more than 150,000 between 1932 and 1941; the proportion of blacks among federal employees was a little higher than their proportion in the general population. Thousands worked in professional and administrative positions, and tens of thousands worked as clerks and secretaries (Sitkoff 1978, 328). This employment opportunity laid the foundation for the growth of a modest-sized black middle class, which expanded gradually from the 1930s to the 1970s.

But the *overall* impact of the Roosevelt administration reinforced the semislave system. Black Americans suffered much discrimination from New Deal agencies. For example in FERA relief programs blacks got lower wages than whites, got employed only as unskilled laborers, and were employed only after whites were taken care of. Wye (1972, 634) argues that the New Deal employment programs "depressed the Negro job structure by engaging many workers in job categories below those that they had filled in the private sector of the economy before the Depression began." New Deal housing programs increased the residential segregation of blacks by restricting Federal Housing Administration loans effectively to segregated areas and by locating public housing in ghetto areas. Moreover, Roosevelt and most of his advisers were unwilling to press for antilynching legislation out of fear of losing the votes of powerful southern congressional members for whom federal legislation was viewed as an assault on states' rights and as northern interference in the South's way of life. As one adviser put it, civil rights was "not to be a primary consideration of the guy at the top. He does his best with it, but he ain't gonna lose his votes for it" (Weiss 1983, 119).

From 1941 to 1965: The Impact of Wars

Most black mobility out of the semislavery employment categories has taken place during war periods, including World War I, World War II, the Korean

War, and the Vietnam War. During the wars employment conditions of black Americans significantly improved. During World War I white immigration subsided, and black workers were needed to produce war goods. During World War II the demand for workers pulled many blacks into better-paying blue-collar jobs for the first time. During the Korean War, and because of domestic prosperity in the early 1950s, black unemployment dropped to low levels; employment in better-paying occupations again expanded. Yet after all three wars the black employment situation declined significantly. Thus white workers from rural areas poured into cities after World War II, and in 1945–46 the black unemployment rate went up twice as fast as the white rate. Most jobs opened to them were again in the unskilled and semiskilled categories in line with their traditional semislave position. In 1950, more than half of all employed blacks were still in laborer and domestic service jobs, but less than a fifth of white workers were in these categories (Harris 1982, 124–31). Again, during the Vietnam War there was a significant black mobility into better-paying jobs, with an assistance this time not only from war and prosperity but also from a major civil rights movement.

Yet in spite of wartime progress, by the early 1960s black workers were *further* behind whites in income, occupation, and unemployment than they were in 1945 (Harris 1982, 131). In 1962, blacks in the prime working groups ages 25–44 had an unemployment rate *three* times that of whites; even among the employed, black workers were much more likely to hold part-time jobs. Further, black workers were more likely to be the first fired when layoffs occurred, to have a higher disability rate than white workers, and thus to have a shorter working life than white workers. Blacks were still in a position of a low-wage and surplus labor supply, to be used only when needed.

Semislavery from the 1960s to the Present

The Optimistic View

An ahistorical view of black America is characteristic of most recent analysis by scholars and other policy analysts. Even those who look at historical periods, such as Wilson in his *The Declining Significance of Race* (1978), see the post-1960 period as quite different from the past. Wilson develops the argument that the rise in the black middle class in the 1950s and 1960s was the result of shifting economic conditions and of dramatic new government policies such as equal employment laws and affirmative-action programs. This equal employment legislation "virtually eliminated the tendency of employers to create a split labor market in which black labor is deemed cheaper than white labor regardless of the work performed" (Wilson 1978, 110–11). The impact of the affirmative-action and equal opportunity laws supposedly increased the number of black Americans holding higher-paying jobs in the expanding service-producing industries, that is, in white-collar jobs. Employment discrimination is viewed as having largely been eliminated. This perspective has often been suggested by prominent analysts. Indeed, in the late 1960s Daniel Patrick Moynihan (1969, 30), scholar and (later) senator, asserted that blacks had advanced so much that he recommended a policy of "benign neglect" to the then-President Nixon; blacks, he argued, "are being transformed into a stable working-class population: truck drivers, mail carriers, assembly-line workers—people with dignity, purpose, and in the United States a very good standard of living indeed."

Optimistic analysts also cite the apparent changes in white attitudes toward blacks. They note a shift to a moderate nondiscrimination stance from a blatant discriminatory stance of just a few decades earlier; this attitudinal shift among whites has paralleled the elimination of legal segregation in the United States and the token penetration of better-paying nontraditional jobs by black Americans. Optimists note too that a white president appointed a black lawyer to the U.S. Supreme Court (Schuman et al. 1985, 200–5).

The Reality

The reality of black America today is quite different from this optimistic portrait.While there have been some important changes, semislavery is still the condition of black America as a whole. The badges of slavery have never been substantially, much less completely, eradicated.

The Center on Budget and Policy Priorities "Falling Behind" report identifies very clearly what that semislavery system means for blacks today. The economic *effects* of persisting institutionalized discrimination are evident. The report documents the point that in terms of real disposable income all categories of black families, from the poor to the affluent, have lost ground since 1980, while 60 percent of the white population has made significant income gains. Thus, the hoary black-white income gap has actually grown during the Reagan years. Both Urban Institute data and Census Bureau data support the conclusion of an increasing black-white income gap. The report also documents the high unemployment and poverty problems of blacks today. It notes that 36 percent of all black Americans, and nearly half of all black children, fell below the official government poverty line in 1983. And the extent of black poverty has worsened since 1980. In 1984, the black unemployment rate was 2.5 times that for whites, a ratio up significantly from 1980. The total black unemployment rate was still 16 percent in 1984. Within the worst-hit group of U.S. workers, the long-term unemployed, nearly one-third are black. These data show there has been a significant deterioration in economic conditions since 1980.

Some of this deterioration has resulted from intentional action on the part of the Reagan administration to improve the tax situation of corporate America, the profits of corporate America, by cutting taxes significantly and by reducing social welfare programs dramatically. Since the late 1960s corporate America has faced intensifying competition from abroad and increased pressure from workers to improve workplace conditions. Corporations have responded by drawing upon the government to improve their profit situation.

The center's "Falling Behind" report shows in detail the impact of governmental action on blacks since 1980. Cutbacks in federal, social, and economic programs have disproportionately savaged black families. Since blacks make up 25 percent to 50 percent of the clients of programs like legal services, Pell grants for needy students, Aid to Families with Dependent Children, subsidized housing, and public service employment programs, it is not surprising that they have been very hard hit by the 10 percent to 100 percent cuts in such programs. In contrast, the massive Reagan tax cuts favor affluent to rich families and, above all, corporations. The total tax burden for poor to moderate-income families rose over the last several years, while the burden for the affluent and for corporations has been reduced very significantly.

The "Falling Behind" report does not discuss the additional problem of reductions in the federal government work force, as well as the ripple effects of cuts in federal aid in the form of layoffs at the local government level. Cutbacks in Washington, D.C., agencies and in state government social programs have in numerous cases meant that a disproportionate number of black employees were laid off. In some cases 30 percent to 70 percent of those laid off in Washington, D.C., have been blacks. Wilson and other optimists are correct about the importance of governmental hiring in expanding the black middle class in the 1960s and 1970s. In 1970 more than half (57 percent) of black male college students were employed by government, compared to just 27 percent of whites. One study of the years 1960–76 found that 55 percent of the growth in nonagricultural employment for black workers was in the governmental sector; this was more than twice the comparable percentage for whites. And many of these governmental jobs have been in the vulnerable social service areas (Anderson 1982, 7).

Thus black Americans who moved up into the middle class because of government employment have been hurt significantly by the Reagan corporate-tax-welfare program. And they have been hurt at all government levels because of cutbacks in social programs. Yet these actions on behalf of corporate America are not the main reason for the many socioeconomic problems of black America today. The aforementioned income and unemployment data show that blacks as a group were in bad shape even in the early 1980s. They have gone from bad to worse in the Reagan period. The major reason for this is that the modest equal opportunity programs of the 1960s and 1970s did not eradicate the semislave system's badges and afflictions. So a reduction in those programs only makes an existing semislavery system much worse.

The Badges and Disabilities of Slavery Today

The civil rights acts of 1964, 1965, and 1968 made many formal acts of discrimination illegal, but they did not end the broad array of blatant, subtle, and covert discrimination in jobs, housing, and education from the 1960s to the 1980s. The spectacle of slavery unwilling to die can be seen today in many examples:

1. restrictions on black voting in many areas of the South;
2. most black children still attend segregated schools;
3. most black families live in segregated residential areas;
4. most blacks seeking housing face informal discrimination by real estate people, landlords, and homeowners;
5. most blacks are tried by all-white juries from which blacks have often been excluded during the selection progress;
6. most blacks face covert and subtle, if not blatant, discrimination in the job market, including promotion barriers.

These features of America are often rationalized as part of a process of voluntary segregation, but that is mostly propaganda for an institutionalized slavery system unwilling to die.

The Job Arena

Many optimistic observers point to the advances that black Americans have made in the job arena. We have just noted the situation in regard to government employment. Now we can look more closely at the general job situation of black Americans. It is true that during the 1960s the number of black professional, technical, managerial, and administrative workers increased dramatically, albeit from a small base. By 1970 just under a fifth held jobs in these categories. And in the 1970s more gains were made in these presumably high-status and white-collar job categories. Yet even here the progress is not what it seems. Nonwhites in white-collar categories are disproportionately concentrated in jobs with lower pay and status than are whites in the same category. For example, within the professional-technical category, blacks today are most commonly found in such fields as social and recreational work, kindergarten teaching, vocational counseling, personnel, dietetics, and health-care work. They are least often found among lawyers and judges, dentists, writers and artists, engineers, and university teachers. Within the managerial-administrative category blacks are most commonly found among restaurant and bar managers, health administrators, and government officials; they are least commonly found among office managers, bank and financial managers, and sales managers. And among "clerical" workers blacks are most often seen among file clerks, shipping clerks, postal clerks, keypunch operators, and typists. Black movement into nontraditional jobs in the 1960s and 1970s was not random. Much of the white-collar growth was in clerical jobs for black women—particularly in central business districts surrounded by black communities—in professional jobs tied to black communities (such as health and educational workers), in departments in private industry that serve black communities, in equal opportunity positions, and in federal government jobs, particularly in cities like Washington, D.C., with large black populations (Feagin 1984, 230–32).

During the 1960s and 1970s younger, better-educated blacks did make significant gains in entry-level jobs of better-paying occupational categories. But in the 1980s it has become clear that many of these gains are much less substantial than initially believed, since entry-level positions have become dead-end jobs with little chance of promotion because of discriminatory promotional barriers. These barriers have been well documented for the corporate world. Jones's (forthcoming) research on black mangers has found that the predominantly white corporate environment, with its intense pressures for conformity, creates regular problems. Jones describes one black manager (Charlie) who was working his way up the lower executive ranks. One day he met with other black managers who wanted his advice on coping with racial discrimination. This was the result:

> Charlie concluded that this should be shared with senior management and agreed to arrange a meeting with the appropriate officers. Two days before the scheduled meeting, while chatting with the President at a cocktail affair, Charlie was sombered by the President's disturbed look as he said, "Charlie, I am disappointed that you met with those black managers. I thought we could trust you."

Black managers are under heavy pressure *not* to support one another even in the face of discrimination. Instances such as this also point up a continuing problem in organizations. The leaders in white organizations are willing, often grudgingly, to bring blacks into important positions but in token numbers and under the existing rules.

Jones (1985) has reported striking racial data from his nationwide survey of a large number of black managers with graduate-level business degrees. Nearly all (98 percent) felt that black managers had not achieved much equal opportunity with white managers. More than 90 percent felt there was much subtle or blatant antiblack hostility in corporations; more than 90 percent felt black managers had less opportunity than whites, or no chance compared to whites, to succeed in their firms solely on the basis of merit and ability. Two-thirds felt that many whites in corporations still believe blacks are intellectually inferior. And most reported that this adverse racial climate had a negative impact on the evaluations, assignments, and promotions of black managers.

Moreover, one study at IBM by Hudson (1978) found that light-skinned blacks were promoted at a higher rate than dark-skinned blacks; the color coding of slave days is still in evidence. Even the penetration of educated blacks into nontraditional (entry-level) jobs has not brought about the necessary internal changes in corporate climate, in evaluation procedures, assignments, and promotions.

Moreover, those black Americans who were able to move into better-paying blue-collar jobs during the late 1960s and 1970s have faced the problems of declining industries. Automation has been one factor. Capital flight is another: many blue-collar jobs, such as those of assembly-line workers in high-tech industries, are being exported to Third World countries where the labor is cheaper. Willhelm has developed this view the most completely of any scholar; while blacks were once needed in the agricultural South, he argues, "today, the economics of corporate capitalism, by turning to automation, makes Black labor unessential; the fact that Blacks still do not own property of production, even though legally possible, and increasingly find their labor is no longer needed for production, they return, once again, to their declassed position under slavery" (Willhelm 1983, 240).

The majority of blacks who find work usually find it in lower-paying job categories. Contrary to the image of a huge black middle class portrayed in some of the media, blacks are still disproportionately concentrated in the low-paying, lower-status work categories as, for instance, private household workers (such as maids), other service workers, nonfarm laborers, and operatives (such as local truck drivers). Brimmer (1976, 17) analyzed employment data for the 1960–75 period and found that the major part of the gains for blacks came between 1960 and 1969, with stagnation in the 1970s. In the 1970s blacks' "occupational center of gravity remained anchored in those positions requiring little skill and offering few opportunities for advancement" (1976, 17).

Voting and Housing

There is much other evidence for the argument that blacks today confront a slavery unwilling to die. Take voting for example. As Table 10.1 makes clear, the exclusion of black voters was a basic feature of slavery's denial of citizenship to black Americans. And that institutionalized attempt to exclude the black vote has been a fundamental feature of this society since slavery. Today blacks are the only large group of minority citizens to face continuing, widespread, and institutionalized attempts to reduce the efficacy of their vote. Davidson (1984) has noted that there are three major types of electoral discrimination: vote dilution, disenfranchisement, and candidate diminution. A major example of vote dilution is the at-large electoral system. This system has been demonstrated, in cities across the nation, to reduce sharply the participation of black candidates and voters in local campaigns. As long as blacks are a minority of local voters in a city, it can be difficult for them to elect officeholders from their own residential areas. The Supreme Court, in *City of Mobile v. Bolden* (1980), put a heavy burden on minority plaintiffs to prove that at-large electoral systems were *intentionally* set up to discriminate against minorities rather than to demonstrate a severe negative impact that could be lessened by an alternative, more democratic system. In effect, the Supreme Court ruled that indirect or subtle direct discrimination is constitutionally permissible.

A variety of other electoral strategies impose discriminatory impacts upon minority candidates, including a runoff rule in at-large elections, gerrymandering districts, decreasing the number of seats in a government body in a single-member district system, and local (white) slating groups that handpick a token black candidate in order to prevent other minority candidates from having a chance at being elected. In addition to discriminatory vote dilution mechanisms, minority workers in some areas face discrimination in the form of such disenfranchisement devices as purges of voter registration rolls, relocation of polling places with either no notice or short notice, the establishment of difficult registration procedures, and threatening voters with retaliation. These practices have been documented in the states of Alabama, Mississippi, and Texas in recent years. Faced with minority dilution strategies, minority voters may further dilute their voting strength by giving up and staying away from the polls. Candidate diminution is yet another form of political discrimination that black Americans face. This involves attempts to keep minority candidates from running for office. Davidson has noted these examples: changing an office from elective to appointive when a minority candidate has a chance to win (Georgia, Alabama); setting high filing and bonding fees (Georgia); abolition of party primaries (Mississippi); and intimidating candidates with threats of violence or of cutting off credit (Alabama, North Carolina, South Carolina, Georgia).

As a result of these acts of discrimination (most of which are institutionalized discrimination), black Americans have not yet achieved full representation in the political sphere, particularly in the Sunbelt.

In regard to housing discrimination today we also see the continuation of *massive* segregation and racial exclusion, North and South. Research on residential segregation in U.S. cities in the 1980s has revealed that high levels of racial separation persist. A study by Taeuber (1983) of twenty-eight central cities in large metropolitan areas found only small declines in residential segregation between 1970 and 1980. There has been some increase in blacks living in suburban areas, but researchers note this is mostly because of black residents of central cities spilling over into adjacent suburbs; most suburbanization was in areas extending out from the traditional black residential areas, with many such suburban areas being "zones of transition" from white to black residences. This research suggests there is more contact between blacks and whites than a decade ago, but the contact is often the short-lived result of turnover and resegregation.

Discrimination by landlords, homeowners, and real estate agents is still significant in the United States. Since the late 1970s there have been a number of important audit studies of housing discrimination mechanisms. The best studies have used a black auditor and a white auditor (of similar backgrounds) who are sent to realtors and apartment rental agents. Studies done in Dallas, Boston, and Denver between 1978 and 1983 found differential treatment favoring the white auditors looking for housing, whether they were owners or renters. In all studies whites were more likely to be shown or told about more housing units than blacks. In a 1981 Boston study white auditors were invited to inspect seventeen units, 81 percent more, on the average, than their black (matched) teammates (Yinger 1984). A 1983 Boston study found a similar pattern.

A key feature of slavery was the residential segregation of slaves to slave quarters. Even the 1968 Civil Rights Act banning discrimination in housing has done very little to eliminate the informal real estate, landlord, and homeowner practices that keep blacks in the modern-day slave quarters we call ghettos. Even a majority upon the U.S. Supreme Court asserted in *Jones v. Mayer* that "when racial discrimination herds men into ghettos and makes their ability to buy property turn on the color of their skin, then it too is a *relic of slavery.*" The promised freedom of the Thirteenth Amendment has not yet been granted, for that freedom includes the right to live wherever a white person can live.

Violence: Another Dimension of Slavery

Violence cuts across all the periods of black experience tabulated in Table 10.1. It was a major dimension of slavery; it has been a major dimension of the semislavery systems that replace slavery. During slavery most white violence aimed at slaves fell short of killing. But there was still very extensive violence in the form of beatings. After slavery, from the 1860s to the 1960s, thousands of black Americans were the victims of lynchings, many of those with the collusion of police and judicial officers. Between 1889 and 1940, according to the Tuskegee Institute, about 3,830 people were lynched; 80 percent were black. Between 1889 and 1916 there were 50 to 161 lynchings of blacks *every* year. The number dropped slowly to 10–24 lynchings per year in the 1930s, with 1–6 a year from 1938 to the 1950s. At least half the lynchings were carried out with police authorities participating; in most of the other cases the police winked at the community action (Myrdal 1964, 2–5). In addition, Wright (1985) estimates that at least half the lynchings of blacks never got counted. This is particularly the case of quiet lynchings without the formation of a mob. One also needs to add to the legal lynchings the cases where, if vigilantes would hold off on a lynching, police and court officials gave a black man a speedy trial and execution.

Violence against blacks was very widespread in the 1920–60 period. Short of murder, much brutality was aimed at black workers in agriculture and industry. In assessing white violence against blacks in the South in the 1930s and 1940s Myrdal noted a continuum, ranging from mild admonition to murder; this violence "has its origin in the slavery tradition" where physical force was used by masters to keep slaves in line. In the 1930s and 1940s this tradition persisted: "if a plantation owner cheats or beats his Negro tenants, 'that's his business'; if a Negro is the victim of a sudden outburst of violence, 'he must have done something to deserve it.' Above all, the Negro must be kept in his 'place' " (Myrdal 1964, 2–559).

There were some lynchings in the North, but more characteristic of antiblack violence were the riots. Numerous riots aimed at keeping blacks in their place occurred in northern cities during the 1900–20 period. For example, in 1908 a crowd of whites moved through the black area of Springfield, Illinois, and burned black-owned buildings, flogged fifty blacks, and lynched two blacks, chanting as they went, "Lincoln freed you, we'll show you your place" (Sitkoff 1978, 15).

Since the 1950s white violence against blacks has attacked civil rights activities and involved policy brutality. During the civil rights movement period, from the mid-1950s to the mid-1960s, more than 100 black and white civil rights activists were killed. And for a century police officials have murdered many blacks. As Willhelm (1983, 261) has noted, when the killings of blacks by police officers "are totaled over a decade it is fair to conclude that they amount to a massacre," for between the late 1960s and the late 1970s some 6,000 people were killed by the police; about 45 percent were black. Police brutality aimed at black Americans is not just a matter of killings; it also involves the widespread use of excessive force, such as beatings, harassment, false arrest, and verbal abuse. Moreover, over half of those executed for all crimes in the U.S. since 1930 have been black. Much of the crime committed by black Americans is, at bottom, an individualized slave revolt. Willhelm (1983, 273) phrases it as follows: "As Blacks become increasingly useless in an automated society, and turn to crime with greater frequency in order to obtain the material needs of life, they confront a White America increasingly determined to meet crime with state violence." High crime areas—the ghetto areas—are often called "combat areas" by the police, and many observers have talked about the undeclared war between youth and the police. Whites meet black crimes with repression rather than a massive job program. Black Americans seem to be the *only large minority* to receive so much violence at the hands of white authorities. This omnipresent violence is not just a contemporary scourge. It is directly linked in a long historical chain to the violence of slavery.

A Future of Slavery?

As the "Falling Behind" report's data makes evident, the modest black progress brought by wars and government intervention programs since the 1940s has begun to erode. The semislave system remains firmly in place in regard to employment, housing, and educational segregation as well as in terms of violence, ideological racism, color coding, and resistance to intermarriage. The likelihood of future change without militant black action is close to zero. The ideological position of white Americans is one of vigorous opposition to any significant government program, whether it be affirmative action in jobs or prosecution of homeowners and realtors who discriminate. If desegregation means a few black employees at work, a few students in the schoolroom, or a few black families in the larger residential neighborhood, that type of desegregation can be tolerated. But more substantial desegregation is not acceptable to most whites, nor do most whites favor federal government intervention to see to it that blacks get fair treatment in jobs or housing. Between 1964 and the mid-1970s public opinion surveys asked whites four times about government intervention to guarantee such fair treatment in jobs. In every survey only 36 percent to 39 percent of whites explicitly supported government action. And the last survey, taken during the 1970s, had the *lowest* percentage. On a similar question about government intervention to get rid of segregation in schools, the proportion of whites supporting federal action *dropped* from 42 percent in 1964 to only 25 percent in 1978. In surveys from 1973 to 1983 the proportion of whites supporting a law prohibiting race discrimination by a homeowner never reached the level of a majority, although unlike the two aforementioned cases the percentage did increase from 34 percent to 46 percent (Schuman et al. 1985).

A majority of white Americans still believe that the tremendous imbalance of power, reflected in the system of semislavery we have discussed here, should *not* be eradicated by race-conscious action. This does not bode well for the future of blacks in the United States.

References

Anderson, B. E. 1982. "Economic patterns in black America." *The State of Black America,* 1–32. New York: Urban League.

Aptheker, H. 1984. Lectures on American History. Minneapolis: University of Minnesota (unpublished).

Blauner, R. 1972. *Racial Oppression in America.* New York: Harper & Row.

Brimmer, A. F. 1976. The Economic Position of Black Americans. Washington, D.C.: National Commission for Manpower Policy.

Center of Budget and Policy Priorities. 1984. *Falling Behind: A Report on*

How Blacks Have Fared Under the Reagan Policies. Washington, D.C.: Government Printing Office.

Daniel, P. 1973. *The Shadow of Slavery*. London. Oxford University Press.

Davidson, C. 1984. "Minority vote dilution: An overview." Report 85-I. Houston: Rice University Institute for Policy Analysis.

Douglas, W. O. 1968. "Concurring opinion." *Jones et ux. v. Alfred H. Mayer Co.*, 392 U.S. 445.

Douglass, F. 1968/1881. "The color line." North America Rev. (June), as excerpted in *Jones et ux. v. Mayer Co.*, 392 U.S. 446–7.

Du Bois, W. E. B. 1935. *Black Reconstruction in America 1860–1880*. New York: World.

Feagin, J. R. 1984. *Racial and Ethnic Relations*. Englewood Cliffs, N.J.: Prentice-Hall.

Harris, W. II. 1982. *The Harder We Run*. New York: Oxford University Press.

Higginbotham, A. L. 1978. *In the Matter of Color*. New York: Oxford University Press.

Hudson, R. L. 1978. "Factors which influence mobility of blacks in an elite corporation." Ph.D. dissertation, City University of New York, New York.

Jones, E. Forthcoming. "What it's like to be a black manager." *Harvard Business Review*.

Jones, E. 1985. "Beneficiaries or victims? Progress or process." Research report. South Orange, N.J.: (unpublished).

Moynihan, D. P. 1969. "Memorandum to President-elect Richard M. Nixon." *New York Times* (11 March): 30.

Myrdal, G. 1964. *An American Dilemma*. Vol. I. New York: McGraw-Hill.

Myrdal, G. 1964. *An American Dilemma*. Vol. II. New York: McGraw-Hill.

Rex, J. 1973. Race, Colonialism and the City. London: Routledge and Kegan Paul.

Ringer, B. 1983. *"We the people" and Others*. New York: Tavistock.

Schuman, H., C. Steeh, and L. Bobo. 1985. *Racial Attitudes in America*. New York: Harvard University Press.

Sitkoff, H. 1978. *New Deals for Blacks*. New York: Oxford.

Taeuber, K. 1983. "Racial residential segregation, 28 cities. 1970–1980." Working Paper. Madison: Univ. of Wisconsin Center for Demography and Ecology.

Weiss, N. J. 1983. *Farewell to the Party of Lincoln: Black Politics in the Age of FDR*. Princeton, N.J.: Princeton University Press.

Willhelm, S. M. 1983. *Black in a White America*. Cambridge: Schenkman.

Wilson, W. J. 1978. *The Declining Significance of Race*. Chicago: University of Chicago Press.

Wright, G. 1985. Personal Communication. Austin: University of Texas.

Wye, C. G. 1972. "The new deal and the Negro community." *J. of Amer. History* 59 (December):630–40.

Yinger, J. 1984. "Measuring racial and ethnic discrimination with fair housing audits." Report, Conference on Fair Housing Testing. Washington, D.C.: HUD. (unpublished).

11

The Continuing Significance of Race: Antiblack Discrimination in Public Places

Joe R. Feagin

Much literature on contemporary U.S. racial relations tends to view black middle-class life as substantially free of traditional discrimination. Drawing primarily on 37 in-depth interviews with black middle-class respondents in several cities, I analyze public accommodations and other public-place discrimination. I focus on three aspects: (1) the sites of discrimination, (2) the character of discriminatory actions; and (3) the range of coping responses by blacks to discrimination. Documenting substantial barriers facing middle-class black Americans today, I suggest the importance of the individual's and the group's accumulated discriminatory experiences for understanding the character and impact of modern racial discrimination.

Title II of the 1964 Civil Rights Act stipulates that "all persons shall be entitled to the full and equal enjoyment of the goods, services, facilities, privileges, advantages, and accommodations of any place of public accommodation . . . without discrimination or segregation on the ground of race, color, religion, or national origin." The public places emphasized in the act are restaurants, hotels, and motels, although racial discrimination occurs in many other public places. Those black Americans who would make the greatest use of these pub-

This chapter is reprinted with minor revisions from Feagin, Joe R. 1991. "The continuing significance of race: Antiblack discrimination in public places." *American Sociological Review,* 56 (February): 101–16.

lic accommodations and certain other public places would be middle-class, i.e., those with the requisite resources.

White public opinion and many scholars have accented the great progress against traditional discrimination recently made by the black middle class. A National Research Council report on black Americans noted that by the mid-1970s many Americans "believed that . . . the Civil Rights Act of 1964 had led to broad-scale elimination of discrimination against blacks in public accommodations" (Jaynes and Williams 1989, 84). In interviews with whites in the late 1970s and early 1980s, Blauner (1989, 197) found that all but one viewed the 1970s as an era of great racial progress for American race relations. With some exceptions (see Willie 1983; Collins 1983; Landry 1987), much recent analysis of middle-class blacks by social scientists has emphasized the massive progress made since 1964 in areas where there had been substantial barriers, including public accommodations. Racial discrimination as a continuing and major problem for middle-class blacks has been downplayed as analysts have turned to the various problems of the "underclass." For example, Wilson (1978, 110–11) has argued that the growth of the black middle class since the 1960s is the result of improving economic conditions and of government civil rights laws, which virtually eliminated overt discrimination in the workplace and public accommodations. According to Wilson, the major problem of the 1964 Civil Rights Act is its failure to meet the problems of the black underclass (Wilson 1987, 146–47).

Here I treat these assertions as problematic. Do middle-class black Americans still face hostile treatment in public accommodations and other public places? If so, what form does this discrimination take? Who are the perpetrators of this discrimination? What is the impact of the discrimination on its middle-class victims? How do middle-class blacks cope with such discrimination?

Aspects of Discrimination

Discrimination can be defined in social-contextual terms as "actions or practices carried out by members of dominant racial or ethnic groups that have a differential and negative impact on members of subordinate racial and ethnic groups" (Feagin and Eckberg 1980, 1–2). This differential treatment ranges from the blatant to the subtle (Feagin and Feagin 1986). Here I focus primarily on blatant discrimination by white Americans targeting middle-class blacks. Historically, discrimination against blacks has been one of the most serious forms of racial/ethnic discrimination in the United States and one of the most difficult to overcome, in part because of the institutionalized character of color coding. I focus on three important aspects of discrimination: (1) the variation in sites of discrimination; (2) the range of discriminatory actions; and (3) the range of responses by blacks to discrimination.

Sites of Discrimination

There is a spatial dimension to discrimination. The probability of experiencing racial hostility varies from the most private to the most public sites. If a black person is in a relatively protected site, such as with friends at home, the probability of experiencing hostility and discrimination is low. The probability increases as one moves from friendship settings to such outside sites as the workplace, where a black person typically has contacts with both acquaintances and strangers, providing an interactive context with greater potential for discrimination.

In most workplaces, middle-class status and its organizational resources provide some protection against certain categories of discrimination. This protection probably weakens as a black person moves from those work and school settings where he or she is well-known into public accommodations such as large stores and city restaurants where contacts are mainly with white strangers. On public streets blacks have the greatest public exposure to strangers and the least protection against overt discriminatory behavior, including violence. A key feature of these more public settings is that they often involve contacts with white strangers who react primarily on the basis of one ascribed characteristic. The study of the microlife of interaction between strangers in public was pioneered by Goffman (1963; 1971) and his students, but few of their analyses have treated hostile discriminatory interaction in public places. A rare exception is the research by Gardner (1980; see also Gardner 1988), who documented the character and danger of passing remarks by men directed against women in unprotected public places. Gardner writes of women (and blacks) as "open persons," i.e., particularly vulnerable targets for harassment that violates the rules of public courtesy.

The Range of Discriminatory Actions

In his classic study, *The Nature of Prejudice,* Allport (1958, 14–5) noted that prejudice can be expressed in a series of progressively more serious actions, ranging from antilocution to avoidance, exclusion, physical attack, and extermination. Allport's work suggests a continuum of actions from avoidance, to exclusion or rejection, to attack. In his travels in the South in the 1950s a white journalist who changed his skin color to black encountered discrimination in each of these categories (Griffin 1961). In my data, discrimination against middle-class blacks still ranges across this continuum: (a) avoidance actions, such as a white couple crossing the street when a black male approaches; (2) rejection actions, such as poor service in public accommodations; (3) verbal attacks, such as shouting racial epithets in the street; (4) physical threats and harassment by white police officers; and (5) physical threats and attacks by other whites, such as attacks by white supremacists in the street. Changing re-

lations between blacks and whites in recent decades have expanded the repertoire of discrimination to include more subtle forms and to encompass discrimination in arenas from which blacks were formerly excluded, such as
formerly all-white public accommodations.

Black Responses to Discrimination

Prior to societal desegregation in the 1960s much traditional discrimination,
especially in the South, took the form of an asymmetrical "deference ritual" in
which blacks were typically expected to respond to discriminating whites with
great deference. According to Goffman (1956, 477), a deference ritual "functions as a symbolic means by which appreciation is regularly conveyed to a recipient." Such rituals can be seen in the obsequious words and gestures—the
etiquette of race relations—that many blacks, including middle-class blacks,
were forced to utilize to survive the rigors of segregation (Doyle 1937). However, not all responses in this period were deferential. From the late 1800s to
the 1950s, numerous lynchings and other violence targeted blacks whose behavior was defined as too aggressive (Raper 1933). Blauner's (1989) respondents reported acquaintances reacting aggressively to discrimination prior to
the 1960s.

Deference rituals can still be found today between some lower-income
blacks and their white employers. In her northeastern study Rollins (1985,
157) found black maids regularly deferring to white employers. Today, most
discriminatory interaction no longer involves much asymmetrical deference,
at least for middle-class blacks. Even where whites expect substantial deference, most middle-class blacks do not oblige. For middle-class blacks contemporary discrimination has evolved beyond the asymmetrical deference
rituals and "No Negroes served" type of exclusion to patterns of black-
contested discrimination. Discussing race and gender discrimination in Great
Britain, Brittan and Maynard (1984) have suggested that today "the terms of
oppression are not only dictated by history, culture, and the sexual and social
division of labor. They are also profoundly shaped at the site of the oppression,
and by the way in which oppressors and oppressed continuously have to renegotiate, reconstruct, and reestablish their relative positions in respect to benefits and power" (7). Similarly, white mistreatment of black Americans today
frequently encounters new coping strategies by blacks in the ongoing process
of reconstructing patterns of racial interaction.

Middle-class strategies for coping with discrimination range from careful
assessment to withdrawal, resigned acceptance, verbal confrontation, or physical confrontation. Later action might include a court suit. Assessing the situation is a first step. Some white observers have suggested that many middle-class
blacks are paranoid about white discrimination and rush too quickly to charges
of racism (Wieseltier 1989, June 5; for male views of female "paranoia" see

Gardner 1988). But the daily reality may be just the opposite, as middle-class black Americans often evaluate a situation carefully before judging it discriminatory and taking additional action. This careful evaluation, based on past experiences (real or vicarious), not only prevents jumping to conclusions, but also reflects the hope that white behavior is not based on race, because an act not based on race is easier to endure. After evaluation one strategy is to leave the site of discrimination rather than to create a disturbance. Another is to ignore the discrimination and continue with the interaction, a "blocking" strategy similar to that Gardner (1980, 345) reported for women dealing with street remarks. In many situations resigned acceptance is the only realistic response. More confrontational responses to white actions include verbal reprimands and sarcasm, physical counterattacks, and filing lawsuits. Several strategies may be tried in any given discriminatory situation. In crafting these strategies middle-class blacks, in comparison with less privileged blacks, may draw on middle-class resources to fight discrimination.

The Research Study

To examine discrimination, I draw primarily on 37 in-depth interviews from a larger study of 135 middle-class black Americans in Boston; Buffalo; Baltimore; Washington, D.C.; Detroit; Houston; Dallas; Austin; San Antonio; Marshall, Texas; Las Vegas; and Los Angeles. The interviewing was done in 1988–1990; black interviewers were used. I began with respondents known as members of the black middle class to knowledgeable consultants in key cities. Snowball sampling from these multiple starting points was used to maximize diversity.

The questions in the research instrument were primarily designed to elicit detailed information on the general situations of the respondents and on the barriers encountered and managed in employment, education, and housing. There were no specific questions in the interpreting schedule on public accommodations or other public-place discrimination; the discussions of that discrimination were volunteered in answer to general questions about barriers to personal goals and coping strategies or in digressions in answers to specific questions on employment, education, and housing. These volunteered responses signal the importance of such events. While I report below mainly on the responses of the thirty-seven respondents who detailed specific incidents of public discrimination, in interpreting the character and meaning of modern discrimination I also draw on some discussions in the larger sample of 135 interviews and in 5 supplementary and follow-up interviews of middle-class blacks conducted by the author and two black consultants.

"Middle class" was defined broadly as those holding a white-collar job (including those in professional, managerial, and clerical jobs), college students preparing for white-collar jobs, and owners of successful businesses. This definition is consistent with recent analyses of the black middle class (Landry 1987). The subsample of thirty-seven middle-class blacks reporting public discrimination is fairly representative of the demographic character of the larger sample. The subsample's occupational distribution is broadly similar to the larger sample and includes nine corporate managers and executives, nine health care or other professionals, eight government officials, four college students, three journalists or broadcasters, two clerical or sales workers, one entrepreneur, and one retired person. The subsample is somewhat younger than the overall sample, with 35 percent under age 35 vs. 25 percent in the larger sample, 52 percent in the 35–50 bracket vs. 57 percent, and 11 percent over 50 years of age vs. 18 percent. The subsample is broadly comparable to the larger sample in income: 14 had incomes under $36,000, 7 in the $36,000–55,000 range, and 16 in the $56,000 or more range. All respondents had at least a high school degree, and more than 90 percent had some college work. The subsample has a somewhat lower percentage of people with graduate work: 39 percent vs. 50 percent for the larger sample. Both samples have roughly equal proportions of men and women, and more than 60 percent of both samples reported residing in cities in the South or Southwest — 37 percent of the overall sample and 34 percent of the subsample resided in the North or West.

Descriptive Patterns

Among the 37 people in the subsample reporting specific instances of public-place discrimination, 24 reported 25 incidents involving public accommodations discrimination, and 15 reported 27 incidents involving street discrimination. Some incidents included more than one important discriminatory action; the 52 incidents consisted of 62 distinguishable actions. The distribution of these 62 actions by broad types is shown in Table 11.1.

Although all types of mistreatment are reported, there is a strong relationship between type of discrimination and site, with rejection/poor-service discrimination being most common in public accommodations and verbal or physical threat discrimination by white citizens or police officers most likely in the street.

The reactions of these middle-class blacks reflect the site and type of discrimination. The important steps taken beyond careful assessments of the situation are shown in Table 11.2. (A dual response is recorded for one accommodations incident).

The most common black responses to racial hostility in the street are withdrawal or a verbal reply. In many avoidance situations (e.g., a white couple crossing a street to avoid walking past a black college student) or attack situations (e.g., whites throwing beer cans from a passing car), a verbal response is

Table 11.1. Percentage Distribution of Discriminatory Actions by Type and Site: Middle-Class Blacks in Selected Cities, 1988–1990

Type of Discriminatory Action	Site of Discriminatory Action	
	Public Accommodations	Street
Avoidance	3	7
Rejection/poor service	79	4
Verbal epithets	12	25
Police threats/harassment	3	46
Other threats/harassment	3	18
Total	100	100
Number of actions	34	28

difficult because of the danger or the fleeting character of the hostility. A black victim often withdraws, endures this treatment with resigned acceptance, or replies with a quick verbal retort. In the case of police harassment, the response is limited by the danger, and resigned acceptance or mild verbal protests are likely responses. Rejection (poor service) in public accommodations provides an opportunity to fight back verbally —the most common responses to public accommodations discrimination are verbal counterattacks or resigned acceptance. Some black victims correct whites quietly, while others respond aggressively and lecture the assailant about the discrimination or threaten court action. A few retaliate physically. Examining materials in these thirty-seven interviews and those in the larger sample, we will see that the depth and complexity of contemporary black middle-class responses to white discrimination

Table 11.2. Percentage Distribution of Primary Responses to Discriminatory Incidents by Type and Site: Middle-Class Blacks in Selected Cities, 1988–1990

Response to Discriminatory Incident	Site of Discriminatory Incident	
	Public Accommodations	Street
Withdrawal/exit	4	22
Resigned acceptance	23	7
Verbal response	69	59
Physical counterattack	4	7
Response unclear	—	4
Total	100	99
Number of responses	26	27

accents the changing character of white-black interaction and the necessity of continual negotiation of the terms of that interaction.

Responses to Discrimination: Public Accommodations

Two Fundamental Strategies: Verbal Confrontation and Withdrawal

In the following account, a black news director at a major television station shows the interwoven character of discriminatory action and black response. The discrimination took the form of poor restaurant service, and the responses included both suggested withdrawal and verbal counterattack.

> He [her boyfriend] was waiting to be seated. . . . He said, "You go to the bathroom and I'll get the table. . . ." He was standing there when I came back; he continued to stand there. The restaurant was almost empty. There were waiters, waitresses, and no one seated. And when I got back to him, he was ready to leave, and said, "Let's go." I said, "What happened to our table?" He wasn't seated. So I said, "No, we're not leaving, please." And he said, "No, I'm leaving." So we went outside, and we talked about it. And what I said to him was, you have to be aware of the possibilities that this is not the first time that this has happened at this restaurant or at other restaurants, but this is the first time it has happened to a black news director here or someone who could make an issue of it, or someone who is prepared to make an issue of it.
>
> So we went back inside after I talked him into it and, to make a long story short, I had the manager come. I made most of the people who were there (while conducting myself professionally the whole time) aware that I was incensed at being treated this way. . . . I said, "Why do you think we weren't seated?" And the manager said, "Well, I don't really know." And I said, "Guess." He said, "Well, I don't know, because you're black?" I said, "Bingo. Now isn't it funny that you didn't guess that I didn't have any money (and I opened up my purse) and I said, "because I certainly have money. And isn't it odd that you didn't guess that it's because I couldn't pay for it because I've got two American Express cards and a Master Card right here. I think it's just funny that you would have assumed that it's because I'm black." . . . and then I took out my card and gave it to him and said, "If this happens again, or if I hear of this happening again, I will bring the full wrath of an entire news department down on this restaurant." And he just kind of looked at me. "Not [just] because I am personally offended. I am. But because you have no right to do what you did, and as a people we have lived a long time with having our rights abridged. . . ." There were probably three or four sets of diners in the restaurant and maybe five waiters/waitresses. They watched him standing there waiting to be seated. His reaction to it was that he wanted to leave. I understand why he would have reacted that way, because he felt that he

was in no condition to be civil. He was ready to take the place apart and....
sometimes it's appropriate to behave that way. We hadn't gone the first
step before going on to the next step. He didn't feel that he could com-
fortably and calmly take the first step, and I did. So I just asked him to
please get back in the restaurant with me, and then you don't have to say
a word, and let me handle it from there. It took some convincing, but I had
to appeal to his sense of, this is not just you, this is not just for you. We
are finally in a position as black people where there are some of us who
can genuinely get their attention. And if they don't want to do this because it's right for them to do it, then they'd better do it because they're
afraid to do otherwise. If it's fear, then fine, instill the fear.

This example provides insight into the character of modern discrimination.
The discrimination was not the "No Negroes" exclusion of the recent past, but
rejection in the form of poor service by restaurant personnel. The black response indicates the change in black-white interaction since the 1950s and
1960s, for discrimination is handled with vigorous confrontation rather than
deference. The aggressive black response and the white backtracking underscore Brittan and Maynard's (1984, 7) point that black-white interaction today
is being renegotiated. It is possible that the white personnel defined the couple
as "poor blacks" because of their jeans, although the jeans were fashionable
and white patrons wear jeans. In comments not quoted here the news director
rejects such an explanation. She forcefully articulates a theory of rights—a response that signals the critical impact of civil rights laws on the thinking of
middle-class blacks. The news director articulates the American dream: she
has worked hard, earned the money and credit cards, developed the appropriate middle-class behavior, and thus has under the law a *right* to be served.
There is defensiveness in her actions too, for she feels a need to legitimate her
status by showing her purse and credit cards. One important factor that enabled
her to take such assertive action was her power to bring a TV news team to the
restaurant. This power marks a change from a few decades ago when very few
black Americans had the social or economic resources to fight back successfully.

This example underscores the complexity of the interaction in such situations, with two levels of negotiation evident. The negotiation between the respondent and her boyfriend on withdrawal vs. confrontation highlights the
process of negotiating responses to discrimination and the difficulty in crafting such responses. Not only is there a process of dickering with whites within
the discriminatory scene but also a negotiation between the blacks involved.

The confrontation strategy can be taken beyond immediate verbal confrontation to a more public confrontation. The president of a financial institution in a Middle Atlantic city brought unfavorable publicity to a restaurant
with a pattern of poor service to blacks:

I took the staff here to a restaurant that had recently opened in the prestigious section of the city, and we waited while other people got waited on. And decided that after about a half hour that these people don't want to wait on us. I happened to have been in the same restaurant a couple of evenings earlier, and it took them about forty-five minutes before they came to wait on me and my guest. So, on the second incident, I said, this is not an isolated incident, this is a pattern, because I had spoken with some other people who had not been warmly received in the restaurant. So, I wrote a letter to the owners. I researched and found out who the owners were, wrote a letter to the owners and sent copies to the city papers. That's my way of expressing myself and letting the world know. You have to let people, other than you and the owner, know. You have to let others know you're expressing your dismay at the discrimination, or the barrier that's presented to you. I met with the owners. Of course, they wanted to meet with their attorneys with me, because they wanted to sue me. I told them they're welcome to do so, I don't have a thing, but fine they can do it. It just happens that I knew their white attorney. And he more or less vouched that if I had some concern that it must have been legitimate in some form. When the principals came in—one of the people who didn't wait on me was one of the owners, who happened to be waiting on everybody else—we resolved the issue by them inviting me to come again. And if I was fairly treated, or if I would come on several occasions and if I was fairly treated I would write a statement of retraction. I told them I would not write a retraction, I would write a statement with regard to how I was treated. Which I ultimately did. And I still go there today, and they speak to me, and I think the pattern is changed to a great degree.

This example also demonstrates the resources available to many middle-class black Americans. As a bank executive with connections in the white community, including the legal community, this respondent used his resources not only to bring discrimination to public attention but also to pressure a major change in behavior. He had the means to proceed beyond the local management to both the restaurant owners and the local newspapers. The detailed account provides additional insight into the black-white bargaining process. At first the white managers and owners, probably accustomed to acquiescence or withdrawal, vigorously resisted ending the blatant discrimination. But the verbal and other resources available to the respondent forced them to capitulate and participate in a negotiation process. The cost to the victor was substantial. As in the first incident, we see the time-consuming and energy-consuming nature of grappling with poor-service discrimination. Compared to whites entering the same places, black Americans face an extra burden when going into public accommodations putatively made hospitable by three decades of civil rights law protection.

The confrontation response is generally so costly in terms of time and energy that acquiescence or withdrawal are common options. An example of the exit response was provided by a utility company executive in an East Coast city:

I can remember one time my husband had picked up our son . . . from camp; and he'd stopped at a little store in the neighborhood near the camp. It was hot, and he was going to buy him a snowball. And the proprietor of the store—this was a very old, white neighborhood, and it was just a little sundry store. But the proprietor said he had the little window where people could come up and order things. Well, my husband and son had gone into the store. And he told them, "Well, I can't give it to you here, but if you go outside to the window, I'll give it to you." And there were other [white] people in the store who'd been served [inside]. So, they just left and didn't buy anything.

Here the act seems a throwback to the South of the 1950s, where blacks were required to use the back or side of a store. This differential treatment in an older white neighborhood is also suggestive of the territorial character of racial relations in many cities. The black response to degradation here was not to confront the white person or to acquiesce abjectly, but rather to reject the poor service and leave. Unlike the previous examples, the impact on the white proprietor was negligible because there was no forced negotiation. This site differed from the two previous examples in that the service was probably not of long-term importance to the black family passing through the area. In the previous sites the possibility of returning to the restaurants, for business or pleasure, may have contributed to the choice of a confrontational response. The importance of the service is a likely variable affecting black responses to discrimination in public accommodations.

Discrimination in public accommodations can occur in many different settings. A school board member in a northern city commented on her experiences in retail stores:

[I have faced] harassment in stores, being followed around, being questioned about what are you going to purchase here. . . . I was in an elite department store just this past Saturday and felt that I was being observed while I was window shopping. I in fact actually ended up purchasing something, but felt the entire time I was there—I was in blue jeans and sneakers, that's how I dress on a Saturday—I felt that I was being watched in the store as I was walking through the store, what business did I have there, what was I going to purchase, that kind of thing. . . . There are a few of those white people that won't put change in your hand, touch your skin—that doesn't need to go on. [Do you tell them that?] Oh, I do, I do. That is just so obvious. I usually [speak to them] if they're rude in the manner in which they deal with people. [What do they say about that?] Oh, stuff like, "Oh, excuse me." And some are really unconscious about it, say "Excuse me," and put the change in your hand, that's happened. But I've watched other people be rude, and I've been told to mind my own business. . . . [But you still do it?] Oh, sure, because for the most part I think that people do have to learn to think for themselves, and demand respect for themselves. . . . I find my best weapon of defense is to educate them, whether it's in the store, in a line at the bank, any situation, I teach them. And you take them by surprise because you tell them and show them what they should be doing, and what they should be saying and how they should be thinking. And they look at you because they don't know how to process you. They can't process it because you've just shown them how they should be living, and the fact that they are cheating themselves, really, because the racism is from fear. The racism is from lack of education.

This excessive surveillance of blacks' shopping was reported by several respondents in our study and in recent newspaper accounts (see Jaynes and Williams 1989, 140). Several white stereotypes seem to underlie the rejection discrimination in this instance—blacks are seen as shoplifters, as unclean, as disreputable poor. The excessive policing of black shoppers and the discourtesy of clerks illustrate the extra burden of being black in public places. No matter how affluent and influential, a black person cannot escape the stigma of being black, even while relaxing or shopping. There is the recurring strain of having to craft strategies for a broad range of discriminatory situations. Tailoring her confrontation to fit the particular discrimination, this respondent interrupted the normal flow of the interaction to call the whites to intersubjective account and make a one-way experience into a two-way experience. Forced into new situations, offending whites frequently do not know how "to process" such an aggressive response. Again we see how middle-class blacks can force a reconstruction of traditional responses by whites to blacks. The intensity of her discussion suggests that the attempt to "educate" whites comes with a heavy personal cost, for it is stressful to "psych" oneself up for such incidents.

The problem of burdensome visibility and the inescapable racial stereotyping by whites was underscored in the reply of a physician in an East Coast city to a question about whether she had encountered barriers:

Yes. All the time. I hate it when you go places and [white] people . . . think that we work in housekeeping. Or they naturally assume that we came from a very poor background. . . . A lot of white people think that blacks are just here to serve them, and [that] we have not risen above the servant position.

Here the discriminatory treatment comes from the white traveller staying in a hotel. This incident exemplifies the omnipresence of the stigma of being black—a well-dressed physician staying in an expensive hotel cannot escape. Here and elsewhere in the interview her anger suggests a confrontational response to such situations.

Middle-class black parents often attempt to protect their children from racial hostility in public places, but they cannot always be successful. A manager at an electronics firm in the Southwest gave an account of his daughter's first encounter with a racial epithet. After describing racist graffiti on a neighborhood fence in the elite white suburb where he lives, he described an incident at a swimming pool:

> I'm talking over two hundred kids in this pool; not one black. I don't think you can go anywhere in the world during the summertime and not find some black kids in the swimming pool. . . . Now what's the worst thing that can happen to a ten-year old girl in a swimming pool with all white kids? What's the worst thing that could happen? It happened. This little white guy called her a "nigger." Then called her a "motherfucker" and told her to "get out of the god-damn pool." . . . And what initiated that, they had these little inner tubes, they had about fifteen of them, and the pool owns them. So you just use them if they are vacant. So there was a tube setting up on the bank, she got it, jumped in and started playing in it. . . . And this little white guy decided he wanted it. But, he's supposed to get it, right? And he meant to get it, and she wouldn't give it to him, so out came all these racial slurs. So my action was first with the little boy. "You know you're not supposed to do that. Apologize right now. Okay, good. Now, Mr. Lifeguard, I want him out of this pool, and you're going to have to do better. You're going to have to do better, but he has to leave out of this pool and let his parents know, okay?"

Taking his daughter back the next day, he observed from behind a fence to make certain the lifeguard protected her. For many decades black adults and children were excluded from public pools in the South and Southwest, and many pools were closed during the early desegregation period. These accommodations have special significance for middle-class black Americans, and this may be one reason the father's reaction was so decisive. Perhaps the major reason for his swift action was because this was the first time that his daughter had been the victim of racial slurs. She was the victim of cutting racist epithets that for this black father, as doubtless for most black Americans, connote segregated institutions and violence against blacks. Children also face hostility in public accommodations and may never shake this kind of experience. At a rather early point, many black parents find it necessary to teach their children how to handle discriminatory incidents.

The verbal responses of middle-class blacks to stigmatization can take more subtle forms. An 80-year-old retired schoolteacher in a southern city recounted her response to a recent experience at a drapery shop:

> The last time I had some draperies done and asked about them at the drapery shop, a young man at that shop—when they called [to him], he asked, and I heard him—he said, "The job for that nigger woman." And I said to

the person who was serving me, "Oh my goodness, I feel so sorry for that young man. I didn't know people were still using that sort of language and saying those sorts of things." And that's the way I deal with it. I don't know what you call that. Is that sarcasm? Sarcasm is pretty good. . . . Well I've done that several times. This being 1989 . . . I'm surprised that I find it in this day and time.

One white clerk translated the schoolteacher's color in a hostile way while the other apparently listened. Suggested here is the way many whites are content to watch overt racist behavior without intervening. The retired teacher's response contrasts with the more confrontational reactions of the previous examples, for she used what might be called "strategic indirection." With composure she directed a pointedly sarcastic remark to the clerk serving her. Mockery is a more subtle tactic blacks can use to contend with antilocution, and this tactic may be more common among older blacks. Later in her interview this angry woman characterizes such recurring racial incidents as the "little murders" that daily have made her life difficult.

Careful Situation Assessments

We have seen in the previous incidents some tendency for blacks to assess discriminatory incidents before they act. Among several respondents who discussed discrimination at retail stores, the manager of a career development organization in the Southwest indicated that a clear assessment of a situation usually precedes confrontations and is part of a repertoire of concatenated responses:

> If you're in a store—and let's say the person behind the counter is white—and you walk up to the counter, and a white person walks up to the counter, and you know you were there before the white customer, the person behind the counter knows you were there first, and it never fails, they always go, "Who's next." Ok. And what I've done, if they go ahead and serve the white person first, then I will immediately say, "Excuse me, I was here first, and we both know I was here first." . . . If they get away with it once, they're going to get away with it more than once, and then it's going to become something else. And you have to, you want to make sure that folks know that you're not being naive, that you really see through what's happening. Or if it's a job opportunity or something like that, too, [we should do the] same thing. You first try to get a clear assessment of what's really going on and sift through that information, and then . . . go from there.

The executive's coping process typically begins with a sifting of information before deciding on further action. She usually opts for immediate action so that whites face the reality of their actions in a decisive way. Like the account of the school board member who noted that whites would sometimes not put money directly in her hand, this account illustrates another aspect of discrimination in public accommodations: For many whites racial hostility is imbedded in everyday actions, and there is a deep, perhaps subconscious, recoil response to black color and persona.

The complex process of evaluation and response is described by a college dean, who commented generally on hotel and restaurant discrimination encountered as he travels across the United States:

> When you're in a restaurant and . . . you notice that blacks get seated near the kitchen. You notice that if it's a hotel, your room is near the elevator, or your room is always way down in a corner somewhere. You find that you are getting the undesirable rooms. And you come there early in the day and you don't see very many cars on the lot and they'll tell you that this is all we've got. Or you get the room that's got a bad television set. You know that you're being discriminated against. And of course you have to act accordingly. You have to tell them, "Okay, the room is fine, [but] this television set has to go. Bring me another television set." So in my personal experience, I simply cannot sit and let them get away with it [discrimination] and not let them know that I know that that's what they are doing. . . .
>
> When I face discrimination, first I take a long look at myself and try to determine whether or not I am seeing what I think I'm seeing in 1989, and if it's something that I have an option [about]. In other words, if I'm at a store making a purchase, I'll simply walk away from it. If it's at a restaurant where I'm not getting good service, I first of all let the people know that I'm not getting good service, then I [may] walk away from it. But the thing that I have to do is to let people know that I know that I'm being singled out for a separate treatment. And then I might react in any number of ways—depending on where I am and how badly I want whatever it is that I'm there for.

This commentary adds another dimension to our understanding of public discrimination, its cumulative aspect. Blacks confront not just isolated incidents—such as a bad room in a luxury hotel once every few years—but a lifelong series of such incidents. Here again the omnipresence of careful assessments is underscored. The dean's interview highlights a major difficulty in being black—one must be constantly prepared to assess accurately and then decide on the appropriate response. This long-look approach may indicate that some middle-class blacks are so sensitive to white charges of hypersensitivity and paranoia that they err in the opposite direction and fail to see discrimination when it occurs. In addition, as one black graduate student at a leading white university in the Southeast put it: "I think that sometimes timely and appropriate responses to racially motivated acts and comments are lost due to the processing of the input." The "long look" can result in missed opportunities to respond to discrimination.

Using Middle-Class Resources for Protection

One advantage that middle-class blacks have over poorer blacks is the use of the resources of middle-class occupations. A professor at a major white university commented on the varying protection her middle-class status gives her at certain sites:

> If I'm in those areas that are fairly protected, within gatherings of my own group, other African Americans, or if I'm in the university where my status as a professor mediates against the way I might be perceived, mediates against the hostile perception, then it's fairly comfortable. . . . When I divide my life into encounters with the outside world, and of course that's 90 percent of my life, it's fairly consistently unpleasant at those sites where there's nothing that mediates between my race and what I have to do. For example, if I'm in a grocery store, if I'm in my car, which is a 1970 Chevrolet, a real old ugly car, all those things—being in a grocery store in casual clothes, or being in the car—sort of advertises something that doesn't have anything to do with my status as far as people I run into are concerned.
>
> Because I'm a large black woman, and I don't wear whatever class status I have, or whatever professional status [I have] in my appearance when I'm in the grocery store, I'm part of the mass of large black women shopping. For most whites, and even for some blacks, that translates into negative status. That means that they are free to treat me the way they treat most poor black people, because they can't tell by looking at me that I differ from that.

This professor notes the variation in discrimination in the sites through which she travels, from the most private to the most public. At home with friends she faces no problems, and at the university her professorial status gives her some protection from discrimination. The increase in unpleasant encounters as she moves into public accommodations sites such as grocery stores is attributed to the absence of mediating factors such as clear symbols of middle-class status—displaying the middle-class symbols may provide some protection against discrimination in public places.

An East Coast news anchorperson reported a common middle-class experience of good service from retailers over the phone:

> And if I was seeking out a service, like renting a car, or buying something, I could get a wonderful, enthusiastic reaction to what I was doing. I would work that up to such a point that this person would probably shower me with roses once they got to see me. And then when I would show up, and they're surprised to see that I'm black, I sort of remind them in conversation how welcome my service was, to put the embarrassment on them, and I go through with my dealings. In fact, once my sister criticized me for putting [what] she calls my "white-on-white voice" on to get a rental

car. But I needed a rental car and I knew that I could get it. I knew if I could get this guy to think that he was talking to some blonde, rather than, you know, so, but that's what he has to deal with. I don't have to deal with that, I want to get the car.

Being middle class often means that you, as many blacks say, "sound white" over the phone. Over the phone middle-class blacks find they get fair treatment because the white person assumes the caller is white, while they receive poorer (or no) service in person. Race is the only added variable in such interpersonal contact situations. Moreover, some middle-class blacks intentionally use this phone-voice resource to secure their needs.

Responses to Discrimination: The Street

Reacting to White Strangers

As we move away from public accommodations settings to the usually less protected street sites, racial hostility can become more fleeting and severer, and thus black responses are often restricted. The most serious form of street discrimination is violence. Often the reasonable black response to street discrimination is withdrawal, resigned acceptance, or a quick verbal retort. The difficulty of responding to violence is seen in this report by a man working for a media surveying firm in a southern industrial city:

> I was parked in front of this guy's house. . . . This guy puts his hands on the window and says, "Get out of the car, nigger." . . . So, I got out, and I thought, "Oh, this is what's going to happen here." And I'm talking fast. And they're, "What are you doing here?" And I'm, "This is who I am. I work with these people. This is the man we want to put in the survey." And I pointed to the house. And the guy said, "Well you have an out-of-state license tag, right?" "Yea." And he said, "If something happened to you, your people at home wouldn't know for a long time, would they?". . . . I said, "Look, I deal with a company that deals with television. [If] something happens to me, it's going to be a national thing. . . . So, they grab me by the lapel of my coat, and put me in front of my car. They put the blade on my zipper. And now I'm thinking about this guy that's in the truck [behind me], because now I'm thinking that I'm going to have to run somewhere. Where am I going to run? Go to the police? [laughs] So, after a while they bash up my headlight. And I drove [away].

Stigmatized and physically attacked solely because of his color, this man faced verbal hostility and threats of death with courage. Cautiously drawing on his middle-class resources, he told the attackers his death would bring television crews to the town. This resource utilization is similar to that of the news director in the restaurant incident. Beyond this verbal threat his response had to be one of caution. For most whites threatened on the street, the police are a sought-after source of protection, but for black men this is often not the case.

At the other end of the street continuum is nonverbal harassment such as the "hate stare" that so traumatized Griffin (1961). In her research on street remarks, Gardner (1980) considered women and blacks particularly vulnerable targets for harassment. For the segregation years Henley (1978) has documented the ways in which many blacks regularly deferred to whites in public-place communications. Today obsequious deference is no longer a common response to harassment. A middle-class student with dark skin reported that on her way to university classes she had stopped at a bakery in a white residential area where very few blacks live or shop. A white couple in front of the store stared intently and hatefully at her as she crossed the sidewalk and entered and left the bakery. She reported that she had experienced this hate stare many times. The incident angered her for some days thereafter, in part because she had been unable to respond more actively to it.

In between the hate stare and violence are many other hostile actions. Most happen so fast that withdrawal, resigned acceptance, or an immediate verbal retort are the reasonable responses. The female professor quoted earlier described the fleeting character of harassment:

> I was driving. This has [happened] so many times, but one night it was especially repugnant. I think it had to be, with my son being in the car, it was about 9:30 at night, and as I've said, my car is old and very ugly, and I have been told by people shouting at intersections that it's the kind of car that people think of as a low-rider car, so they associate it with Mexican Americans, especially poor Mexican Americans. Well, we were sitting at an intersection waiting to make a turn, and a group of middle-class looking white boys drives up in a nice car. And they start shouting things at us in a real fake-sounding Mexican American accent, and I realized that they thought we were Mexican Americans. And I turned to look at them, and they started making obscene gestures and laughing at the car. And then one of them realized that I was black, and said, "Oh, it's just a nigger." And [they] drove away.

This incident illustrates the seldom-noted problem of "cross discrimination" — a black person may suffer from discrimination aimed at other people of color by whites unable to distinguish. The white hostility was guided by certain signals—an old car and dark skin—of minority-group status. The nighttime setting, by assuring anonymity, facilitated the hurling of racist epithets and heightened the negative impact on this woman, who found the harassment especially dangerous and repulsive because she was with her son. She drove away without replying. Later in the interview she notes angrily that in such incidents the ascribed characteristic of "blackness" takes precedence over her achieved middle-class characteristics and that the grouped thinking of racism obscures anything about her that is individual and unique.

For young middle-class blacks street harassment can generate shock and disbelief, as in the case of this college student who recounted a street encounter near her university in the Southwest:

> I don't remember in high school being called a "nigger" before, and I can remember here being called a "nigger." [When was this?] In my freshman year, at a university student parade. There was a group of us, standing there, not knowing that this was not an event that a lot of black people went to! [laughs] You know, our dorm was going, and this was something we were going to go to because we were students too! And we were standing out there and [there were] a group of white fraternity boys—I remember the southern flag—and a group of us, five or six of us, and they went past by us, before the parade had actually gotten underway. And one of them pointed and said, "Look at that bunch of niggers!" I remember thinking, "Surely he's not talking to us!" We didn't even use the word "nigger" in my house. . . . [How did you feel?] I think I wanted to cry. And my friends —they were from a southwestern city—they were ready to curse them, and I was just standing there with my mouth open. I think I wanted to cry. I could not believe it, because you get here and you think you're in an educated environment and you're dealing with educated people. And all of this backward country stuff . . . you think that kind of stuff is not going on, but it is.

The respondent's first coping response was to think the assailants were not speaking to her and her friends. Again we see the tendency for middle-class blacks to assess situations carefully and to give whites the benefit of the doubt. Her subsequent response was tearful acquiescence, but her friends were ready to react in a more aggressive way. The discriminators may have moved on before a considered response was possible. This episode points up the impact of destructive racial coding on young people and hints at the difficulty black parents face in socializing children for coping with white hostility. When I discussed these street incidents involving younger blacks with two older black respondents, one a southern civil rights activist and the other an Ivy-League professor, both noted the problem created for some middle-class black children by their well-intentioned parents trying to shelter them from racism.

It seems likely that for middle-class blacks the street is the site of recurring encounters with various types of white malevolence. A vivid example of the cumulative character and impact of this discrimination was given by another black student at a white university, who recounted his experiences walking home at night from a campus job to his apartment in a predominantly white residential area:

So, even if you wanted to, it's difficult just to live a life where you don't
come into conflict with others. Because every day you walk the streets,
it's not even like once a week, once a month. It's every day you walk the
streets. Every day that you live as a black person you're reminded how
you're perceived in society. You walk the streets at night; white people
cross the streets. I've seen white couples and individuals dart in front of
cars to not be on the same side of the street. Just the other day, I was walking down the street, and this white female with a child, I saw her pass a
young white male about 20 yards ahead. When she saw me, she quickly
dragged the child and herself across the busy street. What is so funny is
that this area has had an unknown white rapist in the area for about four
years. [When I pass] white men tighten their grip on their women. I've
seen people turn around and seem like they're going to take blows from
me. The police constantly make circles around me as I walk home, you
know, for blocks. I'll walk, and they'll turn a block. And they'll come
around me just to make sure, to find out where I'm going. So, every day
you realize [you're black]. Even though you're not doing anything
wrong; you're just existing. You're just a person. But you're a black person perceived in an unblack world. (This quote includes a clarification
sentence from a follow-up interview.)

In a subsequent comment this respondent mentioned that he also endured
white men hurling beer cans and epithets at him as he walked home. Again the
cumulation of incidents is evident. Everyday street travel for young black
middle-class males does not mean one isolated incident every few years.

Unable to "see" his middle-class symbols of college dress and books, white
couples (as well as individuals) have crossed the street in front of cars to avoid
walking near this modest-build black student, in a predominantly white neighborhood. Couples moving into defensive postures are doubtless reacting to the
stigma of "black maleness." The student perceives such avoidance as racist,
however, not because he is paranoid, but because he has previously encountered numerous examples of whites taking such defensive measures. Many
whites view typical "street" criminals as black or minority males and probably
see young black males as potentially dangerous (Graber 1980, 55). This would
seem to be the motivation for some hostile treatment black males experience
in public places. Some scholars have discussed white perceptions of black
males as threatening and the justifiability of that perception (Warr forthcoming), but to my knowledge there has been no discussion in the literature of the
negative impact of such perceptions on black males. This student reports that
being treated as a pariah (in his words, a "criminal and a rapist") has caused
him severe psychological problems. When I discussed this student's experiences with a prominent black journalist in a northeastern city, he reported that
whites sometimes stop talking—and white women grab their purses—on
downtown office-building elevators when he enters. These two men had some-

what different responses to such discrimination, one relatively passive and the other aggressive. In a follow-up interview the student reported that he rarely responded aggressively to the street encounters, apart from the occasional quick curse, because they happened too quickly. Echoing the black graduate student's comments about processing input and missed opportunities, he added: "I was basically analyzing and thinking too much about the incident." However, the journalist reacts more assertively; he described how he turns to whites in elevators and informs them, often with a smile, that they can continue talking or that he is not interested in their purses.

On occasion, black middle-class responses to street hostility from white strangers are even more aggressive. A woman who now runs her own successful business in a southwestern city described a car incident in front of a grocery store:

> We had a new car . . . and we stopped at 7-11 [store]. We were going to go out that night, and we were taking my son to a babysitter. . . . And we pulled up, and my husband was inside at the time. And this person, this Anglo couple, drove up, and they hit our car. It was a brand new car. So my husband came out. And the first thing they told us was that we got our car on *welfare*. Here we are able-bodied. He was a corporate executive. I had a decent job, it was a professional job, but it wasn't paying anything. But they looked at the car we were driving, and they made the assumption that we got it from welfare. I completely snapped; I physically abused that lady. I did. And I was trying to keep my husband from arguing with her husband until the police could come. . . . And when the police came they interrogated them; they didn't arrest us, because there was an off-duty cop who had seen the whole incident and said she provoked it.

Here we see how some whites perceive blacks, including middle-class blacks, in interracial situations. The verbal attack by the whites was laced with the stereotype about blacks as welfare chiselers. This brought forth an angry response from the black couple, which probably came as a surprise to the whites. This is another example of Brittan and Maynard's (1984, 7) point that discriminatory interaction is shaped today by the way in which oppressors and oppressed mediate their relative positions. Note too the role of the off-duty police officer. The respondent does not say whether the officer was white or black, but this detail suggests that certain contexts of discrimination have changed—in the past a (white) police officer would have sided with the whites. This respondent also underscores her and her husband's occupational achievements, highlighting her view that she has attained the American middle-class ideal. She is incensed that her obvious middle-class symbols did not protect her from verbal abuse.

The importance of middle-class resources in street encounters was dramatized in the comments of a parole office in a major West Coast city. He recounted how he dealt with a racial epithet:

> I've been called "nigger" before, out in the streets when I was doing my job, and the individual went to jail. . . . [Ok, if he didn't call you a "nigger," would he have still gone to jail?] Probably not. [. . . Was the person white?] Yes, he was. And he had a partner with him, and his partner didn't say anything, and his partner jaywalked with him. However, since he uttered the racial slur, I stopped him and quizzed him about the laws. And jaywalking's against the law, so he went to jail.

On occasion, middle-class blacks have the ability to respond not only aggressively but authoritatively to street discrimination. This unusual response to an epithet was possible because the black man, unknown to his assailant, had police authority. This incident also illustrates a point made in the policing literature about the street-level discretion of police officers (Perry and Sornoff 1973). Jaywalking is normally a winked-at violation, as in the case of the assailant's companion. Yet this respondent was able to exercise his discretionary authority to punish a racial epithet.

Responses to Discrimination by White Police Officers

Most middle-class blacks do not have such governmental authority as their personal protection. In fact, white police officers are a major problem. Encounters with the police can be life-threatening and thus limit the range of responses. A television commentator recounted two cases of police harassment where he was working for a survey firm in the mid-1980s. In one of the incidents, which took place in a southern metropolis, he was stopped by several white officers:

> "What are you doing here?" I tell them what I'm doing here. . . . And so [he] spread [me] on top of my car. [What had you done?] Because I was in the neighborhood. I left this note on these peoples' house: "Here's who I am. You weren't here, and I will come back in thirty minutes." [Why were they searching you?] They don't know. To me, they're searching, I remember at that particular moment when this all was going down, there was a lot of reports about police crime on civilians. . . . It took four cops to shake me down, two police cars, so they had me up there spread out. I had a friend of mine with me who was making the call with me, because we were going to have dinner together, and he was black, and they had me up, and they had him outside. . . . They said, "Well, let's check you out." . . . And I'm talking to myself, and I'm not thinking about being at attention, with my arms spread on my Ford [a company car], and I'm sitting there talking to myself, "Man, this is crazy, this is crazy."

[How are you feeling inside?] Scared, I mean real scared. [What did you think was going to happen to you?] I was going to go to jail. . . . Just because they picked me. Why would they stop me? It's like, if they can stop me, why wouldn't I go to jail, and I could sit in there for ten days before the judge sees me. I'm thinking all this crazy stuff. . . . Again, I'm talking to myself. And the guy takes his stick. And he doesn't whack me hard, but he does it with enough authority to let me know they mean business. "I told you stand still; now put your arms back out." And I've got this suit on, and the car's wet. And my friend's hysterical. He's outside the car. And they're checking him out. And he's like, "Man, just be cool, man." And he had tears in his eyes. And I'm like, oh, man, this is a nightmare. This is not supposed to happen to me. This is not my style! And so finally, this other cop comes up and says, "What have we got here, Charlie?" "Oh, we've got a guy here. He's running through the neighborhood, and he doesn't want to do what we tell him. We might have to run him in." [You're "running through" the neighborhood?] Yeah, exactly, in a suit in the rain?! After they got through doing their thing and harassing me, I just said, "Man this has been a hell of a week."

And I had tears in my eyes, but it wasn't tears of upset. It was tears of anger; it was tears of wanting to lash back. . . . What I thought to myself was, man, blacks have it real hard down here. I don't care if they're a broadcaster, I don't care if they're a businessman or a banker. . . . They don't have it any easier than the persons on skid row who get harassed by the police on a Friday or Saturday night.

It seems likely that most black men—including middle-class black men—see white police officers as a major source of danger and death (see "Mood of Ghetto America" 1980, 2 June, 32–34; Louis Harris and Associates 1989; Roddy 1990, 26 August). Scattered evidence suggests that by the time they are in their twenties, most black males, regardless of socioeconomic status, have been stopped by the police because "blackness" is considered a sign of possible criminality by police officers (Moss 1990; Roddy 1990, August 26). This treatment probably marks a dramatic contrast with the experiences of young white middle-class males. In the incident above the respondent and a friend experienced severe police maltreatment—detention for a lengthy period, threat of arrest, and the reality of physical violence. The coping response of the respondent was resigned acceptance somewhat similar to the deference rituals highlighted by Goffman. The middle-class suits and obvious corporate credentials (for example, survey questionnaires and company car) did not protect the two black men. The final comment suggests a disappointment that middle-class status brought no reprieve from police stigmatization and harassment.

Black women can also be the targets of police harassment. A professor at a major white university in the Southwest describes her encounters with the police:

When the cops pull me over because my car is old and ugly, they assume I've just robbed a convenience store. Or that's the excuse they give: "This car looks like a car used to rob a 7-11 [store]." And I've been pulled over six or seven times since I've been in this city—and I've been here two years now. Then I do what most black folks do. I try not to make any sudden moves so I'm not accidentally shot. Then I give them my identification. And I show them my university I.D. so they won't think that I'm someone that constitutes a threat, however they define it, so that I don't get arrested.

She adds:

[One problem with] being black in America is that you have to spend so much time thinking about stuff that most white people just don't even have to think about. I worry when I get pulled over by a cop. I worry because the person that I live with is a black male, and I have a teen-aged son. I worry what some white cop is going to think when he walks over to our car, because he's holding on to a gun. And I'm very aware of how many black folks accidentally get shot by cops. I worry when I walk into a store, that someone's going to think I'm in there shoplifting. And I have to worry about that because I'm not free to ignore it. And so, that thing that's supposed to be guaranteed to all Americans, the freedom to just be yourself is a fallacious idea. And I get resentful that I have to think about things that a lot of people, even my very close white friends whose politics are similar to mine, simply don't have to worry about.

This commentary about a number of encounters underscores the pyramiding character of discrimination. This prominent scholar has faced excessive surveillance by white police officers, who presumably view blacks as likely criminals. As in the previous example, there is great fear of white officers, but her response is somewhat different: She draws on her middle-class resources for protection; she cautiously interposes her middle-class status by pulling out a university I.D. card. In the verbal exchange her articulateness as a professor probably helps protect her. This assertive use of middle-class credentials in dealing with police marks a difference from the old asymmetrical deference rituals, in which highlighting middle-class status would be considered arrogant by white officers and increase the danger. Note, too, the explicit theory of rights that she, like many other middle-class blacks, holds as part of her American dream.

Conclusion

I have examined the sites of discrimination, the types of discriminatory acts, and the responses of the victims and have found the color stigma still to be very important in the public lives of affluent black Americans. The sites of racial discrimination range from relatively protected home sites, to less protected workplace and educational sites, to the even less protected public places. The 1964 Civil Rights Act guarantees that black Americans are "entitled to the full and equal enjoyment of the goods, services, facilities, privileges, advantages, and accommodations" in public accommodations. Yet the interviews indicate that deprivation of full enjoyment of public facilities is not a relic of the past; deprivation and discrimination in public accommodations persist. Middle-class black Americans remain vulnerable targets in public places. Prejudice-generated aggression in public places is, of course, not limited to black men and women—gay men and white women are also targets of street harassment (Benokraitis and Feagin 1986). Nonetheless, black women and men face an unusually broad range of discrimination on the street and in public accommo-dations.

The interviews highlight two significant aspects of the additive discrimina-tion faced by black Americans in public places and elsewhere: (1) the cumu-lative character of an *individual's* experiences with discrimination; (2) the *group's* accumulated historical experiences as perceived by the individual. A retired psychology professor who has worked in the Midwest and Southwest commented on the pyramiding of incidents:

I don't think white people, generally, understand the full meaning of racist discriminatory behaviors directed toward Americans of African de-scent. They seem to see each act of discrimination or any act of violence as an "isolated" event. As a result, most white Americans cannot under-stand the strong reaction manifested by blacks when such events occur. They feel that blacks tend to "over-react." They forget that in most cases, we live lives of quiet desperation generated by a litany of *daily* large and small events that whether or not by design, remind us of our "place" in American society.

Particular instances of discrimination may seem minor to outside white ob-servers when considered in isolation. But when blatant acts of avoidance, ver-bal harassment, and physical attack combine with subtle and covert slights, and these accumulate over months, years, and lifetimes, the impact on a black person is far more than the sum of the individual instances.

The historical context of contemporary discrimination was described by the retired psychologist, who argued that average white Americans

. . . ignore the personal context of the stimulus. That is, they deny the historical impact that a negative act may have on an individual. "Nigger" to a white may simply be an epithet that should be ignored. To most blacks, the term brings into sharp and current focus all kinds of acts of racism—murder, rape, torture, denial of constitutional rights, insults, limited opportunity structure, economic problems, unequal justice under the law and a myriad of . . . other racist and discriminatory acts that occur daily in the lives of *most* Americans of African descent—including professional blacks.

Particular acts, even antilocution that might seem minor to white observers, are freighted not only with one's past experience of discrimination but also with centuries of racial discrimination directed at the entire group, vicarious oppression that still includes racially translated violence and denial of access to the American dream. Anti-black discrimination is a matter of racial-power inequality institutionalized in a variety of economic and social institutions over a long period of time. The microlevel events of public accommodations and public streets are not just rare and isolated encounters by individuals; they are recurring events reflecting an invasion of the microworld by the macroworld of historical racial subordination.

The cumulative impact of racial discrimination accounts for the special way that blacks have of looking at and evaluating interracial incidents. One respondent, a clerical employee at an adoption agency, described the "second eye" she uses:

I think that it causes you to have to look at things from two different perspectives. You have to decide whether things that are done or slights that are made are made because you are black or they are made because the person is just rude, or unconcerned and uncaring. So it's kind of a situation where you're always kind of looking to see with a second eye or a second antenna just what's going on.

The language of "second eye" suggests that blacks look at white-black interaction through a lens colored by personal and group experience with cross-institutional and cross-generational discrimination. This sensitivity is not new, but is a current adaption transcending, yet reminiscent of, the black sensitivity to the etiquette of racial relations in the old South (Doyle 1937). What many whites see as black "paranoia" (e.g., Wieseltier 1989, 5 June) is simply a realistic sensitivity to white-black interaction created and constantly reinforced by the two types of cumulative discrimination cited above.

Blacks must be constantly aware of the repertoire of possible responses to chronic and burdensome discrimination. One older respondent spoke of having to put on her "shield" just before she leaves the house each morning. When quizzed, she said that for more than six decades, as she leaves her home, she has tried to be prepared for insults and discrimination in public places, even if nothing happens that day. This extraordinary burden of discrimination, evident in most of the 135 interviews in the large sample, was eloquently described by the female professor who resented having to worry about life-threatening incidents that her "very close white friends . . . simply don't have to worry about." Another respondent was articulate on this point:

... if you can think of the mind as having one hundred ergs of energy, and the average man uses 50 percent of his energy dealing with the everyday problems of the world — just general kinds of things — then he has 50 percent more to do creative kinds of things that he wants to do. Now that's a white person. Now a black person also has one hundred ergs; he uses 50 percent the same way a white man does, dealing with what the white man has [to deal with], so he has 50 percent left. But he uses 25 percent fighting being black, [with] all the problems being black and what it means. Which means he really only has twenty-five percent to do what the white man has fifty percent to do, and he's expected to do just as much as the white man with that twenty-five percent. . . . So, that's kind of what happens. You just don't have as much energy left to do as much as you know you really could if you were free, [if] your mind were free.

The individual cost of coping with racial discrimination is great, and, as he says, you cannot accomplish as much as you could if you retained the energy wasted on discrimination. This is perhaps the most tragic cost of persisting discrimination in the United States. In spite of decades of civil rights legislation, black Americans have yet to attain the full promise of the American dream.

References

Allport, Gordon. 1958. *The Nature of Prejudice*. Abridged. New York: Doubleday Anchor Books.

Benokraitis, Nijole, and Joe R. Feagin. 1986. *Modern Sexism: Blatant, Subtle and Covert Discrimination*. Englewood Cliffs: Prentice-Hall.

Blauner, Bob. 1989. *Black Lives, White Lives*. Berkeley: University of California Press.

Brittan, Arthur, and Mary Maynard. 1984. *Sexism, Racism, and Oppression*. Oxford: Basil Blackwell.

Collins, Sheila M. 1983. "The making of the black middle class." *Social Problems* 30:369–81.

Doyle, Betram W. 1937. *The Etiquette of Race Relations in the South*. Port Washington, N.Y.: Kennikat Press.

Feagin, Joe R., and Douglas Eckberg. 1980. "Prejudice and discrimination." *Annual Review of Sociology* 6:1–20.

Feagin, Joe R., and Clairece Booher Feagin. 1986. *Discrimination American Style* (rev. ed.) Melbourne, Fl: Krieger Publishing Co.

Gardner, Carol Brooks. 1980. "Passing by: Street remarks, address rights, and the urban female." *Sociological Inquiry* 50:328–56.

——. 1988. "Access information: Public lies and private peril." *Social Problems* 35:384–97.

Goffman, Erving. 1956. "The nature of deference and demeanor." *American Anthropologist* 58:473–502.

——. 1963. *Behavior in Public Places*. New York: Free Press.

——. 1971. *Relations in Public*. New York: Basic Books.

Graber, Doris A. 1980. *Crime News and the Public*. New York: Praeger.

Griffin, John Howard. 1961. *Black Like Me*. Boston: Houghton Mifflin.

Henley, Nancy M. 1978. *Body Politics*. Englewood Cliffs, N.J.: Prentice-Hall.

Jaynes, Gerald D., and Robin Williams Jr., eds. 1989. *A Common Destiny: Blacks and American Society*. Washington, D.C.: National Academy Press.

Landry, Bart. 1987. *The New Black Middle Class*. Berkeley: University of California Press.

Louis Harris and Associates. 1989. *The Unfinished Agenda on Race in America*. New York: NAACP Legal Defense and Educational Fund.

"The mood of ghetto America." 1980. *Newsweek*, 2 June, 32–4.

Moss, E. Yvonne. 1990. "African Americans and the administration of justice." In *Assessment of the Status of African-Americans,* edited by Wornie L. Reed, 79–86. Boston: University of Massachusetts, William Monroe Trotter Institute.

Perry, David C., and Paula A. Sornoff. 1973. *Politics at the Street Level*. Beverly Hills: Sage.

Raper, Arthur F. 1933. *The Tragedy of Lynching*. Chapel Hill: University of North Carolina Press.

Roddy, Dennis B. 1990. "Perceptions still segregate police, black community." *The Pittsburgh Press*. 26 August, B1.

Rollins, Judith 1985. *Between Women*. Philadelphia: Temple University Press.

Warr, Mark. Forthcoming. "Dangerous Situations: Social Context and Fear of Victimization." *Social Forces*.

Wieseltier, Leon. 1989. "Scar tissue." *New Republic*. 5 June, 19–20.

Willie, Charles. 1983. *Race, Ethnicity, and Socioeconomic Status*. Bayside: General Hall.

Wilson, William J. 1978. *The Declining Significance of Race*. Chicago: University of Chicago Press.

———. 1987. *The Truly Disadvantaged: The Inner City, the Underclass, and Public Policy*. Chicago: University of Chicago Press.

12

The Continuing Significance of Racism: Discrimination against Black Students in White Colleges

Joe R. Feagin

In the last few years we have seen a growing concern among academic administrators and educational researchers about black student enrollment and attrition rates. A number of survey studies (Astin 1977, 1982) have found that college enrollment and graduation rates for black Americans have declined in many programs. In a recent major review of the literature, George Keller (1988–89), professor at the University of Pennsylvania Graduate School of Education and recipient of the Casey Award in education planning, examined nine books, reports, and special journal issues devoted to assessing the problems of minority access and achievement in higher education. Keller's 1988–1989 analysis (50–54), representative of much social science and policy analysis of minority problems, notes the extensive discussion of minority student attrition and suggests ten reasons that are documented in the literature he reviewed:

1. The campus subculture is hostile to blacks at many institutions, and the faculty and deans remain insensitive.
2. A growing number of blacks are enrolling in the military, in part because of the more hospitable environment there.
3. Financial aid has been declining.

This chapter is reprinted with minor revisions from Feagin, Joe R. 1992. "The continuing significance of racism," *Journal of Black Studies*, 22 (June): 546–78.

4. The decline is mainly among black males; something is wrong with black men, probably drugs, prison, and unemployment.
5. Poor preparation for college work, as seen in SAT scores, is a major factor.
6. With more jobs available, many blacks go to work rather than college.
7. The deterioration of the black family means a lack of discipline and emphasis on education.
8. The high incidence of drug use inhibits study.
9. Attitudes of blacks, such as a lack of effort, are a problem.
10. There is a lack of adult leadership emphasizing education.

Keller (1988–89) notes traces of racism in the college subculture, but plays down the importance of this factor in explaining student attrition and the lack of black advancement in higher education. Like most of the authors he reviews, Keller emphasizes individual and family factors, including black attitudes toward education and the lack of black leadership. He concludes with the argument that no one knows with certainty what to do about attrition; he prefers the interpretive analysis of Glenn Loury, who argues that middle-class blacks bear the "responsibility for the behavior of black youngsters" and are failing to encourage young blacks to study hard (Loury & Anderson 1984, 5). Keller then makes this point:

> White educators and do-gooders outside academe must move beyond their naive pieties onto the treacherous, unknown ground of new realities. Petulant and accusatory black spokespersons will need to climb off their soapboxes and walk through the unpleasant brambles of their young people's new preferences and look at their young honestly. . . . They will need to encourage, lift up, and argue with those youths who do not see the urgency of education in a scientific, international, and information-choked world . . . where knowledge is the principal sword and shield against decline, poverty, and inferiority. Critics will need to stop the fashionable practice of lambasting the colleges as if they were the central problem. (55)

The burden is on black leaders and adults to encourage black youth to view education as the main way to overcome poverty and inferiority. Keller argues in effect that college subcultures no longer play a central role in the problems of black students.

An alternative perspective. Much of the recent educational literature has picked up on this old theme in the analysis of black Americans: the emphasis on racial group deficits in personal, family, intellectual, and moral development as explanations for black problems, in this case college achievement and attrition problems. But there are important exceptions. Some researchers still place racial discrimination near the top of the list in explaining problems of minority student achievement and attrition. For example, in *The Color Line and the Quality of Life in America,* Reynolds Farley and Walter R. Allen (1989) ground their analysis of educational differentials in demographic data and statistical assessments. They present detailed black-white data on educational attainment and SAT scores. The data, which reveal major gaps between white sand blacks, are interpreted as supporting what the authors term the two prevailing interpretations: that "American society has historically discriminated against blacks, and blacks over time come to expect such discrimination as normative," with this mutually reinforcing system undercutting black educational progress (Farley & Allen 1989, 208). This conclusion is plausible in light of the Farley and Allen data showing gaps in black and white educational achievements, but their assessment reads discrimination (behavior) out of data on discrimination's consequences, especially SAT and grade data.

A few research studies have examined the alienation and other attitudinal responses of minority college students, another type of outcome measure suggesting the negative impact of college settings on black attrition and achievement. A study by Loo and Rolison (1986) surveyed 109 minority and 54 white students at a California campus and found that the minority students were more socioculturally alienated than white students, as measured by a four-point alienation scale. The black and Hispanic students reported the greatest isolation and social alienation in the campus subculture (64–67). Suen's (1983, 117–21) study of black and white students at a Midwestern campus found that black students scored higher on an alienation scale and dropped out more often than white students. Coupled with the Farley and Allen (1989) study, these reports on attitudinal outcomes suggest the need to gather in-depth interview data on the situational barriers, including discrimination, that may lead to the alienation and lack-of-achievement outcomes in higher education.

A field research study. The purpose of this research project is (a) to provide a detailed description of the barriers faced by black college students in predominantly white colleges and universities, (b) to suggest a typology of kinds of discrimination, and (c) to offer a tentative theory of cumulative discrimination. The study draws on in-depth interviews with two dozen college students, administrators, and faculty members in a larger sample of 180 middle-class black Americans interviewed in fourteen cities, from Boston and Baltimore to Houston, Dallas, and Los Angeles. The interviewers were black graduate students, undergraduate seniors, and professors. The first respondents were known to the black interviewers as members of white college communities, known to the author, or recommended by knowledgeable informants. Snowball sampling was then used. Those quoted here were interviewed, on average for one to one-and-a-half hours, between July 1988 and October 1989.[1] This type of in-depth interviewing has recently provided much insightful analysis of U.S. race relations (see, for example, Blauner 1989; Collins 1983; Rollins 1985).

A preliminary overview. Discrimination can be defined as the "differential practices carried out by members of dominant racial groups that have a negative impact on members of subordinate racial groups" (see Feagin & Eckberg 1980, 2). Beyond this general definition, one can distinguish an array of different types of discriminatory treatment. Although a detailed typology will be developed later, the following breakdown along the important dimension of potential discriminators will be used to organize the presentation: (a) white students, (b) white faculty members, (c) white administrators and staff members, (d) white alumni. Black students face numerous blatant and subtle discriminatory barriers from these four groups.

Specific Campus Barriers: White Students

Racist comments and racial awareness. Several students discussed in interviews how they became fully conscious of being black only when they entered a white college. In talking about what made her conscious of being black, one student answered:

> I don't remember in high school being called a "nigger" before, and I can remember here being called a nigger.
>
> [When was this?]
>
> In my freshman year, at a university student parade. There was a group of us, standing there, not knowing that this was not an event that a lot of black people went to! [laughs] You know, our dorm was going, and this was something we were going to go to because we were students too! And we were standing out there and [there were] a group of white fraternity boys—I remember the Southern flag—and a group of us, five or six of us, and they went by us, before the parade had actually gotten under way. And one of them pointed and said, "Look at that bunch of niggers!" I remember thinking, "surely he's not talking to us!" We didn't even use the word *nigger* in my house. . . .
>
> [How did you feel?]
>
> I think I wanted to cry. And my friends—they were from a southwestern city—they were ready to curse them, and I was just standing there with my mouth open. I think I wanted to cry. I could not believe it, because you get here and you think you're in an educated environment and you're dealing with educated people. And all of this backward country stuff . . . you think that kind of stuff is not going on, but it is.[2]

This black student's first memory of being called a "nigger" comes from her college years in the 1980s. In this case white fraternity members in a college parade pointed her and her friends out as "bunch of niggers." Note that she first could not believe what they were saying. She gave these white male students the benefit of the doubt. Her sense of fairness is evident. Perhaps because she was inadequately prepared for her encounters with campus racism, she at first did not want to believe that she was being labeled in a derogatory way.

Racist jokes. The student quoted above also commented on the racist jokes that are part of the white campus subculture:

> I hate to say that I've gotten bitter, but I've gotten bitter . . . last summer, I can remember people telling jokes, that's what I remember most, every day there was a racial joke. And they found it necessary to tell me. It might be funny and then I'd laugh, and then I thought about it while reading that book [*Black Power*]. Even if they didn't mean any harm, how can they not mean any harm? How can they not, these people who are your classmates. And supposedly some of them are your friends. How can they not mean any harm? What do you mean they don't mean any harm? Why am I making excuses for their actions? I think that's what I was doing a lot of times was making excuses.

> [Why do you think you were doing that?]

> I think probably that's just the kind of person I am, just really very passive.

> [Do you think it's necessary to be that way as a black person?]

> No, I don't think so. Before I did: Don't make too many waves. And I still think sometimes there's a right way and a wrong way to get certain things accomplished. But if we're talking about [racism] . . . how do I deal with it, let me think, on a day-to-day basis? I don't wake up and give myself a pep talk, "You're black, you're proud!" [laughs] I don't do that, but I think that . . . I feel it now. Maybe there was a time when I didn't feel it, but I feel it now. And yes, I never thought about it, but I don't have to say it because I feel it.

> [What makes you feel black and proud?]

> This university! Every time I had to go across some kind of barrier, whether it was white America-related or not, then that made me stronger, and strengthened one area. This is it. This is the learning tree.

Here we see another aspect of the college subculture: the racist jokes that white students like to tell. Some white students may not realize how offensive and troubling such jokes can be, while others may intentionally tell them because they know the jokes cause pain. For the latter, racial humor is probably an outlet for passive aggression. What makes the jokes even more painful is the experience of a regular diet of them. The student just quoted at first assumed that the joke tellers did not "mean any harm." But on reflection she changed her mind. And her recognition that the white students often do mean harm has made her both bitter and stronger. Note also her interesting description of the white campus climate as "the learning tree" for black students.

Racial aggression against black students is not uncommon across U.S. campuses. And it has escalated beyond individual eipthets and jokes. According to Baltimore's National Institute Against Prejudice and Violence, there were published reports of at least 175 racial incidents on college campuses in 1986 and 1987 alone; and seventy-eight additional incidents were reported for the spring of 1988 (Magner 1989, A27–A29). The campus incidents have involved anti-black graffiti, fraternity parties and parades with racist themes, racist literature passed out on campus, violent attacks on black students, and interracial brawls.

Student opposition to things black. Another undergraduate student explains some one-way integration features of the campus subculture:

> It's a constant battle dealing with racism. It is so much a part of everything. To integrate means simply to be white. It doesn't mean fusing the two cultures; it simply means to be white, that's all. And we spend so much effort in passing into the mainstream of American society. They have no reason to know our culture. But we must, in order to survive, know everything about their culture. Racism is simply preferring straight hair to an Afro; that's certainly more acceptable in our society today. Black vernacular, it's not seen as a cultural expression, it's seen as a speech problem.
>
> When you look at something as simple as just a group of people talking, black people are given much more, a much higher, regard if they are seen in an all-white group than they would if they were to be seen in an all-black group. If you're seen in an all-white group laughing and talking, you're seen as respectable, and probably taking care of something important. You're not wasting time. You're all right. But if you're in an all-black group, regardless if they can even hear your conversation, white people think you're trying to, you're congregated, to take over the world. It's just that basic . . . you're just punished for expressing your black culture . . . you're just constantly forced to take on the culture of white America.

This student expresses a reflective concern with the Procrustean bed aspects of the white campus subculture. Integration has not meant the fusing of two subcultures. Blacks must learn the white subculture, but whites learn little or nothing about black American subculture. So integration, in practice, means racial discrimination. Campus racism means preferring the straight (like-white) hair style to a natural Afro hair style. Campus racism means a preference for white English and slang over black slang. White preferences in these matters provide great pressure on black students to conform.

Particularly insightful is this student's discussion of the group behavior of university students. She suggests that to be respectable as a black student at this large white university involves mostly being seen with, and listening to, whites. One's presence in an all-black group may be taken by whites as a sign of aggressiveness. Whites may feel threatened. black students quickly get the message that congregating in all-black groups is undesirable behavior. There is the constant reminder of one's racial group distinctiveness.

Seeing blacks as "all alike." A student at another university suggested that many white students see black students as "all alike."

> That's the first question they'll ask you: "Are you an athlete?" Professors, students, everybody here will ask you, "Are you an athlete?" When you say, "No," they're like, "Oh!" And it's like you got here because you're black.

In many cases black students were assumed to be athletes. She commented further on her experiences in the dorm:

> Here in my dorm, there are four black girls. Me and my roommate look nothing alike. And the other two are short, and I'm tall. They [white students] called me by my roommate's name the whole semester, and I didn't understand that. [Maybe] I understood it, but I didn't want to have to deal with that whole thing. That's really upsetting. It's like they put their shutters on when they see a black person coming. And the few black people that do get along with the other students, they seem to sort of put on a facade. They pretend to be something they're not.

Noted here is the failure of white students to see very different black students as individuals.

Some white students also assume that black students are not intelligent. One young lawyer in an East Coast city noted this about her law school days:

> In law school, there were some whites who were offended because I was smart. The teacher would ask the question and point to me, and they didn't think I should have an answer. And I would have a correct answer. But then they started to respect me for it, and they would tell me that: "Hey, you beat us on that," "we knew you would have known that;" or "What happened? Did you study all night?"

After she proved herself to be a good student, these white students changed their minds and treated her with respect.

The difficulty of socializing on a white campus. In part as a result of this stereotyping, making close friendships with white students is difficult for black students. Another student with whom we talked had this to say about a question asking, "Do you feel that you can trust white people?"

> I'm sure you could. But I just haven't been in a situation where I could find out, because most of the white people that I've met here at college all

seem to be reacting on a superficial basis. . . . People that I've met living in the dorm—you know most of the time there's a majority of people who are white in the dorm, and most of the people who really develop a close friendship are just white. People I start out knowing, though, I usually get phased out with toward the end of the year. I still don't know why. I've tried to figure it out. But lately I try not to bother with it, because it will just cause me mental anguish, and I don't want to do that to myself.

Now when I was in high school, it was different. We hung out with a lot of different people. We had a lot of Orientals, Mexicans—it was just a whole rainbow of friends I had in high school. I didn't think much of it, but when I came to this university, it seemed to change. I don't know if it was just me, or the environment, but somehow my view of intimacy with other people, especially white people, has soured since then.

This student had a rainbow of friends in his multiethnic high school, but at the white university he has found it difficult to make white friends. In his experience most white students react on a superficial friendship basis; most do not want to become long-term friends with black students.

The ostracism behavior of some whites is illustrated in this report by an attorney in her midtwenties on her predominantly white college:

I had an incident with discrimination, which really, basically took me by surprise . . . I lived in the dorms for a couple of years. And you sit around in the dorms and eat food with the girls, eat popcorn and watch the soaps when you don't have classes. And I remember this particular incident, this girl, we had just socialized the night before, watching T.V., having popcorn, et cetera, and I saw her on campus the next day. And she turned her head to make sure she didn't have to speak to me.

And I had that happen more than once. And I think that was a bout with discrimination which just slapped me in the face, because it doesn't feel real good to be a friend to someone, or an associate to someone at seven o'clock, and then at eight o'clock, or eight-thirty, when they're around friends of their race, they don't know who you are or what you are, and don't even give you the consideration of acknowledging your presence or speaking to you.

A suggested reason here for the socially isolating behavior of some white students is the unwillingness to let other whites see them befriending black students.

Professors

Seeing blacks as "representatives of their race." Much analysis of the attrition rate of black students from white universities and colleges neglects the role of key college actors, especially faculty members and administrators, in that attrition rate. An important aspect of the white campus subculture is the chronic inability, not only of students but also of many white faculty members and administrators to see black students as individuals. Like the students discussed above, many white faculty members view black students in stereotypical group terms. One graduate student described such an experience.

> A black undergraduate in my department is doing some research on black and white achievement in college, and one of her advisers was once the head of a rather prestigious organization in my field, not to mention [being] chair of the department. Apparently she assumed that this one undergraduate somehow spoke for all black people. And this professor would ask her things like, "Well, I don't know what you people want. First you want to be called Negro, then you want to be called black. Now you want to be called African American. What do you people want anyway? And why don't black people show up in class more? Why is it that I can't get enough blacks to sit in on my classes?" So every now and then that sort of racist mentality comes out.

Attempting to do research on blacks and whites, this student went to one of her advisers, but she was treated by this white professor as a spokesperson for her racial group. In this case, the black student was not seen as an individual but rather as a source to explain what black people "want." A common complaint among black students at predominantly white colleges is that they are often not seen as individuals.

Another undergraduate at a major public university echoed this point and set it in a broader context in commenting on what angers her about whites:

> Probably the thing that angers me the most about white people is their insensitivity and their total inability to see you as an individual. You're always seen as a black person. And as a black woman, you're seen as a black person before you're seen as a woman. It's just a constant struggle. You're always trying to assert your personality, or your style, your individuality. If you want recognition you practically have to go overboard to get people to see that you are unique with your own style and your own goals, and your own way of thinking about things.
>
> white people always assume that black people think the same way. I remember this one professor in the sociology department. He was trying to explain something to me about the church, and he said, "Because you're black you'll understand this." And he was saying something about the church, and from what I understood it sounded like the Baptist faith that he was trying to describe.
>
> Well, I didn't understand, primarily because I'm not Baptist. I'm Episcopalian. And he didn't think for a moment that maybe I wasn't Baptist. I had to be Baptist, I was black. I was black and in the South. Of course I'm Baptist. It's that, and the idea that people don't really listen. They always assume what you're going to say, or they'll perceive it a certain

way. It's just they act as if they know you already, like there's nothing new to know about you.

In her college experience she has encountered much insensitivity from white people, including this white sociology professor, who assumed that all black people were Baptists. She notes that "you practically have to go overboard" to get many whites to see you as an individual and to hear what you have to say.

The white model. One black college student described how a college English professor told her that she should not write essays about the black people she liked to write about because those experiences were not universal. She said that he told her

> If a white person, for example, picked up one of my stories he would not understand what the hell was going on. So therefore I shouldn't write about these things. But I should write about [other] things, and he quoted William Faulkner quite liberally. I should write about things that appeal to the human heart, that everybody can appeal to and can relate to. And, see me, in my nice trusting self, I said no, he's not saying that black people aren't people enough to be termed as universal. He's not saying that, he's meaning something else. He couldn't possibly be saying this to my face. I was very, very confused. I did not understand what the hell he meant by it, not just the racial implications, but the whole statement.

The professor regarded her stories about the distinctiveness of the black experience as somehow not as universalizable as classical stories about the white experience. Moreover, by citing Faulkner liberally he was clearly suggesting that the model for good writing is not only white but also male and southern.

In an East Coast city a male banker reported on a recent experience in an English course:

> The only thing that hurt me was certain white institutions. Instead of helping you and educating you, they will browbeat [you] and downplay the educational level that you have. I turned in a paper one time at a college, and I had an instructor tell me that I was speaking black English. I was the only black in the class, and it was a freshmen writing class. And she told me that I was speaking black English. And it kind of, in one sense, made me not want to be black, and, in another sense, wonder what was black English. Because, I had gone to white schools from the sixth grade on, and I had been speaking, not speaking but writing white English all my life.
>
> I couldn't understand what she was talking about . . . if I remember right, she gave me a D in the course. She had given me Ds and Cs on all my papers. And I know for a fact that certain people did less research, less work than me, but she was very hard on me. That really woke me up, because that really taught me to take a lot of English writing workshops.

Where now, I guess you could say, my writing skills are above average. And that's great because by her hurting me, and telling me that I was speaking black English, now I'm able to speak black English in a white format, where I can get my point across and be understood.

This student describes the strong sense of inferiority that came from his teacher stereotyping his English writing patterns as black English without providing him the necessary framework for understanding the racism of making white English the standard. As a young student who had been to integrated schools, he thought he spoke English. Her white bias and insensitivity to the fact that there is not an independent scale for evaluating spoken language—all language is equally valid if it communicates—resulted in the teacher hurting this black student. Interestingly, his reaction was to become an expert in the standard English expected in the white-conformity perspective of such teachers.

A subtle example of the white model being applied to minority students can be seen in the common emphasis on conventional standards such as SAT test scores and on attendance at certain high schools. One student commented on her recent experiences:

When I got here it was an ignorance, a closed-minded ignorance that I didn't know how to handle. One of my professors—I went to him as a freshman asking for help, and he asked me my SAT scores. And I told him. And [he said], "I don't know why they let you in, you're not expected to do well. There are so many people like you here that aren't qualified, and I can try to help you and find a tutor." I [said], "Thanks!"

In this case her score on the SAT test, historically developed as a measure of white middle-class culture and education, was considered to be an excellent measure of a student's quality. The professor also asked her what high school she had gone to. When she told him that she had gone to an elite private white high school, "his face just went every which way, [his] eyes went big, and then he said, 'Well, I'll help you get a tutor, and we'll study, because I know you're prepared for this.' " The student was surprised at the professor's change in attitude toward her when he learned that she had gone to a prominent white high school, not a black high school. She reported that she had similar experiences with several of her professors. One professor even offered to help her with her homework over lunch, after she told him what high school she had gone to. Apparently, the fact that she was tracked through an elite white school meant to these professors that they should take her more seriously.

Stereotyping and the white male model. This practice of holding up the white (or white male) model to nontraditional students can be seen in professional schools as well. A black professional in a New England city recounted the recent experience of her sister:

My sister is a surgical technician, and she's just completed getting her master's degree in nursing. And she's talked about as an older student— again the expectation, being from a black community in the inner city, that she would not be able to sit in the classroom with younger white students and do as well as they could.

But she's proven differently. [I talked] . . . to her about her struggles with her professors, about what she is capable of doing, the course load she is capable of handling, and [her] trying to convince them that she can take on this course load, as opposed to them being supportive and saying, "Whatever you think you can do is fine, and I'll see that you get the kind of guidance and support that you need."

[What exactly did they do?]

Well, limit her course work . . . they said, "You can't take this course." And she got into a fight with the dean.

Another misconception that many white professors and administrators have is that black Americans from "ghetto" communities are not able to handle difficult course loads and educational requirements in the same way that white, or white male, students can. This misconception is probably magnified in this case because not only was this student black, but also she was an older woman returning to school.

The lack of feedback and reinforcement. A problem that many students, black and white, have with their college professors is a lack of appropriate feedback on course performance. But this lack of feedback, and reinforcement is doubly difficult for a black student at sea in a white world. A business executive in a mid-Atlantic city commented on his daughter's experience with two predominantly white universities and a black university:

My daughter, who graduated from Texas Southern University [TSU] in Houston, initially began her college training at an Oklahoma university. . . . she moved back to Houston to be with us, with my wife, and went to a white university there. [She] then decided she needed a little more exposure and went to Texas Southern University.

The thing that was so interesting to her was that at the Oklahoma university and the white Texas university, both good schools, there was a night and day difference on how you were treated by the faculty. The faculty at TSU was interested in you as a person, wanted to ensure that you were successful in completing courses and getting your degree. And at the Oklahoma university and the white Texas university they could care less about you as an individual; you're more or less a number. . . .

She decided in a number of instances that there were some assumptions made by her faculty at these universities that she would not be able to comprehend some of the information they were giving her. Just on an assumption! Of course, she was able to do that, had no problem. But it was just that "Well, I know the university is here, and black students are competing with the white students, and we're really not going to expect you to do too well."

He notes the significant difference among faculty members at the white universities and the black university, not only in the stereotyped assumptions about what the black students could comprehend and attain but also in the feedback provided to students on their progress in higher education.

One graduate student described his undergraduate experiences this way:

And I can think of several courses where I honestly feel that I was very much discriminated against. One class was an honors course in social science. And it just so happened that the criteria for getting in the course was to have made a certain grade in a previous social science course, which I did. So I took the course, which I enjoyed very much.

But when it came time for grades, the grade that I got was not the grade I earned . . . and the professor actually never even respected me enough to sit down and talk to me about my grades. The only feedback I got from the guy was when I approached him after I got the grade. And he talked to me only the amount of time that it took him to walk out of his office and go to where he had to go, and I stood there as he walked through his door. And except for that he wouldn't even give me any feedback.

And essentially what he told me was that, first of all, my attendance was poor in class. And secondly he told me that some work which he gave as optional work—that I had done—was . . . poor work. So what I understood him to say was that he took off of my regular grade for extra credit work. And as far as attendance goes, he said that I never attended class. But in fact I only missed two classes the entire semester, and the only reason I missed those two classes was because I was required by the military to be out of town on those two days. And I think, it seemed like he had, he only had the practice of taking attendance on Fridays. And those were two Fridays because those were the two scheduled times, and I guess he assumed that if you weren't there that Friday that you weren't there that week. But I personally always felt that for a college professor to take attendance was a little bit ludicrous anyway. But that was the explanation that he gave me, that my class attendance was poor, and that my extra credit work was poor. And I think that was no evidence to support the grade.

He gave yet another example:

Another case was in organic chemistry, which in fact I failed. Throughout the semester I would go to the professor, especially before the exams, to see if I could get some help and input for things I expected to encounter on the test. And the professor literally, literally, on several occasions kicked me out of his office, and said he didn't have time to talk to me, and for me to go study with some other students in the class. And so I really think that was racially motivated also. And actually there's probably a million other examples I could give you like that.

And to be real honest, I felt real lucky, because I think a lot of the things I encountered in college were pretty mild and subdued compared to the few black males I knew in college. Some of those guys took a hell of a beating. And to this day, I say, I don't know why they let me finish college, because in fact a lot of guys that I went to college with never even finished.

In some cases a white professor's style may be brusque for all students, black and white, but this cold style brings an especially heavy burden to minority students in a setting that is already difficult for them. In the first case given by the graduate student, the professor did not fairly evaluate the student's attendance record or extra-credit course work. The second case involved a chemistry professor who had no time for the student and ushered him out of the office. Perhaps these professors would have done the same with white students; however, this insensitivity and lack of feedback can have a very negative impact, whether or not it was intentional. A persistent diet of this professional behavior, as this student notes, is a factor in the dropout rate of black males from college.

black students become especially sensitive to negative feedback from faculty members, as yet another graduate student reported:

After a while, I think that you become real sensitive to certain kinds of feedback, and I think that becomes self-defeating. Like, if the message that you receive from someone or some institution, from a school or a class, or a professor is that you're not quite as good, or you're not good enough, or your performance is not up to standard—whether or not that happens to be true—you tend to internalize that. And to the extent that you internalize that, I think that really affects your actual performance. You know, the self-fulfilling prophecy. If you really think that you're dumb, you'll act as a dumb person will.

And so I think that it's only in recent years that I've begun to realize that . . . I think things are starting to surface where I'm beginning to realize that when I got a bad grade and I didn't deserve it, or somebody really gave me a tough time in school, that affected me more than I really realized at the time. But I don't think that's a chronic problem for me, but I certainly think it's something to consider, even if I didn't consider it before, I think it's something that I consider all the time now. Just how valid that kind of feedback is. And I'm making a special effort to distinguish between [when] my performance really is not up to par, and when somebody says it's not up to par, but it really is.

black students in predominantly white colleges and universities generally seem sensitive to the character and quality of the feedback they receive. This is true for most people. Most of us have trouble assessing the feedback we get about our performance. Is the feedback fair or unfair? Is our performance really poor, as negative feedback suggests, or is the evaluator biased? And failure to read the feedback correctly can be a very serious liability in coping with college, and especially with graduate school. This general problem becomes very difficult for black students in a predominantly white college where there is a significant probability of racial bias. The above-quoted graduate student notes that if you are treated as dumb, you may come to see yourself that way. He has realized that he must distinguish between the situation where his performance is good, but not recognized as such, and the situation where his performance is actually subpar. Moreover, a lack of professional feedback can be particularly devastating to minority students because they have often suffered denigration and discrimination in many other areas of college life.

Replying to a question about what you would most like to see changed in the dominant society, one black graduate student made a plea for white faculty members to recognize the differences in resources between whites and blacks:

> On the one hand, I'd like to see an acknowledgment that people bring with them differences in terms of culture, differences in terms of economic advantages, differences in terms of educational advantages. So, if anything, I'd like to see on the part of white Americans some acknowledgment that blacks and other racial minorities bring differences with them into various situations.
>
> Even if those situations are supposedly integrated, the attitude among whites is, "Well, you've made it. You're the epitome of success, you've showed that it can be done, and apparently it's by one's own initiative that things change, there's no need for handouts." That blacks ought to be given nothing more than what whites or anyone else should be given.
>
> And my response to that would be that I don't know of any blacks who are asking for anything more than a fair shake. So, I guess, at a very philosophical type level, I'd just like to see not only an acknowledgment of differences, but also an acknowledgment that we still are not equal, and that it will take more than lip service to achieve equality. It takes active involvement on the part of white America, and right now I don't see that.

Another part of the subculture of white campuses is the failure of many whites there to recognize that minority students who "make it" in the white college world typically do not have the resources of the average white student. Many black students may appear to be middle class in background, but often they are the first generation to attend a white college, and they are less likely to have the deep-pocket resources of typical white students. Most whites inside and outside colleges do not understand the historical background and significance of this resource problem. In our society's educational and economic institutions an individual, whether white or black, does not succeed or fail solely on her or his own merits. Our meritocractic ideology is contradicted by the fact that inherited privileges and wealth provide a leg up the ladder for some, but not for others. Family economic resources are critical in shaping one's educational opportunities—and thus one's educational achievements.

Lack of receptiveness to minority research and issues. Another student, a graduate student in the social sciences, commented on subtle discrimination he has faced from his professors:

> If I go back to my first days as a graduate student, I came in having done some work on stereotypes as an undergraduate. At my undergraduate school, my professor was really supportive and in fact the whole department was supportive of me doing that sort of work. When I got here, literally [on] the first day of class, the very professor who I had been referred to took a look at the work I'd done, and said, "Well, that was fine as an undergraduate, but you're in graduate school now."
>
> And what I didn't realize was that that sort of work basically wasn't done in the department. . . . The example I just gave you where I would be hard-pressed to say well, that's discrimination in itself. But what I found once I began graduate school four years ago was that it was quite difficult to match not only personal interests, but also personalities. . . .
>
> My whole experience of the past four years has been one of pursuing research that isn't tied specifically to ethnicity, and in fact, although I got into social science largely to try to be of some help to other people, especially other black people, I had to pursue that desire outside of the classroom. I guess when I think of opportunity in the way that it's normally presented, academics as being a haven for expressing oneself, that opportunity hasn't been there as far as I can see.

He added this in a similar vein:

> I do remember my first year here being a bit disillusioned. A few faculty within my area were basically up-and-coming types who again gave lip service to notions of equality; [they] seemed not to really take my opinion as seriously as I thought they should have, just in terms of the research we were doing. And in fact, I received some rather negative feedback at the end of that year from those individuals. I thought, for a minute, I haven't heard anything like this before, nobody confronted me with anything like this in my whole first year.
>
> In terms of grades, they didn't have that to complain about; in terms of my involvement in the research they didn't have that to complain about. But there was the notion that what I was doing wasn't quite good enough. It didn't conform enough to what they expected. . . . And this was a person who took a very narrow view of what my field ought to be about, and specifically shied away from ethnic type issues. So, he was ignorant and didn't know how to deal with them. So, yes, that was a bit of a rude awakening.

This graduate student came to the university with enthusiasm for social science research on racial and ethnic issues, for at his undergraduate college he had been encouraged to do research on stereotyping. But he quickly got the message in his graduate department that there was little support for such race-related research. He had gone into this social science field to be of help to black people, but now he has had to go outside the university classrooms to pursue that goal.

The same graduate student noted that his problem was not isolated. He commented on some of his classmates who did not feel welcome in the department:

> I know of people who have been in my department who have left. I can think of a black woman, who I never actually met, who left the year before I got there, who felt that the department was so constricting in terms of not only the types of research that she could do, but in terms of attitudes. Apparently, she was told at one point [that] she wasn't thought of as a black person, largely because she was doing so well. She was outperforming the white students in a class. And apparently a faculty member told her something like, "Well, we don't think of you as one of them anymore."
>
> And I also know someone who was in my department, who received a very cold reception, not only in terms of the type of research he wanted to do, but also in terms of basic politeness. . . . That individual ended up switching departments, he got his doctorate, but never felt at home in that department.

Here we see another reason for the black attrition rate at predominantly white graduate schools. When white faculty members, in blatant or subtle ways, rule out research that minority students consider especially important, they are also likely to force some of those students out of their programs. Another graduate student also talked about the difficulties of doing research on black Americans:

> I guess the other thing that I would say is that obviously I have a vested interest in my heritage, so, although this is not my exclusive focus, there are times and places when I really would want to do some research specifically related to black issues. And my experience to this date is that in the larger educational community, there really is not that much of an interest in that kind of research.
>
> So to the extent that one of my goals is to do research related more to black issues, I can see other obstacles, just because I don't think I'll have the resources and support systems that I would have if my focus were on some other topic. And I guess what I mean by that is in terms of institutions I don't think there's a whole lot of major institutions that are doing a lot of research on black issues.
>
> So what I'll probably wind up doing is going to a predominantly black university. Or universities who have a tangential interest in black re-

search to do any kind of work like that. And I think that's particularly a handicap because I really don't think the resources, research resources, at traditional black schools and smaller minority programs in major universities compare to what the resources are in other research deals.

This student reiterates the point that white professors are not sensitive to the need for research on issues of direct importance to black Americans. In fact, he has come to the conclusion that he will probably have to take a position at a predominantly black university in order to pursue his reasonable research goals.

One black assistant professor recounted her recent experiences with her primary professor in a top West Coast graduate school. The latter pressured her to specialize in a certain period of white literature, not in Afro-American literature, because she would thus be

> doing something he didn't consider most black people did. And that job offers would come in for that reason. And further that doing Afro-American literature was not in and of itself important intellectual work. Well, I insisted . . . and he finally gave in and gave me permission. He never stopped thinking that it was important for me not to do Afro-American literature as evidence that I was a real scholar. You couldn't do Afro-American lit and be a real scholar at the same time. And I ran into that attitude when I was on the job market.

One signal that college and university subcultures are not integrated is the downplaying of research on black Americans. Such research is suspect and not considered to be truly scholarly—an attitude that signals institutionalized discrimination.

Fear of student organization. In talking about effective ways to deal with racial discrimination, one black graduate student commented that

> We set up a meeting of grad students to discuss the recruitment and retention of minorities in the department. And a few of the faculty members there who were pretty much of the old school. . . . We had agreed that the meeting would be open and candid. Their idea of open and candid was that it would be closed to everyone else except those who had been invited to be part of the discussion.
>
> So, in that sense, the department has been quite reactionary. It seems to be acting in good faith now in terms of recruitment, but only because it has been pressured to do so. . . . But it is frustrating to realize how, not only insensitive, but ignorant, a lot of supposedly intelligent white people are. I think [of] the faculty especially in that regard. There seems to be an attitude that things are well enough now for blacks and other minorities that there's no need to rock the boat.
>
> I've certainly seen that in my own department, but I think it extends beyond that department. Indifference to a variety of issues, whether it's investment in South Africa, or faculty recruitment. . . . And when people

come along who want to set things right so to speak, they're the ones that are confronted, they're the ones that are met with everything from excuses, such as divesting from South Africa would be making a political statement where obviously remaining invested is a political statement in itself.

Organizing on campus will often get black students labeled as malcontents or militants by white faculty members and administrators. Ironically, such supportive organizations often keep black students in college and graduate school.

Problems with Administrators and Staff Members

Insensitivity and unwillingness to learn. A black administrator described the insensitivity of a senior white administrator, her supervisor:

One problem that I do have also is that he expects me to be a spokesman for all black people. And that's very difficult, because I've never had to quite deal with someone that closely that has a mind set like that—where they say, "Why do black students do this?" And I'm like, I would never ask you, "Why do white students do this?" because you can't generalize or put them in a group like that. Well, why do black students and white students have different kinds of parties? And I'm like, have you ever been to one? It would help you if you would just go to one. It would help you if you would just go to find out. And I'm looking at this person and thinking, why are you in this position if you don't already know these things?

I've tried very hard, I think. I purchased a video called *Racism 101* and it took me a year to get this man to watch this little one-hour video. . . . I think mostly I have to justify myself and that's our relationship, one in which I'm constantly justifying what I do, constantly trying to educate and enlighten someone I feel should already be at that stage if he's going to supervise my office.

Note this white administrator's tendency to treat the respondent as a black spokesperson and his unwillingness to face his own stereotypes by learning more about the black students whose presence at his university is relatively recent. The tendency to view or treat black students in a stereotypical way is not limited to students and faculty members.

Campus police. Some of the most serious harassment faced by black students at predominantly white colleges and universities has come from the police. At one campus, a student reported that a number of black students had been harassed by white police officers. She has had spotlights put on her by the police; and some male friends, including her boyfriend, have had guns drawn on them. She commented:

As far as my boyfriend. . . . This past year there have been some incidents, some attacks on campus. And he was at the gym playing basketball; and he was going to the gas station. He got out of the car at the gas station down the street. The [police] guy tells him to put his hands up, and he pulled a gun. It wasn't the campus police, but I feel they called him. Their reason was that they saw him leaving the gym, and they thought they heard a woman screaming at him. He said there was no woman.

That doesn't make sense. I think they should be punished, it's just not right. But see, incidents happen to them, especially black men, incidents like this happen to them all the time. Have they written a letter? Have they done anything? No. They [the police] haven't bothered me [physically], but when they do, I will write a letter, and it will be publicized. I will make sure it is. I'm not going to take that. There's no reason that I should have to.

Do you want to see my ID? Give me a reason. You can't just ask me for my ID when I'm just walking down the sidewalk. There are 50 billion other white people walking on the same sidewalk and you didn't ask them for their ID. . . . You don't want to have your friends come here sometime because they'll be harassed. So, it's kind of bad. But I've heard a lot of campuses are like that, white campuses.

In addition to the problems created by white students and faculty members, black students—especially black male students on white campuses in cities with significant black populations—are sometimes treated differently by the campus and local city police. Police officers are trained, formally in classes or informally by older officers, to look for demographic cues or attributes that distinguish potential criminal offenders from other people. High on the list of these attributes are *black* and *male*. black men often do make up a disproportionate percentage of urban criminals, but in most white areas they are not the majority of criminals. And recent research has demonstrated that in general whites tend to exaggerate greatly the role of blacks in crime (see Graber 1980). The consequence of this distorted white perspective is that many innocent blacks, such as black students on white campuses, will be stopped unnecessarily by the police. This differential treatment is clearly discriminatory on campuses, like the above, where there are only a few black students, whose faces could easily be memorized by the campus police.

Other staff members. A black psychologist and counselor at a major university commented on her experience and that of a student treated by a university physician:

In the nine years that I've been here, there have been a couple of times when I've been seated with a client that I'm working with, an Anglo white client, and I've been called a "nigger," or "nigger" has been used in the context of some discussion that the client is making in my office to my face. I've also had clients get up and leave my office. One woman told me she didn't want to work with me because I was black, that she had never worked with, or lived with, or gone to school with blacks, and she just had great difficulty with it.

Another time, I was working with a student at the health center in crisis, a young black student, female. And the student was [getting] a physical exam by a physician. And the physician came out of the examining room after talking with the student and examining her for the physical complaints, and the first thing that the intern asked me was, is she intelligent? Now, it had no connection with the physical exam he had just completed. And it felt very much inappropriate. It was just out in left field. There have been a few others.

She documents the fact that white students verbally harass black staff members as well as black students. And she notes that this white physician operated with a stereotypical conception of a black student as well.

Other Barriers: The Alumni

A former black faculty member at one of our largest universities commented on the weak commitment of the alumni to facilitating the mobility of the black students there:

When I first came to the university . . . [I] was on the advisory committee to the vice president for student affairs, and we met with a member of the alumni association who talked to us about opportunities for graduates, saying that there are so many of our graduates all one needs to do in a particular town is say, "I'm a graduate of your university, can you help me get a job?" My response was, "That's wonderful. [What] if a black student should do this, should go up to one of the white graduates of the university, and say, I'm a university graduate, can you help me. This person who made the presentation said, "I think the person might be insulted." And so I got off the committee.

[The person might be insulted?]

That's right. So, I knew then that was not meant for the benefit of black students, so I resigned from the committee, and yet some of the people on the committee couldn't understand why I resigned. I didn't go back. Those are some of the kinds of things I have faced, but I have not said anything about it, because sometimes you find more difficulties as a result of it. You don't know how many situations that you'll face that are based on what you did at that particular time. Things that you need, opportunities to work for yourself or for somebody else, are denied because they are very angry about what you did, but it's done in another context.

This comment points up the tokenism of the black student and faculty presence at many white colleges and universities. black students are admitted, but once they graduate they cannot expect much help from the predominantly white alumni. This faculty member was angry about the response of his question about black graduates, so angry that he resigned as the token black faculty member on that committee. He also notes his more common strategy of keeping quiet in similar situations in order to work more effectively in later contexts. Eventually, however, this black professor retired early from the university; a major reason was the racial discrimination he endured.

Conclusion: Toward a Theory of Cumulative Discrimination

A typology of discriminatory practices. In *The Theory of Communicative Action*, Jürgen Habermas (1984, 305–87) views macrostructures such as bureaucracy and capitalism as burdensome integrating mechanisms for microlevel human action; in a capitalist society, for example, the macroeconomic structures intrude on the microworld; they thus "colonize the life world." Similarly, the daily white-on-black interactions that involve differential treatment for black college students exemplify the way the macrolevel system of racial inequality and stratification colonizes the everyday micro-lifeworld of black Americans. As we have seen, black students on white college campuses report a different world from that described by scholars and commentators like Keller. In their life worlds black Americans face a broad continuum of discriminatory practices and barriers. In his classic study *The Nature of Prejudice*, Gordon Allport (1958, 14–15) traced out five types of acting out negative prejudice, which he termed antilocution (talking against), avoidance, exclusion (segregation), physical attack, and extermination. Allport was writing at a time (1950s) when exclusion, segregation, and physical attack were the major problems facing black Americans. Today his array of actions and practices needs to be revised to describe discrimination more accurately within formally integrated settings such as white colleges and universities.

In order to describe this contemporary discrimination more accurately, several salient dimensions should be considered. One dimension is the *location* of the discriminatory action. The experience of discrimination and hostility, and thus a black person's vulnerability, varies from the most private to the most public spaces: (a) home with family and friends, (b) work and school settings, (c) stores and public accommodations, (d) streets. If a student is in a protected site, such as with friends at home, the probability of hostile treatment is low. If that same person is in a moderately protected site, such as a black student in a setting within a predominantly white university, then the probability of experiencing racial hostility and discrimination increases. And as that student moves into the public places outside the university, such as stores and streets, the dangers increase.

A second dimension is the type of actor doing the discrimination. There are four classes that we have identified: students, faculty members, administrators and other staff members, and alumni. These make up one dimension of Table 12.1. A third dimension is the type of hostile or discriminatory action directed against blacks. We find the following continuum of practices: (a) aggression, verbal and physical; (b) exclusion, including social ostracism; (c) dismissal of subculture, including values, dress, and groups; (d) typecasting, including assuming blacks are all alike.

By way of summary, the major instances of differential treatment uncovered in the interviews, classified by the perpetrators and the four general types suggested above, are listed in Table 12.1. Some campus obstacles are created mostly by the white students. These include the range of possibilities: verbal aggression, exclusion and ostracism, dismissal of black subculture, and typecasting. Another line of barriers is provided by faculty members. Interviews for this project did not uncover the racist-epithets aggression, but there were examples of exclusion and ostracism, dismissal of black interests and models, and typecasting. Also documented are the common barriers—ranging from

Table 12.1 Barriers in the White Campus World

	Aggression	Exclusion	Dismissal	Typecast
White Students				
Racist epithets	X			
Racist jokes	X			
Denigrating hair, dress, groups			X	
Treating students as athletes or special students				X
Rejection as friends		X		
White Professors				
Treating students as spokespersons for the group (as all alike)				X
Accenting white model for writing			X	
Cursory treatment of students		X		
Rejection of minority research			X	
Rejection of protest organization		X		
White Staff				
Unwillingness to learn about students		X		
Police harassment	X			
Quizzing intelligence of students				X
White Alumni				
Weak support for placement		X		

physical aggression and exclusion to typecasting and stereotyping—that administrators, staff, and alumni create. Each barrier can take different forms. Sometimes the discrimination is blatant and overtly racist. At other times the discrimination is subtle or covert—that is, hidden behind the scenes. Each discriminatory obstacle can vary in its harmful impact, but even one instance can be quite harmful.

Cumulative discrimination: A broad impact. Perhaps most importantly, black students experience the sustained obstacle of *cumulative discrimination.* Discrimination for most of these black students does not mean just the occasional or isolated discriminatory act in one of the enumerated categories, but rather a college career or lifetime series of blatant and subtle acts of differential treatment by whites which often cumulates to a severely oppressive impact. Some particular instances of discrimination may seem minor, or even misperceived, to outside (white) observers, especially if considered one at a time. But when blatant actions combine with subtle and covert slights, and these cumulate over weeks, months, years, and lifetimes, the impact is likely to be far more than the sum of the individual instances.

The cumulative impact of aggression, exclusion, dismissal, and typecasting can be seen in the more general comments of the students about the college environment. One black honors student at a predominantly white college was asked, "What is it like being a black person in white America today?" Situated in her white college environment, she replied:

> Everything, everywhere I look, everywhere I turn, right, left, is white. It's lily white, it's painted with white. And it's funny, because I was reading this article about how America is synonymous with white people. I mean, I'm sure when Europeans—or Asians or Africans for that matter—think of America they think of white people, because white people are mainstream. white people are general. "white is right," as my daddy tells me. white is right, at least they think it is.
>
> So, if you're a black person trying to assert yourself, and express your culture, there's something wrong with you, because to do that is to be diametrically opposed to everything this country stands for. And everything this country stands for is what is white. I'm sorry. I mean, I hate to be that simplistic about it . . . you're a fool if you don't realize that, to a certain degree. I'm not saying that white people are all out to get us, because I don't think they think about us that much, where they sit down and actually plot, in some dark smoke-filled room, how they're going [to] stomp on black people. They don't have to because it's ingrained in the system.
>
> So things are like that. And white people call me paranoid and stuff, because I guess they look at things in regards to like the sixties when black people were like being beaten up every damn day, and crosses [were burned] in front of yards, and it was so blatant. But, now it's

changed. And just because it's not blatant anymore doesn't mean it's not there. In fact, I think it's worse.

Ensconced in a large public college with a student body 97 percent white, she feels hemmed in by the omnipresent white student body and white subculture. When this student asserts herself, she implies, whites ask what is wrong with her. For this honors student the racial discrimination is not less burdensome because it is embedded in the institutional patterns of the society and the subculture of the college and therefore is often less blatant than cross burning or beatings. This student knows that she is expected by some to fail and to leave and by others to conform to the surrounding college subculture, to become, as another student put it, "Afro-Saxon." When she says *white* is an omnipresent problem, she is not just talking about a color or racial identification. When she and other students talk about everything around them being "lily white," they are reporting being at sea in a strange and hostile environment of white ways of being and of thinking.

When asked to comment on the black student's general situation, one black professor responded as follows:

> When a black student walks into a predominantly white environment, that student gets the same feeling that I get when I walk into a predominantly white situation. I immediately become fearful and defensive: fearful that someone will openly show hostility, that someone will openly show that I'm not wanted there; defensive, trying to set myself up so that if I face that, I can deal with it. Students don't have all of the kinds of coping mechanisms held by adults and professional adults; therefore this is more difficult for them.
>
> I still find myself uncomfortable if I walk into a strange environment where they are only whites and I'm the only black. And unfortunately, usually someone, at least one person in that environment or in that situation, will say or do something that's negative, if it's no more than just ignore you. So, you come in defensive . . . your fear is reinforced.
>
> That's what happens to so many of these youngsters on these campuses, they're dealing with kids who are sons and daughters of bigots. And as soon as they find a friend who accepts them, and they feel real good and start to relax, they run into this young bigot who brings back all the pain, all of the hurt, and it almost erases all of the good that's there.
>
> So, they're constantly in a state of stress. There's not a time when they feel that they can afford to let down. And when they let down, they're hurt. They are constantly in a situation where people don't understand, don't know. They don't know black people, they don't know black kids, so you're constantly answering questions.
>
> And everything is predicated on a white norm, so that when the student is in the environment, he is in a situation where the norm is the thinking,

the philosophy, the feelings, the attitudes of whites, and if you deviate from that norm, you're wrong.

From this perspective the college subculture is white-normed; discrimination is reinforced by the everyday, unstated assumptions about the priority of whiteness. As a result, blacks must be on guard; they regularly find themselves, even subconsciously, on the defensive. This array of barriers, ranging from aggression and social exclusion to dismissal of subculture and typecasting, combines to create the white campus subculture and subsociety that daily confront these black students courageous enough to enter the predominantly white colleges.

Notes

1. This project was supported in part by a grant from the Will C. Hogg Foundation. Sections of this report are drawn from a position paper prepared for the Center for Research on Minority Education at the University of Oklahoma.
2. This and later quotations have been edited lightly for clarity. For example, filler words like "you know" and "uh" have been deleted. The locations and names have been disguised or deleted to protect the anonymity of the respondents.

References

Allport, G. 1958. *The Nature of Prejudice*. Garden City, N.Y.: Doubleday Anchor.

Astin, A. W. 1977. *Preventing Students from Dropping Out*. San Francisco: Jossey-Bass.

Astin, A. W. 1982. *Minorities in Higher Education*. San Francisco: Jossey-Bass.

Blauner, B. 1989. *black Lives, white Lives*. Berkeley: University of California Press.

Collins, S. M. 1983. "The making of the black middle class." *Social Problems, 30*, 369–81.

Farley, R. and W. R. Allen. 1989. *The Color Line and the Quality of Life in America*. New York: Oxford University Press.

Feagin, J. R. and D. Eckberg. 1980. Discrimination: Motivation, action, effects, and context. *Annual Review of Sociology, 6*, 1–23.

Graber, D. 1980. *Crime News and the Public*. New York: Praeger.

Habermas, J. 1984. *The Theory of Communicative Action*. Boston: Beacon Press.

Keller, G. 1988–89. black students in higher education: Why so few? *Planning for Higher Education, 17*, 50–56.

Loo, C. M. and G. Rolison. 1986. Alienation of ethnic minority students at a predominantly white university. *Journal of Higher Education, 57,* 76–77.

Loury, G. and B. Anderson. 1984. *black Leadership: Two Lectures.* Princeton, N.J.: Urban and Regional Research Center.

Magner D. K. 1989. blacks and whites on the campuses: Behind ugly racist incidents, student isolation and insensitivity. *Chronicle of Higher Education,* 25 April, A27–A29.

Rollins, J. 1985. *Between Women.* Philadelphia: Temple University Press.

Suen, H. K. 1983. Alienation and attrition of black college students on a predominantly white campus. *Journal of College Student Personnel, 24,* 117–21.

13

Changing Black Americans to Fit a Racist System?[1]

Joe R. Feagin

In this assessment of the Braddock–McPartland and Pettigrew–Martin articles, I will briefly trace out some major contributions, then suggest a few limitations and extensions of their analyses: (1) the need to thoroughly integrate sociopsychological and structural analyses in assessing racial discrimination; (2) the necessity of distinguishing types of discrimination; (3) the limitations of laboratory and survey methodologies in researching discrimination, (4) the problem of mold-victim solutions that do not fully incorporate "Procrustean bed" realities, and (5) race/class codetermination in the black experience.

Contributions

These excellent articles make substantial contributions to the understanding of contemporary race discrimination. As a review of any library catalog will reveal, there is a dearth of 1980s' scholarly literature on black Americans. Much contemporary debate over the condition of blacks has centered on the theme of

---

This chapter is reprinted with minor revisions from Feagin, Joe R. 1987. "Changing black Americans to fit a racist system." *Journal of Social Issues,* 43 (No. 1): 85–89.1.

[1] The articles reviewed in this chapter are Thomas F. Pettigrew and Joanne Martin, "Shaping the organizational context for black American inclusion," *Journal of Social Issues,* 43:1 (1987): 41ff; and Jomills Henry Braddock and James M. McPartland, "How minorities continue to be excluded from equal employment opportunities: Research on labor market and institutional barriers," *Journal of Social Issues,* 43:1 (1987): 5ff.

reverse discrimination, with scholars like Harvard's Nathan Glazer arguing that affirmative action programs discriminate against whites and that whites should perhaps be the concern. It is strange that much scholarly debate took this peculiar turn, given that blacks have not come close to reversing classic white-on-black patterns of discrimination in housing, education, and employment—the latter well demonstrated in the Braddock–McPartland article. A principal contribution of these provocative articles is the opening up of a renewed discussion of racism issues—the microstructure and the macrostructure of discrimination in the employment sphere.

The Braddock–McPartland article presents data from a major survey of 4,078 employers and offers a sustained interpretation of patterns found. They reiterate a distinction, made by previous scholars, between types of employment career stages: the candidate stage, the entry stage, and the promotion stage. Their data reveal that word-of-mouth recruitment networks are very important at both low-paid and higher-paid job levels. When these informal networks are racially segregated, blacks have difficulty securing employment in traditionally white workplaces. Their data show a pattern of group exclusion ("statistical discrimination") and dossier discrimination at the job-entry stage, and of informal procedures favoring whites in promotions. This last finding is similar to that of Jones (1986), who interviewed a large number of well-educated black executives, with huge majorities reporting serious discrimination in white-collar employment. These authors accent as solutions the extension of job information networks to black communities, as well as greater regulation by authorities.

The Pettigrew–Martin article similarly provides an important view of the "triple jeopardy" faced by blacks in the token and solo roles. Examining the sociopsychological literature, they demonstrate that prejudice is still a major barrier to black occupational attainment. Much of their analysis suggests the importance of *cybernetic* feedback in interracial employment settings, such as those where a black employee perceives the subtle undercurrent of prejudice not perceived by white employees. This frustrating situation makes top job performance difficult. Particularly insightful is their discussion of the "ultimate attribution error," of whites opting for stereotyped explanations of black behavior considered to be "bad," rather than choosing a situational explanation. The solutions examined include sanctions by high-ranking authorities, antiprejudice programs, team redesign, and creation of a "critical mass" of black employees.

Some Limitations

While these scholars make suggestive and significant contributions to our understanding of contemporary discrimination, their assessments provide an opportunity for us to consider how the analysis of racism in the workplace might be broadened and extended in future social science research. No article can cover everything of import in this scholarly area, but it would be appropriate, in the mid-1980s, to integrate sociopsychological and structural perspectives in every analysis. Both articles recognize this sociopsychological/structural distinction, but the Pettigrew–Martin piece seems to go the greater distance toward recognizing the problem of separating a sociopsychological approach from a structural one. A society can be visualized as having two basic aspects: a human center made up of interacting persons with different characteristics, attitudes, prejudices, and needs, and a surrounding institutional boundary made up of various economic, political, and other social institutions with traditional and inherited roles and obligations. Any society has a well-defined set of social relations that institutionalize its modes of domination—the *structuring* of society into dominant and subordinated groups. When people shape their personalities and lives to fit the role requirements of the surrounding structures—including racist and capitalistic frameworks—they develop traits and needs that reflect this institutional boundary. This is true of the prejudiced whites examined in the Pettigrew–Martin article and in the responses of blacks examined in both articles. Thus, the contextual frame around particular employment settings and particular employers needs to be incorporated more explicitly into analyses of job discrimination. Future social science researchers should examine these linked features of racist settings in a broader and more holistic perspective.

Types

Another issue is the definition of major types of discrimination. Both articles need to distinguish more clearly between different types of discrimination. Benokraitis and Feagin (1986) have carefully differentiated among three types: overt, subtle, and covert discrimination. *Overt* discrimination is buttressed by the *two* other major types, *subtle* and *covert* discrimination. Overt discrimination is the most blatant type, that most commonly discussed. Subtle discrimination involves unequal treatment which is visible but so internalized as to be considered as "normal" and routine, particularly in bureaucratized settings. Covert discrimination refers to unequal treatment that is *clandestine* and maliciously motivated, an increasing phenomenon in the desegregation of traditionally all-white settings. The latter type of harmful treatment purposely attempts to ensure that black employees fail, while the former involves discrimination subtly built into the normative structure of workplaces.

Broader Methodologies?

There is an implicit methodological bias in these two articles in that neither deals with the historical and societal context of racial discrimination in employment. This is a limitation that they share with much social science research, research often ensconced in laboratory settings or imbedded in surveys limited to a modest array of questions. This limits the depth and significance of the data that can be gathered on many critical aspects of discrimination. Thus there is a major need for a more diversified quiver of research methodologies, including not only historical and contextual analysis but also in-depth interviews with participants in real-world discrimination and participant observation studies of well-chosen organizational settings.

Solutions

To be more specific, we can examine the case of Leanita MacLain, the brilliant young black journalist in Chicago, who took her own life in 1984. She would have been an excellent candidate for an in-depth interview or participant observation study; her daily life combined elements of racism, sexism, and experience with a capitalistic workplace. By the age of thirty-two McLain had won numerous journalism awards and had become the first black to serve on the *Chicago Tribune's* board of editors. In a write-up on her death, Campbell (1984) documented that black workers like McLain have had to don a special cultural mask in order to operate in the traditionally white workplace. She put on the clothes, language, habits of the white professional world, giving up her own cultural heritage for long hours.

This is a common problem for many contemporary black professionals who have had very serious difficulty in adjusting to the white employment world, that culturally rigid Procrustean bed, one that expects the victim to fit the mold, but not the mold to adapt to the black victim. Social science studies on the character of antiblack discrimination should be focused more centrally on this question of the workplace making no adaption to formerly excluded people now being allowed token entry. It is important for *solutions* to change the surrounding structure, to "fit" the characteristics of the new job entrants. If the structure is not significantly changed, then the incorporation of the new employees will not be satisfactory. Furthermore, as a recent analysis (Albert et al. 1986) put it, it appears it is only the oppressed themselves who have the ability to overturn repressive systems, for there is no historical example of a peaceful abdication of racial supremacy: "The oppressors must continue to oppress the subjugated community if they are to maintain their economic, political, and cultural power and privilege. The oppressors cannot renounce their power and privilege *within* a racist relationship; they must *abandon* that relationship" (p.

28). From this perspective, solutions must include the aggressive organization of the oppressed.

Race and Class

A final consideration is the need in both articles for an exploration of the ways in which a capitalistic economic system interrelates with racism in its structural and attitudinal forms. In Anglo-American history, capitalism and racism developed in tandem; each has fed into and reinforced the other, that is, they are *codefined* (Albert et al. 1986, 77). Codefinition means that the different spheres of racism and class subordination jointly characterize basic societal internal roles and relations. The very definition of economic roles reflects influences from racism (and sexism) in the larger society. Higher paying jobs have for more than three centuries been assumed to be the prerogative of white people and lower paying jobs the position of blacks. However, the characteristics of the racial sphere are also determined by the economic sphere. Neither article mentions the critical capitalistic background lying behind racial discrimination. Capitalism was implicated in the creation of racial subordination in the United States from the beginning; early New England merchants sold human beings to southern plantation capitalists who used both wage and slave labor. Ever since emancipation, capitalists have played the central role in developing the exploitative framework within which the patterns of race interaction have been situated.

Without enough jobs being created, black and white workers will routinely be pitted against each other for too few jobs, often to the broad advantage of employers as a class. Such a competitive situation substantially contributes to the discrimination so well described in the Braddock–McPartland study. Without basic changes in the structure of capitalistic workplaces—with their undemocratic, hierarchical, and racial character—there can be no real workplace accommodation between black and white workers. Discrimination in job entry, screening, and promotions is not solely a matter of structured-in or prejudice-generated racial barriers; discrimination has long been shaped by the reality of too few jobs. Those who control most job generation are the investors who decide whether and where to create jobs. When investors go on "strike," as they periodically do in those times euphemistically called "recessions" or "depressions," they hold back on investing capital until the conditions of profitability recur.

It is not sufficient to view racism in employment in isolation from the vested interests of employers, as both articles tend to do. One cannot assume that stronger action by existing authorities or by employers will necessarily improve patterns of discrimination. Behind the tragedy of American race relations lies the failure of the society to provide the kind of democratized investment control that might create enough employment to keep black and white Americans from each other's throats. For too long have scholars of race relations treated the introduction of an economic analysis into these matters as a conceptual aberration.

In summary, then, race relations analysts need to go beyond the usual discussions of interracial prejudice, employment barriers, and tokenism, however excellent these may be, and to extend research to such issues as (1) a holistic integration of structural and sociopsychological models, (2) multifaceted methodologies, (3) differentiated types of discrimination, (4) changing institutions to fit victims, and (5) incorporating the idea of race/class codefinition into both field research and conceptualization.

References

Albert, M., L. Cagan, N. Chomsky, R. Hahnel, M. King, L. Sargent, and H. Sklar. 1986. *Liberating Theory*. Boston: South End Press.

Benokraitis, N. and J. R. Feagin. 1986. *Modern Sexism: Blatant, Subtle, and Covert Discrimination*. Englewood Cliffs, N.J.: Prentice Hall.

Campbell, B. M. 1984. To be black, gifted, and alone. *Savvy*. 5, 69–72.

Jones, E. W. Jr. 1986. Black managers: The dream deferred. *Harvard Business Review, 64* (May/June), 84–93.

V
REVIEW AND REPRISE

14

Urban Sociology: Feagin-style

M. Gottdiener

Urban sociology remains one of the classic fields of American sociology. The early Chicago school scholars, responsible for establishing our profession in the United States during the 1930s, carried out most of their research by using the city of Chicago as a laboratory. Case studies figured prominently in this effort and many urban ethnographies, such as Thrasher's classic study, *The Gang* combined cultural observations with great sensitivity to spatial relations. As Robert Park said of Thrasher's study, it was not about gangs alone, but about "gangland," the sociospatial relations of juvenile groups in Chicago. By the 1970s the insightful sensitivity of the Chicago school researchers had been replaced by a demographically driven discipline that split off ethnography as almost a separate field and focused on the statistical analysis of aggregate census data. Sociospatial relations were now viewed "ecologically," meaning that the distribution of people and resources across the terrain were explained as the patterned reflection of individual preferences for freely chosen locations. Among urban ethnographers, walking the mean streets of American cities, there was still some recognition for the role of class, race, and status influences in determining life chances and personal locations within urban space, but these same considerations were largely ignored by the aggregate data approach of "urban ecology."

In contrast, during the late 1960s and early 1970s, European scholars became fascinated with the study of city life. They even turned to the early Chicago school for inspiration. These same individuals, however, such as Henri Lefebvre, Manuel Castells, and David Harvey, rejected urban ecology in favor of ways of theorizing city relations as extensions of class relations and the structural dynamics of a capitalist political economy. By the 1970s an impressive body of work along these lines was inspiring its own new generation of urbanists to approach the city in a more critical manner. Until the late 1970s and early 1980s, American urban sociology lagged far behind its European counterpart. Since that time, things have changed. Now we have a "new urban sociology" and Joe Feagin is one of its founders.

Here are a few of the underlying assumptions of the "older" urban ecology:

1. Social relations rely on accommodation and social organization being equilibrium seeking.
2. Social change arises through functional adaption to the environment. People differentiate themselves within society according to the structure of functional differentiation and interdependence.
3. Cities are ecological wholes based on functional adaption and interdependence.

In contrast, the new urban sociology sees things differently (see Gottdiener and Feagin, 1988). Some basic concepts are:

1. Societies are not abstract aggregates but are specified according to their modes of production. Agency and individual behavior are specified as manifestations of political/economic relations. Culture is another factor of great importance.
2. Social interaction is dominated by antagonistic relations deriving from inequalities in economic resources. Development is uneven and often contradictory, creating winners and losers that are often based on class.
3. City population patterns are produced by inequalities of power and money. In addition to class, differences in race and gender are also important.
4. All spaces must be analyzed according to their connections to the larger, global system of capitalism and its worldwide dynamics.

In short, the old view was characterized by a descriptive analysis of census data backed up theoretically by appeals to the benevolent logic of some biological imperative to adapt, cooperate, and conform. The new approach studies cities as part of political economy and the global economic system. A very important task of the early founders of the new urban sociology was defining ways of specifying how economic agency translated into domination of sociospatial relations. Each of the famous European urbanists, Lefebvre, Castells, and Harvey, had their own way of addressing this issue. In the United States, people like Joe Feagin used the best ideas of the new Europeans to develop a mode of analysis pertinent to the situation in this country.

I first became aware of Joe Feagin's work in the early 1980s. We met several years after that but had already formed a warm friendship through correspondence. Catching my attention at that time was the way he focused specifically on the actions of real estate speculators and their influence on urban development. From time to time other urban sociologists, such as Homer Hoyt and Everett Hughes from the old Chicago school in the 1930s, had also highlighted this activity. But, Feagin was reviving the practice in an interesting way that the reader can see in chapter 2. Characteristically Joe analyzed the effect of this sector not only in terms of their activities or practices, that is, as a form of agency, but also as an economic *sector*, that is, as a structural form. His approach resonated with my own, although Joe was not aware then of my book-length study of Long Island regional development (Gottdiener, 1977). Attention to the real estate sector as both a mode of agency and an institutional structure differentiated this approach to urban sociology from both the ecological and the "growth machine" variants that were popular at the time.

When I began my relationship with Joe, I had been working out the theoretical aspects of this approach which highlighted the real estate sector as the *leading edge* of urban development. The work of the French urbanist, Henri Lefebvre, figured prominently in this task. Eventually this unique combination of urban theory, current political economy and the American tradition of urban sociology combined to create an approach now known as "The New Urban Sociology." This perspective represents an alternative paradigm to the mainstream approach on this subject taught until very recently in most graduate programs. An article detailing this "paradigm shift" in urban sociology constitutes our one and only collaboration (Gottdiener and Feagin, 1988).

Aside from its unique theoretical and analytical characteristics, the new urban sociology differs from the previous paradigm because of the critical attention paid to factors that were once neglected in urban sociology. Ecologists, for example, notoriously and quite explicitly ignored the factor of class in their analysis. For this reason the mainstream approach was of little help in understanding the place of conflict in the city (see chapter 4). Early efforts among New Urban Sociologists to renew interest in the role of class were often branded by mainstreamers as Marxist inspired, but that was hardly the point. The issue was and remained one of introducing a key analytical concept once and for all to the understanding of urban phenomena. In this light, efforts by ecologists to retain a biologically based metaphor that represented urban relations as "symbiotic" or species specific were quite suspect for their own ideological motives.

Feagin is also responsible for turning our attention to the global context of urban development. He collaborated with Michael Peter Smith on a book explicitly devoted to this subject (see chapter 1). The issue was no longer one of simply displaying descriptive statistics among a list of cities, as was the practice of urban ecology, but of *locating* specific cities within the broader context of an emergent system of global capital. The latter approach did not reify the city itself but specified it as simply a location for the activities of the corporations which embodied the mode of agency operating in the international flow of investment at the base of the global capitalist system. I have my differences with Joe here because of his subscription to the world system and international division of labor thesis as the mode of theorizing this global relation. Nevertheless, Feagin's approach has many useful insights, not the least of which is the use of political economy to analyze comparisons between cities rather than the mainstream practice of simply offering descriptive comparative statistics.

More interesting was the way he wove the global perspective into a discussion of urban development using his case-study materials on Houston. By 1980 Feagin had abandoned fully the urban ecological perspective in favor of one that stressed political economy. Part of this new effort compelled the analysis of individual cities to link with the workings of the global capitalist system. In 1985 Feagin used these themes in the very first paper published by a prestigious sociology journal on the global context of Houston's growth (see chapter 2). Aside from being highly visible within the profession, this piece articulated an early argument that critiqued mainstream urban sociology in favor of the new, emergent paradigm, although at this stage, he favored the world system variant of political economy. Feagin periodizes the growth of Houston according to four distinct stages in the development of capitalism: the commercial period, 1840–1900; the competitive-industrial period, 1901–15; a period of oligopolistic capital, 1916–31; and the phase that he calls "state-assisted" oligopoly capitalism, from 1932 to the present. In sum, Feagin establishes clearly the link between the changing dynamics of Houston's urban development and the changing phases of economic growth. This conceptualization constituted a clean break with the urban ecological tradition.

A second contribution of chapter 2 is the way Feagin highlights the role of the state in the rise of Houston as an important city. Ironically, this place is touted as a paragon of free enterprise. For decades the ruling elite propagated the ideology of free-market capitalism as a legitimation of their actions. Yet, Feagin shows meticulously how false this ideology was. At every phase of Houston's growth massive infusions of government spending were used to promote development. The ecological approach conceptualized city growth as if the state simply did not exist. Feagin undercuts that perspective with a tour de force analysis focusing on the close relationship between the local ruling class, the extraction of huge fortunes through urban development, and the explicit role of government spending to subsidize capital.

Feagin's subsequent work is noteworthy for the way he teases out the factor of government intervention as a critical contributor to urban development patterns. The chapters in section III are devoted to an exploration of the state's role in city growth and decline. A number of important themes emerge from this work, all of which had been neglected by the mainstream approach to urban sociology. Feagin examines the conditions under which state-supported redevelopment occurred; the relationship between class and conflict relations and government intervention; and the specification of how local economic elites collaborate with state officials to promote specific aspects of growth, principally for the pursuit of individual profit. A hallmark of Feagin's approach to the state is its multidimensional conception. Whereas other writers may focus on government as a manager of capitalist relations, on the state as a reflection of economic interests, or, state officials as relatively autonomous from other social interests, Feagin uses each of these aspects when they are relevant to his analysis. Instead of forcing us to choose among variant theorizations of the state's role in society, he argues for a multifaceted perspective that illuminates rather than constrains the analysis of urban development within the context of a political economic approach.

Chapter 3 is noteworthy for the way Feagin combines his interest in the state and the global context of urban growth. He draws on a comparative case study between Houston, the "oil capital of the United States," and Aberdeen, Scotland, the "oil capital of Western Europe" (see also chapter 9). In both cities active state intervention combined with venture-capital interests to exploit oil resources for profit. In this sense the two cities are alike. They are both growth poles in the worldwide fuel-extraction and processing industry. Neither could have developed or allowed specific factions of capital to enjoy substantial profits without the aid of government subsidies. So much for the ideology of free enterprise. But, Feagin pushes the analysis further. He asks how government also responded to the uneven development of these growth poles. Did it intervene to ameliorate the costs of growth? If so, how and under what circumstances? In short, were there any redeeming aspects of the state subsidization of capital, or contrarily were the economic elites the only ones to benefit.

Feagin's answer to this question is instructive and, at the same time, he shows us the value of comparative case studies. The social costs of growth were obvious in both places. Development attracted people, causing population to expand rapidly. Housing shortages, school overcrowding, and the straining of infrastructure, especially sewer and water supply, were some of the costs of growth in Aberdeen. Houston also had crises following expansion of a similar nature. Characteristically, as an American city, it also suffered from a specific shortage of low-income housing and immense traffic problems from cars due to the lack of adequate public transportation facilities. However, here the gross similarities end. Located in different structures of political economy, the response to growth differed between the two cities. On balance Aberdeen's planning capability acted quickly and comprehensively. Master planning was deployed to "rationalize" the effects of rapid growth and to minimize its collective costs. Considerable government spending was devoted to bolstering planning activities. These not only aided local residents but also the oil industry itself because of the greater efficiency it brought to the operation of the city.

The case of Houston contrasts with Aberdeen's record and reveals "a weak defense against social costs." Comprehensive planning was not even part of the local government function due to the ideology of free enterprise. Little money was devoted to the Department of Planning which was restricted to contend with short-range requirements alone. Sewage, housing, and traffic needs were all neglected. In short, the costs of development were born by the citizens in the form of periodic infrastructure crises and immense time delays, not to mention the dollar cost, of an intractable gridlock problem on the city's highways, especially during rush hour. While the state acts often as a collective agent of capital, given the appropriate political-economic arrangements, it can also perform in the pursuit of the social good by addressing the costs of profit taking.

Perhaps the most significant contribution to the new urban sociology is the way Feagin introduces the factor of race into the discussion. Appreciating the special aspect of Feagin's approach to race requires some contextualization. The bloody ghetto riots of the 1960s, broadcast to every American home, set the stage for a soulful reexamination of society's race problem. The "wild city" phenomenon, the sense that urban conflict had gotten out of control, belied the serene, organic view of the city espoused by ecologists and certainly set the stage for the reception of the political-economic approach that was to follow. A new image emerged of our cities, one that did not harbor a consensual accommodation among various ethnic groups in varying stages of struggle, but of searing rifts in the population caused by class restrictions and racial prejudice. Our society responded to this crisis with a series of legislative acts that established equal-opportunity employment, proactive affirmative action policies, and the conscious effort to channel much-needed resources to inner-city areas.

By the 1970s a certain complacency had settled into academic discourse regarding the issue of race. People pointed to statistics that showed remarkable gains by African Americans in rising to status positions within the labor force. Urban sociologists of all persuasions focused on the imperatives of economic growth and especially the implications from the startling statistics on deindustrialization and city decline. Within this context even famous African-American sociologists, such as William Julius Wilson, argued that class was more relevant a factor than race in understanding the situation of blacks living in central cities. Furthermore, some social scientists celebrated the gains of African Americans and the growing presence of the black middle class. The impact of social legislation attacking racial discrimination and supporting the proactive creation of jobs and educational opportunities, was believed by some to have ameliorated the effect of race even if class disparities persisted within cities.

During the last decade Joe Feagin addressed these issues and is responsible for a renewed interest in the independent effects of racial distinctions in perpetuating social problems. Despite the robust nature of economic growth during the Reagan years, for example, Feagin argued that the black–white income gap had widened in the 1980s (see chapter 10). Furthermore, in keeping with the new urban perspective, Feagin shows how this disparity was very much a consequence of government policies that subsidized the actions of corporations in the pursuit of profits. Cuts in taxes and social welfare programs were particularly singled out by Feagin in this regard. Most importantly, Feagin demonstrates that the very same social restrictions on free access to resources that had constrained African Americans in the past, such as discrimination in housing, voting, education, and employment, remained effective in the 1980s, despite the gains of a small middle-class segment. Black America was particularly besieged by the effects of inner-city violence, as well. In sum, Feagin reintroduced concerns about racial discrimination and demonstrated, in the 1980s, that race remained a significant independent factor in the uneven development of our society.

Another contribution came in the early 1990s when Feagin published a paper in the prestigious *American Sociological Review* (see chapter 11). Using the case study/interview method, Feagin documents the way middle-class blacks, the ones that many others believed had escaped from the grinding cycle of despair within ghetto areas, were victimized by racial prejudice. One interesting aspect of his contribution is the way Feagin specifies the role of spatial location in discrimination. According to case-study materials, successful African Americans still had to be aware of open, public spaces where their class status availed them little protection from racists and their remarks. Attention to this spatial dimension is very much like studying crime using "opportunity theory" and exposes the potency of latent racist attitudes even in the most urbane places.

Feagin uses case-study materials to document the varying responses of blacks to acts of discrimination or racism. These ranged from no response at all to stages of aggressive reaction. An important aspect of this discussion is the way he shows how middle-class status can, in certain circumstances, ameliorate and serve to minimize the threat of an encounter with racism. As a society we still must deal with the "cumulative effect" of racist encounters on black middle-class professionals that reinforce the legacy of prejudice and discrimination which remains our heritage from the days of slavery.

There is a particular "Feagin" style of approach to the new urban sociology. He shares in common with others working in the new vein the fundamental commitment to discuss all urban phenomena within the larger context of the society's political economy. Beyond that feature, however, Feagin has been particularly effective in specifying the many ways government intervention is implicated in perceived patterns of urban growth and decline. This contribution also characterizes his masterful and classic case study of Houston (1988), not reproduced here. Finally, Feagin's work is particularly sensitive to the issue of race, more so than most other new urban sociologists. Contributing to a multi-dimensional view of the effects of racism, he explored the way prejudice operates within space as well as by affecting the lives of African Americans through the reproduction of a "slavery that refuses to die."

References

Feagin, Joe R. 1988. *Free Enterprise City: Houston in Political-Economic Perspective*. New Brunswick, N.J.: Rutgers University Press.

Gottdiener, Mark. 1977. *Planned Sprawl: Private and Public Interests in Sub urbia*. Newbury Park, Calif.: Sage.

Gottdiener, Mark, and Joe R. Feagin. 1988. "The paradigm shift in urban sociology." *Urban Affairs Quarterly*, 24:163–88.

15

The New Urban Paradigm: Can It Revive Urban Sociology?

John I. Gilderbloom

For too long conventional urban sociology has paid an inordinate amount of attention to the differences between urban and rural life. As society is largely urban, the key is to examine differences among and within cities and to explain why they exist. To this end, books should embrace comparative perspectives that examine managerial or entrepreneurial approaches to capitalist cities, or should examine capitalist versus socialist cities. Indeed, students are fascinated by comparing cities such as Houston (where no zoning exists and elites control the urban agenda) and Santa Monica (which has enacted an array of progressive planning proposals and is run by a coalition of tenant and environmental groups). Students are equally interested in cities like Madrid, Stockholm, Amsterdam, Havana, Bucharest, and Shanghai in terms of urban spatial design and distribution of "collective consumption" items. Discrimination in the allocation of essential goods exists in all these cities—whether communist, socialist, or capitalist. Why?

The chief focus for the urban sociologist is not the aesthetics of a city but *how* basic necessities are distributed, *who* decides on this allocation, and *what* impact these choices have on an individual's life. In the end, the major question for the urban sociologist becomes distributive justice.

Urban sociology textbooks need to be completely recast. Chapter after chapter is spent on the human ecology perspective in explaining how cities developed, how they are organized, how they change, how they affect people, and what they might look like in the future, but radically different answers to these important questions are provided by neo-Weberian and Marxist urban paradigms. Moreover, questions that concern the neo-Weberian and Marxist perspectives, particularly housing, growth, transportation, neighborhood movements, and environmental aspects of urban life, are not given serious attention in most urban sociology textbooks on the market. This is a serious error in scholarship, and it prevents students from pursuing issues they find both intellectually and emotionally relevant.

One common explanation for why textbooks shrink away from integrating Weber and Marx into urban sociology is the "midwest mentality." Major book editors claim that the universities in the midwest and south are conservative and are "put off" by the power/conflict perspectives, but the editors' stereotype of what is acceptable to these universities is off the mark. Having taught in Wisconsin, Kentucky, and Texas, I find that students are open to the Weberian and Marxist urban perspectives, especially as a critique of human ecology. Another argument is that the human ecology perspective makes sociology respectable because of a "scientific" appearance, whereas the power/conflict perspective is seen as nonscientific and ideological. It is obvious that an urban sociology textbook is needed that integrates the three major perspectives in one book; I suspect, however, that most editors will disregard this advice and produce urban sociology books that remain generally the same in content— only the pictures and graphs are different.

At the heart of good teaching is a willingness to explore a variety of perspectives regardless of a person's ideological position. In sociology, three major paradigms have emerged at the macro level, rooted in the works of Marx, Durkheim, and Weber. These "ways of seeing" receive serious consideration and discussion in the core course requirements of sociology; students generally are given books or chapters to read on each of these perspectives.

Unfortunately American urban sociology, for the most part, leaves out the critical perspectives of Weber and Marx and concentrates on a neofunctionalist view surrounded by a hodgepodge of descriptive fillers on urban life and history. Urban sociology's denial of these important schools of critical thought prevents students from attaining a well-rounded understanding of contemporary urban sociology.

American urban sociology textbooks, as well as the chapters in introductory books focusing on urbanism, play a major hegemonic role in defining the proper boundaries of urban sociology. Textbooks have the dubious distinction of determining whether a sociologist's contribution is important as well as lasting. Our colleagues learn that "legitimate" urban sociological inquiry has a functionalist approach, and infer incorrectly that the conflict approach has little to offer on urban issues. This conventional wisdom challenged as well as changed.

The teaching of American urban sociology is in crisis. An adequate textbook should at least provide space for the various perspectives and should include at least one chapter each on the contributions of functionalists, neo-Marxist urban theory, and neo-Weberian urban theory.

British sociologist Ray Pahl, in his book *Whose City?* (1975), argued that urban sociology was slowly dying and needed a new direction that went beyond the traditional Chicago school of urban ecology. He pointed out that much of the current work in urban sociology is redundant, and has failed to make major advances beyond the traditional concerns of patterns of city growth and urban culture. Urban sociology, according to Pahl, was disappearing from introductory sociology and theory courses, as well as sociological course offerings. This decline in urban sociology occurred despite the fact that eight out of ten citizens in industrialized countries live in urban areas. Indeed, Saunders' words echo Pahl's concerns.

> For many years following the Second World War, urban sociology was unmistakably in decline as it became increasingly isolated from developments within the discipline as a whole. Following the Chicago ecology and the lingering but finally inevitable collapse of the rural-urban continuum, urban sociology staggered on as an institutionally recognized subdiscipline within sociology departments, yet its evident lack of theoretically specific area of study resulted in a diverse and broad sweep across a range of concerns that shared nothing in common save that they could all be studied in cities. . . . The "urban" was everywhere and nowhere, and the sociology of the urban thus studied everything and nothing. [Saunders 1981, 110]

Pail argued that urban sociology must define its intellectual mission in order to legitimate its continued existence as an area of inquiry. The central concern of urban sociology is to develop an understanding of the social and spatial constraints on scarce basic necessities such as housing, jobs, health care, and transportation that are distributed on a nonrandom basis. Pahl argues that a person's opportunities to secure adequate schooling, jobs, health care, and a safe neighborhood are shaped by the spatial and social allocation of housing and transportation services. Pahl further asserts that an individual's life chances are powerfully influenced by "managers" who determine the use of space. A person's life is not determined solely by his or her relationship to the means of production but by their spatial location in the urban system, which creates its own set of classes and conflicts. Inequalities are generated within and among cities. Why is it that certain cities can provide affordable housing and others cannot? What is the role of government, banks, developers, landlords, and tenants in the allocation of housing needs? While an economist might explain the cause of homelessness as a supply and demand problem, the sociologists would look at the institutional constraints on the allocation of decent and affordable housing. In order to pump new life into urban sociology, a critical examination must be made of how essential human needs are distributed within and across urban systems. Urban sociologists should identify the social and spatial constraints faced by consumers who cannot obtain adequate housing and transportation. Inequality in the distribution of goods is not purely a function of the "free market," as suggested by human ecology, but a social result of certain actors (bankers, city councilors, developers, commercial businesspersons) making key decisions that affect the urban environment and the life chances of individuals. This, in turn, produces conflict at the neighborhood level, which promotes urban social movements.

The urban sociologist should attempt to understand how access to these fundamental needs varies among urban areas and identify why certain urban places have problems allocating necessities while others do not. Pahl argued that "access to such resources is systematically structured in a local context" (1975,203). In terms of housing, urban sociologists should focus on the key actors who manage the urban housing system (owners of property) and the recipients of their housing (tenants—"those who must rent") (Pahl 1975,244–46). According to Pahl,

> It is evident that I have taken as my starting point the fact that the whole society is urban, but that, since people's life chances are constrained to a greater or lesser degree by the non-random distribution of resources and facilities, urban sociology is concerned with the understanding of the causes and consequences of such distribution for relevant populations. The values and ideologies of the distributing, organizing and caretaking professions, or the relations between the formal and informal patterns of social relationships, are of central concern to urban sociology. (1975,206)

Pahl's argument that urban sociologists should attempt to explain the "causes and consequences" of resource allocation provides a new direction and meaning for urban sociology. An urban sociologist, according to Pahl, examines only those resources that are "fundamental" and have a "spatial" dimension: "Housing and transportation are elements in my view of the city, family allowances and pension schemes are not" (1975,10). Pahl argues that since the allocation of space is inherently unequal (no two persons can occupy the same space), urban sociology must examine how these spatially derived resources are distributed. The urban sociologist should also focus on the "gatekeepers" and "urban managers" as conscious social forces molding the urban environment, and abandon the human ecology assumption of subsocial urban forces competing against one another.

A final important implication of Pahl's approach is that the unequal distribution of scarce and vital resources creates conflict among social classes: "Fundamental life chances are affected by the type and nature of access to facilities and resources and this situation is likely to create conflict in a variety of forms and contexts" (1975,204). Inequalities within the urban system help to foster urban movements.

Instead of drawing from a simple Marxist model of a two-class society based on relations of production, Pahl refers to the work of Weberians Rex and Moore (1967), who argued that the working class could be further broken down by market relations, including housing—revealing fundamental conflicts over the allocation of housing between tenants and landlords. If the distribution of jobs and wage rates is the primary focus of much Marxist scholarship, the allocation of housing and housing costs is also of concern to Weberians. Inequalities do not only exist in the workplace, but in the consumption of basic necessities as well. For Pahl, a framework for a revived urban sociological analysis must "examine three elements—spatial constraints on, social allocation of, and conflict over, the distribution of life chances in the urban system" (Saunders 1981,118). Pahl argues that "urban problems are too big to leave to traffic engineers, economists and what have you" (1975,200). Urban sociology can play a vital and progressive role in affecting how the means to fulfill fundamental needs are allocated within the urban system.

One advantage of the sociological perspective is its willingness to adopt an interdisciplinary approach to the study of social issues. While concerned with macro-level structural processes, it acknowledges that institutions are shaped by individual actors—at the same time that institutions constrain individuals' actions. It is such a sociological perspective that we have attempted to bring to the institutional analysis of the rental housing markets. We have combined structural analysis with an effort to understand the social relationships that constitute the world of landlords and tenants.

The potential for a significant sociological contribution to the study of the city has yet to be fully realized. This is unfortunate, for sociology has historically played a pivotal role in providing analysis and even direction on a variety of critical issues, including civil rights, sexism, poverty, and inequality in its various forms. Sociology loses its importance and vitality when it ignores the important social problems of the day. A review of sociology journals and conventional textbooks amplifies this point. Too often, the gatekeepers of sociological knowledge appear to believe that market behavior is the proper province of economists, or that the role of the state is best analyzed by political scientists. In the case of housing, sociology has forfeited an important opportunity to look at a major problem, affecting millions of Americans, by turning the issue over to the discipline.

Sociology should be on the cutting edge, probing and investigating the most important social problems of the day. As Collins (1986,1336) recently commented:

There is a rather widespread feeling that sociology in recent years has been in a depression. There are many complaints from many directions: that the field has grown repetitive, stagnant, fragmented; that it has lost public impact or even its impulse to public action; that it lacks the excitement; that it no longer gets good students or has good ideas.

Collins (1986,1354) concludes that "there must be new ideas, new results, new models and visions of the world," and he calls for a "sociological economics."

> Economics is in crisis on both theoretical and empirical fronts, and its idealized mathematical models are going to be challenged, especially from our discipline. This will provide some of the frameworks of the near future. [Collins 1986,1352–53]

Freeman and Rossi (1984,571) have similarly called for a redirection of sociology, to a more closely applied concern with the major political and social issues of the day. The fear is that if this is not done, sociology will lose its relevance, not to mention its funding base:

> We have been faulted by many in influential positions for the lack of relevance of our work to the solution of contemporary social and political problems. The criticism has been used to undermine governmental and foundation support for sociological research and training. An increased commitment among sociologists to work on solutions to contemporary social problems and critical policy issues would help to counter such criticism and advance our discipline in the queue for extra-academic support.

Cummings (1986,193), in a provocative and bold critique of the status of contemporary urban and applied sociology, argues that the legacy of urban sociology has been conservative for the most part:

> Social scientists, including sociologists, can no longer afford to view themselves as detached, objective observers of social phenomena. Nor should sociology, in the face of mounting pressures to serve the interests of the business classes, abandon its allegiance with those groups and classes most severely impacted by the problems of industrial society. . . . A social science capable of enhancing the human condition is a vision worthy of preservation.

In the present political climate, sociology appears to have lost its purpose and direction. Indeed, the sociological imagination has been lost.

I began this introduction by arguing that urban sociology in particular is badly in need of rejuvenation. Joe Feagin's work ranks as the best expression of the new "urban paradigm" because of its integration of the following components: (1) class and race as powerful factors in shaping the city; (2) public and private "gatekeepers" who shape the urban environment; (3) the importance of culture, norms and values in shaping cities; (4) urban social movements that can play a pivotal role in shaping the urban environment; and (5) cities structured by a global capitalist economy. Feagin convincingly integrates these powerful forces into the new urban paradigm. Feagin's work ranks as the best American expression of the "new urbanism," with nearly 40 books and 139 scholarly articles. His book *White Racism: The Basics* recently won the Gustavus Myer Center Outstanding Human Rights Book Award, and his book *Ghetto Revolts* was nominated for the Pulitzer Prize. That's why Feagin is considered the most important urban thinker of our time.

Of particular importance is Feagin's insistence on the powerful role race plays in the shape and opportunities of our cities. The much ballyhooed claim of the "declining significance of race" in our cities is repeatedly tested by Feagin, who finds that racism is one of the most pressing problems in American cities today. Marxist scholars were too quick to lump issues of race as a class issue. Feagin corrects this problem by showing that racism is not just a burden of the poor blacks but of the black middle class as well.

A second important point is how urban social movements can be a powerful weapon in changing the city. San Antonio's grass-roots movement, for example, fought for greater equity, opportunity, and fairness for the Mexican-American working class. The Los Angeles riots of 1992 show what happens when politicians, bureaucrats, and the rich neglect the poor and working class. Feagin never gets trapped by pessimism that is too often a trademark of traditional Marxists analysis. He shows how capitalism can be redirected to create a more sustainable economy that will benefit everyone.

A third important point of Feagin's work is his insistence that it is not just the powerful and rich capitalist actors who create many of the problems found in the inner city, but also the elected officials, bureaucrats, and assorted gate-keepers. Too often conventional social science relies on sanitized and biased newspaper accounts of what is going on. The real story is not what is portrayed on the front stage but the backstage. Feagin, unlike most urban scientists, has the keys to the backstage and opens the doors to investigating what is really going on.

A fourth important point is Feagin's perspective of the world economy as a persuasive force shaping not only New York and Los Angeles but Louisville and Ames along with smaller towns such as Leichtfield and Oskaloosa. Kentucky must contend with multinational firms that determine what, where, and how something gets built and distributed. Increasingly, what is built in Japan, woven in India, planted in Mexico; and mined in South Africa have begun to show a major impact on our cities in what must be understood as a "global market place."

The "new urban paradigm" has been essential in our successful efforts to help revitalize inner-city neighborhoods. SUN (Sustainable Urban Neighborhoods) at the University of Louisville is considered the best project of its kind. Our project has helped spark new investment, jobs, and homes. These houses follow the planning principles of sustainable neighborhoods: attractive, affordable, accessible homes that incorporate environmentally sensitive architecture, deter criminal activity, and respect the diversity of community. This past year the *New York Times* ran a highly complimentary article on our partnership. Our partnership is on the cutting edge of the "new urbanism" with a proven record that is unmatched.

SUN focused on a neighborhood with the highest concentration of urban poverty in the Commonwealth of Kentucky. The East Russell neighborhood located in downtown Louisville has a host of problems: high unemployment, crime, and welfare dependency. One out of every two adults is without a job and on welfare. The leading businesses are funeral homes, pawn shops, liquor stores, and hair salons; illegal enterprises such as drugs and prostitution have flourished for years.

SUN, along with its minority partners, promotes human and economic development through business/technology training, entrepreneurship training, micro-enterprise lending/incubation, homeownership, crime prevention, and neighborhood planning. Our efforts target nonprofit organizations operating within the Louisville Empowerment Zone. SUN provides capacity building and expert technical assistance by utilizing student and faculty advisers from a broad range of disciplines in university–community partnership projects. Through SUN, students and professors experience firsthand knowledge of the challenges faced by the poor and promote workable and sustainable alternatives to improve their grim situation.

This partnership has resulted in real changes to real people. Since January of 1996 nearly 800 families have been serviced by our SUN outreach workers in the West End to get assistance for food, shelter, health, education, jobs, and businesses. SUN and its partners have assisted the development of 33 new minority businesses. In the neighborhood where we place most of our resources (East Russell between Eighth and Thirteenth Streets), crime in 1996 fell compared to adjacent neighborhoods have seen felonies and misdemeanors increased. These newly woven seams of a once fragmented community have been united to form a viable and livable neighborhood.

The success of the partnership can be transferred from Louisville's impoverished West End to other neighborhoods throughout Kentucky, the United States, and the world at large. SUN has helped create and sustain greater economic development activity.

The success of the partnership can best be measured by the amount of economic development activity that was generated. The community is undergoing a rebirth with new houses and jobs. With cutbacks in government programs (from welfare, to housing, to health and even food), new strategies that emphasize sustainable human, community, and economic development must be promoted. Sustainable development integrates environmental, empowerment, and equity concerns by building partnerships that maximize the resources necessary to build on the human capital of inner-city neighborhoods. The university has created the neutral ground where all stakeholders can join together to develop the "common ground."

SUN is now recognized as a leader in sustainable development by creating bold, imaginative, responsive, and pragmatic university-community partnerships. Thousands of Internet explorers, researchers, and world citizens have visited our Web site.

While reactionary racists are a visible threat, a more important problem is greedy, smooth-talking majority-based groups that block grass-roots change. Our successful efforts were mostly done without the support of majority-based housing groups that would try to interfere with our neighborhood work or would refuse to endorse it. In one instance, a powerful majority-based organization (who was not given its "cut" of the grant) tried to block university-community partnership federal grant applications. When their initial efforts failed, they went to the local newspaper and fed them a negative story on the university-community partnership effort. The story was so biased, error-ridden, and emotional that it never was successful in derailing efforts to rebuild the inner-city neighborhoods. After almost five years of growing success, these same opposition groups continue to try to undermine our programs to create African-American empowerment.

Can we have hope about the future of American cities? Are ghettos and hopelessness inevitable? Do urban social movements matter? Is government intervention harmful to the workings of the market, or will economic democracy generate the "good city?" And what do tenants' movements reveal about the answers to any of these questions? As we head into the 1990s, can a more comprehensive, more engaging, and perhaps more optimistic theory of the city be embraced? These are the kinds of questions we should be addressing as we seek to develop an urban paradigm with greater explanatory power.

Feagin provides a coherent and credible argument for the new urban paradigm by uniting into a whole contributions made by French, English, American, and Spanish academics. Feagin's important new book advances considerably our understanding of the city. He shows us "why" things are and "how" to change them. The problems of the city are too big to be left to economists, traffic engineers, and cops. The new urban paradigm provides us some key answers to some of our most vexing problems in the city.

Cities must be remade for all to enjoy. Goodman (1956,97) observed that an individual "has only one life and if during it he has no great environment, no community, he has been irreparably robbed of a human right." Urban tenants' movements, with all of their limitations, have pushed forward the public dialogue centering on human rights and what constitutes a fair and just society. They have rendered problems and social relations visible that are often hidden from view by the heartfelt belief that a free market unleashed can solve all problems. This question is symbolic of a much larger debate about democracy, community, and the economic rights that will determine what kind of society the United States becomes as it enters the next century.

As an activist, consultant, and educator, who has worked in a wide range of roles in revitalizing inner-city neighborhoods, I believe that contemporary urban scholars never seem to capture the dynamics of what is going on in our cities. The new urban paradigm can revive moribund urban sociology with a theory that is grounded in reality not on a computer simulation. Feagin's book is perhaps the spark that can reignite academic urban analysis with a truly breakthrough paradigm.

Contact SUN and John I. Gilderbloom at http://www.louisville.edu/org/sun.

References

Collins, Randall. 1986. "Sociology in the Doldrums?" *American Journal of Sociology.* 91:6:1336–55.

Cummings, Scott. 1986. "Urban Policy Research and the Changing Fiscal Focus of the State: Sociology's Ambiguous Legacy and Uncertain Future." In Mark Rosentraub (ed.), *Urban Policy Problems: Federal Policy and Institutional Change.* New York: Praeger, 167–200.

Freeman, Howard, and Peter Rossi. 1984. "Furthering the Applied Side of Sociology." *American Sociological Review* 49 (Aug.): 571–80.

Goodman, Paul. 1956. *Growing Up Absurd.* New York: Random House.

Pahl, Ray E. 1975. *Whose City?* Middlesex, England: Penguin.

Rex, J. and R. Moore. 1967. *Race, Community and Conflict.* Oxford: Oxford University Press.

Saunders, Peter. 1981. *Social Theory and the Urban Question.* New York: Holmes and Meier.

Index

Aberdeen, Scotland, extraction
  economy of:
boom-bust cycles in, 103–104
boomtown, costs of, 224–25
  defense against, 226–33
capitalist historical periods,
  94
downside of, 101
development of, 87, 93–94, 107,
  222–23
multinationals' dominance of,
  97–98, 100
political linkages, 100, 108
employment paradox, 98
as field-office management city,
  107
and Houston, 98, 100–101
multilayered economy of, 94–95
Dutch disease, threat of,
  105–106
Adair, Red, 98
Addams, Jane, 2
American City Planning Institute,
  and large developers, 7

apartheid:
demographic trends and, 10–13
economic repression, 13
federal government decentralization and, 13
in housing, 122
See also segregation; suburbanization
Atlanta, and public-private coalition
  to combat economic decline,
  45

Birmingham (Alabama), and regional economic restructuring, 41–42
Burgess, Ernest. *See* Chicago
  school of urban sociology,
  2–4

capital, centralization of, 33–36
multinational corporations and,
  88–89
real estate speculators and,
  138

349

About the Author

Joe R. Feagin is professor of sociology at the University of Florida. He is the author of numerous books, including *The Agony of Education: Black Students at White Colleges and Universities* and *Living with Racism: The Black Middle-Class Experience*.